W9-BVQ-324

TEACHING WRITING
Balancing Process and Product

Gail E. Tompkins
California State University, Fresno

Merrill Publishing Company
A Bell & Howell Information Company
Columbus   Toronto   London   Melbourne

Cover Illustration: Leslie Beaber

Published by Merrill Publishing Company
A Bell & Howell Information Company
Columbus, Ohio 43216

This book was set in Korinna.

Administrative Editor: Jeff Johnston
Developmental Editor: Linda James Scharp
Production Editor: Ben Ko
Art Coordinator: Vincent A. Smith
Cover Designer: Brian Deep
Photo Editor: Terry Tietz

Library of Congress Catalog Card Number: 89–
63048
International Standard Book Number: 0–675–
20926–9
Printed in the United States of America
1 2 3 4 5 6 7 8 9—94 93 92 91 90

CHILDREN'S ACKNOWLEDGMENTS

Chapter 1 p. 14—"Beowulf Simulated Journal," Bucky Black, grade 7, Anadarko Middle
School, Anadarko, OK; p. 5—"A Martian," "Peanut Butter and Jelly Sandwich . . ." and "Dear
Mom . . ." John Lamm, age 5, Norman, OK; p.
8—"Plant Journal," Adam Gibson, grade 2, Eisenhower Elementary School, Norman, OK; p.
8—"Black and White Horse," Melanie Gilmer,
grade 1, Eisenhower Elementary School, Norman, OK; p. 10—"The Runaway Crayon," Sarah
Hamilton, age 5, Stillwater, MN; p. 12—"The
Promise of Blueberries," Tiffanie Myers, grade 3,
Cyril Elementary School, Cyril, OK; p. 13—"Solstices and Equinoxes," Kary Moorman, grade 7,
Central Junior High School, Lawton, OK.

Chapter 2 pp. 30–32—"Reading Log," Veron-
ica Stockton, grade 6, Briarwood School, Moore,
OK; p. 35—"Personal Journal," Kerry Melott,
grade 3, Jefferson Elementary School, Norman,
OK; pp. 35–36—"Personal Journal," Andrea
Jones, grade 3, Jefferson Elementary School,
Norman, OK; p. 36—"Personal Journal," Micah
Hunt, grade 3, Jefferson Elementary School, Nor-
man, OK; p. 36—"Personal Journal," Michael
Holzer, grade 3, Jefferson Elementary School,
Norman, OK; p. 36—"Personal Journal," Jenna
Alsip, grade 3, Jefferson Elementary School, Nor-
man, OK; pp. 39–40—"Dialogue Journal," Dan-
iel, grade 5, Monroe Elementary School, Norman,
OK; p. 45—"Journal on Betsy Ross," Lisa Nye,
grade 4, Pioneer Intermediate School, Noble, OK;
p. 60—"Coldness," Mark Ramsey, grade 7, Choc-
taw Junior High School, Choctaw, OK; p. 37—
"Mandy's Journal," Mandy, grade 3, Cyril Ele-
mentary School, Cyril, OK; p. 41—"Dialogue
Journal," Alisa Richmond, grade 2, Winding
Creek Elementary School, Moore, OK; p. 47—
"Football" Brandon Barrett, Kindergarten, Eisenhower Elementary School, Norman, OK; p. 47—
"I spent the night . . .," Jessica Mendoza, Kindergarten, Eisenhower Elementary School, Norman,
OK; p. 47—"Halloween," Marc Trammell, Kinder-
garten, Eisenhower Elementary School, Norman,
OK; p. 47—"My mom . . .," Becky Lee, Kinder-
garten, Eisenhower Elementary School, Norman,
OK; p. 53—"Florence Nightengale," Christina

Randy Roman Nose, grade 6, Watonga Middle School, Watonga, OK; p. 167—"Heart," Thaja Berglan, grade 4, James Griffith Intermediate School, Choctaw, OK; p. 177—"Key," Kim Mulligan, grade 7, Anadarko Middle School, Anadarko, OK; p. 177—"Lightbulb," Bucky Black, grade 7, Anadarko Middle School, Anadarko, OK.

Chapter 6 pp. 200–202—"Petrologists," Matt, grade 6, James Griffith Intermediate School, Choctaw, OK; p. 209—"Lord Eagle," Chris Nelson, grade 6, Irving Middle School, Norman, OK; pp. 225–226—"Daniel Boone," Charles Perez, grade 3, Western Hills Elementary School, Lawton, OK; p. 245—"Dear William," Adam Wilcox, grade 3, Jefferson Elementary School, Norman, OK; pp. 206–07—"The Sea Animals," David McDaniel, grade 1, Eisenhower Elementary School, Norman, OK; p. 212—"The World of the Dinosaurs," Dustin Smith, grade 4, Pioneer Intermediate School, Noble, OK; pp. 220–22—"A Story about Me," Eddie Heck, grade 2, Hubbard Elementary School, Noble, OK; pp. 223–24—"All About Me," Kasey Tompkins, grade 1, Whittier Elementary School, Lawton, OK; p. 226—"Are You Married?" Estelle Willingham, grade 2, Western Hills Elementary School, Lawton, OK; pp. 232–233—"My Life," Brian Spencer, grade 4, Blanchard Elementary School, Blanchard, OK; pp. 239–40—"Dear Annie," Allison Dawson, grade 3, Jefferson Elementary School, Norman, OK; p. 241—"Dear Marci," Amy Jacob, grade 4, Ranchwood Elementary School, Yukon, OK; p. 241—"Dear Amy," Marci Gamble, grade 6, Ranchwood Elementary School, Yukon, OK; p. 241—"Dear Dr. Seuss," Sara Boehme, grade 1, Lincoln Elementary School, Norman, OK; p. 245—"Dear Ms. Lichty," Kyle Johnson, grade 4, Horace Mann Elementary School, Duncan, OK.

Chapter 7 p. 252—"Miss McDonnell," Linda, grade 1, Fairfax County Public Schools, VA; p. 258—"Refreshments," Michael Quillin, grade 6, Deer Creek School Oklahoma City, OK; p. 258—"Sports for Girls," Amy, grade 6, Deer Creek School, Oklahoma City, OK; pp. 259–60—"Dear Mike," Tom Bogges, grade 6, Bethel School, Shawnee, OK; p. 260—"I am in favor of the American Revolution . . . ," Marshall Cole, grade 5, Pioneer Intermediate School, Noble, OK; pp. 260–61—"I'm Against the American Revolution . . . ," Tim Stecklin, grade 5, Pioneer Intermediate School, Noble, OK; pp. 264–65—"Dear Uncle Bobby," Lance Coker, grade 5, Bethel School, Shawnee, OK; p. 269—"Gamble with Drugs," Steve Spain, grade 6, Bethel School, Shawnee, OK; p. 268—"Missing," Trisha Zech, grade 4, Horace Mann Elementary School, Duncan, OK; p. 275—"Dear Mom," John, grade 1, Wayne Elementary School, Wayne, OK.

Chapter 8 p. 278—"Pen Pal Letter," Stephanie Craig, grade 4, Pioneer Intermediate School, Noble, OK.

Chapter 9 p. 322—"Digging Up Dinosaurs," Russell, grade 4, Pioneer Intermediate School, Noble, OK; p. 330—"Trophies," Matt, grade 5, James Griffith Intermediate School, Choctaw, OK; p. 333—"Reading Log," Emily, grade 2, Monroe Elementary School, Norman, OK; p. 333—"Reading Log," Christen, grade 2, Monroe Elementary School, Norman, OK; p. 333—"Reading Log," Melissa, grade 2, Monroe Elementary School, Norman, OK; pp. 334–40—"Beowulf Interview," Matt Polly, grade 7, Anadarko Middle School, Anadarko, OK; p. 341—"The Peacock and the Mouse," Felton Frueh, grade 6, Irving Middle School, Norman, OK; p. 354—"Math Story Problem," Suzy Stubblefield, grade 6, Longfellow Middle School, Norman, OK; p. 335—"Sounder," Jamie Battles, grade 5, Horace Mann Elementary School, Duncan, OK; pp. 347–49—"Seed Experiment Log," Tyler Crow, grade 1, Eisenhower Elementary School, Norman, OK; p. 353—"Changing to Improper Fractions," Lenora Cowell, grade 6, Longfellow Middle School, Norman, OK.

Chapter 10 p. 368—"A, B, C, D, or U," Megan Dill, grade 6, Western Hills Elementary School, Lawton, OK.

Appendix p. 403—"I Wish I Were an Astronaut . . . ," David Creveling, grade 5, Lincoln Elementary School, Norman, OK; p. 403—"I Wish I Could Fly . . . ," Josh Utter, grade 5, Lincoln Elementary School, Norman, OK; p. 404—"I Wish,"

Craig Edsall, grade 8, Watonga Middle School, Watonga, OK; p. 404—"I Wish," Becky, grade 6, Watonga Middle School, Watonga, OK; p. 404—"Blue Is," David, grade 4, James Griffith Intermediate School, Choctaw, OK; pp. 404–05—"White," Todd Wells, grade 7, Anadarko Middle School, Anadarko, OK; p. 405—"Being Heartbroken," Kim Thomas, grade 6, Watonga Middle School; pp. 405–06—"Electricity," Don Strasbaugh, grade 6, Watonga Middle School, Watonga, OK; p. 406—"If I Were," Leslie Jones, grade 4, Lindsay Elementary School, Lindsay, OK; pp. 406–07—"If I were a glove . . . ," by Devin Gilbert, grade 5, Lincoln Elementary School, Norman, OK; p. 407—"Me," Cassidy Gentile, grade 6, Irving Middle School, Norman, OK; pp. 407–08—"I Used to Be a Giraffe . . . ," by Kevin Lively, grade 8, Watonga Middle School, Watonga, OK; p. 408—"Our Freaky Family," Amber, grade 4, James Griffith Intermediate School, Choctaw, OK; p. 408—"Me," Eric, grade 4, James Griffith Intermediate School, Choctaw, OK; p. 409—"Sadness Is," Chelsa Songer, grade 5, Lincoln Elementary School, Norman, OK; p. 409—"Beside the building . . . ," Kevin, grade 4, Santa Fe Elementary School, Moore, OK; p. 410—"Dear Teacher," Brandon, grade 7, Anadarko Middle School, Anadarko, OK; p. 410—"Superman," Mike, grade 7, Anadarko Middle School, Anadarko, OK; pp. 410–11—"The Dinosaur Poem," by John Lamm, age 5, Norman, OK; p. 411—"Herskey's Kiss," by Mark Hooper, age 7, Lawton, OK; pp. 411–12—"Ode to the American Flag," Jenny Bryant, grade 5, Nicoma Park Intermediate, Nicoma Park, OK; p. 413—"An Innocent Victim . . . ," Angela, grade 7, Choctaw Junior High School, Choctaw, OK; p. 413—"Ghost," Kelsey Cox, grade 5, Horace Mann Elementary School, Duncan, OK; p. 413—"Chicago," April Jump, grade 6, Watonga Middle School, Watonga, OK; p. 414—"Mosquito," Jeff Grove, grade 7, Watonga Middle School, Watonga, OK; p. 414—"Icicles," Jason Howry, grade 8, Watonga Middle School, Watonga, OK; p. 414—"Fall," Vickie Loewen, grade 8, Watonga Middle School, Watonga, OK; pp. 414–15—"Butterflies," Amy Huff, grade 6, Watonga Middle School, Watonga, OK; p. 415—"The Rose Seems Anxious . . . ," Tiffany Davis, grade 7, Watonga Middle School, Watonga, OK; p. 415—"Brother," Audrey Osburn, grade 3, Woodrow Wilson School, Norman, OK; p. 415—"Pool," Amanda Ross, grade 3, Woodrow Wilson School, Norman, OK; p. 415—"Raccoon," James Mitchell, grade 5, Lincoln Elementary School, Norman, OK; p. 415—"Twister," Josh Utter, grade 5, Lincoln Elementary School, Norman, OK; p. 416—"Abandoned House," Jennifer Brickman, grade 8, Watonga Middle School, Watonga, OK; p. 416—"People," Gabrial Bedolla, grade 3, Woodrow Wilson School, Norman, OK; p. 417—"There Once Was a Thing at the Zoo . . . ," Jason, grade 6, Watonga Middle School, Watonga, OK; p. 417—"Mrs. Hobb has a hat with a feather . . . ," Carrie, grade 6, Watonga Middle School, Watonga, OK; p. 417—"The Egyptian Mummy," Nicole Dobbins, grade 8, Watonga Middle School, Watonga, OK; p. 417—"Albert Einstein," Heather, grade 6, Watonga Middle School, Watonga, OK; p. 417—"Mickey Mouse," Carrie Thomas, grade 8, Watonga Middle School, Watonga, OK; pp. 417–18—"Clint Eastwood," Bobby Hoffpauir, grade 8, Watonga Middle School, Watonga, OK; p. 418—"Oh Cookie Jar . . . ," Krystal, grade 4, James Griffith Intermediate School, Choctaw, OK; p. 418—"Dear Chair," Tony, grade 5, Nicoma Park Intermediate School, Nicoma Park, OK; p. 418—"The Truck," Jeff, grade 7, Anadarko Middle School, Anadarko, OK; p. 419—"My Place," B. J., grade 7, Anadarko Middle School, Anadarko, OK; p. 419—"Come with Me," Amy, grade 7, Anadarko Middle School, Anadarko, OK; p. 419—"The Kangaroo's Prayer," Chad, grade 2, Grand Avenue Elementary School, Chickasha, OK; p. 420—"The Mouse's Prayer," Jason, grade 2, Grand Avenue Elementary School, Chickasha, OK; pp. 420–21—"If I Were in Charge of the World, I . . . ," Jack, grade 5, Horace Mann Elementary School, Duncan, OK; p. 421—"If I Were in Charge of the World," Tracy, grade 5, Horace Mann Elementary School, Duncan, OK.

For Dick, I love you.

Preface

More than 50 years ago Alvina Burrows and her colleagues (1938) recognized that "they all want to write," but not until Donald Graves' pioneering work in process writing (1975, 1983) did the movement to empower children in the elementary grades through writing take hold. In the last decade, teachers and researchers have extended Graves' work in different contexts, with varied types of writing, and at all grade levels. *Teaching Writing: Balancing Process and Product* integrates this recent research and theory about the writing process, collaborative learning, reading and writing connections, and writing instruction to assist teachers who are striving to teach students to write in kindergarten through eighth grade. This book provides practical strategies for teaching writing—with specific step-by-step directions—and presents student writing samples to illustrate the teaching strategies. It is unique because of its focus on pedagogy. It can be used as a text for undergraduate or graduate writing courses or as a supplementary text for reading and language arts courses. Also, teachers participating in inservice workshops will find it useful. Special features have been included to increase the book's useability:

- Specific teaching strategies are provided for varied writing forms, including stories, poems, reports, and advertisements.
- Over 200 writing samples, written by students in kindergarten through eighth grade are used to illustrate the types of writing possible using the teaching strategies.
- Question-and-answer sections at the end of each chapter include questions most commonly asked by preservice and inservice teachers.
- Techniques for assessing students' writing are presented as a part of each teaching strategy and an entire chapter is devoted to the assessment of writing.
- Vignettes are included to illustrate more concretely how teachers implement the ideas set forth in this book. Names of the teachers are included for authenticity as well as to acknowledge their expertise and willingness to share their classrooms with me.

- Across the curriculum connections are made throughout the book, and one chapter is devoted to ways to connect writing to reading, social studies, science, and math.
- Lists of recommended books to use in teaching varied types of writing activities are presented. These lists include short stories that illustrate point of view that students can examine as they experiment with viewpoints in their own writing. Students can also read books in which main characters keep journals, something students will find interesting as they begin keeping their own journals.

The focus throughout the book is on writing; it is not intended to be a comprehensive language arts methods textbook.

Instructors can use *Teaching Writing* chapter by chapter, in the order in which the chapters are presented or in an order varied to fit the instructor's preferences or teaching style. For those instructors who wish to vary the sequence of the chapters, it might be useful to think of the book in three parts. The first three chapters present the foundation for the book, and I recommend that they be read in order. Chapter 1 presents an overview of writing in elementary and middle schools. Chapter 2, "Informal Writing," focuses on journal writing and informal writing strategies, such as clustering and freewriting, that students often use when gathering and organizing ideas before writing more formal pieces that move through the writing process. Chapter 3 focuses on the writing process. Chapters 4 through 7 are the second part of the text, and they deal with how to teach elementary students to write stories, poems, reports, biographies and autobiographies, letters, persuasive essays, and other forms of writing. Chapters 4 through 7 can be taught in any order, depending on personal preference. The last three chapters, "Writers' Tools," "Writing Across the Curriculum," and "Assessing Students' Writing" can be read in any sequence, but because they include references to the writing process and particular writing forms, they will be more easily understood when read after the first seven chapters.

ACKNOWLEDGMENTS

My heartfelt thanks go to the many people who have encouraged me and provided invaluable assistance as I wrote this text. *Teaching Writing: Balancing Process and Product* is a reflection of what the undergraduate and graduate students with whom I worked at the University of Oklahoma and the teachers across the state of Oklahoma have taught me. This book is testimony to their excellence and dedication. First, I want to recognize Carol Ochs, a fourth grade teacher at Pioneer Intermediate School in Noble, Oklahoma, who has worked with me for the past seven years as we explored children's potential to express themselves as writers. She and her students welcomed me into their classroom and demonstrated all that a writing-oriented classroom could be. Next, Jennifer Reno, principal of Western Hills Elementary School in Lawton, Oklahoma and her faculty of innovative teachers who blazed a new direction in writing instruction for the state of Oklahoma deserve special recognition. Kay Preston, Glenna Jarvis, Eunice Edison, Betty Jordan, Mary Ann Comeau, Pat Blackburn, Judy Reeves, Linda Riley, Carolyn Mayes, Marilyn Williams, Kaye Hicks, Pat Pittman, and Sue Wuestner have worked for the past three years to implement a holistic, integrated approach to language arts in their school. Third, I want to acknowledge the teacher/consultants in the Oklahoma Writing Project and Claudette Goss of the Oklahoma State Department of Education and Assistant OWP Director. Together we have studied and applied writing theory and research in Oklahoma classrooms. And, I want to thank my masters and doctoral students for challenging me to think, investigate, write, and learn as I have striven to challenge them: Donna Camp, Shirley Carson, Patricia Daniel, Christine Edge-Christensen, Sandra Harris, Mary Hitchcock, Lisa Lawrence, Glenda LoBaugh, Katherine Matthews, Debra Myers, Jo Ann Pierce, Annette Van Dusen, Brenda Wilkins, and Robert Wyatt.

I want to express my appreciation to the children whose writing samples and photographs appear in this text and to the teachers, administrators, and parents who shared writing samples with me: Max Ballard, Nicoma Park Intermediate School, Nicoma Park, OK; Anita Beard, Norman, OK; Marc Bell, Monroe Elementary School, Norman, OK; Kathy Bending, Highland Elementary School, Downers Grove, IL; Linda Besett, Sulphur Elementary School, Sulphur, OK; Gracie Branch, Eisenhower Elementary School, Norman, OK; Juli Carson, Jefferson Elementary School, Norman, OK; Pam Cottom, James Griffith Intermediate School, Choctaw, OK; Jean Davis, James Griffith Intermediate School, Choctaw, OK; Deanie Dillen, Putnam City Schools, Oklahoma City, OK; Polly Dwyer, University of Oklahoma, Norman, OK; Charlotte Fleetham, Pioneer Intermediate School, Noble, OK; Parthy Ford, Whittier Elementary School, Lawton, OK; Debbie Frankenberg, Purcell, OK; Chuckie Garner, Kennedy Elementary School, Norman, OK; Mendy Gipson, Eisenhower Elementary School, Norman, OK; Peggy Givens, Watonga Middle School, Watonga, OK; Teri Gray, James Griffith Intermediate School, Choctaw, OK; Garett Griebel, Chickasha, OK; Carole and Bill Hamilton, Stillwater, MN; Debbie Hamilton, Irving Middle School, Norman, OK; Lori Hardy and Kay Hughes, James Griffith Intermediate School, Choctaw, OK; Ernestine Hightower, Whittier Elementary School, Lawton, OK; Linda Hopper, Wilson Elementary School, Norman, OK; Annette Jacks, Blanchard Elementary School, Blanchard, OK; Suzie Jennings, Lindsay, OK; Martha and Rob Lamm, Norman, OK; Helen Lawson, Deer Creek School, Oklahoma City, OK; Diane Lewis, Irving Middle School, Norman, OK; Mark Mattingly, Central Junior High School, Lawton, OK; Pam McCarthy, Hubbard Elementary School, Noble, OK; Tissie McClure, Nicoma Park Intermediate School, Nicoma Park, OK; Gina McCook, Whittier Middle School, Norman, OK; Gloria McDonnell, Fairfax County Public Schools, VA; Mary Oldham, University of Oklahoma, Norman, OK; Teresa Ossenkop, Eisenhower Elementary School, Norman, OK; Sandra Pabst, Monore Elementary School, Norman, OK; Alice Rakitan, Highland Elementary School, Downers Grove, IL; Jelta Reneau, Lincoln Elementary School, Norman, OK; Martha Rhynes, Stonewall, OK; Bobby Russell, Seiling Schools, Seiling, OK; Becky Selle, Bethel School, Shawnee, OK; Linda Shanahan, Nicoma Park Intermediate School, Nicoma Park, OK; Jo Ann

Steffen, Nicoma Park Junior High School, Nicoma Park, OK; Gail Warmath, Long-fellow Middle School, Norman, OK; MaryBeth Webeler, Highland Elementary School, Downers Grove, IL; Lynnda Wheatley, Briarwood Elementary School, Moore, OK; Linda White, University of Oklahoma, Norman, OK; Vera Willey, Lincoln Elementary School, Norman, OK; Jean Winters, Irving Middle School, Norman, OK; and Susie Wood, Marlow, OK.

I also want to thank my parents, friends, and colleagues at the University of Oklahoma for their encouragement and understanding of my preoccupation with this project. My secretary, Challis Coulston, deserves special recognition for her tireless efforts in typing and proofreading the manuscript and dealing with a myriad of details so that I had time to write.

I also want to thank the colleagues across the United States who served as reviewers, carefully reading and critically reacting to the manuscript: Linda B. Amspaugh, University of Cincinnati; Jill Fitzgerald, University of North Carolina; Shirley Haley-James, Georgia State University; James L. Hoot, University of Buffalo; and Ruth Justine Kurth, North Texas State University.

Finally, I want to express my sincere appreciation to my editors at Merrill Publishing Company. I thank Jeff Johnston for providing the opportunity for me to pursue this project and Linda James Scharp for her caring and nurturing encouragement and support. I also want to thank Ben Ko for his patience with me and for moving the book so efficiently through the maze of production details, and Cindy Peck for wielding her red pen so skillfully to smooth out the rough spots.

Gail E. Tompkins

Contents

10   *ASSESSING STUDENTS' WRITING*   *367*

APPENDIX   *403*

TITLE AND AUTHOR INDEX   *422*

SUBJECT INDEX   *427*

AUTHOR PROFILE   *432*

1

Why Teach Writing?

Why teach writing in the elementary grades? It's a reasonable question. The elementary curriculum is already so crowded that it is nearly impossible to squeeze additional subject matter into it. Yet, there are significant reasons for including writing in the elementary school curriculum, and numerous benefits of writing instruction for children can be cited.

First, students need to learn to communicate effectively with others through written language as well as through oral language. This language ability is known as *communicative competence* (Hymes, 1974), and it is composed of two components. The first is the ability to transmit meaning through talking and writing; the second is to comprehend meaning through listening and reading. Communicative competence also refers to students' fluency in the different *registers,* or varieties, of language as well as knowing when it is socially appropriate to use language in each register (Smith, 1982). For example, we write letters to close friends in a less formal register than we would use in writing a letter to the editor of the local newspaper. Students need to know how to record thoughts on paper and how to make their papers "optimally readable" (Smith, 1982) so that others will read and understand their writing.

A second reason for teaching writing is that through writing, students learn and apply language skills. Mechanical skills, such as punctuation, capitalization, spelling, and usage, are used in writing, and it is through such practice that these skills are learned. In fact, students learn language skills more readily when they use them in genuine communication activities than simply in textbook drills (Calkins, 1980).

Another benefit is that through writing, students gain valuable knowledge about reading. Reading and writing are both meaning-making processes, and experience with one process provides a scaffold or framework to support the learning of the other (Hansen, 1987; Jensen, 1984; Kucer, 1985). Butler and Turnbill (1984) draw parallels between what readers and writers do before, during, and after reading and writing and the cognitive strategies that they use. Strong relationships exist between comprehending and composing, and Frank Smith (1983) reminds us that, in order for students to be writers, they must read like writers.

A fourth benefit of writing instruction is that students learn critical thinking skills as they write. Indeed, writing *is* thinking (Langer & Applebee, 1987). As students make choices about taking a point of view, organizing their writing, appealing to their audience, and revising their writing, they are using higher level critical thinking skills.

A fifth reason for teaching writing is that writing is a valuable tool for learning, and through writing students learn content better (Barr et al., 1981; Emig, 1977; Fulwiler & Young, 1982; Gere, 1985; Martin et al., 1976). Through informal writings, such as learning logs, students think about what they are learning, relate it to what they know, and raise questions about information that is unclear. Formal writing activities, such as research reports, biographies, and simulated newspapers and letters can also be integrated with content area study. For example, as a part of a unit on the American Revolution, students can write and publish a simulated newspaper that might have been published on April 20, 1776 (the day after the Battles of Lexington and Concord), December 26, 1776 (the day after Washington and his troops crossed the Delaware and surprised the Hessians at Trenton), or October 20, 1781 (the day after General Cornwallis surrendered at Yorktown).

A final reason for including writing in the elementary school curriculum is that writing is fun. Many people—both children and adults—write for enjoyment. Children enjoy writing stories to share with classmates and letters to exchange with pen pals while adults find pleasure in keeping journals to chronicle their lives, sharing opinions through letters to the editor of the local newspaper, writing church newsletters, or composing poetry and publishing it in literary magazines.

This chapter presents an overview of writing instruction in the elementary grades. In the next section, you will see samples that illustrate the range of writing that children produce in primary, middle, and upper grades. Later in the chapter, I will identify the components of a writing program and then elaborate on them throughout the textbook. The chapter concludes with a report on the current status of writing instruction in American schools and a look toward the future as writing becomes an integral part of the elementary school curriculum.

CHILDREN'S WRITING IN THE ELEMENTARY GRADES

The first time I explored in detail how children learn to write, I was tempted to conclude that it was, like the flight of bumblebees, a theoretical impossibility (Smith, 1988, p. 17).

The notions that students in the elementary grades cannot write, that they must learn to read before they can write, or that they must learn to write words and sentences before writing longer texts are antiquated. Classroom teachers as well as writing researchers have discovered that even young children communicate through writing, and they begin writing as they are learning to read or even before they read (Bissex, 1980; Chomsky, 1971; Graves, 1983). Children first write to communicate a message and only later do they examine the parts of the message. Moreover, developmental trends can be observed as children learn to express more complex thoughts using varied writing forms and learn to use standard spelling and other mechanical considerations.

In kindergarten through eighth grade, children's writing assumes many different forms as it is written for varied functions and audiences. For instance, during the elementary grades children write letters, and the function, form, and audience of these letters vary. The first letters that many young children write are notes and letters to parents, grandparents, and Santa Claus. Through these letters, children learn about the social uses of language and the conventions used in letter writing. In the primary grades, they extend letter writing to include notes to classmates and to the teacher as they focus on the personal or instrumental dimensions of language use. In the primary and middle grades, students also write letters to pen pals, and through these letters they learn to include questions in their letters so that they will get a response. During the middle and upper grades, students write business letters to rock and movie stars, governmental leaders and agencies, and businesses to share ideas or request information. Older students also write persuasive letters to the editor of school and community newspapers in which they argue their point of view.

Writing in the Primary Grades (Kindergarten Through Grade 2)

Many children become writers before entering kindergarten while others are introduced to the power of written language during their first year or two of school (Harste, Woodward, & Burke, 1984; Temple, Nathan, Burris, & Temple, 1988). Planned opportunities for writing should begin the first day of kindergarten regardless of whether children have learned to read or to spell words using standard English. From the first day, using a combination of art and scribbles or letter-like forms, children communicate in a written form. While some children are using letters or words to label pictures they have drawn, others are writing personal narratives in which they describe experiences, letters to family members, or books to share information. In their writing, children use a combination of adult spelling and invented spelling, or an idiosyncratic approach of using letters and other marks to represent words. Three samples of 5-year-old John's writing are presented in Figure 1-1. In the first sample, John drew a picture of a creature from outer space and labeled it "A Martian." The second sample is a menu, listing the foods John ate for lunch. It reads, "Peanut butter and jelly sandwich, applesauce." The third sample is a letter John wrote to his mother: "Dear Mom, I hope you are having a very Merry Christmas. Me."

Through listening to stories read aloud to them by the teacher and reading stories themselves, students in the primary grades learn about stories and the kinds of information that authors use in constructing stories. This increasing awareness of stories and narrative structure is called *a concept of story,* or story schema (Applebee, 1978). In the primary grades, children write their own retellings of familiar stories in which they apply their knowledge about stories and experiment with the conventions that authors and storytellers use, such as the traditional opening, "Once upon a time . . . ." In Figure 1-2, a kindergartner named David retells the story of "The Little Red Hen." On the first two pages, David dictated his retelling and then because he tired of waiting for the teacher to return to take his dictation, he continued writing on his own. Through these experiences with stories, children develop a sense of authorship and come to think of themselves as authors (Graves & Hansen, 1982).

The physical demands of writing can become burdensome for young children, but teachers can help by taking children's dictation. The idea of transcribing children's talk was originally introduced as the language experience approach to reading (Van Allen, 1976). Through dictation, children see a teacher writing in a conventional form from left-to-right and top-to-bottom on a sheet of paper and using standard spelling. At the same time, dictated writing is a hard act for children to follow. They can't write as quickly or as neatly as adults can, they can't spell as many words using conventional spelling, and they can't punctuate as well. While children should do much of their own writing, dictation is an alternative for

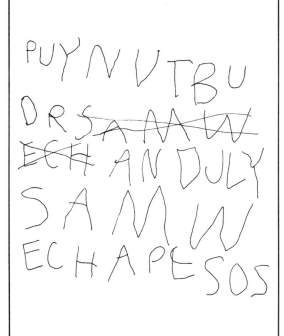

FIGURE 1-1 Samples of a 5-Year-Old's Writing
John, age 5

FIGURE 1-2 A Kindergartner's Retelling of "The Little Red Hen"
David, Age 5, Tompkins & McGee, 1989, p. 71.

Once upon a time, there lived a hen, a dog, a cat and a mouse. One day the hen found some grains of wheat and she decided to plant the grains.

2

Now, who will help me chop the wheat?

Not I. said the Dog.

Not I. Said the cat,
Not I. said the Mouse
then I shall,
Said the hen.

3

NOW WHO Will help me
carry the wheat. to the mill?
Not I. Said the DoG.
Not I. Said the cat.
Not I. said the Mwse.
then I shall, said the hen

2

NOW Who Will
help me Eet the Bead!
I will! said the DoG.
I will! Said the CAT.
I will! said the Mouse,
I will! No! you wont. Iwill. said the hen.

4

Now, Who will help me
cook the Bread?
Not I said the Dog.
Not I. Said the cat.
Not I. Said the Mouse.
then I shall, said the hen.

times when the physical demands of writing become too great or when the writing needs to meet adult standards of correctness.

During the primary grades, children explore a number of the functions, forms, and audiences that older students and adults have for writing. From writing about personal experiences and interests, children move to writing letters, making "All about _____ " booklets of animals, colors, and other concepts, writing autobiographies, retelling favorite stories, and writing original stories and poetry. They write to respond to literature and they write to learn all across the curriculum. Figures 1-3 and 1-4 present examples of writing done by children in the primary grades. Figure 1-3 includes the label "Black and White Horse" that a kindergart-

FIGURE 1-3 Samples of Writing by Primary-Grade Students
Top: Melanie, grade 1. Bottom: Adam, grade 2. Right: Anonymous.

ner put on a drawing, a page from a second grader's learning log on plants, and a page from a wish booklet written by a first grader. Figure 1-4 features a story dictated by a kindergartner.

As soon as children begin to write, they want to share their writing with others. In many primary classrooms, one chair is designated as the *Author's Chair* (Graves & Hansen, 1982), and children sit in this chair to share their writing with classmates. They read their texts aloud just as teachers read books aloud to them and show their illustrations. Then classmates take turns offering comments and compliments. Sometimes children also offer suggestions for revising a piece of writing. Through this sharing, children learn that writing is a social activity and that their classmates can provide an important audience and a source of feedback about their writing.

Writing in the Middle Grades (Grades 3 Through 5)

Students' writing assumes more specialized forms in the middle grades—letters, simulated journals, biographies, genre stories, and reports—and more closely approximates adult writing conventions. Writing is a part of the school day at this level—in language arts class to learn language and in content area classes to learn social studies, science, and other content. In language arts, for example, children learn letter-writing skills by writing letters to pen pals. To learn mechanical skills, such as using commas in a series, they locate examples in their own personal journal entries.

The students in Mrs. Myers' third-grade class are studying Indians and as part of the unit, the teacher is reading Indian legends to the students such as Tomie dePaola's *The Legend of the Paintbrush* (1988) and *The Legend of the Bluebonnet* (1983). After reading five or six legends, the students examine the legends they have read to decide what the unique characteristics of legends are. With this knowledge, they compose their own legends to explain other things, much like the Indians might have. Tiffanie's legend about "The Promise of Blueberries" is presented in Figure 1-5. (For more information about reading and writing legends, see Chapter 9, "Writing Across the Curriculum.")

In Mrs. Alonzo's fourth-grade class, the students use writing to learn as they study about the Alamo. To participate in the unit, each student chooses a figure of that period to "become." They begin their study by reading one or more biographies about the person and developing a timeline of that person's life. Then they keep a simulated journal as that character, through that person's eyes, focusing on how their person would have reacted and acted during the events of the turbulent era. Later, they will write a biography of their person, focusing on memorable events in the person's life. Entries from a fourth grader's simulated journal written as though he were Jim Bowie are presented in Figure 1-6, p. 13.

Writing in the Upper Grades (Grades 6 Through 8)

In the upper grades, students apply what they have learned about writing and make conscious choices about function, form, and audience as they write. The organization of schools typically changes for grades 6 through 8 into either a middle school or junior high school arrangement. Students change classes, and language arts becomes one period of the school day. The emphasis is on reading-writing connections in language arts class and on writing to learn or writing across the curriculum in content area classes. Sometimes, language arts and content area teachers plan joint writing projects.

FIGURE 1-4 Sample Story Dictated by a Kindergartner

Then Mommy tried to catch him. But she couldn't catch him.

Then Sebastian tried to chase him. But he couldn't catch him.

Then Peter tried to catch him. And he did. And Peter put him back in the box.

FIGURE 1-5 An Indian Legend

The Promise of Blueberries

The sunrise glittered on the meadows and forests. As Blue Moon and Little Star were going to the meadow to pick blueberries they were talking too.

Little Star said, "I don't think we should go do this because we might get in trouble. The blueberries are so rare. Let's make a promise that we won't eat blueberries for fourteen days and nights because they are so rare. The Great Spirit will be so proud of us for doing this.

"It's getting dark now. We better go back to camp." "You're right, Little Star." Blue Moon and Little Star had been doing about the same thing all week except they were not eating blueberries as usual. It was hard but they did it. The Great Spirit was getting more and more proud of them.

It is the fourteenth day now but they forgot to look at the day stone. When they went to bed that night they looked at the day stone and saw that it was the fourteenth day. The next morning when they woke up they knew it was the fifteenth day since they made the promise. So they were going to pick some blueberries.

The Great Spirit spoke, "Blue Moon and Little Star, I'm rewarding you and your people from now on by enriching your meadows with blueberries." And their people always had blueberries to eat.

Tiffanie, grade 3

For example, the students in Mrs. Harris' seventh-grade language arts class use writing as they read and discuss literature. Mrs. Harris selects a children's version of the Old English epic poem *Beowulf* (Keeping, 1982) to read aloud. Her students are excited; they know a little about the Middle Ages, and castles have always excited them. Writing will be important before, during, and after Mrs. Harris reads the poem aloud. Before reading, students work in small groups to brainstorm lists of words related to the Middle Ages. Then the groups share their lists and a lively discussion develops about this era. Mrs. Harris clarifies misconceptions and provides some additional information specifically about the Anglo-Saxons and British life in the 700s. As Mrs. Harris reads the epic poem aloud, students keep a reading log in which they reflect on the events in the poem, the qualities that Beowulf possesses, and the use of alliteration rather than rhyme in the poem. After reading, they will each create a project that involves writing. Together Mrs. Harris and her students develop a list of the possible projects to choose from. Here are 10 ideas from that list:

1. Choose a character from the poem and write five simulated journal entries as that character.
2. Compose the lyrics for a song inspired by *Beowulf.*
3. Rewrite *Beowulf* in comic book form.
4. Update *Beowulf* to the present time.

5. Together with several of your classmates, develop a news broadcast depicting events described in *Beowulf.*
6. Design a movie poster for *Beowulf* and assign parts to well-known actors.
7. Do a short research project on one aspect of life in the Middle Ages, such as clothing, transportation, food, housing, or weaponry.
8. Design a crossword, seek-and-find, or jigsaw puzzle using ideas from *Beowulf.*

FIGURE 1-6 Simulated Journal

February 23, 1836

Dear Journal,
It's very cold and rainy out. I've been on guard duty now since 24:00. Now it's 2:00. Well, the Mexicans sure won't get by me.

February 26, 1836

Dear Journal,
Well, here I am again on guard duty. The Mexicans have calmed down a little bit but not much. Boy, I wish I could just go down to their fort, and I would tell 'em a piece of my mind (without getting killed!). I wonder how ma and pa are doing out there in Louisiana. Ma sent me a telegram a short time ago. She said pa was getting sicker every day. Well, if I would just go home for a while, it should make him feel better. Boy do I miss them.

February 29, 1836

Dear Journal, No food. Seven dead. I'm scared!

March 4, 1836

Dear Journal,
Am I going to live or die? The war's going to be over soon. We have 57 men left but the Mexicans have 3,578 men. We know we're going to lose. It's just sad to think if we're going to die.

March 5, 1836

Dear Journal,
Here I am lying in bed. I got shot six hours ago. They said I didn't have a chance! I told them if I didn't give up I would live.

Kary

9. Design the front page of a newspaper using information from *Beowulf.*
10. Construct puppets and a stage depicting the characters and the setting from *Beowulf.* Then act out a scene for the class.

Bucky chose to write a simulated journal in the character of Beowulf, and the first three entries in his journal are presented below:

Marz 7, 750 A.D.

Today a wanderer came and spoke of a half-wolf, half-man known as Grendel the death shadow. This night-stalker dwells in the land ruled by King Hrothgar known as Denmark. He told how this evil creature prowled into King Hrothgar's Hall, hating all humans and killing 30 of his most noble warriors. He told how Grendel keeps coming back hoping for the day that men sleep again in Heorot Hall. I knew I had to repay the favor the King Hrothgar had paid to my father Ecgtheow years ago. So I asked King Hygelac his leave to go on a seafaring trip. I told him of the debt waiting to be paid and the wish was granted.

Marz 8, 750 A.D.

I've chosen 14 other warriors and today we shall embark on our dangerous journey across the mysterious seas to Denmark. We are full of spirit and ready to come to King Hrothgar's aid.

Marz 9, 750 A.D.

When we arrived in Denmark my warriors and I were made welcome by King Hrothgar. A great feast was held in Heorot Hall. We feasted upon steaming boar's head and eel pie. And I was given a golden cup to drink from as a token of thanks for coming so valiantly to King Hrothgar's aid. But my companions and I were careful not to rejoice too quickly. For we knew that there was still a battle to be fought. We barred the doors of Heorot Hall and prepared for what was to come. Time passed and the torches were burning slowly. And suddenly Grendel barged in and tore one of my warriors limb from limb and drank his warm red blood. Then I jumped from the darkness of my resting bench and grasped the beast firmly. We struggled back and forth constantly until finally with a last effort to try to escape Grendel's arm was torn from the roots. He fled in pain. In triumph we nailed up the huge gruesome limb on the roof beam above the high seat of Hrothgar. We thought that the beast was surely dead.

Another seventh-grader's response activity, an interview with Beowulf, is presented in Chapter 9, "Writing Across the Curriculum." These reading-writing connections increase students' interest in the piece of literature and provide the opportunity for students' to apply what they are learning.

Mr. Mattingly used writing in his eighth-grade science class for an end-of-year project. As a review, his students brainstormed a list of the scientific concepts they had learned during the school year, and then each student chose one concept to develop into a picture book. The completed books were to be presented to the local elementary school and placed in their school library to augment their small selection of science books. One student chose solstices and equinoxes as her topic, and an excerpt from her book is presented in Figure 1-7.

The Role of Writing in the Elementary Grades

M. A. K. Halliday (1980) identified three components of language arts as learning language, learning about language, and learning through language. These components can be rephrased specifically to describe the role of writing in the elementary grades: learning to write, learning about written language, and learning through writing.

Learning to Write. Through experiences with writing, students learn to write. Informal writing activities, such as journal writing, brainstorming, and freewriting, provide opportunities for students to acquire writing fluency. For more formal writing activities, such as writing stories, reports, and poems, students use the writing process. This process is a multistep strategy through which students learn how to gather and organize ideas for writing, how to write a rough draft, and how to refine and polish that piece of writing.

Learning About Written Language. As students learn to write, they discover the uniqueness of written language and the ways in which it differs from oral language and other types of graphics. They develop an appreciation for the interrelatedness of function, audience, and form in writing and learn to consider these three elements as they write. At the same time, students are introduced to the mechanics of writing, and they learn to use some of the basic conventions of written language, including standard spelling and usage, capitalization, and formatting considerations.

Learning Through Writing. Writing is a valuable learning tool that has many applications across the curriculum. Students write informally to analyze and synthesize their learning as Mrs. Harris' seventh graders did when they kept reading logs to reflect on *Beowulf.* Similarly, students write formally and apply their knowledge when they write reports, as Mr. Mattingly's students did when they applied their knowledge of scientific concepts through the picture book reports.

Children's writing changes during the elementary grades as they tackle a variety of writing activities and the content of their writing becomes more sophisticated. Also, they become better able to consider the function, audience, and form of their writing and to manage the mechanics and other conventions of writing.

FRAMEWORK FOR A WRITING PROGRAM

Most of the writing activities provided for children in the elementary grades have fallen under the rubric of "creative writing." Using this traditional approach, teachers often provided a creative topic or story starter such as, "One spooky Halloween night, I was walking up the stairs to a haunted house and . . . ," for their students to finish. This approach was often unsatisfactory, and students wrote

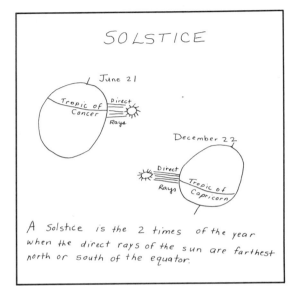

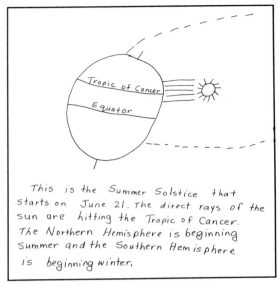

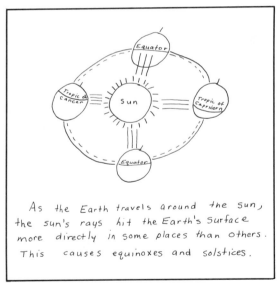

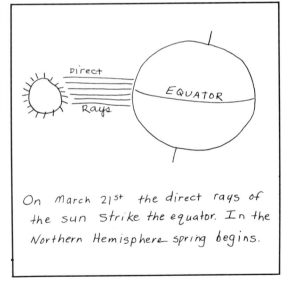

FIGURE 1-7 Excerpt from an Eighth-Grader's Picture Book Report on Solstices and Equinoxes

poorly developed compositions. Unsuccessful experiences with writing often led teachers to believe that their students could not write and needed to learn the mechanics of written language—capitalization, punctuation, grammar, and spelling—before attempting to write again. This logic that teaching mechanical skills would prepare students for writing was faulty; what the traditional approach lacked was instruction. Teachers did not teach students how to write; instead, through the creative writing approach, students practiced writing.

An alternative to the creative writing approach to writing instruction is the writing process approach (Britton, 1970; Calkins, 1983, 1986; Emig, 1971; Flower & Hayes, 1977, 1981; Graves, 1975, 1983). By using the writing process, students learn how to write, not how to fail at writing. In the process approach, writers move recursively through a series of stages as they compose. These five stages are prewriting, drafting, revising, editing, and sharing. Students participate in a variety of activities as they gather and organize information, pour out ideas in a rough draft, get feedback on how well they are communicating, and locate and correct mechanical errors before sharing their writing with a genuinely interested audience. Elementary students can learn to use these activities just as teenage and adult writers do. As elementary students learn these stages and the activities involved in each, they are learning strategies they can use for "attacking" any writing assignment. In short, they are becoming writers.

The writing process approach was used to create many of the examples shared throughout this textbook. Students who use the writing process become deeply involved in their own writing activities and develop a strong sense of ownership and responsibility toward their writing. Some activities such as journal writing activities, however, are informal, and the entire writing process is not used. However, material from the journals may serve as prewriting and be used later in more formal writing activities in which the entire writing process is used.

The approach I advocate in this book is the process approach to writing. It involves 10 components that are delineated in this section and then expanded on in the following chapters. The list is remarkably similar to a list of research-based instructional recommendations for teaching learning disabled students (Graham & Harris, 1988). Writing that emerges from this process approach is described as "authentic" (Edelsky & Smith, 1984) because students are involved in real-life writing activities for genuine audiences. In contrast, "inauthentic" writing occurs when the writing process and the other components of the writing framework are ignored.

1. Students Learn and Use the Writing Process. Teaching students to use the writing process is the first and most important component of a writing program in the elementary grades (Hoskisson & Tompkins, 1987). Instruction in the writing process begins in kindergarten as students gather and organize ideas before writing and share their writing with classmates and other audiences. By second grade students have been introduced to all five stages. Once students understand the five stages, they then apply the process to different types of writing activities, such as letters to pen pals, stories, reports, and poems. (The writing process and the activities involved in each stage will be more fully described in Chapter 3, "The Writing Process.")

2. Students Write Every Day. Time should be set aside every day for writing in each elementary classroom (Tway, 1984). Writing informally in journals and learning logs is one way to provide this daily practice. Students also need larger chunks of time for more formal writing activities such as stories, poems, reports, and persuasive essays that involve the writing process. Writing about complex and powerful ideas cannot be chopped up into half-hour periods, nor can expression be called forth by giving a few directions and the dictum, "Now get busy." For students to write, to find out about themselves and what they think and feel, they must be given adequate time to write. Finding time in the school day for this writing may mean throwing away the fill-in-the-blank workbooks and dittoes that clutter students' in-school world. (See Chapter 2 "Informal Writing" for more information about journals and learning logs and Chapters 4 through 7 for information about more formal writing activities.)

3. Students' Writing Is Based on Their Experiences. Students must know a topic well to write about it. However self-evident this maxim appears on the surface, it is rarely acknowledged in practice (Hoskisson & Tompkins, 1987). Personal experience is the best source of information, and much of children's writing comes from their personal experiences—a pet they've cared for, a television program viewed last night, or a fishing trip with granddad. For other types of writing, teachers need to provide students with the background for writing. Reading literature and content area books are two additional sources of experience. Students may write about what they are reading in reading logs during reading. After they read, they may apply what they have learned in response activities. Similarly, in social studies and science classes, students keep learning logs and apply what they have learned in writing stories, biographies, poems, and reports. In prewriting, the first stage of the writing process, students gather and organize ideas for writing. Sometimes this gathering is no more than a reflection on past experiences. At other times it involves more extended reading and study in content areas. Whether it involves a brief period of reflection and listing ideas or more lengthy study, writers must have a background of experiences.

4. Students Consider the Function, Form, and Audience of Writing. As they write, students make choices about function, form, and audience—three considerations that influence each other and the compositions students produce (Murray, 1985, 1987). As they consider function, students think about why they are writing. Is it to entertain, to persuade, to provide information? Or for some other purpose? Students must choose among many different forms of writing—stories, poems, reports, letters, for example—and use the conventions of the form they select. A piece of writing that is intended to entertain, for instance, may begin as a story and change into a poem or a script. As these changes in form occur, students switch to the conventions of the new form. Audience is the third major consideration, and students should write for many different audiences, including their classmates, other children, their parents, the local community, and more distant and less well-known audiences. As students write for varied audiences they learn about the social registers of the English language and how to vary the language in informal and formal writing.

5. *Students Write Across the Curriculum.* *Writing across the curriculum* is a new movement that involves writing in all content areas. Writing is a powerful tool for learning as well as a strategy for applying learning in social studies, science, and other content area classes (Britton et al., 1975; Emig, 1977; Gere, 1985; Hembrow, 1986). For example, students can keep learning logs to describe and reflect on the concepts they are learning and to clarify misconceptions. Students apply what they have learned through writing stories, reports, persuasive essays, and other formal types of writing. The ideas for these compositions may come from social studies, science, or other content areas. (For more information about the connections between content area study and writing, see Chapter 9, "Writing Across the Curriculum.")

6. *Students Work Collaboratively with Classmates.* In the process approach to writing, students work in pairs and small groups as they prewrite, draft, revise, and edit their writing. This type of collaborative learning is an effective way for students to assume responsibility for their own learning. By talking and sharing ideas as they work together, students learn from each other and enjoy writing (Bruffee, 1984; Dewey, 1938; Fine, 1987; Freire, 1968).

In her study of fourth graders' collaboration in writing, "Do 1 and 1 Make 2?", Collette Daiute (1986) found that students enjoyed exchanging writing strategies and experimenting with writing conventions and instructions. She cited a fourth grader's explanation of the value of collaborative writing:

> It's [writing with a partner] easier than writing by yourself . . . because it's easier to get ideas. You have someone to argue with and get better ideas . . . When you write with someone you don't get all the credit but that doesn't really matter and you have two points of view on the story. (p. 384)

While peer feedback is the most common type of collaboration in writing, students may also participate in a variety of other collaborative activities as they write.

- Conferencing to help a classmate choose a topic for writing
- Working together to gather and organize ideas before writing
- Drafting a group composition
- Participating in a writing group to share and critique writing
- Proofreading each other's writing to locate and correct mechanical errors
- Collaborating in writing and illustrating the final copy (Elbow, 1973; Golub, 1988; Graves, 1983)

To write together productively, students need to develop specific collaborative learning skills, and teachers must establish guidelines for group behavior, model the behaviors appropriate in group work, and monitor students as they work in groups. As well as providing immediate feedback about writing concerns and allowing for continuous, informal learning, working collaboratively makes writing less isolated and a more social experience.

7. *Teachers Provide an Instructional Scaffold.* Teachers play several different roles in the various stages of the writing process. They serve as a guide or coach as they encourage students who are moving through the writing process stages. They encourage, guide, and meet with students in writing conferences. They respond to and reflect on writing as any interested audience would. Also, teachers may model the writing process by leading the class in writing a group composition called a class collaboration. The model the teacher supplies is an example to learn from, not a sample to copy (Cazden, 1983).

Through these roles, teachers provide a "scaffold," or framework, to support students as they tackle complex learning tasks (Applebee & Langer, 1983; Bruner, 1978; Cazden, 1980). As students' writing skills improve, the need for this scaffolding diminishes. However, teachers must continue to be responsive to children's growing competencies. It is important that teachers appreciate the power of their interactions with students and how they support students' learning.

8. Skills Are Taught in Context. In the process approach to writing, students are taught language skills as the need to know these skills occurs in writing (Atwell, 1987; Graves, 1983). This is an opportunistic approach in which teachers must seize the "teachable moment" when students want or need to learn a particular language skill to communicate effectively in writing. In contrast, in the traditional approach to language arts instruction students were taught skills according to a scope and sequence chart, in the order they were presented in a textbook or workbook without any consideration for the skills students may have been using or needing in their writing. Too often students saw these textbook and workbook drills as unrelated to real life and not worth their time and effort. Sometimes teachers feel that they lose control of students with the opportunistic approach, but they can develop a tracking system to record when students are introduced to a skill, apply it successfully or unsuccessfully in their writing, and demonstrate mastery of it. As students collaborate in groups and when teachers and students have conferences about writing, introducing, practicing, and applying language skills become part of the writing process. Teachers can also plan mini-lessons in which they provide a quick review of a skill for one or more students.

9. Mechanics Are Writers' Tools. Spelling, handwriting, and grammar are tools for writers and courtesies for readers (Graves, 1983). Correct spelling, neat handwriting, and standard English in and of themselves will not produce a memorable piece of writing. The ideas and content in a composition are more important, and students focus on them during the first three stages of the writing process. During the fourth stage, attention shifts from content to mechanics, and writers proofread their compositions to identify and correct these mechanical errors. Too early an emphasis on these tools in the writing process will send a false message to students about their importance and will hinder children's creative expression rather than facilitate it. (For more information about the role of spelling, handwriting, and grammar as tools for writers, see Chapter 8, "Writers' Tools.")

10. Teachers Focus Assessment on Process, Not Product. When teachers assess students' achievement in writing, they should focus more on the writing process students use than on the product that students create (Johnston, 1987; McKenzie & Tompkins, 1984). In the past, teachers have tried to evaluate student writing by comparing the quality of one student story or to another or by counting the number of errors in a piece of writing. These attempts have been futile. However, when the writing process is used, teachers focus their assessment on how well their students use the writing process and participate in various collaborative writing activities. Teachers can develop checklists of activities that students participate in as they complete specific writing assignments, such as "student draws a plot diagram," "student shares the rough draft in a writing group," or "student includes at least three chapters in the report." Then teachers assess students' writing by comparing the writing with the criteria listed on the checklist. (For more information on assessment, see Chapter 10, "Assessing Students' Writing" and the sections on assessment in Chapters 4 through 7 in which assessment checklists for specific writing assignments are delineated.)

These 10 components for a writing program in the elementary grades are based on current research in cognitive learning, written discourse, and sociolinguistics. To further clarify the application of these areas of research to the writing process, it is worthwhile to describe not only what an effective process-oriented program *is,* but what it is *not.*

Writing Is Not Skill-and-Drill Exercises in Capitalization, Punctuation, Spelling, Grammar, or Usage. Writing is communication and while these mechanical skills are important in making writing readable, they are not as important as the content of a piece of writing. Moreover, research has shown that these writing mechanics are best learned when they are being applied in genuine and functional writing activities, not as practice sheets.

Writing Is Not Handwriting. Handwriting is a tool for graphically representing thoughts just as dictation and entering text on a microcomputer are; the goal of handwriting is legibility. Having students copy sentences or paragraphs from the chalkboard is not writing and does not contribute significantly to teaching students about writing. It is also questionable that copying from the chalkboard improves handwriting skills unless the teacher models the formation of each letter while the students watch.

Writing Should Not Be Used As Punishment. Requiring students to write an essay or complete the sentence "I will not . . . " and write it over and over as punishment for misbehavior, tardiness, or poor work habits is ineffective and inappropriate. Both concerned educators and the National Council of Teachers of English are fighting to prohibit the use of writing as punishment because it neither solves the problem that precipitated the punishment nor teaches students how to write.

Writing Is Not Dependent on Any One Program or Textbook. Too often educators and parents are looking for a "quick fix"—one program or textbook—that will teach students how to write. However, writing is much more complex than that, and no one approach or gimmick will adequately teach students how to write. Rather, a writing program that includes the 10 components presented in this section provides the best basis for teaching students in the elementary grades. Gimmicky story starters, imaginary pen pals, or skill-and-drill workbook exercises will not take the place of the process approach to writing in which students learn how to write and write for different functions and audiences using various writing forms.

STATUS OF WRITING INSTRUCTION TODAY

In the last decade writing has received an increasing amount of attention from the American public as well as concerned educators. This interest in writing is due to several factors. First, writing is an important communication skill, and in a technologically complex world, the ability to communicate effectively with others has become crucial (Smith, 1988). Writing is becoming increasingly recognized as the flip-side of the literacy coin and the meaning-making relationship between the reading and writing processes is being acknowledged (Jensen, 1984). This reading-writing connection is a second reason for the growth of interest in writing by reading educators. Next, writing is being recognized for its potential as a tool for learning, and "writing to learn" or "writing across the curriculum" is an important part of any instructional program, whether at the elementary, secondary, or college level (Gere, 1985; Langer & Applebee, 1987).

The word processing capability of computers is also responsible for spurring interest in writing (Knapp, 1986). Educators are optimistic that these writing tools will facilitate writing for students. Even though recent research with computers has not demonstrated that word processing actually improves the quality of students' writing, the ease with which revisions and editorial corrections can be made on computers should be a boon to writers at all ages.

Last, the process approach to writing is revolutionizing writing instruction (Proett & Gill, 1986). Teachers who in the past merely provided students with *opportunities* to practice writing are now teaching students *how* to write. In a recent U.S. Department of Education booklet, *What Works: Research About Teaching and Learning* (1986), the writing process was described as "the most effective way to teach writing" (p. 27). Information about the writing process is increasingly being presented in the most recently published language arts textbooks (DeGroff & Leu, 1988), and reading-writing connections are also being included in reading textbooks. Even with this new emphasis on writing, however, students need more opportunities to write extended discourse and to share their writing with classmates.

State-Mandated Writing Assessments

Writing assessments have been added recently to the batteries of achievement tests mandated by the legislatures in almost every state. This addition to state-wide testing programs demonstrates the increased interest in this part of the elementary curriculum. Most writing assessments on these tests require students to write sample compositions rather than to answer questions about grammar and usage, spelling, capitalization, and punctuation. This emphasis on the content of writing rather than on isolated mechanical skills is clear evidence of the widespread acceptance of the writing process as an important part of the elementary curriculum.

The National Writing Project

The National Writing Project (NWP) has had a tremendous impact on focusing attention on writing instruction. The NWP began as the Bay Area Writing Project at the University of California at Berkeley in 1974. It was conceived by James Gray and a group of English teachers who wanted to improve the quality of writing instruction in elementary and secondary schools. In less than two decades, the NWP has spread to more than 170 affiliate groups located in almost every state as well as in Canada, Europe, and Asia. For example, the Gateway Writing Project serves the St. Louis area, the Capital Writing Project serves the Washington, D.C. area, and the Oklahoma Writing Project serves the state of Oklahoma. In-service workshops are scheduled in school districts located near each affiliate group. One of the principles on which the NWP is based is that the best teacher of other teachers is a teacher, and teachers who have been trained by the affiliate groups give presentations at the in-service workshops.

Each NWP affiliate group recruits experienced elementary teachers who have special interest and expertise in teaching writing to participate in special summer training institutes. These teachers then serve as teacher/consultants and make presentations at the in-service workshops. Many NWP affiliate groups also sponsor other workshops, study tours, young author conferences, workshops for student writers, and teacher-as-researcher projects that have direct classroom applications.

■ ANSWERING TEACHERS' QUESTIONS ABOUT TEACHING WRITING

1. How can I fit writing into my already overcrowded curriculum?

Don't think of writing as a separate subject that must have its own 30 or 45 minutes during the school day; instead, writing should be integrated into language arts and other curricular areas. Writing can become a valuable learning tool, with language skills being taught and learned through writing. Similarly, students write about the books they are reading and about the content they are learning in science and social studies. Check Chapter 9, "Writing Across the Curriculum," for specific ideas about integrating writing into other curricular areas.

2. I teach kindergarten, and young children who don't even know how to read can't write, can they?

Yes, young children can write! The notion that language learning progresses from listening and talking to reading and then to writing is outdated. Recent research suggests that some young children begin to write before learning to read, and certainly the two—reading and writing—go hand in hand. Young children use invented spelling, or writing in which they use scribbles or a few letters to represent entire words. Such writing may not use standard spelling, but it is writing, nevertheless. Writing should be an important part of kindergarten and first-grade programs, not postponed until students are independent readers.

3. How can I learn more about how to teach writing?

First, most schools or school districts provide in-service or staff development programs, some of which will likely be devoted to writing. Contact your administrator or local staff development coordinator and request an in-service program on writing.

Second, two organizations are dedicated to improving the quality of instruction in the language arts, including writing. These two organizations are the National Council of teachers of English (NCTE) and the International Reading Association (IRA). Both organizations publish journals that include articles related to writing instruction. *Language Arts* is published by NCTE and *The Reading Teacher* by IRA. A list of these and other journals that publish articles about writing and writing instruction are presented in Figure 1-8.

NCTE and IRA also organize yearly national conferences held in major cities around the United States on a rotating basis. At these conferences, teachers can listen to presentations given by authorities on writing instruction and by classroom teachers who have developed innovative techniques for teaching writing in their classrooms.

Third, teachers can learn more by reading books about writing and writing instruction. In recent years, a number of excellent books have been written both by classroom teachers who have special expertise in writing as well as by experts in the field of writing research. A list of books you may want to consult is presented in Figure 1-9.

FIGURE 1-8 Journals That Publish Articles About Writing and Writing Instruction

Language Arts
English Journal
College Communication and Composition
Research in the Teaching of English
National Council of Teachers of English
1111 Kenyon Road
Urbana, IL 61801

The Reading Teacher
Journal of Reading
International Reading Association
800 Barksdale Road
P.O. Box 8139
Newark, DE 19714

The ALAN Review
The Adolescent Literature Assembly of
   National Council of Teachers of English
1111 Kenyon Road
Urbana, IL 61801

The Bulletin
The Children's Literature Assembly of
   National Council of Teachers of English
1111 Kenyon Road
Urbana, IL 61801

Journal of Teaching Writing
425 Agnes Street
Indianapolis, IN 46202

Learning
530 University Avenue
Palo Alto, CA 94301

The New Advocate
Christopher-Gordon Publishers
P.O. Box 809
Needham Heights, MA 02194-0006

The Writing Teacher
P.O. Box 791437
San Antonio, TX 78279

Written Communication
Sage Publications
275 South Beverly Drive
Beverly Hills, CA 90212

FIGURE 1-9   Books About Writing and Writing Instruction

Atwell, N. (1987). *In the middle: Writing, reading, and learning with adolescents.* Upper Montclair, NJ: Boynton/Cook.

Barr, M., D'Arcy, P., & Healy, M. K. (1982). *What's going on? Language/learning episodes in British and American classrooms, grades 4–13.* Montclair, NJ: Boynton/Cook.

Calkins, L. M. (1986). *The art of teaching writing.* Portsmouth, NH: Heinemann.

Cooper, C. R., & Odell, L. (1978). *Research on composing: Points of departure.* Urbana, IL: National Council of Teachers of English.

Emig, J. (1983). *The web of meaning: Essays on writing, teaching, learning and thinking.* Upper Montclair, NJ: Boynton/Cook.

Graves, D. H. (1983). Writing: *Teachers and children at work.* Portsmouth, NH: Heinemann.

Graves, D. H. (1984). *A researcher learns to write: Selected articles and monographs.* Exeter, NH: Heinemann.

Harste, J., Woodward, V. A., & Burke, C. L. (1984). *Language stories and literacy lessons.* Portsmouth, NH: Heinemann.

Hillocks, G. (1986). *Research on written composition.* Urbana, IL: ERIC Clearinghouse on Reading and Communication Skills and the National Conference on Research in English.

Johnson, D. M., & Roen, D. H. (1989). *Richness in writing: Empowering ESL students.* New York: Longman.

Kirby, D., & Liner, T. (1981). *Inside out: Developmental strategies for teaching writing.* Montclair, NJ: Boynton/Cook.

Knapp, L. R. (1986). *The word processor and the writing teacher.* Englewood Cliffs, NJ: Prentice-Hall.

Murray, D. M. (1982). *Learning by teaching: Selected articles on writing and teaching.* Montclair, NJ: Boynton/Cook.

Murray, D. M. (1987). *Write to learn* (2nd ed.). New York: Holt.

Newkirk, T., & Atwell, N. (1988). *Understanding writing: Ways of observing, learning, and teaching K–8* (2nd. ed.). Portsmouth, NH: Heinemann.

Petrosky, A. R., & Bartholomae, D. (1986). *The teaching of writing* (85th Yearbook of the National Society of the Study of Education). Chicago: National Society for the Study of Education.

Proett, J., & Gill, K. (1986). *The writing process in action: A handbook for teachers.* Urbana, IL: National Council of Teachers of English.

Rhodes, L. K., & Dudley-Marling, C. (1988). *Readers and writers with a difference: A holistic approach to teaching learning disabled and remedial students.* Portsmouth, NH: Heinemann.

Fourth, National Writing Project affiliate groups sponsor in-service programs for elementary teachers as well as summer training institutes. For the location of the NWP affiliate group nearest you, contact the National Writing Project, School of Education, University of California, Berkeley, CA 94720.

A final source is local authors who give presentations about writing and talk about their own writing processes. Many authors will also talk to students and present demonstration lessons.

4. I'm not much of a writer. I don't think I know enough about writing to teach writing.

You don't have to have a degree in English or have published a novel to be able to teach writing. Similarly, it is not necessary to be able to identify a gerund or a comma splice to teach writing. Instead, teachers need to know how to teach the *writing process* and how to guide students as they strive to communicate their thoughts. However, if you want to review the guidelines for effective writing, an excellent resource is William Strunk Jr. and E. B. White's *The Elements of Style* (1979). These authors provide the basic guidelines for effective writing in a very readable little book, only 85 pages in length.

■ REFERENCES

Applebee, A. N. (1978). *The child's concept of story: Ages 2–17.* Chicago: University of Chicago Press.

Applebee, A. N., & Langer, J. A. (1983). Instructional scaffolding: Reading and writing and natural language activities. *Language Arts, 60,* 168–175.

Atwell, N. (1987). *In the middle: Writing, reading, and learning with adolescents.* Upper Montclair, NJ: Boynton/Cook.

Barr, M., D'Arcy, P., & Healty, M. (Eds.). (1981). *What's going on: Language/learning episodes in British and American classrooms, grades 4–13.* Montclair, NJ: Boynton/Cook.

Bissex, G. L. (1980). *Gyns at wrk: A child learns to write and read.* Cambridge, MA: Harvard University Press.

Britton, J. L., Burgess, T., Martin, N., McLeod, A., & Rosen, H. (1975). *The development of writing abilities, 11–18.* London: Macmillan.

Bruffee, K. A. (1984). Collaborative learning and the "conversation of mankind." *College English, 46,* 635–652.

Bruner, J. (1978). The role of dialogue in language acquisition. In A. Sinclair, R. J. Jarvelle, & W. J. M. Levelt (Eds.), *The child's concept of language.* New York: Springer-Verlag.

Butler, A., & Turnbill, J. (1984). *Towards a reading-writing classroom.* Rozelle, New South Wales (Australia): Primary English Teaching Association and Portsmouth, NH: Heinemann.

Calkins, L. M. (1980). When children want to punctuate: Basic skills belong in context. *Language Arts, 57,* 567–573.

Calkins, L. M. (1983). *Lessons from a child: On the teaching and learning of writing.* Portsmouth, NH: Heinemann.

Calkins, L. M. (1986). The art of teaching writing. Portsmouth, NH: Heinemann.

Cazden, C. B. (1980). Peekaboo as an instructional model: Discourse development at home and at school. *Papers and Reports of Child Language Development, 17,* 1–29.

Cazden, C. B. (1983). Adult assistance to language development: Scaffolds, models, and direct instruction. In R. P. Parker & F. A. Davis (Eds.), *Developing literacy: Young children's use of language,* pp. 3–18. Newark, DE: International Reading Association.

Chomsky, C. (1971). Write now, read later. *Childhood Education, 47,* 296–299.

Daiute, C. (1986). Do 1 and 1 make 2? Patterns of influence by collaborative authors. *Written Communication, 3,* 382–408.

de Paola, T. (1983). *The legend of the bluebonnet: An old tale of Texas.* New York: Putnam.

de Paola, T. (1988). *The legend of the Indian paintbrush.* New York: Putnam.

DeGroff, L. C., & Leu, Jr. D. J. (1988). An analysis of writing activities: A study of language arts textbooks. *Written Communication, 4,* 253–268.

Dewey, J. (1938). *Experience and education.* New York: Collier.

Edelsky, C., & Smith, K. (1984). Is that writing—Or are those marks just a figment of your curriculum? *Language Arts, 61,* 24–32.

Elbow, P. (1973). *Writing without teachers.* Oxford: Oxford University Press.

Emig, J. (1971). *The composing processes of twelfth graders.* Champaign, IL: National Council of Teachers of English.

Emig, J. (1977). Writing as a mode of learning. *College Composition and Communication, 28,* 122–128.

Fine, E. S. (1987). Marbles lost, marbles found: Collaborative production of text. *Language Arts, 64,* 474–487.

Flower, L. S., & Hayes, J. R. (1977). Problem-solving strategies and the writing process. *College English, 39,* 449–461.

Flower, L. S., & Hayes, J. R. (1981). A cognitive process theory of writing. *College Communication and Composition, 32,* 365–387.

Freire, P. (1968). *Pedagogy of the oppressed.* New York: Seabury.

Fulwiler, T., & Young, A. (Eds.). (1982). *Language connections: Writing and reading across the curriculum.* Urbana, IL: National Council of Teachers of English.

Gere, A. R. (Ed.). (1985). *Roots in the sawdust: Writing to learn across the disciplines.* Urbana, IL: National Council of Teachers of English.

Golub, J. (Ed.). (1988). *Focus on collaborative learning* (Classroom Practices in Teaching English, 1988). Urbana, IL: National Council of Teachers of English.

Graham, S., & Harris, K. R. (1988). Instructional recommendations for teaching writing to exceptional students. *Exceptional Children, 54,* 506–512.

Graves, D. H. (1975). An examination of the writing processes of seven-year-old children. *Research in the Teaching of English, 9,* 227–241.

Graves, D. H. (1983). *Writing: Teachers and children at work.* Exeter, NH: Heinemann.

Graves, D. H., & Hansen, J. (1982). The author's chair. *Language Arts, 60,* 176–183.

Halliday, M. A. K. (1980). Three aspects of children's language development: Learning language, learning through language, learning about language. In Y. M. Goodman, M. M. Haussler, & D. S. Strickland (Eds.) *Oral and written language development research: Impact on the schools* (pp. 7–19). Proceedings from the 1979–1980 IMPACT Conferences sponsored by the International Reading Association and the National Council of Teachers of English.

Hansen, J. (1987). *When writers read.* Portsmouth, NH: Heinemann.

Harste, J. C., Woodward, V. A., & Burke, C. L. (1984). *Language stories and literacy lessons.* Portsmouth, NH: Heinemann.

Hembrow, V. (1986). A heuristic approach across the curriculum. *Language Arts, 63,* 674–679.

Hoskisson, K., & Tompkins, G. E. (1987). *Language arts: Content and teaching strategies.* Columbus, OH: Merrill.

Hymes, D. (1974). *Foundations in sociolinguistics: An ethnographic approach.* Philadelphia: University of Pennsylvania Press.

Jensen, J. M. (Ed.). (1984). *Composing and comprehending.* Urbana, IL: National Conference on Research in English and the ERIC Clearinghouse on Reading and Communication Skills.

Johnston, P. (1987). Teachers as evaluation experts. *The Reading Teacher, 40,* 744–748.

Keeping, C. (1982). *Beowulf.* Oxford: Oxford University Press.

Knapp, L. R. (1986). *The word processor and the writing teacher.* Englewood Cliffs, NJ: Prentice-Hall.

Kucer, S. L. (1985). The making of meaning: Reading and writing as parallel processes. *Written Communication, 2,* 317–336.

Langer, J. A., & Applebee, A. N. (1987). *How writing shapes thinking: A study of teaching and learning* (NCTE Research Report No. 22). Urbana, IL: National Council of Teachers of English.

Martin, N., D'Arcy, P., Newton, B., & Parker, R. (1976). *Writing and learning across the curriculum, 11–16.* London: Ward Lock Educational.

McKenzie, L., & Tompkins, G. E. (1984). Evaluating students' writing: A process approach. *Journal of Teaching Writing, 3,* 201–212.

Murray, D. M. (1985). *A writer teaches writing* (2nd ed.). Boston: Houghton Mifflin.

Murray, D. M. (1987). *Write to learn* (2nd ed.). New York: Holt.

Proett, J., & Gill, K. (1986). *The writing process in action: A handbook for teachers.* Urbana, IL: National Council of Teachers of English.

Smith, F. (1982). *Writing and the writer.* New York: Holt.

Smith, F. (1983). Reading like a writer. *Language Arts, 60,* 558–567.

Smith, F. (1988). *Joining the literacy club: Further essays in education.* Portsmouth, NH: Heinemann.

Strunk Jr., W., & White, E. B. (1979). *The elements of style* (3rd ed.). New York: Macmillan.

Temple, C., Nathan, R., Burris, N., & Temple, F. (1988). *The beginnings of writing* (2nd ed.). Boston: Allyn and Bacon.

Tompkins, G. E., & McGee, L. M. (1989). Teaching repetition as a story structure. In K. D. Muth (Ed.), *Children's comprehension of text: Research into practice* (pp. 58–78). Newark, DE: International Reading Association.

Tway, E. (1984). *Time for writing in the elementary school* (TRIP Booklet). Urbana, IL: ERIC Clearinghouse on Reading and Communication Skills and the National Council of Teachers of English.

United States Department of Education. (1986). *What works: Research about teaching and learning.* Washington, DC: United States Department of Education.

Van Allen, R. (1976). *Language experiences in communication.* Boston: Houghton Mifflin.

2

Informal Writing

Mrs. Wheatley asks her sixth graders, "Would you like to live forever?" After a lively discussion of the advantages and disadvantages of immortality, she becomes more specific and asks students to write their answers to this question: "If I offered you a drink of water from a magic spring that would allow you to stay the same age you are right now forever, would you drink it?" Veronica answers:

I think I would save the water until I finish college and started my career. Then I would drink it because I would like to know how the world would be in about 200 years, and if I lived forever I could become a very important person.

After Veronica and her classmates share their writings, Mrs. Wheatley introduces the book she will read aloud to them, Natalie Babbitt's *Tuck Everlasting* (1975). This novel is about the Tuck family who unknowingly drank from a magic spring that stopped them from growing any older, a condition they found to have some surprising disadvantages. As the story begins, a young girl named Winnie comes upon the spring, and the Tucks kidnap her to keep her from drinking from it. Later, the Tucks explain to Winnie why they took her away from the spring and their story is overheard by an evil man who plans to expose them and make a profit from selling the magic spring water. The Tucks must prevent the man from doing this or risk having everyone find out about them and their immortality.

Mrs. Wheatley explains that *Tuck Everlasting* is a "think-about" story, and she suggests that the students make reading logs in which they can write their thoughts about the story. Students then compile individual booklets of paper stapled together with construction paper covers, which they decorate as Mrs. Wheatley begins reading the story. What the students have already written about drinking from the magic spring will become the first page in their logs. Like their impromptu writing about immortality, their other writings in this log will be informal and personal, written for and about themselves rather than for the teacher. They will be thinking on paper, she explains, because by writing about the story, they will understand it better.

Each day Mrs. Wheatley reads one chapter aloud, and after she reads, students spend approximately 10 minutes writing an entry in their logs. Rather than having them simply summarize the chapter, she asks them to relate the story to their own lives and gives them this list of possible writing topics:

- Who is your favorite or least favorite character?
- Does one character remind you of a friend or family member?
- Does one character remind you of yourself?
- Do any of the events in this story remind you of your own life?
- What event would you have handled differently if you were the character?
- Does anything puzzle you about the story? If so, explain.
- Does the setting remind you of somewhere you have been?
- What do you like best or least about the story?
- How does this story make you feel?
- What other stories that you have read does this story remind you of?
- What would you change about this story, if you could?

After writing, some students will eagerly share their entries with the class, while others will keep their entries private. Excerpts from Veronica's reading log are presented below to illustrate how students think about and respond to the novel:

Chapter 1:   I found the book quite boring although the author did use a lot of imagination in making the animals seem like real people.

Chapter 4:   At this point of the story I am beginning to like it a lot. My favorite character right now is Winnie. She seems like quite a little girl and the elf music I think is coming from Mae's music box. Winnie's grandmother seems pretty funny also.

Chapter 6:   Winnie has been kidnapped by the Tucks and you can tell she has a big imagination when you think about how she imagined the kidnappers. In a way I think she kind of enjoys this but as they go farther she begins to become more scared. Mae started playing the music box and the music was the same music her grandmother had told her was elf music.

Chapter 8:   indomitable-unstoppable
eddies of dust-small whirlpools or swirls
mirage-illusion, trick of eyes
I did notice the food they ate is rarely eaten today. I never really though about chewing but now that I do think about it, it is kind of a personal thing. I don't really like people watching me chew.

Chapter 18:   Right now in the story I like Jesse the best because he has big dreams and seems intent on making them come true. He's always looking at the bright side of things.

Chapter 22:   Winnie is feeling really guilty about Mae so she is going to help them get her out of jail. If I was Winnie I think I might run away with them because they are really nice people and she has grown to love them. She would probably miss her family a lot but if she drank the water, they wouldn't have to worry about her getting hurt.

Chapter 24:   I wish I was more like Winnie in a way. She is a very brave person and would do anything to help someone. "Stone walls do not a prison make" means there are other kinds of prisons besides rock walls and you can put yourself in a prison by shutting out others and not helping other people.

Epilogue: I think Tuck is happy that Winnie died and didn't have to live forever. I think it was neat that they saw the toad that lived forever. I liked the way the story ended but I kind of wanted Winnie to find Jesse and the Tucks and to drink the water and live forever.

Veronica's use of the first person pronoun *I* in this log demonstrates that she wrote about what she thought, what she liked, and what was meaningful to her in this log. She didn't try to second-guess what author Natalie Babbitt intended or what Mrs. Wheatley thought. She wrote for herself. Also, Veronica used the log to note unfamiliar words and phrases (e.g., "eddies of dust" in Chapter 8) and sayings (e.g., "stone walls do not a prison make" in Chapter 24).

After finishing the story, Mrs. Wheatley asks the students to respond again to the question, "If I offered you a drink of water from a magic spring that would allow you to stay the same age you are right now forever, would you drink it?" and Veronica writes:

■ If someone offered me some magic water that would let me live forever, I wouldn't take it because I believe if the Lord wanted us to live forever he would let us. And I wouldn't want to because forever is an awful long time.

The about-face in Veronica's second response demonstrates the power of a reading log to stimulate thinking and verifies Toby Fulwiler's (1987) statement that "when people write about something they learn it better" (p. 9). Having read and thought about immortality, Veronica has become less egocentric and more perceptive in her response.

Reading logs are one type of informal writing. The writing is personal and private as students think aloud on paper and explore their feelings. The focus is on the writer. Students' writing is spontaneous, loosely organized, and may contain many mechanical errors because the students are focusing on thinking, not spelling, capitalization, and punctuation. James Britton and his colleagues (1975) compare this type of writing to a written conversation, and that conversation may be with oneself or with someone who is interested in the writer.

Students use informal writing for many reasons. Romano (1987) has identified seven purposes:

■ Writing to get ready to learn
■ Writing to explore thinking
■ Writing to make learning personal
■ Writing to struggle with difficult learning
■ Writing to think independently
■ Writing to wonder
■ Writing to engage the imagination

Two other purposes that are more typical of younger children's writing might be added to Romano's list:

■ Writing to record experiences
■ Writing to share experiences with a trusted reader

Veronica and the other students in Mrs. Wheatley's sixth-grade class wrote for many of these purposes in their reading logs. Students were writing to get ready to learn when they wrote in response to Mrs. Wheatley's question about immortality before reading the novel; they were writing to record experiences and information as well as to explore thinking when they made entries in their logs. In addition, they were writing to make learning personal as they related the experiences in the novel to their own lives in their reading logs.

In this chapter, journal writing and other types of informal writing will be examined. These types include brainstorming, clustering, freewriting, and cubing:

four types of informal writing that are often thought of as prewriting activities. In these types of writing, students write informally for themselves or for a trusted audience of classmates, friends, family members, and the teacher. They write to record and share experiences, to think about what they are learning, and to personalize learning. Because this writing is informal and spontaneous, teachers should focus only on the thinking that inspired the writing. Students can refine and polish their writing using the writing process when it is important that the writing be mechanically correct—when it is made public. (See the discussion of the writing process in Chapter 3.)

JOURNAL WRITING

All sorts of people—artists, scientists, dancers, politicians, writers, assassins, and children—keep journals (Mallon, 1984). In most of these journals, people record the everyday events of their lives and the issues that concern them. These journals, typically written in notebook form, are personal records, not intended for public display. Other journals might be termed "working" journals in which writers record observations and other information that will be used for another purpose. For example, farmers might record weather or crop data or gardeners the blooming cycle of their plants.

The journals of some well-known public figures have survived hundreds of years and provide a fascinating glimpse of their authors and the times in which they lived. For example, the Renaissance genius Leonardo da Vinci recorded his daily activities, dreams, and plans for his painting and engineering projects in more than 40 notebooks. In the 1700s, Puritan theologian Jonathan Edwards documented his spiritual life in his journal. In the late 1700s American explorers Meriwether Lewis and George Rogers Clark, kept a journal of their travels across the North American continent, more for geographical than personal use. In the nineteenth century, the American writer Henry David Thoreau filled 39 notebooks with his essays. French author Victor Hugo carried a small pocket notebook to record ideas as they came to him—even at inopportune moments while talking with friends. American author F. Scott Fitzgerald filled his notebooks with snippets of conversation that he overheard, many of which he later used in *The Great Gatsby* and other novels. Anne Frank, who wrote while hiding from the Nazis during World War II, is the best-known child diarist.[1]

Journals may be used for a variety of purposes in elementary classrooms just as adults use them differently; however, for all types of journals, teachers should set aside specific periods for writing daily or at least several times a week. The frequency of the writing varies according to the purpose of the journal. If students keep personal journals or reflect on what they are learning in learning logs, they

---

[1]The terms *diary* and *journal* are often used synonymously, with diaries sometimes considered the more personal and private of the two. Whether the records that children write are called diaries or journals is unimportant. For convenience, I will use the term *journal* to refer to this type of informal writing.

may wish to record events daily. If they want to converse with the teacher in dialogue journals, write stories and poems in writing journals, or take the role of historical figures in simulated journals, they may wish to write two or three times a week. Young children may even want to combine writing and drawing in their journals.

The Tchudis (1984) suggest possible writing activities that explore students' experiences, investigate the world around them, and play with language:

- Recording past experiences
- Recording dreams
- Analyzing opinions to better understand one's values and beliefs
- Using the senses—seeing, hearing, feeling, smelling, tasting—to write more vividly
- Recording impressions about people, places, and new experiences
- Analyzing experiences by asking how and why
- Responding to newspaper/magazine articles, TV shows, or movies
- Collecting examples of dialogues and dialects
- Conducting a dialogue with oneself, friends, or historical personalities
- Collecting words, puns, riddles, and other word plays
- Copying quotes
- Making lists of possible writing topics

Toby Fulwiler (1985) shared excerpts from his daughter Megan's third-grade journal in *Language Arts,* demonstrating how she used writing for many of these functions. More recently, Megan Fulwiler (1986), now a teenager, reflected on her journal writing experience and her reasons for writing as reflected in the Tchudis' list. Most importantly, Megan described her journal as "an extension of my mind" that she used to "work out my feelings, ask questions, and find answers and write down and organize all my floating thoughts" (p. 809). She noted that as she grew up, her entries grew more personal and became a record of her growing up . Like Megan, students can gain valuable practice in writing through journal writing. They gain fluency and confidence that they can write. They also can experiment with new writing styles and formats without worrying too much about the conventions of writing that must be considered in more public writing. If they decide to make an entry "public," students can later revise and edit their writing.

Characters in children's literature, such as Harriet in *Harriet the Spy* (Fitzhugh, 1964), Leigh in *Dear Mr. Henshaw* (Cleary, 1983), and Catherine Hall in *A Gathering of Days* (Blos, 1979), keep journals in which they record the events in their lives, their ideas, and dreams. A list of stories in which characters keep journals is presented in Figure 2-1. In these stories, the characters demonstrate the process of journal writing and illustrate both the pleasures and difficulties of keeping a journal (Tway, 1981). A good way to introduce journal writing is by reading one of these books.

FIGURE 2-1   Stories in Which Characters Keep Journals

Anderson, J. (1987). *Joshua's westward journal.* New York: Morrow. (M)

Blos, J. (1979). *A gathering of days: A New England girl's journal, 1830–1832.* New York: Scribner. (U)

Bourne, M. A. *Nabby Adams's diary.* New York: Coward. (U)

Cleary, B. (1983). *Dear M. Henshaw.* New York: Morrow. (M)

Crusoe, R. (1972). *My journals and sketchbooks.* New York: Harcourt. (U)

Fisher, L. E. (1972). *The death of evening star: Diary of a young New England whaler.* New York: Doubleday. (M-U)

Fitzhugh, L. (1964). *Harriet the spy.* New York: Harper. (M)

Frank, A. (1952). *Anne Frank: The diary of a young girl.* New York: Doubleday. (U)

George, J. C. (1959). *My side of the mountain.* New York: Dutton. (M-U)

Glaser, D. (1976). *The diary of Trilby Frost.* New York: Holiday House. (U)

Mazer, N. F. (1971). *I, Trissy.* New York: Delacorte. (U)

Oakley, G. (1987). *The diary of a church mouse.* New York: Atheneum. (M)

Orgel, D. B. (1978). *The devil in Vienna.* New York: Dial. (U)

Reig, J. (1978). *Diary of the boy king Tut-Ankh-Amen.* New York: Scribner. (M)

Sachs, M. (1975). *Dorrie's book.* New York: Doubleday. (M)

Wilder, L. E. (1962). *On the way home.* New York: Harper. (M)

Williams, V. B. (1981). *Three days on a river in a red canoe.* New York: Greenwillow. (P-M)

P = primary grades (K–2)
M = middle grades (3–5)
U = upper grades (6–8)

Personal Journals

Students can keep personal journals in which they recount the events in their lives and write about topics of their own choosing. These third graders' entries show the variety of topics students may choose. Kerry reviews the events of a school day:

■   I came to school and cleaned out my desk and got my work all done and put a layer on a pumpkin and went to lunch. On recess me, Rex, Ray and Tray got chased and then we came in and worked.

Andrea tells about Thanksgiving vacation:

■   Yesterday was the end of Thanksgiving break. I went to the church crafts fair and they served soup. I got a gingerbread cookie and it was about 6 inches long. We had for Thanksgiving dinner: mashed potatoes, turkey, stuffing, sweet potatoes, pumpkin pie, Dutch apple pie, oregano beans, and water. We put up our Christmas tree. So far it has almost drunk a gallon of water and we have some presents.

Micah describes a grandparent's death:

■ My PaPa had a heart attack by sitting down and he could not get up. My Grandma called the ambulance and I saw the people in the ambulance help. And he died.

Michael shares a problem:

■ Today I made a friend an enemy, and I am glad of it, too. It all started about the beginning of the year. My brother and somebody else and me started a club, so the person that I am mad at was jealous. He started hanging around us and we didn't like it so we didn't pay attention to him. So yesterday he started a club. Today I talked some of his people in his club into being in my club. That's why he is mad at me and I am mad at him.

Micah writes about his plans for the future:

■ I am going to be a golfer when I grow up. Now I can hit a golf ball almost 80 yards. My dad can hit a golf ball almost 300 yards. I go golfing almost every 2 months. And I might be a baseball player or a basketball player.

And Jenna writes about a disappointment:

■ My class all got pen pals. My pen pal's name is Eric. He is 8-1/2 years old and lives in Washington. See I wanted a girl but when I went up to Mrs. Carson she was fresh out of girls.

An excerpt from another third grader's personal journal is presented in Figure 2-2. In this journal, Mandy ends each entry by saying good-bye as many children do, but her arrangement of entries on the page is unusual unless you know that her class writes a monthly newspaper which is formatted the same way.

It is often helpful to list possible journal-writing topics on a chart in the class-room or on sheets of paper clipped inside each student's journal notebook. A list of possible journal-writing topics developed by a class of fourth- and fifth-graders is presented in Figure 2-3. Throughout the year, students may add topics to their list, which may include more than one hundred topics by the end of the school year. In personal journals, students choose their own topics. Although they can write about almost anything, some students will complain that they don't know what to write about. A list of topics provides a crutch to students who believe they have nothing to write about. Referring students to the list or asking them to brain-storm a list of topics encourages them to become more independent writers and discourages them from becoming too dependent on teachers for writing topics.

Privacy is an important issue as students grow older. Most primary grade stu-dents are very willing to share what they have written, but by third or fourth grade, some students become reluctant to share their writing with classmates. Usually they are willing to share their personal journal entries with a trusted teacher.

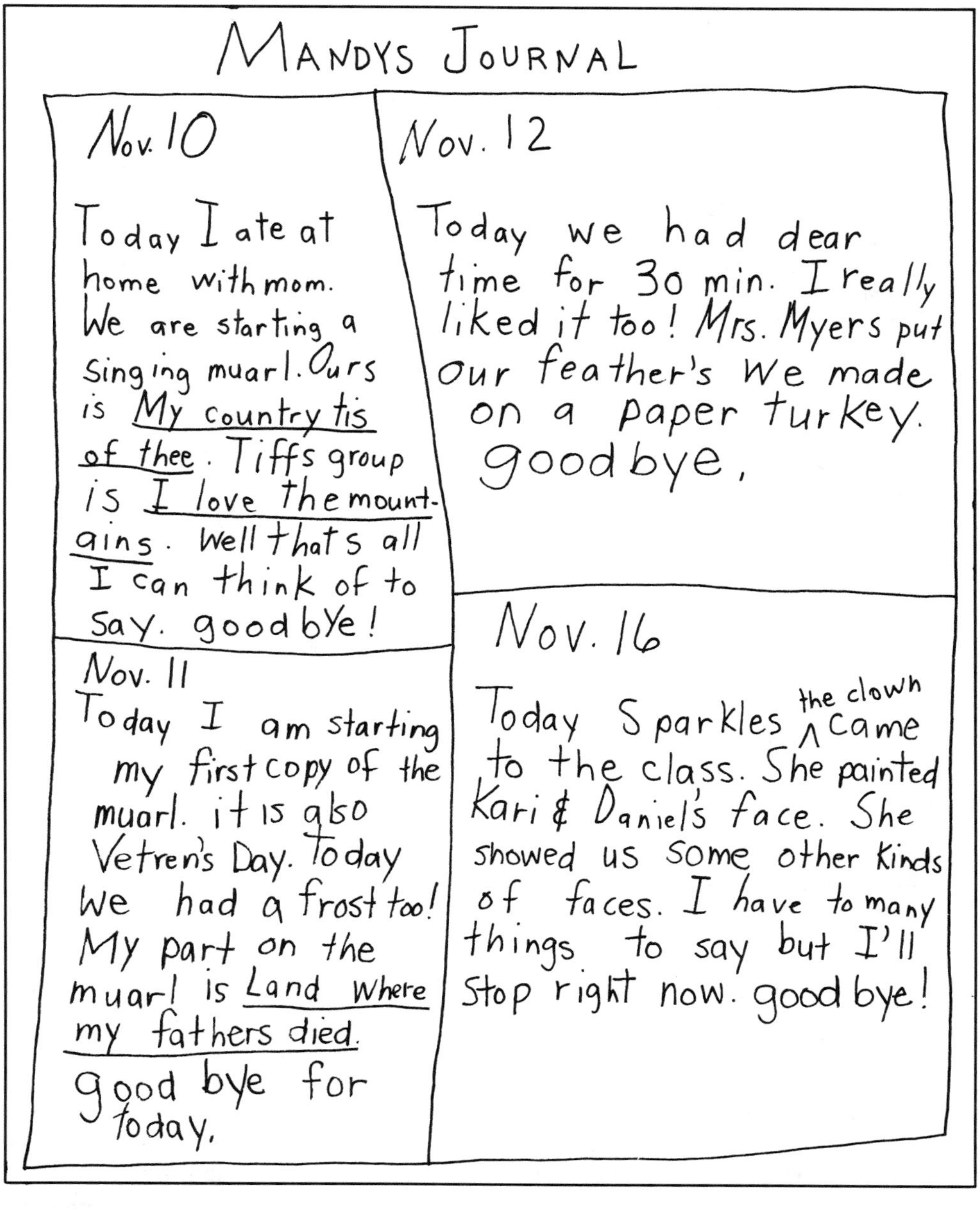

MANDYS JOURNAL

Nov. 10

Today I ate at home with mom. We are starting a singing muarl. Ours is <u>My country tis of thee</u>. Tiffs group is <u>I love the mountains</u>. Well thats all I can think of to say. good bYe!

Nov. 11

Today I am starting my first copy of the muarl. it is also Vetren's Day. Today We had a frost too! My part on the muarl is <u>Land Where my fathers died.</u> good bYe for today,

Nov. 12

Today we had dear time for 30 min. I really liked it too! Mrs. Myers put our feather's We made on a paper turkey. goodbye,

Nov. 16

Today Sparkles the clowh ^ Came to the class. She painted Kari & Daniel's face. She showed us some other Kinds of faces. I have to many things to say but I'll stop right now. good bye!

FIGURE 2-2 Entries from a Third Grader's Personal Journal
Mandy, grade 3

FIGURE 2-3   A List of Possible Writing Topics

my favorite place in town	if I had three wishes
boyfriends/girlfriends	my teacher
things that make me happy or sad	TV shows I watch
music	my favorite holiday
an imaginary planet	if I were stranded on an island
cars	what I want to be when I grow up
magazines I like to read	private thoughts
what if snow were hot	how to be a super hero
dreams I have	dinosaurs
cartoons	my mom/my dad
places I've been	my friends
favorite movies	my next vacation
rock stars	love
if I were a movie/rock star	if I were an animal or something
poems	else
pets	books I've read
football	favorite things to do
astronauts	my hobbies
the president	if I were a skydiver
jokes	when I get a car
motorcycles	if I had a lot of money
things that happen in my school	dolls
current events	if I were rich
things I do on weekends	wrestling and other sports
a soap opera with daily episodes	favorite colors
	questions answered with "never"

or ANYTHING else I want to write about

Fourth- and fifth-graders

Teachers must be scrupulous about protecting students' privacy and not insist that students share their writing when they are unwilling to do so. It is also important to insist that students respect each other's privacy and not read each other's journals. To protect students' privacy, many teachers keep personal journals on a shelf out of the way when they are not being used.

When students share personal information with teachers through their journals a second issue also arises. Sometimes teachers may learn details about students' problems and family life that they may not know how to deal with. Entries about child abuse, suicide, or drug use may be the child's way of asking for help. While teachers are not counselors, they do have a legal obligation to protect their students and report possible problems to appropriate school personnel. Occasionally a student may invent a personal problem in a journal entry as an attention-getting tactic. However, asking the student about the entry or having a school counselor do so will help to ensure that the student's safety is being fully considered.

Dialogue Journals

Another approach to journal writing is dialogue journals. In this approach, students and teachers—at any grade level—carry on a private conversation with each other through writing (Bode, 1989; Gambrell, 1985; Staton, 1980, 1987; Staton & Shuy, 1987). These journals are interactive, conversational in tone, and provide the opportunity for real student-teacher communication, something that is too often missing in elementary classrooms (Shuy, 1987). Each day students write informally to the teacher about something of interest or a concern, and the teacher responds. Students choose their own topics for writing and usually control the direction that the writing takes. Staton (1987) offers these suggestions for responding to students' writing and continuing the dialogue:

1. Acknowledge students' ideas and encourage them to continue to write about their interests.
2. Support students by complimenting them about behavior and school work.
3. Provide new information about topics, so that students will want to read your responses.
4. Write less than the students do.
5. Avoid nonspecific comments like "good idea" or "very interesting."
6. Ask few questions; instead encourage students to ask you questions.

Teachers' responses do not need to be lengthy; a sentence or two is often enough. Even so, it is very time-consuming for teachers to respond to 25 journal entries every day. Often teachers read and respond to students' journal entries on a rotating basis. They might respond to one group of students' writing one week and another group the next week.

In this fifth grader's dialogue journal, Daniel shares the events and problems in his life with his teacher, and she responds sympathetically:

■ Over spring break I went down to my grandma's house and played basketball in their backyard and while we were there we went to see some of my uncles who are all Indians. Out of my whole family down there they are all Indians except Grandpa Russell.

And Daniel's teacher responds:

■ What a fun spring break! That is so interesting to have Indians in your family. I think I might have some Indian ancestors too. Do you still plan to go to Padre Island for the summer?

The next day Daniel writes:

■ My family and I plan to go to Padre Island in June and I imagine we will stay there for quite a while. I think the funnest part will probably be swimming or camping or something like that. When we get there my mom says we will probably stay in a nice motel.

Daniel's teacher responds:

■ That really sounds like a fun vacation. I think swimming is the most fun, too. Who will go with you?

Daniel continues to talk about his family, now focusing on the problems he and his family are facing:

■ Well, my mom and dad are divorced so that is why I am going to court to testify on Tuesday but my mom, me, and my sister, and brother are all going and that kind of makes me sad because a couple of years ago when my mom and dad were together we used to go a lot of places like camping and hiking but now after what happened we hardly go anywhere.

His teacher responds:

■ I am so sorry your family is having problems. It sounds as if your mom and dad are having problems with each other, but they both love you and want to be with you. Be sure to keep talking to them about how you feel.

Daniel replies:

■ I wish my mom and dad did not have problems because I would have a lot more fun and get to go and do a lot more things together, but since my mom and dad are divorced I have to take turns spending time with both of them.

His teacher offers a suggestion:

■ I'm sure that is hard. Trevor and Carla have parents who are divorced, too. Maybe you could talk to them. It might help.

This journal is not a series of teacher questions and student answers. Instead, Daniel and his teacher are having a dialogue or conversation, and the interchange is built on mutual trust and respect. Another series of entries from a dialogue journal is presented in Figure 2-4. These entries are written by a second-grade learning disabled student and the student teacher working in her classroom.

Dialogue journals can be used effectively to deal with students who are misbehaving or having almost any type of problem in school (Staton, 1980). The teacher and student write back and forth about the problem. To begin, the teacher may ask the student to explain the problem and identify ways to solve it. In later entries, the student reflects on progress made toward solving the problem. The teacher responds to the student's message, asks clarifying questions, or offers sympathy and praise.

Joy Kreeft (1984) suggests that the greatest value of dialogue journals is that they bridge the gap between talking and writing; they are literally written conversations. A second value must be the strong bonds that develop between students and the teacher as a result of writing to each other.

I am glad to be a Browney.
My friend gave me a Stickr.
My friend invide me to her sluber parte.

Wow! A slumber party is so much fun
to go to. I was a Brownie, too. It was fun.

My dad is making me and my
Sistre a treehouse. My mom is going
to by me and my sister a eyraer.
it is like a pinsel but thers a
eyraer. Its all that is in it.
We had so much fun.
My dog ran a way. To
night my moms birth day.

So, what are you going to do tonight for
your mom's birthday? Are you going to
have a party with cake and ice cream?

I am going to arecnsall. We have
a bumbed ther. yes we had a
parte for my moms birth day. It wa fun,
fun, fun, fun. I gave my mom a
present.

I'm glad you had fun!

I am going to bring a
trofey tomaro. I can spell my
Name in crsiv. See Alila.

What did you do to get a trophy?
I've got a couple of trophies at home.

I got it from chilrden.
I 10 or 9 of them. How do you
get them? How many do you hav?

I don't have as many as you do. I have
4 of them. I got one for softtball, one
for dance team and 2 for cheerleading.

My dog was going craszey with
Smorineg. Do you have a dog?
What cined is it? Myimg is a
dover rpincher.

I used to have a dog. I have a
cat now. Its name is Sebastian.

Writing Notebooks

Writing notebooks are a specialized type of journal in which students record a variety of information about writing. They can include information about content and mechanics that authors need to know to write well, such as:

- Lists of ideas for future compositions, interesting settings, or character descriptions
- Snippets of dialogue (overheard or invented)
- Notes about the elements of story structure including the characteristics of beginnings, middles, and ends of stories
- Charts describing poetic formulas
- Lists of comparisons that they locate in books they are reading
- Synonyms for overused words such as *said* or *pretty* or *nice*
- Capitalization and punctuation rules
- Lists of commonly misspelled words
- Lists of homonyms (e.g., *their-there-they're*)

By recording this information about writing in a journal notebook, students create a permanent reference book.

Two sample pages from a fifth grader's writing notebook are presented in Figure 2-5. On the first page, the student lists synonyms for the overused word *said* that she collected over a period of several months from words found in books she was reading and from a thesaurus. On the second page, the words are organized into five categories, ranging from *loud* to *soft,* that she developed to locate the synonyms more easily.

Writing notebooks also function much like writing folders or portfolios in which students write drafts of stories, poems, and other pieces of writing. Some students write long stories in chapters or episodes, which they work on during daily journal writing or free activity periods.

Learning Logs

Students can also use journals to record or react to what they are learning in language arts, science, math or other content areas (Fulwiler, 1985). These journals are known as learning logs. Students use writing in these journals to reflect on their learning, to discover gaps in their knowledge, and to explore relationships between what they are learning and their past experiences. Paulo Freire (1973) used the term "critical consciousness" to explain that writing in learning logs is valuable because knowledge must be constructed by learners, not supplied by teachers.

In language arts, learning logs can be used by students to respond to the literature they are reading. As students read stories or listen to them read aloud, they react to the story or relate it to events in their own lives as Veronica did in the *Tuck Everlasting* reading log described at the beginning of this chapter. They can list unfamiliar words and jot down quotable quotes in their reading logs. Students can also take notes about characters, plot, or other elements of the story.

FIGURE 2-5 Excerpts from a Fifth-Grader's Writing Journal

Words for *Said*

screamed	called	talked
remarked	screeched	giggled
insisted	hollered	warned
sighed	yelled	bellowed
answered	barked	ordered
cried	quoted	shrieked
pleaded	replied	whined
sobbed	wondered	mumbled
whimpered	moaned	responded
whispered	shouted	hissed
exclaimed	commanded	reminded
directed	raved	muttered
grumbled	questioned	murmured
bawled	argued	snapped
proclaimed	repeated	explained
bragged	laughed	

Words for *Said* Arranged According to Loudness

Loudest				*Softest*
yelled	snapped	questioned	whined	moaned
shouted	reminded	laughed	giggled	whispered
raved	called	answered	grumbled	muttered
bellowed	exclaimed	insisted	sighed	murmured
cried	commanded	wondered	sobbed	mumbled
hollered		pleaded		whimpered
screamed		replied		
screeched				
shrieked				

In science, students can make daily records of the growth of seeds they have planted or animals they are observing, such as meal worms, gerbils, or caterpillars. For instance, a fourth-grade class observed mealworms as they changed to beetles over a period of 4 to 6 weeks. Students each kept a daily log, describing the changes they observed using texture, color, size, and other property words. Excerpts from a fourth grader's log documenting the mealworm's growth and change are presented in Figure 2-6. As students write in these science logs, they are assuming the role of scientists, learning to make careful observations and to record them accurately in their logs.

Students can also use learning logs to write about what they are learning in math (Salem, 1982). They record explanations and examples of concepts pre-

FIGURE 2-6 Entries from a Fourth-Grader's Learning Log on Mealworms

Day 1
My mealworm has 6 legs. I fed it a potato. My mealworm is rough. It has 13 sections. It runs around in cornflakes and it will eat a potato and cornflakes. It has eyes. Sometimes it will walk backwards. It will get on its hind legs and look up. It also has antennas. It is a fast and sometimes a slow crawler. It eats tiny, tiny bites.

Day 2
My mealworm has shrunk a little bit. His bottom half has gotten fatter. He has tiny legs in his bottom half, too.

Day 3
My mealworm is in a cocoon. It shrunk a bunch. I guess it ate a bunch before it made its cocoon. The cornflakes are moist too.

Day 7
My mealworm has shrunk a little and it's blacker and when I touch it, it will breakdance. I have to feed it cornflakes.

Day 14
My mealworm is a beetle now. It's brown and big.

Day 23
My beetle isn't doing much. It's just black like usual.

Day 28
My beetle is black, big, and frisky. It's 3 cm. long.

Day 30
It's not moving much. It's just not. Erica's is dead. Katrina's is in a cocoon.

Day 33
My black beetle is fine, eating, but just fine. Erica's is dead and gone. Katrina's mealworm is in its cocoon and it's turning black.

Day 36
My beetle is fat and black. It sucked the juice or moisture out of the cornflakes.

sented in class and react to any problems they may be having. Some upper-grade teachers allow students the last 5 minutes of math class to summarize the day's lesson and react to it in their learning logs. Through these activities, students practice taking notes and writing descriptions and directions. They also learn how to reflect on and evaluate their own learning (Stanford, 1988). For more information about learning logs, see Chapter 9, "Writing Across the Curriculum."

Simulated Journals

In simulated journals students assume the role of another person and write from that person's viewpoint. As students read biographies or study social studies units, they can assume the role of a historical figure. As they read stories, they can assume the role of a character in the story. In this way, students gain insight into the lives of other people and into historical events. A series of diary entries written by fourth-grade Lisa, who has assumed the role of Betsy Ross, is presented below. Lisa chose the date for each entry carefully. She picked important dates in Betsy's life and wove factual information into each entry.

■ May 15, 1766
Dear Diary,

   This morning at 5:00 o'clock I had to wake up my husband John to get up for work but he wouldn't wake up. I immediately called the doc. He came over as fast as he could. He asked me to leave the room so I did. An hour later he came out and told me he had passed away. I am so sad. I don't know what to do.

June 16, 1776
Dear Diary,

   Today General Washington visited me about making a flag. I was so surprised. Me making a flag! I have made flags for the navy, but this is too much. But I said yes. He showed me a pattern of the flag he wanted. He also wanted six-pointed stars but I talked him into having five-pointed stars.

July 8, 1776
Dear Diary,

   Today in front of Carpenter Hall the Declaration of Independence was read by Tom Jefferson. Well, I will tell you the whole story. I heard some yelling and shouting about liberty and everyone was gathering around Carpenter Hall. So I went to my next door neighbors to ask what was happening but Mistress Peters didn't know either so we both went down to Carpenter Hall. We saw firecrackers and heard a bell and the Declaration of Independence being read aloud. When I heard this I knew a new country was born.

July 14, 1777
Dear Diary,

   Today was a happy but scary day. Today the flag I made was adopted by Congress. I thought for sure that if England found out that a new flag was taking the old one's place something bad would happen. But I'm happy because I am the maker of the first American flag and I'm only 25 years old!

   Ira Progoff (1975) uses a similar approach, called "dialoging," in which students converse with a historical figure or other character in a journal by writing both sides of the conversation. He suggests focusing on a milestone in the person's life and starting the journal at an important point. A dialogue with Martin Luther King, for instance, might take place the day he gave his "I Have a Dream" speech in Washington D.C.

Young Children's Journals

Teachers have used journals effectively with preschoolers, kindergartners, and other young children who are emergent readers or who have not yet learned to read (Elliott et al., 1981; Hipple, 1985; Nathan, 1987). Young children's journal entries include drawings as well as some type of text. Some children write scribbles, random letters and numbers, simple captions, or extended texts using invented spelling. These invented spellings often seem bizarre by adult standards, but are reasonable in terms of children's knowledge of phoneme-grapheme correspondences and spelling patterns. Other children want parents and teachers to take their dictation and write the text. After the text is written, children can usually read it immediately, and they retain recognition of the words several days later.

Four journal entries made by kindergartners are presented in Figure 2-7. In his journal entry, Brandon focuses on the illustration, drawing a detailed picture of a football game (note that the player in the middle right position has the ball), and adds five letters for the text so his entry will have some writing. Becky's entry is about her dog and she writes a text vertically to accompany her illustration. She writes the first letter (or an important letter) in each word, except that she writes the entire word *dog* because she knows how to spell it. Becky reads her text this way: "My mother would like our black dog very much." Jessica and Marc's entries are more similar to personal journal entries because they describe events in the five-year-olds' lives. Jessica writes, "I spent the night at my dad's," and her picture shows her sleeping at her dad's house. Marc writes that "I'm going to be a phantom for Halloween" and draws a picture of himself in his Halloween costume going trick-or-treating.

Journal writing takes a variety of different forms and can be used for a number of purposes, but through each one, elementary students discover the power of writing to record information and explore ideas. Students usually cherish their informal journals and are amazed by the amount of writing they contain.

TEACHING STUDENTS TO WRITE IN JOURNALS

Journals are typically written in notebooks. Spiral-bound notebooks are used for long-term personal and dialogue journals and writing notebooks, while small booklets of paper stapled together are more often used for learning logs and simulated journals. Students often decorate the covers for these short-term journals as Mrs. Wheatley's students who kept reading logs for *Tuck Everlasting* did. Most teachers prefer to keep the journals in the classroom so they will be available for students to write in each day.

Students usually write in journals at a particular time each day. Many teachers have students make personal or dialogue journal entries while they take attendance or immediately after recess. Writing notebooks are often used in the language arts curriculum to record information about topics such as poetic forms or quotation marks. Learning logs and simulated journals can be written in as part of a daily assignment or as part of social studies or science class. For ex-

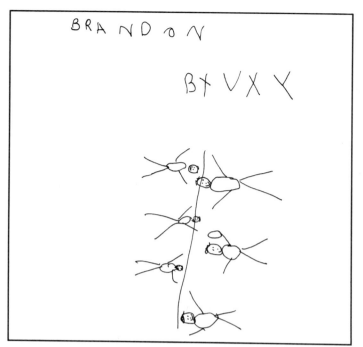

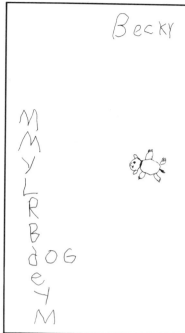

FIGURE 2-7 Entries from Young Children's Journals
Brandon, Becky, Jessica, and Marc, kindergartners

ample, students may go over to an incubator of quail eggs, observe them, and then make an entry in their learning log during their daily reading/language block. Students who are writing simulated journals as part of a social studies unit on the Crusades may make their entries during reading/language block or during social studies class.

Introducing Students to Journal Writing

Teachers introduce students to journal writing by explaining the purpose of the journal-writing activity and writing a sample entry—often a class collaboration—on the chalkboard. This sample demonstrates that the writing is to be informal, with content being more important than mechanics. Then students make their own first entries, and several read their entries aloud. Through this sharing, students who are still unclear about the writing activity have additional models on which to base their own writing.

A similar introduction is needed for each type of journal. While all journals are informal writing activities, the purpose of the journal, the information included in the entry, and the point of view of the writer vary according to the type.

Sustaining Journal Writing

Students write in journals on a regular schedule, usually daily. Once students know how to write the type of entry, they can write independently. While some children prefer to write private journals, others will volunteer to read their journal entries aloud each day no matter what type of journal they are writing. Young children should share their picture journal entries and talk about them. If the sharing becomes too time-consuming, several children can be selected each day on a rotating basis to share. Teachers and classmates may offer compliments about the topic, word choice, humor, and so on.

Students can select entries from their journals and develop them into polished compositions if they wish. However, the journal entries themselves are rarely revised and edited because the emphasis is on writing fluency and self-expression rather than on the correctness of mechanics.

Students may continue to write in personal journals throughout the school year while their writing in other types of journals starts and stops with particular assignments. Sometimes students seem to lose interest in personal journals, and many teachers find it useful to put these journals away for several weeks and substitute another type of journal or free reading in lieu of personal journals.

Assessing the Journals that Students Write

Students can write in journals independently with little or no sharing with the teacher, or they can make daily entries that the teacher monitors or reads regularly (Tway, 1984). Typically, students are accustomed to having teachers read all or most of their writing, but the quantity of writing that students produce in their journals is often too great for teachers to keep up with. Some teachers try to read all entries, while others read selected entries and monitor remaining entries. Still others rarely check their students' journals. These three management approaches can be termed *private journals, monitored journals,* and *shared journals.* When students write private journals, they write primarily for themselves, and sharing with classmates or the teacher is voluntary. The teacher does not read the journals unless invited to do so by students. When students write monitored journals, they write primarily for themselves, but the teacher monitors the writing to ensure that entries are being made on a regular basis. The teacher may simply check that entries have been made and not read the entries unless they are specially marked as "read me." When students write shared journals, they write primarily for the teacher. The teacher regularly reads all entries except for those personal journal entries marked "private" and offers encouragement and suggestions.

How to grade journal entries is a concern. Because the writing is informal and usually not revised and edited, teachers should not grade the quality of the entries. One option is to give points for each entry made, especially with personal journals. For learning logs and simulated journals, though, some teachers grade the content because they can check to see if particular pieces of information are included in the entries. For example, when students write simulated journals about the Crusades, students can be asked to include five pieces of historically accurate information in their entries. (It is often helpful to ask students to identify the five pieces of information by underlining and numbering them.) Rough draft journal entries should not be graded for mechanical correctness. Students need to complete the writing process and revise and edit their entries if they are to be graded for mechanical correctness.

INFORMAL WRITING STRATEGIES[2]

When students make lists of ideas, organize information with a diagram, and write paragraphs to clarify their thinking, they are writing informally and using informal writing strategies. Sometimes this writing serves as prewriting and is expanded into more formal stories, reports, and poems; at other times, it is more like taking notes or keeping a journal. As with journal writing, these strategies are informal and the emphasis is on content, not spelling, punctuation, or capitalization. In this section four informal writing strategies—brainstorming, clustering, freewriting, and cubing—will be presented and a variety of uses will be suggested.

Brainstorming

One good way to generate ideas is through brainstorming, a strategy that includes the following steps:

1. Choose a topic.
2. Quickly list all words and phrases that come to mind in response to the topic.
3. Make no value judgments about items in the list; instead look for unusual relationships among the items.

---

[2]Adapted from Tompkins & Camp, 1988, pp. 209–214.

Students can brainstorm as a class, in small groups, or individually to help them discover what they already know about a topic. Brainstorming encourages the free flow of ideas. Introduce brainstorming with an activity for the whole class, in which the teacher records students' ideas on the chalkboard or on a chart. After several whole-class brainstorming activities, students can brainstorm in small groups and later individually. By first using this strategy in a large group, students can observe the process and learn how to use the strategy before having to use it independently. Brainstorming in small groups also provides another rehearsal before students work independently. Even though brainstorming is a commonly used strategy, it needs to be introduced and practiced several times before students feel comfortable using it.

Using Brainstorming in the Classroom. Brainstorming can be used to generate ideas for writing. For example, students can use brainstorming to develop a list of signs of spring to prepare for writing a poem about spring, they can list the causes of the American Revolution before writing a chapter in a report about that war, or they can list the characteristics of mysteries before writing their own mystery stories. Brainstorming takes only a few minutes, but helps students generate many ideas and words to use in their writing.

Similarly, students use brainstorming when they are identifying a writing topic. For example, after reading Judith Viorst's *Alexander and the Terrible, Horrible, No Good, Very Bad Day* (1972), students might be asked to write about a very bad, no good day they have had. Brainstorming is an effective way to identify a topic. Students begin by listing some bad days they may have had. They then choose from the list the most promising recollection for their topic. Or, after studying community helpers, students might brainstorm a list of all the helpers they have learned about and then select one helper to write about.

Students can also use brainstorming before they write in social studies, science, or other content area units. For example, on the day that a class of upper-grade students began a social studies unit on Egypt, the teacher asked the students to brainstorm a list of all the words they knew about Egypt to put in their newly decorated Egypt learning logs. The students suggested *mummy, Africa, Nile River, pyramids, slaves, tomb, hieroglyphics,* and *desert.* Students continued to add to their list until, five weeks later, their lists contained more than 100 words. The brainstormed list provided one measure of students' learning about Egypt, and students used the list to provide ideas for posters, journal entries, spelling words, acrostic poems, and research projects. While students used the brainstormed list of words for many activities, the list itself was a piece of informal writing that students used to help them learn, not a polished piece of writing that was graded by the teacher. The teacher required that students have a list of words about Egypt in their Egypt learning logs and it was graded simply as done or not done.

Clustering. Another technique that students can use to help them start writing is clustering (Rico, 1983). The process is similar to brainstorming except that all the words generated are circled and linked to a nucleus word. The result is a web-like diagram, rather than a list. This strategy includes the following steps:

1. Choose a topic.
2. Write the topic or nucleus word in a circle centered on a sheet of paper.
3. Draw rays from the circle and add main ideas.
4. Add branches with details and examples to complete each main idea.

Clustering is designed to capture as many associations as possible in a short amount of time. This strategy helps students discover what they know about a topic. In clustering, ideas are triggered by associating one idea with another.

A cluster about clustering is presented in Figure 2-8. *Cluster* is the nucleus word, and the three main ideas are *easy, effective,* and *informal writing strategy.* Details are added to complete each main idea. Two details are added to one main idea, three to another main idea, and four to the third main idea. The number of details added to each main idea is not important; rather, each main idea should be explored, expanded, and developed as fully as possible.

Outlining. The main ideas in a cluster are the same as main ideas in an outline (labeled with Roman numerals) and the details in a cluster are the same as details in the outline (labeled with uppercase letters). A biographical cluster is presented in Figure 2-9 with the same information presented in an outline. While upper-grade elementary students often feel outlining is a meaningless activity, these same students enjoy clustering and recognize its usefulness in organizing ideas before writing. Outlining is a traditional prewriting activity that has outlived its usefulness. Too many older students, when required to have an outline as part of a high school or college writing assignment, construct the outline *after* writing the composition. In contrast to clustering, which helps students be better writers, outlining is thought of as an unnecessary requirement. Whenever possible, students should use clustering rather than outlining to organize ideas before writing. When outlining must be taught, it should be described to students as the formal rewriting of a cluster. Students first make a cluster as they gather and organize ideas for writing. Then the cluster can be rewritten as an outline, with the main ideas and details sequenced in the outline as they will be in the composition.

Using Clusters in the Elementary Classroom. Clusters take many different forms, depending on their purpose. For example, a cluster for a story may include three rays, one for the beginning of the story, one for the middle, and one for the end. In contrast, a cluster for a research report on an animal might have five rays, one ray to answer each of the following questions:

1. What does the animal look like?
2. Where does the animal live?
3. What does the animal eat?
4. How does the animal protect itself?
5. What is special about the animal?

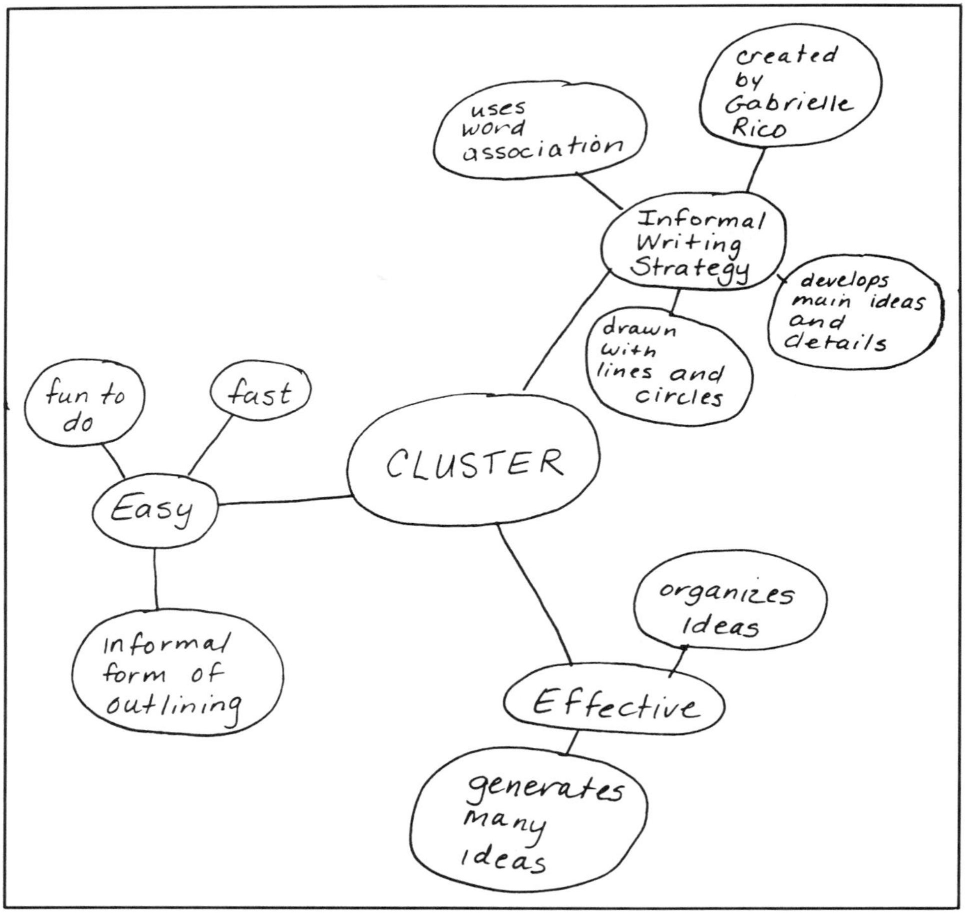

FIGURE 2-8 A Cluster About Clusters

A third type of cluster is a five senses cluster in which each of the senses is used as a main idea. Sensory clusters are useful for making abstract topics, such as the United States Constitution, more concrete. A fourth type of cluster is the "5Ws plus one" cluster that journalists and student reporters use. In this cluster, the words *Who? What? Where? Why? When?* and *How?* are used as the main ideas. This type of cluster is useful in writing newspaper articles as well as describing historical and autobiographical events. A fifth type of cluster is a biographical cluster with information about a person's life and accomplishments. Examples of these five forms of clusters are presented in Figure 2-10.

These clusters are informal writing because students are writing for themselves. Students may develop the cluster to help them understand what they are

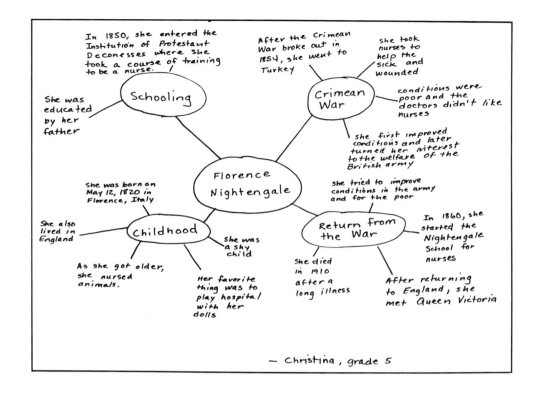

In 1850, she entered the Institution of Protestant Deconesses where she took a course of training to be a nurse.

She was educated by her father

Schooling

After the Crimean War broke out in 1854, she went to Turkey

she took nurses to help the sick and wounded

Crimean War

conditions were poor and the doctors didn't like nurses

she first improved conditions and later turned her interest to the welfare of the British army

Florence Nightengale

She was born on May 12, 1820 in Florence, Italy

she tried to improve conditions in the army and for the poor

She also lived in England

Childhood

she was a shy child

Return from the War

In 1860, she started the Nightengale School for nurses

As she got older, she nursed animals.

Her favorite thing was to play hospital with her dolls

She died in 1910 after a long illness

After returning to England, she met Queen Victoria

— Christina, grade 5

Florence Nightengale

I. Childhood
   A. She was born on May 12, 1820 in Florence, Italy.
   B. She also lived in England.
   C. She was a shy child.
   D. As she got older, she nursed animals.

II. Schooling
   A. She was educated by her father.
   B. In 1850, she entered the Institution of Protestant Deconesses where she took a course of training to be a nurse.

III. Crimean War
   A. After the Crimean War broke out in 1854, she went to Turkey.
   B. She took nurses to help the sick and wounded.
   C. Conditions were poor and the doctors didn't like the nurses.
   D. She first improved conditions and later turned her interest to the welfare of the British army.

IV. Return from the War
   A. She tried to improve conditions in the army and for the poor.
   B. In 1860, she started the Nightengale School for nurses.
   C. After returning to England, she met Queen Victoria.
   D. She died in 1910 after a long illness.

FIGURE 2-9 Biographical Information Presented as a Cluster and as an Outline
Christina, grade 5

learning or to use as information in a writing activity. Sometimes the cluster is re-copied as a piece of formal writing. For instance, the biographical cluster pre-sented in Figure 2-9 was recopied on a large sheet of posterboard as a book report. The student added the title of the book, illustrations, and a quotable quote from the book.

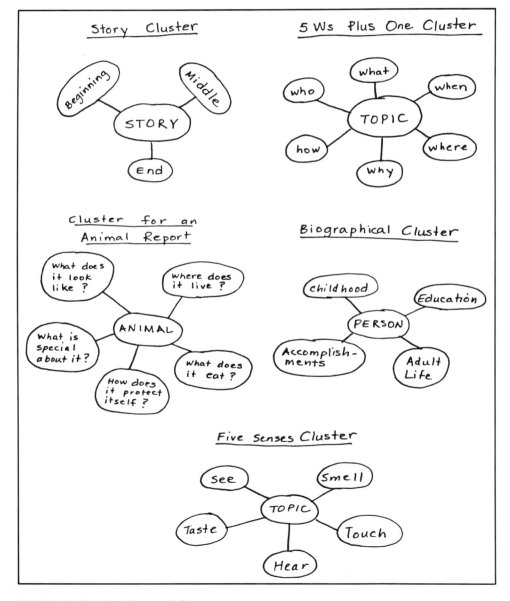

FIGURE 2-10 Five Types of Clusters

Nonhierarchical Clusters. Clusters can also be developed that are not organized in a hierarchical arrangement. In these clusters, all words radiate out from the nucleus word, like rays from the sun. This type of cluster is much like brainstorming, in that the words are not organized into main ideas and details. This nonhierarchical cluster can be used any time you might use brainstorming. Examples of two nonhierarchical clusters are presented in Figure 2-11. Fourth graders developed these two clusters describing the hare and the tortoise after reading Paul Galdone's retelling of the familiar fable *The Hare and the Tortoise* (1962).

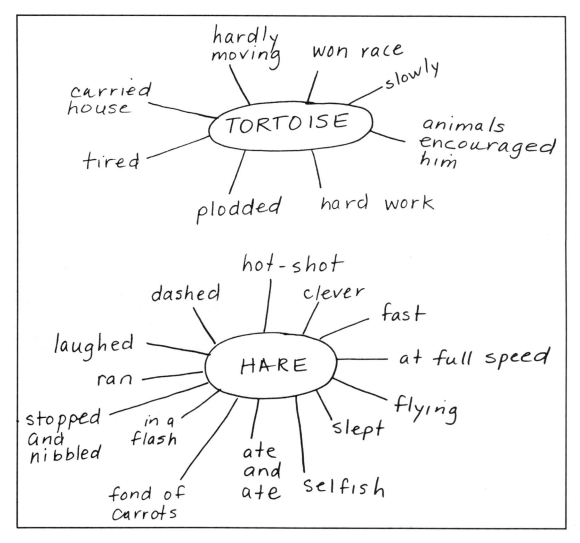

FIGURE 2-11 A Nonhierarchical Cluster
Fourth-graders

Freewriting

Freewriting is just what the name suggests, a strategy in which students simply begin to write and let their thoughts flow freely without focusing on mechanics or revisions. Freewriting includes the following steps:

1. Choose a topic.
2. Write for 5 to 10 minutes without pausing to think, to reread the writing, to make corrections, or for any other reason.
3. Write "I don't know what to write about" or a similar phrase over and over until a new idea comes.
4. *Optional:* At the end of the writing time, reread the writing and circle a specific and promising idea that can be expanded in another freewriting session.
5. *Optional:* Write again for another 5 to 10 minute period on the circled idea without pausing for any reason.

Through freewriting, students ramble on paper, generating words and ideas and developing writing fluency. This strategy, popularized by Peter Elbow (1973), helps students focus on content rather than on mechanics. Even by second or third grade, students have learned that many teachers and parents prize correct spelling and careful handwriting over the content of a composition. Elbow explains that focusing on mechanics makes writing "dead" because it does not allow students' natural voices to come through. In freewriting, students focus on content and later, if they choose, can revise and polish their compositions using the writing process.

A sixth grader's freewriting is presented in Figure 2-12. In this sample, the student has allowed his mind to wander, focusing briefly on several different things—exotic automobiles, school, and a book he is reading—before returning to exotic automobiles, his original idea. In many ways, this student's freewriting is like a personal journal entry. In both types of writing, students write about their thoughts, experiences, and feelings. There is also a similar lack of emphasis on mechanics. The major difference is that in freewriting students write continuously for a specified period of time.

Student and adult writers often suffer from the "blank page syndrome" or an inability to start writing. Too often when writers begin writing, they look at the clean, blank sheet of writing paper and freeze. They discard sentence after sentence as they try to create a "perfect" first sentence, an imposing task for any writer! Freewriting is a good prescription for the blank page syndrome because writers simply begin to write imperfectly with the confidence that after three or four sentences, a usable, if not perfect, sentence will emerge (Elbow, 1981). Experienced writers often return to freewriting whenever they are stuck for ideas or words. They know that freewriting gives them writing power.

Unfocused and Focused Freewrites. Elbow has developed two types of freewriting—unfocused and focused. In unfocused freewriting, students let their thoughts ramble from topic to topic. The sixth-grader's writing sample presented in Figure 2-12 is an example of unfocused freewriting. Freewriting can end after

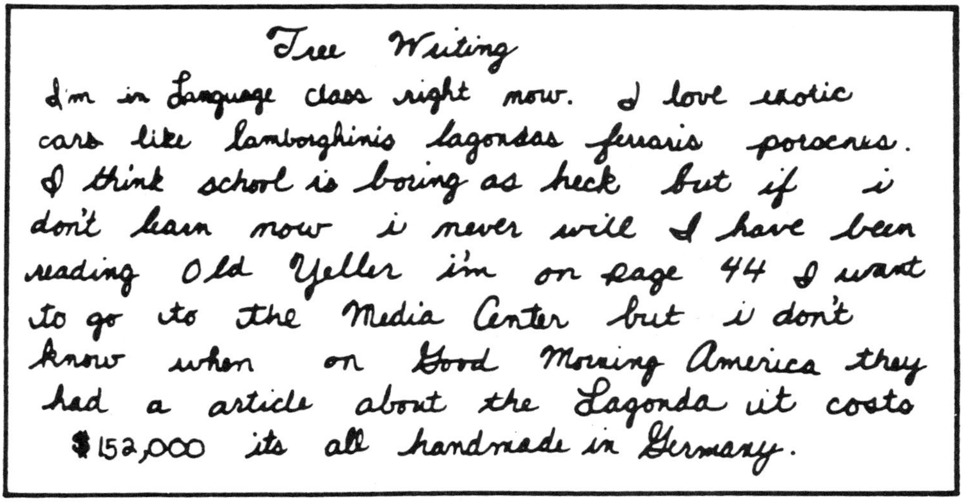

> Free Writing
>
> I'm in Language class right now. I love exotic cars like lamborghinis lagondas feraris porsches. I think school is boring as heck but if i don't learn now i never will I have been reading Old Yeller i'm on page 44 I want to go to the Media Center but i don't know when on Good Morning America they had a article about the Lagonda it costs $152,000 its all handmade in Germany.

FIGURE 2-12 A Sixth-Grader's Freewrite
Sam, age 11

the first freewrite, or students can write a second, more focused, freewrite that develops and expands one of the ideas mentioned in the first attempt. For example, in the sample unfocused freewrite, the topic of exotic cars might have been expanded in a focused freewrite.

If students are going to continue with a second freewrite, they reread what they have written and choose one idea to develop in the second try. Students should circle a word, phrase, or sentence in the first freewrite to specify the topic for the second freewrite. Then students write again for a period of 5 to 10 minutes, following the guidelines presented for unfocused freewriting. This time students try to write on a single topic, probing as many dimensions of the topic as possible.

A set of unfocused and focused freewrites written by a seventh grader is presented in Figure 2-13. In the first freewrite, the student mentioned a variety of topics and then selected one topic, the upcoming project on Beowulf, as the topic for the second freewrite.

Using Freewriting in the Classroom. Students freewrite for a variety of purposes. First, they can freewrite as they do in personal journal entries, letting their minds wander from topic to topic as they write. This develops writing fluency because, in far too many classrooms, students rarely fill up a page with writing. After these freewrites, students are often amazed at how much they have written. Often when the timer rings, students sigh and ask, "Do we have to stop?"

Second, teachers can assign specific topics for students to explore in freewriting. Before starting a new unit of study, teachers might ask students to freewrite on the topic of the unit. This activity has several purposes: to check students' knowledge about the topic, to relate students' personal experiences to the topic,

FIGURE 2-13 A Seventh-Grader's Unfocused and Focused Freewrites

---

Unfocused Freewrite

I am doing a freewrite. We are about to start doing things on Beowulf the warrior and Grendel the werewolf monster. We can do reports, comic books, magazines, newspapers, movies, soap operas, and many other things. I just got through with my report on the snake-killing mongoose. It was a fun report to write. My hand and arm are starting to ache. Today is the last day of school for the week—T.G.I.F. day! Well, I almost got everything down. I am in my third hour Language Arts class. My next class is Science, then Band, and then lunch. I wonder what I am going to do on the Beowulf project. Surely I'll find something to do. In science there's a hard report I need to get started on soon. It is on the planet Uranus.

Focused Freewrite
Beowulf

In Language Arts we are listening to the teacher read *Beowulf.* I have heard about Beowulf before this book. I have read several of the Time-Life books. Beowulf was into dragons and night creatures. He was killed fighting a cave-dwelling dragon. In *Dragons and Night Creatures,* he battled with Grendel and his wife (two werewolfs). Although the book *Beowulf* is based mainly on the fight between the valiant warrior and Grendel, he is more famous as a dragonslayer, having destroyed many menacing dragons. Both books are quite different from each other. To know the truth, you would have to have lived in the seventh century.

Faron, grade 7

and to stimulate students' interest in the topic. For example, students can participate in the following freewrites in connection with current events, literature, social studies, and science units:

- Freewrite on freedom or a geographic location before discussing a current events topic
- Freewrite on the theme of friendship before reading *Bridge to Terabithia* (Paterson, 1977)
- Freewrite on a trip students have taken before studying the Oregon Trail
- Freewrite on snakes before studying reptiles
- Freewrite on junk food before studying nutrition

After completing the unit, students freewrite again on the same topic, applying what they have learned in this second freewrite, and compare the two freewrites as one measure of what they have learned in the unit.

Through this informal and unstructured writing, students collect ideas and words that probe topics and eventually may be used in a polished composition. Even if the writing is never developed, however, the freewriting experience is valuable because students are developing writing fluency, learning a strategy to use when they don't know how to start a writing assignment, and learning that they usually *do* have something to say on almost any topic.

Cubing

When students want to explore a topic from several dimensions, cubing (Neeld, 1986) is a useful strategy. Cubing involves the following steps:

1. Choose a topic.
2. Examine it from all six sides of the cube and write informally about each side:

    - Describe it. (Describe its colors, shapes, and sizes.)
    - Compare it. (What is it similar to or different from?)
    - Associate it. (What does it make you think of?)
    - Analyze it. (Tell how it is made or what it is composed of.)
    - Apply it. (What can you do with it? How is it used?)
    - Argue for or against it. (Take a stand and list reasons for sup-
      porting it.)
3. Move quickly, spending only 5 to 10 minutes on each side of the cube.

Students can brainstorm words, take notes, or freewrite about each side of the cube, or they can use a specially designed sheet of paper that can be cut and folded into a cube.

Cubing is the most complex informal strategy described in this chapter and it requires students to be flexible and change their points of view as they examine a topic from the six sides of the cube. This strategy is more appropriate for older students. Because it is a more difficult strategy, begin by demonstrating cubing to the entire class and then have small groups of students cube a topic. A sixth-grade class examined the topic of junk food by cubing and their collaborative writing is presented in Figure 2-14.

In the cubing on junk food, the students composed each paragraph together by first brainstorming a list of ideas. The teacher served as scribe, writing their ideas on the chalkboard. Then students used these ideas to create sentences for the paragraph that they dictated to the teacher. As a last step, students refined the paragraph by checking the sequence of ideas, combining sentences, and choosing more appropriate vocabulary.

Using Cubing in the Classroom. Middle- and upper-grade students divide into groups to cube a social studies topic, such as the American Revolution, a book, or a scientific concept. They describe the topic, compare it to another, and focus on the topic from varied points of view. This activity encourages students to become more flexible in their thinking and helps to expand their understanding of a topic. While adults write all six sides of the cube individually, it is more reasonable for elementary students to work together in groups, each group writing one side of the cube. If students write their side of the cube on a square piece of posterboard, the squares can be taped together to create a cube. Also, when working individually, students can construct their own cubes. By sharing their writings, children benefit from the thinking that went into the cubing exercise.

A seventh-grade class cubed the topic of cold on a winter afternoon and, after sharing the six sides of the cube, students wrote individually about cold, incorporating ideas developed through cubing. Mark wrote:

FIGURE 2-14   A Sixth-Grade Collaborative Cubing on Junk Food

Junk Food

1. Describe it.

Junk food is delicious! Some junk food is made of chocolate, like chocolate ice cream and brownies. Some junk food is salty, like potato chips and pretzels. Other junk food is usually sweet or sugary, like sugar cookies, sweet rolls, or soft drinks. Junk food packages are colorful and often show you what's inside to get your attention. Most of the packages are made of paper or plastic, and they make crinkly sounds.

2. Compare it.

Junk food tastes better than nutritious food, but nutritious food is better for you: Nutritious food is less sweet and salty. Parents would rather you eat nutritious food than junk food because nutritious food keeps you healthy, but kids would rather eat junk food because it tastes better and is more fun to eat.

3. Associate it.

Most often you eat junk food at get-togethers with friends. At parties, junk food such as chips and dip and soft drinks are served. At movies, you can buy popcorn, candy, nachos, and many other kinds of junk food. Other places where people get together and eat junk food are skating rinks, sporting events, and concerts.

4. Analyze it.

Junk food is not good to eat because of all the oils, sugar, salt, and calories. Most of them have artificial colorings and flavorings. Many junk foods are low in vitamins and protein, but they have a high percentage of fats.

5. Apply it.

The most important thing you can do with junk food is to eat it. Some other uses are popcorn decorations at Christmas time, Halloween treats, and Easter candy. You can sell it to raise money for charities, clubs, and schools. Last year we sold junk food to raise money for the Statue of Liberty.

6. Argue for or against it.

We're for junk food because it tastes good. Even though it's not good for you, people like it and buy it. If there were no more junk food, a lot of people would be unemployed, such as dentists. Bakeries, convenience stores, fast food restaurants, grocery stores, and ice cream parlors would lose a lot of business if people didn't buy junk food. The Declaration of Independence guarantees our rights and freedoms, and Thomas Jefferson might have said, "Life, Liberty, and the Pursuit of Junk Food." We believe that he who wants something pleasing shall have it!

Tompkins & Camp, 1988, p. 213.

Coldness

The smell of the chimney on a cold day. Like ice cold snowballs. Ice on your windshield at six o'clock in the morning. Shattering ice coming from the overhang of your house. The taste of snow coming in your mouth while throwing snow balls. Coldness is similar to loneliness. It is different from a warm blanket. Many cold December days I have played in snow. You can make small balls or large balls out of snow. It is really good because you get to know people by playing in the snow.

Mark's writing rambles as informal writing often does, focusing on the senses, on comparisons, and then moving on to remembered experiences. After writing, Mark read his piece aloud to the class, and students complimented him on his strong images and then suggested that his writing could be arranged as a poem.

TEACHING STUDENTS TO USE INFORMAL WRITING STRATEGIES

Students need to learn how and when to use each of the informal writing strategies—brainstorming, clustering, freewriting, and cubing. These strategies can be used informally when children begin to discuss a topic, when they are listing facts, when a new concept is being introduced and students need information, in response to their reading, and in preparing to write. Teachers can help students apply these strategies by following these steps:

1. *Introduce the strategy.* Introduce an informal writing strategy by demonstrating it through a whole-class activity. It is best to use a familiar topic for students' first experience with the strategy since it is difficult for students to focus on learning to use a strategy at the same time they are struggling with difficult content. Then review the steps in the strategy and work through the steps with the students, serving as a scribe and recording the writing on the chalkboard. After completing the steps, then review the steps in the strategy again.
2. *Apply the strategy first with the class, then in small groups, and finally with individuals.* After introducing the strategy and working through the steps together as a class, have students practice using the strategy, first in small groups and later individually. These class and small group activities allow students to practice the strategy and clarify any misconceptions before using it individually. Those students who understand the strategy quickly move on to use it in small groups, pairs, and individually, while students who need more support continue to work in a small group.

   The four informal writing strategies can be used equally well in class, small group, or individual arrangements. For example, eighth graders can brainstorm about dreams before reading Martin Luther King's "I Have a Dream" speech as a class, in small groups, or individually. The arrangement for the brainstorming is not important and depends more on the classroom context and time constraints than on anything else. What matters is that the students appreciate that Martin Luther King (and all black Americans) have dreams just as they do. Similarly, kindergartners who are studying the color red, can make a cluster of "red things" as a class, in a small group, or individually. Children add words and pictures of red things to the nonhierarchical cluster, and the decision about how to arrange the activity depends on the students' independence and their previous experiences with clustering.
3. *Learn when to use each strategy.* Once students have learned to use these four informal writing strategies as a class, in small groups, and individually,

they need to learn how to choose an appropriate strategy. Through a variety of experiences with the four strategies, students gain an intuitive awareness of the usefulness of each. It is best to talk about the strategies and ask students to choose which strategy to use, rather than tell them which one to use for a specific writing activity. This practice helps students develop the ability to choose writing strategies. Brainstorming, for instance, is a good choice when a list is needed, while freewriting is more appropriate for exploring a topic.

After viewing a film about animals in the arctic, for instance, the teacher may ask students to write informally about the film. Any of the four strategies could be used. In a small group, students might brainstorm a list of concepts or facts remembered from the film, or they might freewrite individually about what they learned from the film. Together as a class, the teacher and students might identify the main ideas presented in the film for a cluster. Then students individually complete the cluster by adding details. As another alternative, the class might do a cubing about arctic animals using information from the film and other sources.

■ ANSWERING TEACHERS' QUESTIONS ABOUT INFORMAL WRITING

1. Sometimes my second graders get tired of writing in their personal journals. What can I do?

Many teachers report this problem. During the first month or two of the school year, students are eager to write in their journals and then they get tired of it. There are several things you might try. First, you can alternate journal-writing with free reading activities so that students only write every other day in their journals, or give students a choice of reading a book or writing in journals during this time. Second, change from personal journals to dialogue journals. Corresponding with you might add new interest to journal-writing activities. Third, read aloud a book in which the main character keeps a journal, such as Beverly Cleary's *Dear Mr. Henshaw* (1983) (check the list of suggested books in Figure 2-1), and ask students to reflect on their journal-writing activities by comparing them to the character's.

2. How does freewriting differ from personal journals? They seem like the same thing to me.

You're right. These two types of expressive writing are very similar, and the differences between them can be confusing. Freewriting is a specific strategy that students use to write more fluently. They can use the freewriting strategy to write a journal entry but they can use it for other informal writing activities as well. In contrast, a personal journal is a place where students write informally for themselves about almost any topic. They may use freewriting or any other approach to writing these entries.

3. Which type of journal should I use with my fifth-grade class?

Choosing a type of journal depends on your purpose for using journals with your students. If you want your students to develop writing fluency, or if this is your students' first experience with journals, the personal journal is a good choice. If you want your students to gain writing practice and you also want to get to know your students better, you might try dialogue journals. In connection with your language arts class, try writing journals. If you want to use journals in content area classes, learning logs or simulated journals are two possible options. Many teachers have students keep personal (or dialogue) and writing journals in separate notebooks throughout the school year, and have them staple together booklets of paper for learning logs and simulated journals for particular units of study.

4. I have to disagree with you about not correcting errors in students' informal writing. I'm a teacher and it's my job to correct students' spelling, capitalization, punctuation, and other errors.

Many teachers agree with you, and it's difficult for me to ignore many of the errors I see in students' journal entries and other informal writings. But what good would the corrections do? Would the effect of your corrections be to teach students how to spell or use punctuation marks correctly; or would your overemphasis on correctness convince students that they're "no good at this writing thing," a conclusion that causes many students to stop writing? Many teachers have found that focusing on students' mechanical errors rather than on the content of their writing teaches students that correctness is more important than mean-

ing, and that is just not true. Journal entries are personal and private writing, in contrast to public writing in which mechanical correctness counts. In more formal types of writing, mechanics do count and in the next chapter, you will learn about the writing process and how to help students identify and correct their mechanical errors. If you focus on errors, you are defeating the purpose of expressive writing.

5. I don't like having my students work in groups because I feel as if I lose control. What can I do?

Many teachers who work with the class as a whole group feel the same way you do. While the classroom will be a bit noisier when students work in groups, if students have a specific task to complete, you will not lose control. Before you break the students into groups, you need to set some guidelines for behavior, identify areas for groups to meet, and appoint a group leader who will keep the group members on task. Halfway through the working period, you also might try stopping the groups—by ringing a bell or blinking the lights—and ask each group leader for a progress report. You also might want to visit another classroom where the students work in groups and watch how that teacher operates the groups. Collaborative work is an important component in the elementary classroom because students take more responsibility for their learning, and by working together students learn more effectively.

■ REFERENCES

Babbitt, N. (1975). *Tuck everlasting.* New York: Farrar.

Blos, J. (1979). *A gathering of days: A New England girl's journal, 1830–1832.* New York: Scribner.

Bode, B. A. (1989). Dialogue journal writing. *The Reading Teacher, 42,* 568–571.

Britton, J., Burgess, T., Martin, N., McLeod, A., & Rosen, H. (1975). *The development of writing abilities (11–18).* London: Macmillan.

Cleary, B. (1983). *Dear Mr. Henshaw.* New York: Morrow.

Elbow, P. (1973). *Writing without teachers.* Oxford: Oxford University Press.

Elbow, P. (1981). *Writing with power.* New York: Oxford University Press.

Elliott, S., Nowosad, J., & Samuels, P. (1981). 'Me at home,' 'me at school': Using journals with preschoolers. *Language Arts, 58,* 688–691.

Fitzhugh, L. (1964). *Harriet the spy.* New York: Harper and Row.

Freire, P. (1973). *Education for critical consciousness.* New York: Continuum.

Fulwiler, M. (1986). Still writing and learning, grade 10. *Language Arts, 63,* 809–812.

Fulwiler, T. (1985). Writing and learning, grade 3. *Language Arts, 62,* 55–59.

Fulwiler, T. (1987). *The journal book.* Portsmouth, NH: Boynton/Cook.

Galdone, P. (1962). *The hare and the tortoise.* New York: Seabury.

Gambrell, L. B. (1985). Dialogue journals: Reading-writing interaction. *The Reading Teacher, 38,* 512–515.

Hipple, M. L. (1985). Journal writing in kindergarten. *Language Arts, 62,* 255–261.

Kreeft, J. (1984). Dialogue writing—Bridge from talk to essay writing. *Language Arts, 61,* 141–150.

Mallon, T. (1984). *A book of one's own: People and their diaries.* New York: Ticknor & Fields.

Nathan, R. (1987). I have a loose tooth and other unphotographic events: Tales from a first-grade journal. In T. Fulwiler (Ed.), *The journal book* (pp. 187–192). Portsmouth, NH: Boynton/Cook.

Neeld, E. C. (1986). *Writing.* Glenview, IL: Scott Foresman.

Paterson, K. (1977). *Bridge to Terabithia.* New York: Crowell.

Progoff, I. (1975). *At a journal workshop: The basic text and guide for using the intensive journal process.* New York: Dialogue House.

Rico, G. L. (1983). *Writing the natural way.* Los Angeles: Tarcher.

Romano, T. (1987). *Clearing the way: Working with teenage writers.* Portsmouth, NH: Heinemann.

Salem, J. (1982). Using writing in teaching mathematics. In M. Barr, P. D'Arcy, & M. K. Healy (Eds.), *What's going on? Language/learning episodes in British and American classrooms, grades 4–13,* (pp. 123–134). Montclair, NJ: Boynton/Cook.

Shuy, R. W. (1987). Research currents: Dialogue as the heart of learning. *Language Arts, 64,* 890–897.

Stanford, B. (1988). Writing reflectively. *Language Arts, 65,* 652–658.

Staton, J. (1980). Writing and counseling: Using a dialogue journal. *Language Arts, 57,* 514–518.

Staton, J. (1987). The power of responding in dialogue journals. In Toby Fulwiler (Ed.), *The journal book* (pp. 47–63). Portsmouth, NH: Boynton/Cook.

Staton, J., & Shuy, R. W. (1987). Talking our way into writing and reading: Dialogue journal practice. In B. Rafoth & D. Rubin (Eds.), *The social construction of written communication.* Norwood, NJ: Ablex.

Tchudi, S., & Tchudi, S. (1984). *The young writer's handbook: A practical guide for the beginner who is serious about writing.* New York: Scribner.

Tompkins, G. E., & Camp, D. E. (1988). Rx for writer's block. *Childhood Education, 64,* 209–214.

Tway, E. (1981). Come, write with me. *Language Arts, 58,* 805–810.

Tway, E. (1984). *Time for writing in the elementary school.* Urbana, IL: ERIC Clearinghouse on Reading and Communication Skills and the National Council of Teachers of English.

Viorst, J. (1972). *Alexander and the terrible, horrible, no good, very bad day.* New York: Atheneum.

3

The Writing Process

The fourth graders in Mrs. Ochs' class are studying about life in ancient Egypt. Their study occupies much of the school day because language arts and social studies are integrated into one unit. Instead of reading in basal readers and writing in workbooks, the students in Mrs. Ochs' class read books about life in ancient Egypt, and they write in response to their reading. The type of response varies— it may be a simulated journal or learning log, an essay or report, or a biography or a simulated letter. Students work cooperatively in small groups on projects that may involve reading, writing, talking, art, music, and drama in addition to social studies. Students learn language arts and writing skills as they need them to respond to their reading or work on their projects. Some of the specific activities include:

- Students read informational books and keep a reading log.
- The weekly spelling list is developed with words from the unit (e.g., pyramid, goddess, tomb).
- Each student is researching one Egyptian god or goddess and will make a poster to share the information.
- Mrs. Ochs is reading *The Egypt Game* (Snyder, 1967) aloud to the students, one chapter a day.
- Students are working in small groups on various projects. One group is creating a salt map of ancient Egypt; one is dressing dolls in clothes like those worn by ancient Egyptians; one is making a timeline, chronicling the major events in the period; another is designing a chart of the hieroglyphic symbols.

One day several students share with the class what they have learned about Howard Carter's discovery of King Tut's tomb in 1922 from *In Search of Tutankhamun* by Piero Ventura and Gian Paolo Ceserani (1985). Mrs. Ochs capitalizes on the class's interest and shows a videotaped film of Carter's discovery that she rented from a local store. Several students express the wish that they could have been with Carter when the tomb was discovered. They discuss what this would have been like. The students' interest gives Mrs. Ochs an idea: She asks if the students would like to write a first-person "I was with Howard Carter" narrative of the discovery. Are the students interested? You bet they are!

Mrs. Ochs suggests that their writing, like the film, evoke a strong mood and focus on a description of the tomb. To gather words and ideas for writing, she and the students create on the chalkboard a five senses cluster in which they brainstorm words about the sights, sounds, smells, tastes, and feelings as the tomb is entered. A copy of this collaborative cluster is presented in Figure 3-1. *Taste* was the most difficult sense for the students because the explorers did not eat in the tomb, but students recognized that the explorers might have tasted dryness, sandy grit, and even fear. The *feel* sense evoked perhaps the most powerful images as students suggested that the explorers might have felt guilt about their trespassing.

With the background of experiences from the unit on ancient Egypt and the clustering experience, students wrote the rough draft of their first-person narratives. After the students finished their rough drafts, they met in groups to share

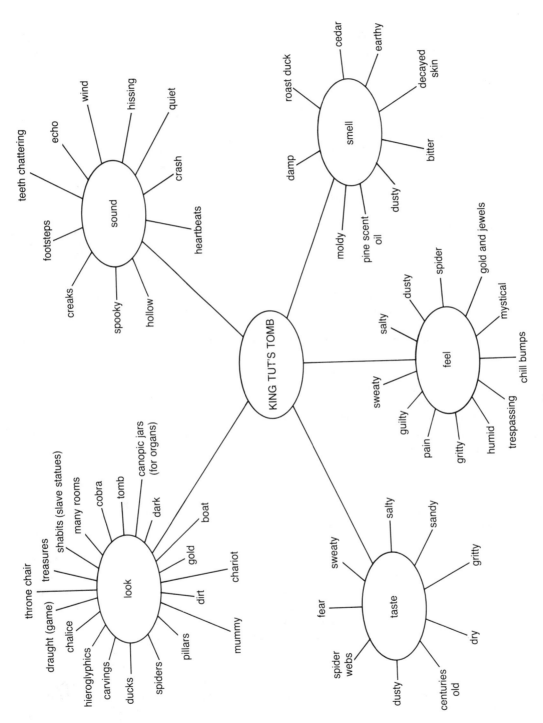

FIGURE 3-1 Fourth-Grade Collaborative Cluster on King Tut

their writing. Mrs. Ochs asked students to focus on the mood created in the writing and the use of description as writing-group members commented about each other's writings.

In his writing group, Josh read first:

It was November 1922 and I was in Egypt with Howard Carter. We had uncovered one step in the Sahara Desert and then 15 more leading downward. As Howard and I walked down we heard the echo of our footsteps. When we got to the bottom we could not see our hands nor each other. I called, "Are you there, Howard?" And he called, "Yes." Both our voices echoed.

As we waited for our eyes to adjust to the darkness we listened. It was quiet, so quiet. I could hear my heartbeat, and I think Howard could hear his too.

My eyes had adjusted and I was amazed at what I saw. There was gold and jewels everywhere. There was a boat and a chariot. There were canopic jars, statues, tools, some kind of gameboards that looked like chess, and a child-size throne chair.

Suddenly it hit me. I turned around and there it was—Tut's tomb!

There was a silence and then his writing group members begged, "Read it again." Josh willingly read his piece a second time, this time more dramatically. When he finished, Matt said, "I've got chill bumps like I was with Howard Carter. That's my compliment." Then Amber told Josh she liked the part about hearing his heartbeat, and Becky Lee liked the dialogue.

Next it was Josh's turn, as the writer, to ask a question. He asked if his classmates thought he had included enough details as Mrs. Ochs had suggested. They counted the details from the cluster that he had included and after they reached 10, they quit counting and concluded that he had.

Finally, Josh asked the writing group members for suggestions to improve his writing. "I think you should keep writing and get to the part about the cobra," suggested Matt. "That's the best part and you could give it a lot of mood!" Becky Lee suggested that Josh call the game by its real name *draught* instead of describing it and saying it was like chess. Josh agreed to continue writing but explained to Becky Lee that he hadn't named the game on purpose because if he were just exploring with Howard Carter, not studying Egypt in fourth grade, he might not know the name!

The other students took turns sharing their rough drafts, listening to compliments and suggestions from the writing-group members, and asking questions themselves. After everyone in the group had shared, they moved back to their desks to make revisions. Later, they would edit and recopy these "I was with Howard Carter" writings and add them to a bulletin board display about King Tut.

Mrs. Ochs' approach to teaching writing is very different from the traditional approach in which the teacher selects a creative topic such as, "If I were a leprechaun," writes it on the chalkboard, and directs the students to write a story about being a leprechaun without providing a background of experiences. In such a class, students would typically write a single-draft composition during a 30-minute period, after which teachers would collect the papers to grade. Sadly, the teacher is usually disappointed with the results. There might be four papers in which students have written clever and creative stories. These papers are fun to read, and the teacher feels gratified. Next, three students might turn in papers with only several words or a single sentence written. This is not surprising because these students never complete assignments. The teacher's biggest disappointment, however, is in the remaining twenty papers; they are mediocre. These writings include a few descriptive sentences but lack interesting ideas and are not stories. The problem is not with the students, but with the traditional approach to writing. These students, in contrast to Mrs. Ochs' students, are not learning how to write; they are simply trying to perform their best on a difficult task that has not been explained to them.

The traditional approach to writing, often called *creative writing,* has been used in elementary schools for the past 30 years and is characterized by its emphasis on the finished product, not on what students *do* as they write. Students practice writing; they do not learn how to write. Because of recent research about writing, the emphasis in writing instruction has shifted from the product of writing to the process involved in creating that product. The teacher's role in this process has shifted from merely assigning and assessing a product to working with students throughout the writing process as Mrs. Ochs does. A number of contrasts between the traditional and process approaches to teaching writing are summarized in Figure 3-2.

Models of the Writing Process

The process approach to writing is based both on classical rhetoric and cognitive psychology. Cognitive theorists including Piaget (1959), Vygotsky (1986), and Bruner (1966) have provided crucial insights by describing the impact of thought and language on writing. The emphasis in the writing process has shifted from analyzing students' finished products to investigating what students think and do as they write.

James Britton (1970) and Janet Emig (1971) were two of the first researchers to examine students' writing processes. In her study, Emig interviewed eight 12th graders as they wrote, and she studied one student's writing in-depth using a case study approach. Through this examination, she described the writing processes that these students used. At the same time, Britton and his colleagues examined 2,000 essays written by British high school students and found that students' writing processes differed according to the type of writing. Several years later, Donald Graves (1975) examined young children's writing and documented that 7-year-olds, like high school students, used a variety of activities as they wrote.

These researchers generally divided the writing process into three activities, subprocesses, or stages. James Britton (1970) labeled them as conception, incubation, and production. In the conceptual stage, writers choose topics and decide to write; in the incubation stage, they develop the topic by gathering

FIGURE 3-2 Contrasts Between the Traditional and Process Approaches to Writing Instruction

	The Traditional Approach	**The Process Approach**
Topic Selection	A specific creative writing assignment is made by the teacher.	Students choose their own topics, or topics are drawn from content-area study.
Instruction	Teachers provide little or no instruction. Students are expected to write as best they can.	Teachers teach students about the writing process and about writing forms.
Focus	The focus is on the finished product.	The focus is on the process that students use when they write.
Ownership	Students write for the teacher and feel little ownership of their writing.	Students assume ownership of their writing.
Audience	The teacher is the primary audience.	Students write for genuine audiences.
Collaboration	There is little or no collaboration.	Students write collaboratively and share writing in groups.
Drafts	Students write single-draft compositions in which they must focus on content and mechanics at the same time.	Students write rough drafts to pour out ideas and then revise and edit these drafts before making final copies.
Mechanical Errors	Students are required to produce error-free compositions.	Students correct as many errors as possible during editing but a greater emphasis is on content than on mechanics.
Teacher's Role	The teacher assigns the composition and grades it after it is completed.	The teacher teaches about writing and provides feedback during revising and editing.
Time	Students complete most compositions in less than an hour.	Students may spend one, two, or three weeks working on a composition.
Assessment	The teacher assesses the quality of the composition after it is completed.	The teacher provides feedback while students are writing so they can use it to improve their writing. Assessment focuses on the process that writers use and the finished product.

information; and in the production stage they write, revise, and edit the composition. Donald Graves (1975) described a similar process using three different labels: prewriting, composing, and postwriting. In prewriting, writers choose topics and gather ideas for writing; in the composing stage, they write the composition; and in the postwriting stage, they share their writing. The single biggest drawback of these descriptions of the writing process is that they suggest a linear, lock-step progression through the three activities (Flower & Hayes, 1981).

Linda S. Flower and John R. Hayes (1977, 1981, 1986) studied college students' writing using a research technique called *protocol analysis.* They asked students to talk about their thought processes while they composed, and then they analyzed the transcripts (or protocols) of the talk to examine the activities and strategies used in writing. Through this analysis, Flower and Hayes (1981) developed a model of the writing process that described writing as a complex problem-solving process. Their model included three major elements: the task environment, the writer's long-term memory, and the writing processes. The task environment is the assignment and the text the writer is writing; the writer's long-term memory is the knowledge of the topic, audience, and writing; and the writing processes involve three activities:

1. Planning: writers set goals to guide the writing.
2. Translating: writers put the plans into writing.
3. Reviewing: writers evaluate and revise the writing.

These three activities are not three linear stages, according to Flower and Hayes, because writers continually monitor their writing and move back and forth among the activities. This monitoring might be considered a fourth component of the writing process. An important finding from their research is that writing is recursive. Using this monitoring mechanism, writers jump back and forth from one subprocess to another as they write.

Researchers have examined particular writing process activities or stages. Nancy Sommers (1980, 1982) described writing as a revision process in which writers develop their ideas, not polish their writing. Less experienced writers, according to Sommers, focus on small word-level changes and error-hunting. This emphasis on mechanics rather than content may be due to teachers' behavior. Sondra Perl (1979, 1980) examined how the writing process is used in high school and college classrooms and concluded that teachers place inordinate importance on mechanical errors. Flower and Hayes (1977) found that less successful writers have a limited repertoire of alternatives for solving problems as they write, and Bereiter and Scardamalia (1982) found that even though children participated in writing process activities, they were less capable of monitoring the need to move from activity to activity.

This research has confirmed the importance of the process approach to writing and that the examination of what writers do as they write is at least as important as the products they produce. Even though there is much more to study about the writing process and the social contexts of composing, the conclusions drawn from the recent research can guide instructional practice today. Four precepts that guide the presentation of the writing process in this chapter are:

Elementary Students Can Write. Research on first graders' writing demonstrates that elementary students, even at the primary grade level, can write and that they use activities representative of the various stages of the writing process.

Elementary Students Need to Develop a Repertoire of Writing Strategies. According to research findings, less experienced writers have a smaller repertoire of writing activities and monitor the strategies less effectively than do more experienced writers. In a process approach to writing, students learn a variety of writing strategies, and teachers provide a supportive environment to help students learn to monitor them.

Elementary Students Separate Revising and Editing Activities. The three-stage versions of the writing process combine revising and editing activities, even though research has shown that when they are grouped together, the emphasis of both teachers and students will be on editing—the error-hunting activity. The two activities should be separated so that proper attention can be given to each in the writing process.

Elementary Students Learn a Problem-Solving Approach to Writing. Writing is a form of problem-solving in which students experiment with a variety of alternative activities as they try to communicate effectively. These activities—the writing process—can be organized in a multicomponent model that researchers have attempted to describe in various ways. While there is no consensus on the names of the stages or the activities involved in each stage there is agreement that writers use a variety of activities and move back and forth among them.

The five-stage writing process presented in this chapter incorporates activities identified through the research. These stages are (a) prewriting, (b) drafting, (c) revising, (d) editing, and (e) sharing. The key features of each stage are presented in Figure 3-3. The labeling and numbering of the stages should not be construed to suggest that this writing process is a linear series of neatly packaged categories. Research has shown that the process is cyclical, involving recurring cycles, and labeling is only an aid to use in identifying and discussing the activities that represent each stage. In the classroom, the stages merge and cycle as students write. Moreover, students personalize the process to meet their own needs, and they vary the process according to the writing assignment.

PREWRITING

Prewriting is the getting-ready-to-write stage. The traditional notion that writers have thought out their topic completely is ridiculous. If writers wait for the ideas to be fully developed, they may wait forever. Instead, writers begin tentatively, talking, reading, and writing to see what they know and what direction they want to go. Pulitzer prize-winning writer, Donald Murray (1985, 1987) calls this the discovery of writing. You begin writing to explore what you know and to surprise yourself.

Prewriting has probably been the most neglected stage in the writing process; however, it is as crucial to writers as a warm-up is to athletes. Donald Murray (1982) believes that 70% or more of writing time should be spent in prewriting. During the prewriting stage, students:

FIGURE 3-3 Overview of the Writing Process

Stage 1: Prewriting

Students write on topics based on their own experiences.
Students engage in rehearsal activities before writing.
Students identify the audience to whom they will write.
Students identify the purpose of the writing activity.
Students choose an appropriate form for their compositions based on audience and
   purpose.

Stage 2: Drafting

Students write a rough draft.
Students emphasize content rather than mechanics.

Stage 3: Revising

Students share their writing in writing groups.
Students participate constructively in discussions about classmates' writing.
Students make changes in their compositions to reflect the reactions and comments
   of both teacher and classmates.
Between the first and final drafts, students make substantive rather than only minor
   changes.

Stage 4: Editing

Students proofread their own compositions.
Students help proofread classmates' compositions.
Students increasingly identify and correct their own mechanical errors.

Stage 5: Sharing

Students publish their writing in an appropriate form.
Students share their finished writing with an appropriate audience.

- Choose a topic
- Consider purpose, form, and audience
- Use informal writing strategies to generate and organize ideas for writing
- Write a collaborative composition

Choosing a Topic

Choosing topics for writing can be a stumbling block for students who have become dependent on teachers to supply their topics. In the traditional approach,
teachers supplied the topics by suggesting gimmicky story starters and relieving
students of the "burden" of topic selection. Often, these "creative" topics stymied
students who were forced to write on topics they knew little about or were not interested in. Donald Graves (1976) calls this traditional approach of supplying top-

ics for students "writing welfare." Instead, students need to take responsibility for choosing their own topics for writing.

At first, dependent students will argue that they do not know what to write about; however, teachers can help them brainstorm a list of three, four, or five topics and then identify the one topic they are most interested in and know the most about. Students who feel they cannot generate any writing topics are often surprised that they have so many options available. Then through prewriting activities, students talk, draw, read, and even write to develop information about their topics.

Asking students to choose their own topics for writing does not mean that the teachers never give writing assignments. Rather, teachers provide general guidelines. Teachers may specify the writing form—journals, stories, poems, reports, and so on. At other times they may establish the function—for example, to share what students have learned about life in ancient Egypt—but students should choose their own specific content. For instance, students can demonstrate what they have learned about life in ancient Egypt by writing a report about how people were mummified; by assuming the persona of a person who lived in ancient Egypt and writing a simulated journal, or by writing a biography of Queen Nefrititi; by writing an acrostic poem on the word *pyramid;* or by writing a story set in ancient Egypt.

Considering Function

As students prepare to write, they need to identify their function or purpose for writing. Are they writing to entertain? To inform? To persuade? This decision about function influences other decisions students make about audience and form. M.A.K. Halliday (1973, 1975) has identified seven language functions that apply to both oral and written language. These seven functions are:

1.	Instrumental Language	Language to satisfy needs, such as in business letters
2.	Regulatory Language	Language to control the behavior of others, such as in directions and rules
3.	Interactional Language	Language to establish and maintain social relationships, such as in pen pal letters and dialogue journals
4.	Personal Language	Language to express personal opinions, such as in learning logs and letters to the editor
5.	Imaginative Language	Language to express imagination and creativity, such as in stories, poems, and scripts

6. Heuristic Language	Language to seek information and to find out about things, such as in learning logs and interviews
7. Informative Language	Language to convey information, such as in reports and biographies

Frank Smith (1977) has observed that these language functions are learned through genuine communication experiences rather than through practice activities that lack functional purposes. Moreover, skill in one function does not generalize to other functions, so students need to learn to use each one. Language is rarely used for just one function, according to Smith; typically, two or more functions are involved in any composition.

Considering Audience

Students may write primarily for themselves to express and clarify their own ideas and feelings or they may write for others. Possible audiences include classmates, younger children, parents, foster grandparents, children's authors, and pen pals. Other audiences are more distant and less well known. For example, students may write letters to businesses to request information, write articles to be published in the local newspaper, or submit stories and poems to be published in literary magazines.

Children's writing is influenced by their sense of audience. James Britton (Britton et al., 1975) defines sense of audience as "the manner in which the writer expresses a relationship with the reader in respect to the writer's understanding" (pp. 65–66). When students write for others, they adapt their writing to fit their audience, just as they vary their speech to fit the audience. This variance is called "register" (Smith, 1982). Students must be aware of their audience while writing in order to choose the appropriate register. In contrast, when students write only to complete assignments, they lack a sense of audience.

Elementary students demonstrate their relationship with the audience in a variety of ways, often by adding parenthetical information or an aside. For example, a seventh grader begins "George Mudlumpus and the Mystery of the Golden Spider," his sixth mystery featuring George Mudlumpus, the detective with the outrageous rates, this way:

I had decided to take my vacation, as you already know from the last story I told you. So, I packed, got my airplane ticket, and got on a 747 jetliner. I was off to San Francisco!

This student feels a close relationship, that of a storyteller, with his unknown audience. He often includes asides in his stories, and George sometimes comments to his readers, "I know! You think I should have recognized that clue!"

Also, there are times when students need to learn a new register, one which they may not have been exposed to through oral language or through previous writing experiences. For example, children recognize that the closings "Love" or "Your friend" may not be appropriate to end a business letter but they may not be familiar with a more appropriate way to close the letter.

When students write for others, teachers are the most common audience and they can assume several roles. How writers perceive these roles are crucial. Teachers can assume the role of trusted adult, a partner in dialogue, or judge (Britton et al., 1975). In writing to a trusted adult, students feel secure because they can rely on their reader to respond sympathetically. When writing a dialogue with a teacher, students are secure in the teacher's presence and assume that the teacher will be interested in the writing, responding to *what* has been written, not to *how* it has been written. Unfortunately, the teacher's most common role is that of judge, and this role is least conducive to good writing. When a teacher acts as a judge, students produce writing only to satisfy a teacher's requirement or to receive a grade.

Considering Form

One of the most important considerations is the form the writing will take. A story? A letter? A poem? A journal entry? A writing assignment could be handled in any one of these ways. As part of a science unit on hermit crabs, for instance, students could write a story about a hermit crab, draw a picture of a hermit crab and label body parts, write an explanation of how hermit crabs obtain shells to live in, or keep a log of observations about the hermit crabs living in the classroom.

There is an almost endless variety of forms that children's writing may take. Figure 3-4 lists approximately 100 of them. Too often students' writing is limited to writing stories, poems, and reports. Instead, they need to experiment with a wide variety of writing forms and to explore the functions and formats of these forms. The forms can be used in both creative and traditional ways. Recipes are a good example. Most adults think of recipes as simply a list of instructions and ingredients for preparing food, and they may question why students are writing recipes. However, students can write creative recipes, such as a recipe for a war in conjunction with a social studies unit. This activity probes students' understanding of the causes and events leading to wars. Other possible recipes include a recipe for a best friend or a hero. As they write recipes, students learn to write directions clearly and in sequence.

Through reading and writing, students develop a strong sense of these forms and how they are structured. Langer (1985) found that by third grade, students responded in clearly different ways to story and report writing assignments. They organized the writing differently and included varied kinds of information and elaboration, depending on the form. Similarly, Hidi and Hildyard (1983) found that elementary students could differentiate between stories and persuasive essays. Because children are clarifying the distinctions between various writing forms during the elementary grades, it is very important that teachers use the correct terminology and not label all children's writing as "stories."

While most writing forms look like the text on this page does—block form written from left-to-right and from top-to-bottom—some writing forms require a special arrangement on a page or special language patterns. For example, scripts, recipes, poems, and letters are four writing forms that have very recognizable for-

FIGURE 3-4   A Variety of Writing Forms

ABC books	diagrams	paragraphs
advertisements	dictionaries	personal narratives
"All About the Author"	directions	persuasive letters
announcements	editorials	poems
anthologies	essays	postcards
apologies	evaluations	posters
applications	explanations	proverbs
autobiographies	fables	puzzles
awards	fairy tales	questionnaires
ballots	folktales	questions
bibliographies	freewrites	quizzes
biographies	greeting cards	recipes
book jackets	hink-pinks	research reports
book reports	instructions	reviews
books	interviews	riddles
brochures	invitations	schedules
bumper stickers	jokes	scripts
campaign speeches	journals	sentences
captions	lab reports	signs
cartoons	labels	slogans
catalogues	learning logs	stories
certificates	letters	study guides
character sketches	letters to the editor	tall tales
charts	lists	telegrams
comics	lyrics	telephone directories
comparisons	maps	thank you notes
complaints	menus	thesauruses
computer programs	mysteries	thumbnail sketches
coupons	myths	tongue twisters
crossword puzzles	newspapers	valentines
definitions	notes	word-finds
descriptions	obituaries	wordless picture books
dialogue	oral histories	words

mats. Examples of writing that use special language patterns would be a story that begins with "Once upon a time . . . " or letters that require "Dear . . . " and "Sincerely." As children are introduced to these writing forms and have opportunities to experiment with them, they will learn about the unique requirements of the formats.

Teaching children about these three considerations—function, audience and form—is an important component of writing instruction. Children need to learn to make decisions about these considerations and they need to know the range of options available to writers.

Decisions about function, audience, and form impact on each other. For example, if the function is to entertain, a form such as a story, poem, or script might be selected. These three forms look very different on a piece of paper. While a story is written in the traditional block format, scripts and poems have unique page arrangements. For example, in a script, the character's name appears first and is followed by a colon and then the dialogue. Action and dialogue, rather than description, carry the storyline in a script. In contrast, poems have unique formatting considerations and words are used judiciously. Each word and phrase is chosen to convey a maximum amount of information.

Audience also plays an important role. Audiences for stories, scripts, and poems are often unknown or large while the audience for a letter is usually one particular person. While the function of a letter may be to request information or share personal information, it is customized according to audience. Children might share the same information with their pen pal and with their grandparents, but the way they present the information varies according to their degree of familiarity.

While these decisions may change as students write and revise, writers must begin with at least a tentative concept of function, audience, and form as they move into the drafting stage.

Prewriting Activities

Donald Graves (1983) has labeled as "rehearsal" the activities that students engage in to gather and organize ideas for writing. These activities help students prepare for writing. Two types of prewriting or rehearsal activities include background activities and informal writing strategies. Background activities provide the knowledge students need to write because it is impossible to write well about a topic you don't know well. Rehearsal activities take many forms, including drawing, talking, reading, interviewing, informal drama, field trips, and other content area experiences.

Drawing. For very young children, drawing is the way they gather and organize ideas for writing. Kindergarten and first-grade teachers often notice that students draw before they write. When young children are asked to write before drawing, for example, students explain that they can't write yet because they don't know what to write until they see what they draw. As young children become writers, they use drawing and other symbol systems as they grapple with the uniqueness of writing (Dyson, 1982, 1983, 1986).

Talking. Too often the value of talk is ignored in the classroom, but as students write, talk is necessary. Students talk with their classmates to share ideas about possible writing topics, try out ways to express an idea, and ask questions. They read and react to each other's writing. They also participate in class discussions about writing forms, elements of story structure, and other writing-related issues. Talk continues throughout the writing process as students discuss their compositions in conferences and proofread each other's writing.

Reading. Reading and writing are symbiotic, mutually beneficial processes. Through reading, children gather ideas for writing and investigate the structure of various written forms. Reading is a form of experience and writers need a variety of experiences to draw on as they write. Often students will retell a favorite story in writing, write new adventures for favorite story characters, or experiment with repetition, onomatopoeia, or another poetic device used in a book they have read.

Reading informational books also provides the raw material necessary for writing. For example, if students are studying polar bears for a writing assignment, they need to gather background information about the animal, its habitat, and predators. If they are interested in Olympic athletes, they may read biographies of Jesse Owens, Nadia Comaneci, Ray Leonard, or Mary Lou Retton and then share what they learn by writing a collection of biographical sketches.

Interviews. Students can interview people in the community who have special knowledge about the topic they will write about. Interviewing involves three steps: planning the interview, conducting the interview, and sharing the results. In the first step, students arrange for the interview and develop a list of questions to ask during the interview. Next, students conduct the interview and take notes or tape-record the answers. Last, students share the information they gathered in the interview. This sharing can take many different forms, ranging from newspaper articles to reports to books.

Students can invite someone with special expertise, such as a police officer, the manager of the local McDonald's restaurant, or a scientist from a nearby college to visit the classroom to be interviewed. For example, a class of first graders invited the local high school principal to visit their class and be interviewed as part of a unit on the five senses. The principal, who had been blinded several years earlier, brought his guide dog with him. The children asked questions about how visually impaired people manage everyday tasks and how he performs his job as a principal. They also asked questions about his guide dog. After the interview, students drew pictures and wrote summaries. One first grader's report is shown in Figure 3-5.

Informal Drama. Through informal drama, children discover and shape ideas that they will use in their writing (Wagner, 1983). According to Mills (1983), having students role-play an experience provides energy and purpose for writing. Often writing grows out of dramatic play and role-playing stories. One way children

Mr. Kirtley came down.
We asked him questions. He
answered them. He is
blind. His dog's name is
Milo.

FIGURE 3-5 A First Grader's Report
Tomara, age 7

learn to write directions is to write directions for an activity, such as making a peanut butter sandwich. Typically, children omit crucial steps, such as opening the
jar of peanut butter, when they write directions; however, when they write directions after dramatizing the activity, the directions they write are better organized
and more complete. Students can also assess the effectiveness of their directions
by having a classmate try to follow the directions. In this way, children learn about
the steps they have omitted.

Similarly, in social studies units and after reading stories, students can re-enact events to bring the experience to life. British educator Dorothy Heathcote

(Wagner, 1976, 1983) advocates an approach in which teachers choose a dramatic focus, or a particular critical moment for students to reenact. The improvisation begins as students assume roles, and the teacher becomes a character, too. As they role play the event, questions are used to draw students' attention to certain features and to prove their understanding. For example, after reading *Sarah Plain and Tall* (MacLachlan, 1985), children might re-enact the day that Sarah took the wagon to town. This is the critical moment in the story: Does Sarah like them and their prairie home well enough to stay? Through role playing, students become immersed in the event, and by reliving it, they are learning far more than mere facts.

Informal Writing Strategies. The second type of prewriting activities are informal writing strategies. Students use the informal writing strategies—brainstorming, clustering, freewriting, and cubing—that were presented in Chapter 2 to gather and organize the information learned through the background experiences. They brainstorm lists of words and ideas, cluster main ideas and details, freewrite to discover what they know about a topic and what direction their writing might take, and cube a complex topic to consider it from several different dimensions. Many young children (and some older students) use drawing to gather and organize ideas for writing.

Collaborative Compositions. Another prewriting activity is writing a collaborative or group composition. When students write a composition together with the teacher, they have the opportunity to rehearse before writing a similar composition independently. The teacher reviews concepts and clarifies misconceptions as the group composition is written, and students offer ideas for writing and suggestions about how to tackle common writing problems. In addition, the teacher models or demonstrates the writing process and provides an opportunity for students to practice the process approach to writing in a supportive environment.

First, the teacher introduces the idea of writing a group composition and reviews the assignment. Students compose the class collaboration composition, moving through the drafting, revising, editing, and publishing stages of the writing process. The teacher records students' dictation, noting any misunderstandings students may have about the writing assignment or the writing process. When necessary, the teacher reviews concepts and offers suggestions. Students first dictate a rough draft which the teacher records on the chalkboard or on chart paper. Then the teacher and students read the composition and identify ways to revise it. Some parts of the composition will need to be reworked, and other parts may be deleted or moved. More specific words will be substituted for less specific ones and redundant words and sentences will be deleted. Also, students may want to add new parts to the composition. After making the necessary content-related changes, students proofread the composition, checking for mechanical errors, paragraph breaks, and for sentences to combine. Errors are corrected and changes are made. Then the teacher or a student copies the completed composition on chart paper or on a sheet of notebook paper. Copies can be duplicated and given to each student.

In "Marbles Lost, Marbles Found: Collaborative Production of Text," Esther Fine (1987) described how her middle grade class of students with behavior disorders wrote a novel collaboratively. All of the students contributed to the writing and through the experience learned that they could write and that they had valuable contributions to make. Fine summed up the experience this way: "Collaboration is learning to learn and to work together . . . Collaboration is a great solution" (p. 487).

Collaborative compositions are an essential part of many writing experiences, especially when students are learning to use the writing process or a new writing form. Group compositions serve as a "dry-run," and students' questions and misconceptions are clarified.

DRAFTING

In the process approach to writing, students write and refine their compositions through a series of drafts. During the drafting stage, students focus on getting their ideas down on paper. Because writers do not begin writing with their compositions already composed in their minds, they begin with tentative ideas developed through prewriting activities. The drafting stage is the time to pour out ideas, with little concern about spelling, punctuation, and other mechanical errors.

Writing a Rough Draft

Students should skip every other line as they write their rough draft to leave adequate space for revising as they draft and in the later stages of the writing process. They use arrows to move sections of text, crossouts to delete sections, and scissors and tape to cut apart and rearrange text just as adult writers do. Similarly, students should only write on one side of a sheet of paper so that the paper can be cut apart or rearranged. As word processors become more accessible in elementary classrooms, revising, with all its shifting and deletion of text will be made much easier. However, at present, for students who handwrite their compositions, the wide spacing is crucial. Make small *x*'s on every other line of young children's papers as a reminder to skip lines as they draft their compositions.

Students label their drafts by writing the words *ROUGH DRAFT* in ink at the top of their papers or by stamping the papers with a *ROUGH DRAFT* stamp. This label indicates to the writer, other students, parents, and administrators that the composition is a draft in which emphasis has been placed on content, not mechanics. It also explains why teachers have not graded the paper or marked mechanical errors. Also, some students who are just learning the writing process and have been writing single-draft compositions secretly plan to continue to write this way and plan to make this rough draft their final draft if they write carefully. The words *ROUGH DRAFT* stamped in ink at the top of the paper negates that idea and further emphasizes that writing involves more than one stage.

As students draft their compositions, they may need to modify their earlier decisions about function, audience, and especially the form their writing will take. For example, a composition that began as a story may be transformed into a report, letter, or a poem. The new format may allow the student to communicate more effectively. This process of modifying earlier decisions also continues into the revising stage.

Writing Leads

The lead, or opening sentences, of a composition is crucial. Think of the last time you went to a library to choose a novel to read. Several titles or book jacket pictures may have caught your eye, but in making your selection, you opened the book and read the first paragraph or two. Which one did you choose? You chose the one that "hooked" you or "grabbed" your attention. The same is true for children's writing. Students who consider audience as they write will want to grab the attention of the audience. Nothing is such a failure as a piece of writing that no one wants to read! Children may use a variety of techniques to appeal to their audience, such as questions, facts, dialogue, brief stories, and problems.

Donald Graves (1983) and Lucy McCormick Calkins (1986) recommended that students create several leads and try them out on classmates before choosing one. As students write these leads they gain valuable knowledge about how to manipulate language and how to vary viewpoint or sequence in their writing.

Emphasize Content, Not Mechanics

It is important in this stage not to emphasize correct spelling and neatness. In fact, when teachers point out mechanical errors during the drafting stage, they send a false message to students that mechanical correctness is more important than content (Sommers, 1982). Later, during editing, students can clean up mechanical errors and put their composition into a neat, final form.

REVISING

During the revising stage, writers refine ideas in their compositions. Often students break the writing process cycle as soon as they complete a rough draft, believing that once their ideas are jotted down the writing task is complete. Experienced writers, however, know they must turn to others for reactions and revise on the basis of these comments. Revision is not just polishing writing; it is meeting the needs of readers through adding, substituting, deleting, and rearranging material. By definition, the word *revision* means "seeing again," and in this stage writers see their compositions again with their classmates and the teacher helping them. The activities in the revising stage are:

- Rereading the rough draft
- Sharing the rough draft in a writing group
- Revising on the basis of feedback received from the writing group

Rereading the Rough Draft

Writers are the first to revise their compositions. Some revision occurs during drafting when writers make choices and changes as they write. After finishing the rough draft, writers need to distance themselves from the draft for a day or two and then reread the draft from a fresh perspective, as a reader might, not as writers who know what they intended to say. As they reread, students make changes—adding, substituting, deleting, and moving—and place question marks by sections that they need help with. It is these trouble spots that students ask for help with in their writing group.

Writing Groups[1]

Students meet in writing groups to share their compositions with small groups of classmates. Because writing cannot occur in a vacuum and must meet the needs of readers, feedback is crucial. Mohr (1984) has identified four general functions of writing groups: to offer the writer choices, to give the writers responses, feelings, and thoughts, to show different possibilities in revising, and to speed up revising. Writing groups provide a "scaffold," or supportive environment, in which teachers and classmates talk about plans and strategies for writing and revising (Applebee & Langer, 1983; Calkins, 1983).

Writing groups can form spontaneously when several students have completed drafts and are ready to share their compositions, or writing groups can be formal groupings with identified leaders. In Mrs. Preston's first-grade classroom, for example, writing groups form spontaneously. When students finish writing, they go to the reading rug and sit in a chair designated as the "author's chair" (Graves & Hansen, 1983). As soon as a child with writing to share is sitting in the chair, others who are available to listen and respond to the writing to and sit on the floor in front of the author's chair. When three or four children have arrived for the writing group, the writer reads the writing and the other children listen and respond to it, offering compliments and relating this piece of writing to their own experiences and writing. Sometimes Mrs. Preston joins the listeners on the rug to participate in the writing group; other times when she is involved in another activity, the children work independently. In contrast, in Mrs. Blackburn's second-grade classroom, writing groups are formal groupings. Reading groups become writing groups when children have completed a rough draft and are ready to share their writing with classmates and the teacher. Mrs. Blackburn participates in these groups, providing feedback with the students. In Mrs. Hicks' sixth-grade classroom, the groups function independently. Four or five students are assigned to each group, and a list of the groups and their members is posted in the classroom. On the list, Mrs. Hicks puts a star by one student's name and that student serves as a group leader. Every quarter she changes the leader.

Once writing group arrangements are set, students meet in writing groups to share their writing through these activities:

[1]Adapted from Tompkins & Friend, 1988, pp. 4–9.

- The writer reads the composition aloud to the group.
- Listeners respond with compliments about the composition.
- The writer asks listeners for assistance with trouble spots.
- Listeners offer comments and suggestions about how to improve the composition.
- Each writer in the group repeats the process.
- Writers each identify two or three revisions they will make to improve their compositions.

The Writer Reads. Students take turns reading their compositions aloud to writing group members. Everyone listens politely, thinking about the compliments and suggestions for improvement they will make after the writer has finished reading. Typically, only the writer looks at the composition as it is read, because when classmates and the teacher look at it, they quickly notice and comment on mechanical errors even though the emphasis during revising is on content. Listening to the writing without looking at it keeps the focus on content.

Listeners Offer Compliments. After reading, writing group members offer compliments, stating what they liked about the writing. These positive comments should be specific, focusing on strengths rather than the often-heard "I like it" or "It was good." Even though these are positive comments, they do not provide effective feedback because they are not specific. When teachers first introduce revision, they should model appropriate types of responses because students may not know how to offer specific and meaningful responses. Working together, the teacher and students brainstorm a list of acceptable comments and post it in the classroom for students to refer to. The acceptable comments may focus on organization, leads, word choice, voice, sequence, dialogue, theme, and other elements of writing. Figure 3-6 presents a list of sample compliments.

The Writer Asks Questions. After a round of positive comments, writers ask their classmates for assistance on trouble spots they identified earlier when they reread their writing, or they may ask questions that reflect more general concerns about how well they are communicating. Admitting that they need help from their classmates is a major step in learning to revise. Encourage students to ask for help using a specific context, as these students did:

> "When I was trying to explain that the dinosaurs all died off, well I didn't know what to say. What's that word that means they all died off?"

> "Well, I put this part first, about how lions are the giraffe's main enemy. I don't know if that part should go before where giraffes live. Or I could say that male giraffes are 18 feet tall. Is it best to start there?"

> "I don't have very much information to put in this first chapter about Betsy Ross's childhood. It seems so short. What can I do?"

A list of sample questions that writers can use in asking their classmates for assistance is also presented in Figure 3-6. The teacher can model some of these questions, prefacing them with "If I were the writer, I might ask . . . ," and when the

FIGURE 3-6   Writing Group Responses

Listeners' Compliments

I like the part where . . .
I'd like to know more about . . .
I think your main idea is . . .
You used some powerful words, like . . .
I like the way you described . . .
I like the way you explained . . .
I like the way you wrote . . .
Your writing made me feel . . .
I like the order you used in your writing because . . .
I think your dialogue was realistic, the way (*character*)
said . . .
Your writing reminded me of . . .

Writer's Questions

What do you think the best or strongest part is in my writing?
What did you learn from my writing?
What do you want to know more about?
What part doesn't make sense?
Is there a part that I should throw away?
Can you tell what my main idea is?
How can I make my writing clearer?
What details can I add?
Did I use some tired words that I need to change?
Are there some sentences I should combine?

Listeners' Comments and Suggestions

What is your favorite part?
What part are you having trouble with?
Could you write a lead sentence to "grab" your readers?
Do you need a closing?
I got confused in the part about . . .
Could you add more to this part because . . .
Could you leave this part out because . . .
Could you use a different word for _____
because . . .
Is this paragraph on one topic?
Do your paragraphs seem to be in the right order?
Could you combine some sentences?
What do you plan to do next?

Adapted from Tompkins & Friend, 1988

students understand what is expected of them, they can brainstorm a list of questions and add this list to their list of compliments. Many students find it difficult to ask questions about their writing, but when they work with their writing to the extent that they ask questions as in the examples above, they have become writers who look to their classmates for assistance.

Listeners Offer Suggestions. Next, members of the writing group ask questions about things that were unclear to them and make suggestions about how to revise the composition. Almost any writer resists constructive criticism, and it is especially difficult for elementary students to appreciate these comments and suggestions. However, this approach is far more constructive than the traditional approach in which the teacher graded the paper and covered it with comments and corrections. Students ask the same types of questions that writers ask about their own trouble spots, for example:

> "Up here at the top you said that birds migrate. But later on you said that ducks live at ponds in our town all year long. Well, ducks are birds, aren't they? What did you mean?"

> "You say 'It is . . . ' 'It is . . . ' 'It is . . . ' I think that you could put all of those together because it is boring to read the same words over and over."

> "Here you tell why junk food is bad for you. Then you say 'Junk food is fun to eat." That doesn't really go there. You need to put it somewhere else. Maybe where you talk about why junk food is good."

Figure 3-6 also includes a list of sample questions that writing group members can use in making comments and suggestions. Here again the teacher should model some of these questions, and when the students understand what is expected of them, they can brainstorm a list of comments and suggestions and add this to their lists of compliments and questions. It is important to take time to teach students what kinds of comments and suggestions are acceptable so that students can phrase their comments in a helpful rather than a hurtful way.

Repeat the Process. After everyone in the writing group offers feedback, the process is repeated as each student reads his or her composition and receives feedback. This is the appropriate time for teachers to provide input as well. They should react to the piece of writing as any other listener would, not with red pen in hand, error-hunting (Sommers, 1982). In fact, most teachers prefer to listen to students read their compositions aloud rather than to read them themselves and become frustrated by numerous misspelled words and nearly illegible handwriting common in rough drafts.

Writers Plan for Revision. At the end of the writing group, students each make a commitment to revise their writing based on the comments and suggestions of their writing group members. The final decision on what to revise always rests with the writers themselves, but with the understanding that their rough drafts are not perfect comes the realization that some revision will be necessary. When students verbalize their planned revisions, they are more than likely to complete the revision stage. Some students also make notes for themselves about their revision plans. After the group disbands, students make the revisions.

Students' Revisions

As they make revisions, students add words, substitute sentences, delete paragraphs, and move phrases. They cross out, draw arrows, and write in the space they left between the lines of writing when they double-spaced their rough drafts. Students move back and forth into prewriting to gather additional information, into drafting to write a new paragraph, and back into revising to substitute an often-repeated word. Messiness is inevitable, but despite the scribbles, students are usually able to decipher what they have written.

Students' changes can be classified as the kinds of changes (e.g., additions, substitutions, deletions, and movements) and the level of changes (e.g., whether a word, a phrase/clause, a sentence, a paragraph, or the entire text (Faigley & Witte, 1981). There is a hierarchy of complexity both in the four types of revisions and in the levels of revision as illustrated in Figure 3-7. The least complex change is the addition of a word and the most complex change is at the text level. Elementary students often focus at the word and phrase/clause level and make more additions and substitutions than deletions and movements.

Teachers can examine the types and levels of revisions that students are making by examining their revised rough drafts, and the revisions that students make is another gauge of their growth as writers. Teachers also might want to share this hierarchy with upper-grade students so that they know the revision options they have available. Students should be encouraged to keep a record of their own revisions. Even though some revisions might be considered more sophisticated than others, students should make the change that is most effective for their writing. They should not move a paragraph when adding a sentence is the more effective revision.

EDITING

Editing is putting the piece of writing into its final form. Until this stage, the focus has been primarily on the content of students' writing. Once the focus changes to mechanics, students polish their writing by correcting spelling and other mechanical errors. The goal here is to make the writing "optimally readable" (Smith, 1982). Writers who write for readers understand that if their compositions are not readable, they have written in vain because their ideas will never be read.

Mechanics are the commonly accepted conventions of written standard English. They include capitalization, punctualization, spelling, sentence structure, usage, and formatting considerations specific to poems, scripts, letters, and other writing forms. The use of these commonly accepted conventions is a courtesy to those who will read the composition.

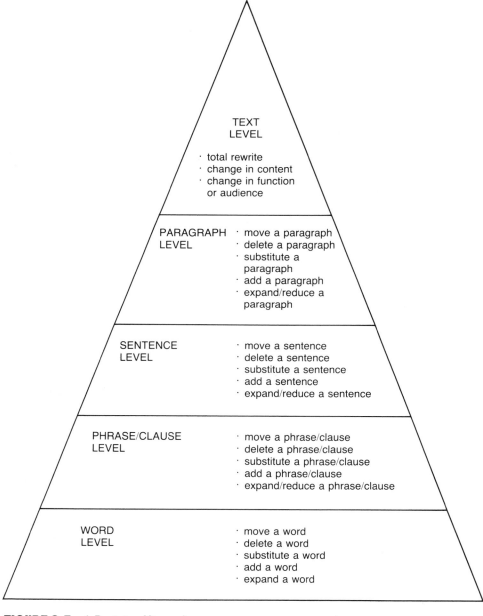

FIGURE 3-7 A Revision Hierarchy

The most effective way to teach mechanical skills is during the editing stage of the writing process rather than through workbook exercises. When editing a composition that will be shared with a genuine audience, students are more interested in using mechanical skills correctly so that they can communicate effectively.

In a study of 2 third-grade classes, Calkins (1980) found that the students in the class who learned punctuation marks as a part of editing could define or explain more marks than the students in the other class who were taught punctuation skills in a traditional manner with instruction and practice exercises on each punctuation mark. In other words, the results of this research as well as other studies (Bissex, 1980; Elley et al., 1976; Graves, 1983) suggest that a functional approach to teaching the mechanics of writing is more effective than practice exercises.

Students move through three activities in the editing stage:

- Getting distance from the composition
- Proofreading to locate errors
- Correcting errors

Getting Distance

Students are more efficient editors when they set the composition aside for a few days before beginning to edit. After working so closely with the piece of writing during drafting and revising, they are too familiar with it to be able to locate many mechanical errors. With the distance of a few days, children are better able to approach editing with a fresh perspective and gather the enthusiasm necessary to finish the writing process by making the paper optimally readable.

Proofreading

Students proofread their compositions to locate and mark possible errors. Proofreading is a unique form of reading in which students read word-by-word and hunt for errors rather than for meaning (King, 1985). Concentrating on mechanics is difficult because of our natural inclination to read for meaning. Even experienced proofreaders often find themselves reading for meaning and overlooking errors that do not inhibit meaning. It is important, therefore, to take time to explain proofreading and to demonstrate how it differs from regular reading.

To demonstrate proofreading, teachers take a piece of student writing and copy it on the chalkboard or display it on an overhead projector. The teacher reads it several times, each time hunting for a particular type of error. During each reading, the composition is read slowly, with the teacher softly pronouncing each word and touching the word with a pencil or pen to focus attention on it. The teacher marks possible errors as they are located.

Errors are marked or corrected with special proofreader's marks. Students enjoy using these marks, the same ones that adult authors and editors use. A list of proofreader's marks that elementary students can learn and use in editing their writing is presented in Figure 3-8.

Editing checklists also help students focus on particular categories of error as they proofread their compositions. Teachers can develop these checklists with two to six items appropriate for students' grade level. A first-grade checklist, for example, might include only two items, one about capital letters at the beginning of sentences and a second about periods at the end of sentences. In contrast, a middle-grade checklist might include items including using commas in a series, paragraph indentation, capitalizing proper nouns and adjectives, and spelling homonyms correctly. During the school year, teachers revise the checklist to focus attention on skills that have recently been taught. A sample third-grade editing checklist is presented in Figure 3-9. In this checklist, the writer and a classmate work together as partners to edit their compositions. First, students proofread their own compositions, searching for errors in each category listed on the checklist and, after proofreading, they check off each item. After completing the checklist, students sign their names and trade checklists and compositions. Now they become editors and complete each other's checklist. Having the writer and editor sign the checklist helps to impress on them to take the activity seriously.

Function	*Mark*	*Example*
Delete	ℰ	The boy was at in home.
Insert	∧	The weather today is cold and windy.
Indent paragraph	¶	¶ Spiders are not insects. They are arachnids.
Capitalize	≡	I was born in dallas, Texas.
Change to lower case	/	Why do beached Whales die?
Add period	⊙	The princess lived in a castle high in the mountains⊙
Add comma	∧	I have two cats a dog and a parakeet.
Add apostrophe	∨	My brothers name is Bill.

FIGURE 3-8 Proofreader's Marks

FIGURE 3-9 A Third-Grade Editing Checklist

EDITING CHECKLIST

Author   Editor

1. I have circled the words that might be misspelled.

2. I have checked that all sentences begin with capital letters.

3. I have checked that all sentences end with punctuation marks.

4. I have checked that all proper nouns begin with a capital letter.

Signatures:

Author: _____ *Editor:* _____

Correcting Errors. After students proofread their compositions and locate as many errors as possible, they correct these errors individually or with their editor's assistance. Some errors are easy to correct, some require the use of a dictionary, and others involve instruction from the teacher. It is unrealistic to expect students to locate and correct every mechanical error in their compositions. Not even published books are error-free! Once in a while, students may even change a correct spelling or punctuation mark and make it incorrect, but overall they correct far more errors than they create.

Editing can end after students and their editors correct as many mechanical errors as possible, or students may meet with the teacher in a conference for a final editing. When mechanical correctness is crucial, this conference is important. Teachers proofread the composition with the student, and they identify and correct the remaining corrections together, or the teacher makes checkmarks in the margin to note errors that the student corrects independently.

Mini-lessons. Many teachers use the editing stage to informally assess students' mechanical and spelling skills and to give mini-lessons on a skill that a child or several children are having trouble with. The teacher notes students are having difficulty with a particular skill—for example, paragraphing, capitalizing proper nouns, or using the apostrophe in possessives. The teacher then conducts a brief mini-lesson using the students' writing instead of a language textbook. In this brief 5- to 10-minute lesson, the teacher reviews the particular skill and students practice the skill in their classmates' writing. Then they may practice the skill a few more times on sentences they create or using text from their journals or another writing project. If additional work is needed, they might develop a lesson on it to teach to their classmates or students in another class. Using this procedure, teachers individualize instruction and teach the skill at a time when learning it matters to students.

SHARING

In this final stage of the writing process, sharing, students bring the composition to life by publishing their writing or sharing it orally with an appropriate audience. As they share their writing with real audiences of their classmates, other students, parents, and the community, students come to think of themselves as authors.

Concept of Author

Most of the time children assume the role of "student" in school. However, they take more interest in a subject and learn more about it when they assume a more active role. The real-life role for writing is "author." Authors write for real purposes and for genuine audiences. Students, in contrast, often write so that the teacher will have something to grade. Explaining to students that the writing process they are using is similar to the one that authors use is one way to help students think of themselves as authors.

Another way to help children move from the "student" role to the "author" role is by helping them develop the concept of an author. Donald Graves and Jane Hansen (1983) suggest that primary classrooms should have a special chair designated as the "author's chair." Whenever someone—either the teacher or a child—reads a book, that person sits in the author's chair. At the beginning of the year, most of the books read from that chair are picture books written by Dr. Seuss, Steven Kellogg, and other authors of children's books. However, as children begin to write and construct their own books, they sit in that chair to share the books they write. Through sitting in the special author's chair and sharing their books, children gradually realize that they too are authors! Graves and Hansen describe children's transition from "student" to "author" in three steps:

1. *Replication: Authors write books.* Students develop the concept that authors are the people who write books after hearing many books read to them and reading books themselves.
2. *Transition: I am an author.* Students view themselves as authors as they share the books they have written with classmates from the author's chair.
3. *Option awareness: If I wrote this published book now, I wouldn't write it this way.* Students learn that they have options when they write, and this awareness

grows after experimenting with various writing functions, forms, and audiences.

In classrooms where reading, writing, and sharing writing are valued activities, students become authors. Often they recopy a story or other piece of writing into a stapled booklet or hardcover book. These published books are added to the classroom or the school library. Sometimes students form a classroom publishing company and add the name of the publishing company and the year the book was made on the title page. In addition, students can add an "All About the Author" page with a photograph at the end of their books, just as information about the author is often included on the jackets of books written by adult authors. A fifth grader's "All About the Author" page from a collection of poetry he wrote is presented in Figure 3-10. Notice that Brian used the third person pronoun *he* in writing about himself as is used in adult biographical sketches.

Ways to Share Writing

Students read their writing to classmates, or share it with larger audiences through hardcover books that are placed in the class or school library, class anthologies, letters, newspaper articles, plays, filmstrips and videotapes, or puppet shows. A list of these and other ways to share children's writing is presented in Figure 3-11. Through this sharing, students communicate with genuine audiences who respond to their writing in meaningful ways.

Sharing writing is a social activity, and through sharing, children develop sensitivity to the audience and confidence in themselves as authors. When students share writing, Dyson (1985) advises that teachers consider the social interpretations—students' behavior, teacher's behavior, and interaction between students and the teacher—within the classroom context. Individual students will naturally interpret the sharing event differently. More than just providing the opportunity for students to share writing, teachers need to teach students how to respond to their classmates. Also, teachers themselves serve as a model for responding to students' writing without dominating the sharing.

Bookmaking. One of the most popular ways for children to share their writing with others is by making and binding books. Simple booklets can be made by folding a sheet of paper into quarters like a greeting card. Students write the title on the front and have three sides remaining for their compositions. They can also construct booklets by stapling sheets of writing paper together and adding construction paper covers. Sheets of wallpaper cut from old sample books also make good, sturdy covers. These stapled booklets can be cut into various shapes, too. Students can make more sophisticated hardcover books by covering cardboard covers with contact paper, wallpaper samples, or cloth. Pages are sewn or stapled together, and the first and last pages (endpapers) are glued to the cardboard covers to hold the book together. The directions for making one type of hardcover book are presented in Figure 3-12.

all About the Author

Brian was born on August 22, 1976 in Woodward, Ok. He is going to be a USAF pilot and Army L.T., and a college graduate. He is also wanting to be a rockstar singer. He is going to write another book hopefully about the Air Force or Army. In his spare time he likes to run, ride his motorcycle, skate board, and play with his dogs. He also wrote "How the Hyena Got His Laugh."

FIGURE 3-10 A Fifth-Grader's "All About the Author" Page
Brian, grade 5

Magazines that Publish Student Writing. Students can also submit their stories, poems, and other pieces of writing to magazines that publish children's writing. Some magazines also accept artwork accompanying the compositions. A list of these magazines is presented in Figure 3-13, pp. 98–99. Students should check a recent issue of the magazine or write to the editor for the specific guidelines before submitting a contribution. General guidelines for submitting students' writing include:

FIGURE 3-11 Twenty-five Ways to Share Writing

Read writing aloud in class
Submit to writing contests
Display as a mobile
Contribute to class anthology
Contribute to the local newspaper
Place in the school library
Make a shape book
Read the writing on a cassette tape
Submit to a literary magazine
Read at a school assembly
Share in writing groups
Share with parents and siblings
Produce a videotape

Display poetry on a "poet-tree"
Send to a pen pal
Make a hardbound book
Produce a roller movie
Display on a bulletin board
Make a filmstrip
Make a big book
Design a poster
Read to foster grandparents
Share as a puppet show
Display at a public event
Read to children in other classes

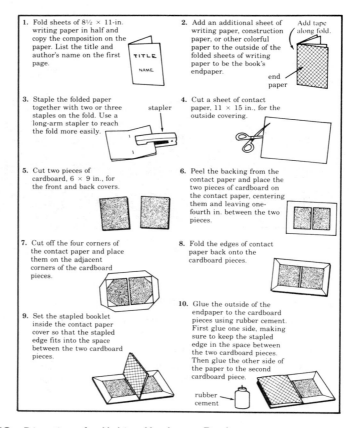

1. Fold sheets of 8½ × 11-in. writing paper in half and copy the composition on the paper. List the title and author's name on the first page.

2. Add an additional sheet of writing paper, construction paper, or other colorful paper to the outside of the folded sheets of writing paper to be the book's endpaper.

3. Staple the folded paper together with two or three staples on the fold. Use a long-arm stapler to reach the fold more easily.

4. Cut a sheet of contact paper, 11 × 15 in., for the outside covering.

5. Cut two pieces of cardboard, 6 × 9 in., for the front and back covers.

6. Peel the backing from the contact paper and place the two pieces of cardboard on the contact paper, centering them and leaving one-fourth in. between the two pieces.

7. Cut off the four corners of the contact paper and place them on the adjacent corners of the cardboard pieces.

8. Fold the edges of contact paper back onto the cardboard pieces.

9. Set the stapled booklet inside the contact paper cover so that the stapled edge fits into the space between the two cardboard pieces.

10. Glue the outside of the endpaper to the cardboard pieces using rubber cement. First glue one side, making sure to keep the stapled edge in the space between the two cardboard pieces. Then glue the other side of the paper to the second cardboard piece.

FIGURE 3-12 Directions for Making Hardcover Books

1. Read the information in the magazine about the types of contributions the editor wants to receive. Send the contribution to magazines that publish that type of writing.
2. Follow the information regarding submissions in the magazine in submitting the contribution.
3. Write a cover letter to send with the contribution, giving the author's name, address, telephone number, and age. Also state in the letter that the contribution is original.
4. Send a self-addressed, stamped envelope with the contribution so that the editor can return the contribution if it will not be published.
5. Keep a copy of the contribution in your files.
6. Expect to wait 3 months or more before learning whether or not the contribution has been accepted for publication.

Children should be cautioned that the competition is very stiff in many publications and that their contributions may not be accepted even though they are well written. Also, children should not expect to receive monetary compensation for their writing; the honor is in seeing their name in print!

Responding to Student Writing

The teacher's role should not be restricted to that of evaluator. Again and again researchers report that although teachers are the most common audience for student writing, they are one of the worst because they read with a red pen in their hands (Lundsteen, 1976). Instead, teachers should read students' writing for information, for enjoyment, and for all of the other purposes that other readers do. Much of students' writing does not need to be assessed; instead it should simply be shared with the teacher as a "trusted adult" (Martin, D'Arcy, Newton, & Parker, 1976).

When children use a process approach to writing, there is less chance that students will *plagiarize,* or copy work from another source and pass it off as their own. The reason is that students will have developed their compositions, step by step, from prewriting and drafting to revising and editing. However, almost every teacher has come across a composition that they fear is not the student's own work. Jackson, Tway, and Frager (1987) cite several reasons why children may plagiarize. First, some students may simply internalize a piece of writing through repeated readings so that they do not realize that it is not their own work, months or years later, when they write it. Second, some students may plagiarize because of the competition to succeed. Third, some students plagiarize by accident, not realizing the consequences of their actions. A final reason that some students plagiarize is that they have not been taught how to write using a process approach, and they may not know how to synthesize information for a report from published sources. There are two excellent ways to prevent plagiarism. One is to teach students how to write using the writing process and the second is to have students write at school rather than at home. When students write at school and move through the various writing process activities, they know how to complete the writing project.

FIGURE 3-13 Magazines that Publish Children's Writing

MAGAZINE	AGES	TYPES OF WRITING ACCEPTED
American Girl 830 Third Avenue New York, NY 10022	12–14	Short stories, poems, and letters to the editor
Boys' Life 1325 Walnut Hill Lane Irving, TX 75602	all	Short stories, poems, and nonfiction
The Children's Album P.O. Box 262 Manchester, CA 95459	all	Short stories, poems, and nonfiction
Children's Digest P.O. Box 567 Indianapolis, IN 46206	8–10	Poetry, short stories, riddles, and jokes
Child Life P.O. Box 567 Indianapolis, IN 46206	7–9	Short stories, poetry, riddles, jokes, and letters to the editor
Cricket 1058 8th Street LaSalle, IL 61301	6–12	Letters and Cricket League monthly; short story and poetry contests
Ebony Jr! 820 S. Michigan Ave. Chicago, IL 60605	all	Essays, short stories, poems, jokes, riddles, and cartoons
FLIP Magazine (Future Literature in Progress) The Art Center of Battle Creek 265 East Emmett Street Battle Creek, MI 49017	all	Poetry and short stories
Highlights for Children 803 Church Street Honesdale, PA 18431	5–10	Poetry, short stories, jokes, riddles, and letters to the editor
Jack and Jill P.O. Box 567 Indianapolis, IN 46206	5–10	Short stories, poems, riddles, and letters to the editor
Kids Magazine P.O. Box 3041 Grand Central Station New York, NY 10017	all	Short stories, reports, poems, cartoons, puzzles, and most other forms of writing

FIGURE 3-13 *continued*

The McGuffey Writer 400A McGuffey Hall Miami University Oxford, OH 45056	all	Poetry, short stories, essays, and cartoons
Merlyn's Pen P.O. Box 716 East Greenwich, RI 02818	12–14	Essays, poems, and short stories
Prism Magazine 1040 Bayview Drive, Suite 223 Ft. Lauderdale, FL 33304	10–14	Poetry, short stories
Scholastic Scope 50 West 44th Street New York, NY 10036	13–14	Poems, stories, plays
Scholastic Voice 50 West 44th Street New York, NY 10036	13–14	Short stories and poems; also writing contests
Spinoff (for gifted children) P.O. Box 115 Sewell, NJ 08080	all	Stories, poems, essays, and word games
Stone Soup Children's Art Foundation P.O. Box 83 Santa Cruz, CA 95063	all	Poetry, short stories, and book reports (books to be reviewed are provided by the magazine)
Wombat 365 Ashton Drive Athens, GA 30606	all	Short stories, poems, essays, puzzles, cartoons, and book reports
Young Author's Magazine 3015 Woodsdale Blvd. Lincoln, NB 68502	all	Short stories, essays, other nonfiction, poetry, and drama
Young World P.O. Box 567 Indianapolis, IN 46206	10–14	Poetry, short stories, jokes, and letters to the editor

To measure students' growth in writing, it is not always necessary to assess their finished products (Tway, 1980). Teachers make judgments about students' progress in other ways. One of the best ways is by observing students as they write and noting whether they are prewriting, whether they are focusing on content rather than mechanics in their rough drafts, and whether they are participating in writing groups.

When as assessment of students' writing is necessary, teachers can judge whether students have completed all components of the writing project and can assess the quality of the final product. Information about how to assess stories, poems, reports, and other forms of writing is included in the chapters discussing these forms, and a more complete description of assessment alternatives is provided in Chapter 10, "Assessing Students' Writing."

THE WRITING PROCESS IN ACTION

The stages of the writing process were described as though they were five separate ingredients that must be combined in sequence to complete a recipe, but this is an unfortunate oversimplification. In practice, writers move back and forth through the stages as they develop, refine, and polish their compositions, and they participate in some activities such as revising and editing *throughout* the writing process (Hayes & Flower, 1980). Not all writing needs to go through all the stages. A journal entry, for example, may be abandoned after drafting, and editing will receive less attention when a story will be shared orally as a puppet show.

Introducing the Writing Process

Introducing students to the writing process—whether they are first graders or eighth graders—and helping them learn the activities involved in each stage is crucial. The teacher explains the stages and has students develop a short composition as they practice each stage. The following guidelines may be useful:

1. *Teach the informal writing strategies before introducing the writing process.* When teachers introduce the writing process, there are so many things to explain, and students can get bogged down as they move through the five stages the first time. One way to shorten the time needed to complete the first writing process experience is to teach students to use the informal writing strategies before introducing the writing process.
2. *Use the writing process terminology.* As teachers introduce the process approach, they should use the names of the stages and the other terminology introduced in this chapter. Students, even young children, will learn to use the terminology quickly and easily.
3. *Write class collaborations.* Too many teachers ignore the class collaboration step of the prewriting stage. While students do not need to write class collaborations for every writing project, it is an important step because the teacher models all of the activities that students will soon be doing individually. Sometimes teachers omit this step because they worry they can't lead a class collaboration. This is a needless fear as many students have good ideas and will be eager to share them.
4. *Keep first writings short.* Students' first process writings should be short pieces—one or two paragraphs in length—so that they can move through the writing process rather quickly. A seven-page biography of King George III is not a good first process writing project because of the time and effort involved in gathering information, writing the rough draft, sharing it in writing groups,

locating and correcting mechanical errors, and recopying the final draft. Personal narratives in which students write about an event in their own lives work well for these first writings.

5. *Practice critiquing compositions as a class.* As students work in writing groups, they learn new activities—giving compliments, asking judicious questions of the author, and offering suggestions. Because these activities are unfamiliar to most students, teachers will want to introduce the activities and practice them as a class before having students work in writing groups. Read aloud a sample (and anonymous) composition and critique the composition together as a class. After listening to it read aloud, students offer compliments, the teacher role plays the author and asks a question or two about trouble spots, and then students make suggestions for improvement.

6. *Begin with compliments in writing groups.* During the first two or three writing group sessions, teachers may have students cut short the procedure and stop after giving compliments to the writer. Once students feel comfortable giving compliments, the next step, having the writer ask questions, is added. Finally the remaining steps are added. Introducing writing group activities in a step-by-step approach gives students the opportunity to learn each activity.

7. *Keep writing folders.* Students' writing is kept in manila folders. Students put prewriting activities, informal writings, rough drafts, writing group notes, and editing checklists into this file. When the writing project is completed, all materials are organized, stapled together and clipped to the final copy. A new folder is prepared for the next writing project.

Learning the writing process takes time. Students need to work through the entire process again and again until the stages and activities become automatic. Then students can manipulate the activities to meet the differing demands of particular writing projects and modify the process to accommodate their personal writing style.

Using the Writing Process in Elementary Classrooms

Once students learn the stages of the writing process and some of the activities involved in each stage, they use their knowledge to write stories, poems, and other forms listed in Figure 3-4. It would be convenient if this five-stage model equated to prewriting on Monday, drafting on Tuesday, revising on Wednesday, editing on Thursday, and sharing on Friday, but it does not. In fact, it is difficult to predict how long a writing project will last because of variations in how students write.

As students write, they are engaged in various activities during each writing process stage. The activities vary according to the function, audience, and form of the writing. The activities involved in writing myths, animal reports, color poems, and business letters are outlined in Figure 3-14. For example, when students write myths, they read myths, and analyze the characteristics of a myth. They record these characteristics in a list. Then students refer to this list as they write a class collaboration myth. These activities represent the prewriting stage in which students gather ideas for writing. Then students write a rough draft of their myth during the drafting stage. In revising, students meet in writing groups to share their myths and get feedback on how to improve them. Then students revise based on the feedback they received. Students may move on to the editing stage or they may do more prewriting, drafting, or meet again in a writing group for additional feedback. When they move into editing, students proofread their myths with a classmate and then correct as many mechanical errors as possible before meeting with the teacher for a final editing. Students complete the writing process by recopying the myth into a hardbound book and reading the myth to students in another class. As an alternative, a small group of students might prepare a dramatic presentation of the myth, videotape it, and show it to students in other classes.

Similar activities are shown in Figure 3-14 for the other three writing projects. While students may use brainstorming for one writing project and clustering in another, these activities are prewriting because they prepare students to write. Variance in each stage is due to differences in the function, audience, and form of the writing project. Figure 3-14 is just an overview, and in the next four chapters information about how to write these and other forms will be described in detail.

The Teacher's Role

Teachers are involved in many different activities during the writing process, and their role varies according to the stage. Mary Simpson (1986) described the role as forming a partnership with students, instructing, listening, encouraging, challenging, and responding. The teacher's role during each stage is described below, and a list of questions based on these descriptions that teachers can use to monitor their own behavior as students write is presented in Figure 3-15.

Prewriting. During prewriting, teachers make plans for the writing project, provide the necessary background experiences, and arrange for rehearsal activities. They also teach students about informal writing strategies or about the writing form (e.g., biographies) that students will write. Teachers also provide a scaffold for students through class collaborations.

Drafting. Teachers provide support and encouragement as students pour out their ideas during drafting. They have conferences with students as they search for words to express themselves, to clarify their thinking, and to search for voice. It is important in this stage not to emphasize correct spelling and neatness. In fact, when teachers point out mechanical errors during the drafting stage, they send a false message to students that mechanical correctness is more important than content.

Revising. During the revising stage, the teacher is a reader and reactor just as students are, responding, as Somers suggests, "as any reader would, registering questions, reflecting befuddlement, and noting places where we are puzzled about the meaning" (1982, p. 155). Teachers participate in writing groups and conferences and model appropriate responses, both admiring students' efforts and seeing potential as well as providing feedback about how to improve writing.

It is in this stage, rather than at the end of the process, that teachers offer suggestions for improvement because students still have the opportunity to benefit from the suggestions and incorporate changes in their writing.

Editing. It is unrealistic to expect students to locate and correct every mechanical error in their compositions during editing. Many teachers find it more practical to focus on particular categories of error in each composition. In a conference, they can quickly review a particular problem area such as quotation marks with a student and help that student make the necessary corrections. Using this mini-lesson procedure, instruction is individualized, and during the school year, teachers review the mechanical skills that each student needs. When correctness is crucial in a composition, teachers can make the corrections or put checkmarks in the margin to note any remaining errors so that students can complete the correcting.

Sharing. Teachers need to make sure students have genuine audiences to share their reading with. Sending letters to pen pals, reading picture books students have written to the kindergarten class, compiling a class anthology, and submitting a newspaper article to the local newspaper all require behind-the-scenes work by the teacher. Most importantly, teachers should enjoy students' writing as other audiences do, not simply serve as an evaluator.

■ ANSWERING TEACHERS' QUESTIONS ABOUT THE WRITING PROCESS

1. This writing process seems very time-consuming. I just don't have time for it.

The process approach to writing is time-consuming, but it is worth the investment because through the writing process students learn a problem-solving approach to writing that they will use for the rest of their lives. When it is integrated into the language arts program and into content area study, the process approach is less time-consuming than adding a separate class to the curriculum. This integration benefits students' learning in all content areas. The reading-writing connection is well documented, and when students write about they are learning in social studies, science, and other content areas, they learn that content better. Also, when students use the writing process, they write fewer compositions and each one takes longer to write, revise, and edit. However, the quality of their writing improves dramatically because students refine and polish their writing rather than churning out many single-draft compositions.

2. The writing process is just for older students, isn't it?

No, the writing process is for all students. Kindergartners and first graders participate in prewriting activities just as older students do and they share their compositions in writing groups and use the author's chair. At first young children may write only one draft, but they like hearing compliments about their writing, and before long a suggestion for improvement is intermingled with a series of compliments. For example, "I really liked all the facts you told about gerbils, but you didn't say that they are mammals." And the writer responds, "Oh, I forgot. I think I can put it here. Thanks!" With the realization that

FIGURE 3-14 An Analysis of Four Writing Projects

	Write a Myth	Write an Animal Report	Write a Color Poem	Write a Business Letter
Function: **Form:** **Audience:**	Imaginative Story Classmates	Informative Report Younger children (books to be replaced in school library)	Imaginative Poem Classmates and family	Instrumental Business letter Unknown
Stage 1 **Prewriting**	Read myths. Analyze characteristics of myths. Brainstorm a list of characteristics. Write a collaborative myth.	Design research questions. Gather and organize information on a cluster. Interview an expert and add information to cluster.	Review the form of a color poem. Read examples of color poems written by students. Write a collaborative color poem.	Review the form of a business letter. Brainstorm a list of the information to include in the letter.
Stage 2 **Drafting**	Write a rough draft of the myth.	Write a rough draft of the report.	Write a rough draft of the color poem, beginning each line or stanza with a color.	Write a rough draft of the letter.
Stage 3 **Revising**	Share the rough draft in a writing group. Listeners offer compliments and suggestions.	Share the rough draft in a writing group. Listeners offer compliments and suggestions.	Share the rough draft in a writing group. Listeners offer compliments and suggestions.	Share the rough draft in a writing group. Listeners offer compliments and suggestions.

	Myth	Report	Poem	Letter
	Ask questions about the content and form of the myth. Make revisions based on classmates' suggestions.	Ask questions about the completeness of the information in the report. Make revisions based on classmates' suggestions.	Ask questions about the content and form of the poem. Make revisions based on classmates' suggestions.	Ask questions about the completeness of the information in the letter and appropriateness of language. Make revisions based on classmates' suggestions.
Stage 4 Editing	Proofread with a classmate and the teacher to locate and correct errors.	Proofread with a classmate and the teacher to locate and correct errors. Add a bibliography.	Proofread with a classmate and the teacher to locate and correct errors.	Proofread with a classmate and the teacher to locate and correct mechanical and formatting errors.
Stage 5 Sharing	Recopy the myth and share with classmates. Alternative: Videotape a dramatic presentation of the myth.	Construct a hardbound book. Recopy the report in the book. Share the book with younger children and add to the school library.	Recopy the poem and add to a personal anthology. Share with classmates.	Recopy the letter. Address the envelope. Mail the letter.

FIGURE 3-15 The Teacher's Role in the Writing Process

Prewriting

The teacher:

Provides background experiences so students will have the prerequisite knowledge to write about the topic

Allows students to participate in decisions about topic, function, audience, and form

Defines the writing project clearly and specifies how it will be assessed

Teaches information about the writing form

Provides opportunities for students to participate in idea gathering and organizing activities

Writes a class collaboration with students

Drafting

The teacher:

Provides support, encouragement, and feedback

Emphasizes content over mechanics

Teaches students how to draft

Encourages students to cycle back to prewriting to gather more ideas or ahead to revise when needed

Revising

The teacher:

Organizes writing groups

Teaches students how to function in writing groups

Participates in a writing group as any listener and reactor would

Provides feedback about the content of the writing and makes suggestions for revision

Insists that students make some revisions

Encourages students to cycle back to prewriting or drafting when necessary

Editing

The teacher:

Teaches students how to edit with partners

Prepares editing checklists for students

Assists students in locating and correcting mechanical errors

Diagnoses students' errors and provides appropriate instruction

Corrects any remaining errors that students cannot correct

Sharing

The teacher:

Arranges for genuine audiences for student writing

Does not serve only as a judge when receiving student writing

readers provide worthwhile suggestions and that students need to revise their writing, these youngsters become full-fledged members of the writing process club.

3. I don't feel comfortable with the writing process. Really, I'm afraid I'll lose control.

A writing process classroom is different from a traditional classroom. There is more noise as students work in groups and move around the classroom. This environment stimulates learning because students are actively involved and assuming responsibility for their own learning, but at the same time teachers can feel they are losing control because there is noise and students are involved in many different activities. To ensure that students are learning, teachers can move about the classroom, observing and talking with students as they write, talk, revise, and share their writing. If the noise or movement becomes too great, teachers can stop students for a class meeting. At the meeting, they discuss the problem and consider ways to solve it.

Teachers might observe in a classroom that is already using the writing process approach. They will observe a teacher who serves as a guide or a facilitator and students who know how to use the writing process and are actively involved in a writing project. In spite of the freedom to talk, move, and work independently, there is discipline and techniques for monitoring students' behavior and the work they complete.

4. My students aren't mature enough to work in groups.

Students are every grade level can work successfully in groups when guidelines have been set, when students understand the project they are involved in, and when the assignment is interesting and appropriate for students' background of experiences. To avoid problems, teachers carefully select students who will work together in a group to minimize potential conflicts, and they limit the size of groups to four or five members. To develop a team spirit, students can name their groups. When a problem does arise, a group meeting can help to resolve it.

5. But don't you have to teach parts of speech before students can write?

No, students do not need to know the parts of speech in order to write. By the time they enter kindergarten, children have internalized the structure of English and have the syntactic knowledge to allow them to write sentences, paragraphs, and longer texts. The traditional notion that grammar instruction must precede writing has been challenged for more than 25 years (Braddock, Lloyd-Jones, & Schoer, 1963). Any grammatical or usage problems that arise can be dealt with during the editing stage of the writing process—at a time when students are interested in getting their writing mechanically correct. In fact, students are more interested in grammar when they are writing for an genuine audience than when they are completing exercises in a language textbook.

■ *REFERENCES*

Applebee, A. L., & Langer, J. A. (1983). Instructional scaffolding: Reading and writing and natural language activities. *Language Arts, 60,* 168–175.

Bereiter, C., & Scademalia, M., (1982). From conversation to composition: The role of instruction in the developmental process. In R. Glaser (Ed.), *Advances in Instructional Psychology* (2 vols.), vol. 2, pp. 1–64.

Bissex, G. L. (1980). *Gnys at wrk: A child learns to write and read.* Cambridge, MA: Harvard University Press.

Braddock, R., Lloyd-Jones, R., & Schoer, L. (1963). *Research in written composition.* Champaign, IL: National Council of Teachers of English.

Britton, J. (1970). *Language and thought.* Harmondsworth: Penguin.

Britton, J., Burgess, T., Martin, N., McLeod, A., & Rosen, H. (1975). *The development of writing abilities (11–18).* London: Schools Council Publications.

Bruner, J. S. (1966). *Toward a theory of instruction.* Cambridge: Harvard University Press.

Calkins, L. M. (1980). When children want to punctuate: Basic skills belong in context. *Language Arts, 57,* 567–573.

Calkins, L. M. (1983). *Lessons from a child: On the teaching and learning of writing.* Portsmouth, NH: Heinemann.

Calkins, L. M. (1986). *The art of teaching writing.* Portsmouth, NH: Heinemann.

Dyson, A. H. (1982). The emergence of visible language: Interrelationships between drawing and early writing. *Visible Language, 6,* 360–381.

Dyson, A. H. (1983). Early writing as drawing: the developmental gap between speaking and writing. Presentation at the Annual Meeting of the American Educational Research Association, Montreal, CA.

Dyson, A. H. (1985). Second graders sharing writing: The multiple social realities of a literacy event. *Written Communication, 2,* 189–215.

Dyson, A. H. (1986). The imaginary worlds of childhood: A multimedia presentation. *Language Arts, 63,* 799–808.

Elley, W. B., Barham, I. H., Lamb, H., & Wyllie, M. (1976). The role of grammar in a secondary school English curriculum. *Research in the Teaching of English, 10,* 5–21.

Emig, J. (1971). *The composing processes of twelfth graders.* Champaign, IL: National Council of Teachers of English.

Faigley, L., & Witte, S. (1981). Analyzing revision. *College Composition and Communication, 32,* 400–410.

Fine, E. S. (1987). Marbles lost, marbles found: Collaborative production of text. *Language Arts, 64,* 474–487.

Flower, L. S., & Hayes, J. R. (1977). Problem-solving strategies and the writing process. *College English, 39,* 449–461.

Flower, L. S., & Hayes, J. R. (1981). A cognitive process theory of writing. *College Composition and Communication, 32,* 365–387.

Graves, D. H. (1975). An examination of the writing processes of seven-year-old children. *Research in the Teaching of English, 9,* 227–241.

Graves, D. H. (1976). Let's get rid of the welfare mess in the teaching of writing. *Language Arts, 53,* 645–651.

Graves, D. H. (1983). *Writing: Teachers and children at work.* Exeter, NH: Heinemann.

Graves, D. H., & Hansen, J. (1983). The author's chair. *Language Arts, 60,* 176–183.

Halliday, M. A. K. (1973). *Explorations in the functions of language.* London: Edward Arnold.

Halliday, M. A. K. (1975). *Learning how to mean: Explorations in the development of language.* London: Edward Arnold.

Hayes, J. R., & Flower, L. S. (1980). Identifying the organization of writing processes. In L. W. Gregg and E. R. Steinberg (Ed.), *Cognitive processes in writing,* pp. 3–30. Hillsdale, NJ: Erlbaum.

Hayes, J. R., & Flower, L. S. (1986). Writing research and the writer. *American Psychologist, 41,* 1106–1113.

Hidi, S., & Hildyard, A. (1983). The comparison of oral and written productions in two discourse modes. *Discourse Processes, 6,* 91–105.

Jackson, L. A., Tway, E., & Frager, A. (1987). Dear teacher, Johnny copied. *The Reading Teacher, 41,* 22–25.

King, M. (1985). Proofreading is not reading. *Teaching English in the Two-year College, 12,* 108–112.

Langer, J. A. (1985). Children's sense of genre. *Written Communication, 2,* 157–187.

Lundsteen, S. W. (Ed.). (1976). *Help for the teacher of written composition: New direc-*

tions in research. Urbana, IL: National Conference on Research in English and ERIC Clearinghouse on Reading and Communication Skills.

MacLachlan, P. (1985). *Sarah plain and tall.* New York: Harper and Row.

Martin, N., D'Arcy, P., Newton, B., & Parker, R. (1976). *Writing and learning across the curriculum 11–16.* London: Schools Council Publication.

Mills, B. S. (1983). Imagination: The connection between writing and play. *Educational Leadership,* 41, pp. 50–53.

Mohr, M. M. (1984). *Revision: The rhythm of meaning.* Upper Montclair, NJ: Boynton/Cook.

Murray, D. H. (1982). *Learning by teaching.* Montclair, NJ: Boynton/Cook.

Murray, D. H. (1985). *A writer teaches writing* (2nd ed.). Boston; Houghton Mifflin.

Murray, D. H. (1987). *Write to learn* (2nd ed.). Boston: Houghton Mifflin.

Perl, S. (1979). The composing processes of unskilled college writers. *Research in the Teaching of English, 13,* 317–336.

Perl, S. (1980). Understanding composition. *College Composition and Communication, 31,* 363–369.

Piaget, J. (1959). *Language and thought of the child.* London: Routledge & Kegan Paul.

Russell, C. (1983). Putting research into practice: Conferencing with young writers. *Language Arts, 60,* 333–340.

Simpson, M. K. (1986). What am I supposed to do while they're writing? *Language Arts, 63,* 680–684.

Smith, F. (1977). The uses of language. *Language Arts, 54,* 638–644.

Smith, F. (1982). *Writing and the writer.* New York: Holt.

Snyder, Z. K. (1967). *The Egypt game.* Boston: Atheneum.

Sommers, N. (1980). Revisions strategies of student writers and experienced writers. *College Composition and Communication, 31,* 378–388.

Sommers, N. (1982). Responding to student writing. *College Composition and Communication 33,* 148–156.

Tway, E. (1980). Teacher responses to children's writing. *Language Arts, 57,* 763–772.

Ventura, P., & Cesarani, G. P. (1985). *In search of Tutankhamun.* Morristown, NJ: Silver Burdett.

Vygotsky, L. (1986). *Thought and language.* Cambridge: MIT Press.

Wagner, B. J. (1976). *Dorothy Heathcote: Drama as a learning medium.* Washington, DC: National Education Association.

Wagner, B. J. (1983). The expanding circle of informal classroom drama. In B. A. Busching and J. I. Schwartz (Eds.), *Integrating the language arts in the elementary school,* pp. 155–163. Urbana, IL: NCTE.

4

Narrative Writing

"Clever Trick #4!" cries LaWanda. "That mean ol' crocodile is pretending to be a picnic bench."

"Don't worry, Trunky is going to warn the kids," replies Ashton. The children in Ms. Dillen's first-grade classroom are listening to their teacher reread a favorite story, Roald Dahl's *The Enormous Crocodile* (1978). They eagerly listen to the enormous crocodile's four clever (but unsuccessful) attempts to catch a fat and juicy child to eat for supper, and they join in as Ms. Dillen reads, predicting the failure of the crocodile's tricks again and again. While many adults find the story repulsive, these first graders love it.

Recognizing the students' interest in this story, Ms. Dillen decides to use the story to introduce her first graders to the most basic element of story structure, beginning-middle-end. She explains that stories have three parts, a beginning, a middle, and an end. She then makes a chart to hang in the classroom with this information. She and the children retell the beginning, middle, and end of *The Enormous Crocodile*. Next, she draws a cluster on the chalkboard with the title of the story in a circle and three rays marked *beginning, middle,* and *end.* The children identify the events that belong in each story part and complete the following story cluster shown in Figure 4-1.

The following day, Ms. Dillen asks the children if they want to write their own version of the story in a big book (a large book made out of sheets of posterboard that the class can read together). They shout and clap their enthusiasm. Ms. Dillen begins by reviewing the story with the children, using the story cluster to organize the retelling. The children decide to write a six-page book, with one page for the introduction, one page for each of the four tricks, and one page for the end. (Later a title page will be added.) Next, she divides the chalkboard into six columns and asks the students to dictate the story. She records their dictation on the chalkboard, page by page. Then the children reread their story, and several children suggest changes. Ms. Dillen, using proofreader's marks, incorporates the changes agreed upon by the class. After a final reading, the children create a big book for their story. They volunteer to complete various tasks. Some children draw illustrations for each page of the story on large sheets of posterboard and other children write the text, above or below the illustrations on each page. Another illustrator and writer create the title page. Then the pages are compiled, holes are punched on the left margin of the pages, and metal rings are used to bind the story. Here is their completed story:

The Enormous Crocodile
as Retold by Ms. Dillen's First-Grade Class

Page 1: The enormous crocodile wanted to eat the children in Ms. Dillen's class.
Page 2: The enormous crocodile made himself look like a coconut tree. The trick didn't work.
Page 3: The crocodile tried another trick. He made himself into a seesaw. But Muggle-Wump warned the children.
Page 4: The crocodile turned himself into a merry-go-round. The Roly-Poly Bird warned the kids. Clever trick three didn't work!

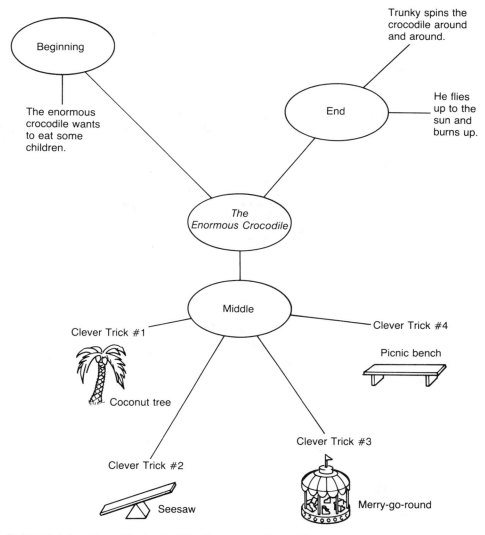

FIGURE 4-1 Story Cluster for *The Enormous Crocodile*

Page 5: The crocodile was a picnic bench. Trunky warned the children. Clever trick four did not work either.

Page 6: Trunky spun the enormous crocodile around and around. He threw him up into the sun.

Notice how the children personalized the story by having the enormous crocodile want to eat the children in their class rather than the children in the nearby town, as Roald Dahl wrote in his version of the story. Also, they use the repetition of clever tricks to organize the story and recall the story events.

Several days later, the children participate in a variety of activities related to the story. Some of the children make finger puppets to use in retelling the story. They draw pictures of the characters, cut them out, and tape the pictures to strips of paper that they fit around their fingers. As soon as the puppets are made, students break into small groups to tell the story to each other. Other children draw and write retellings of the story, with one page for the beginning, four pages for the middle, and one page for the end. Then they add a cover and staple their completed booklets together. Barry's retelling is presented in Figure 4-2.

Next, Ms. Dillen suggests that they write another class story using clever tricks. As a class, they brainstorm a list of clever tricks and discuss possible plots. The class decides to write a story about six hungry rabbits who use clever tricks to fool a fox so they can eat the vegetables in the garden. They decide on three clever tricks and develop a story cluster with a beginning, middle, and end. With this preparation, they dictate it to Ms. Dillen, who records it on the chalkboard. They refine their story and then Ms. Dillen makes copies for each child. Here is their story:

The Hungry Rabbits
written by Ms. Dillen's First-Grade Class

Page 1: Once there were six rabbits. They wanted carrots and lettuce. But the fox chased the rabbits out of the garden.

Page 2: The rabbits think of clever tricks. They tell the fox there's a deer in the forest so the fox will chase the deer instead of them. But the trick didn't work.

Page 3: The rabbits dig a hole trying to get to the garden but they didn't dig far enough. They were only by the fence.

Page 4: Then the rabbits ran to the briar patch and jumped over it. The fox tried to jump over it but landed in it. "Ouch, ouch," cried the fox. He couldn't get out.

Page 5: So the rabbits jumped real high over the briars and got the carrots and lettuce. And they lived happily ever after.

As the children are finishing their class story, many are already talking about clever trick stories they want to write. Ms. Dillen provides the guidelines. Like their class story, children's individual stories should have a beginning, three (or more) clever tricks in the middle, and an ending. Children pile up five, six or more pages of paper on their desks and begin to work. Some begin to illustrate their stories; some begin to write; and others mark their papers with the words *beginning, middle-1, middle-2, middle-3,* and *end* before writing or drawing.

Eddie has his story already in mind. He quickly sets to work drawing a picture in the top half of each page. Then he writes his story, using the pictures he has drawn much like an adult uses an outline. As he writes, using a combination of invented and standard spelling, Eddie becomes more and more animated. As soon as he finishes writing, he gets construction paper for a cover and staples his storybook together. He goes over to Barry's desk to share his story with his best

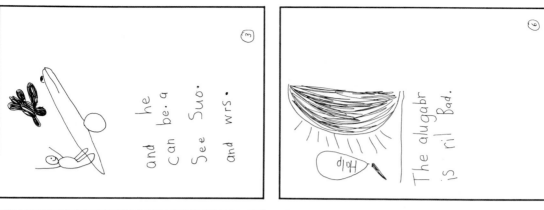

③

and he
can be. a
See Suo.
and wrS.

⑥

Help

The alugabr
is ril Bad.

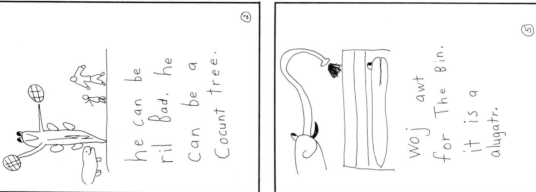

②

he can be
ril Bad. he
Can be a
Cocut tree.

⑤

Woj awt
for The Bin.
it is a
alugatr.

①

There in The
jugul. is a
Bad alugadr.

④

iT is not
a goob.ibi
to be a
more go rod.

FIGURE 4-2 A Child's Retelling of *The Enormous Crocodile*

friend. "Hey, Bar', listen to this. You're gonna love it," he says. And Barry does. Other children crowd around to read Eddie's story and soon Ms. Dillen moves this group of children over to the Author's Chair circle to share their stories. They clap as each story is read and offer compliments about the first-grade authors' use of clever clues and surprise endings.

This is Eddie's story, written in standard spelling:

The Dog

Page 1: The little dog is very, very hungry and he sees a little rabbit. He chases the rabbit but he ran too fast.

Page 2: Clever trick no. 1. The dog jumped on the rabbit's tail but the trick didn't work.

Page 3: Clever trick no. 2. He hid under the bushes and jumped out of the bush but he missed the rabbits and they ran away.

Page 4: Clever trick no. 3. The dog dressed up into a carrot and the rabbit walked by the dog and the dog ate him.

Page 5: That's the end.

Eddie's "The Dog" is a well-developed story. He established a conflict between the hungry dog and the rabbit in the beginning; in the middle he presented three attempts to catch the rabbit; and with the third attempt, the dog is successful. While the ending is not as elaborated as it might be, it follows the style often used in folktales (e.g., "Snip snap snout, This tale's told out!") and on television cartoon shows (e.g., "That's all folks!").

These first graders in Ms. Dillen's class are learning about stories by listening to stories read aloud, examining how authors organize their stories, and by writing stories themselves. In a recent article, distinguished British educator Harold Rosen (1986) pleaded for elementary teachers to provide more opportunities, or "generous space," for storytelling—both oral and written—to teach children about narrative discourse, its meaning, voice, and seduction.

CONCEPT OF STORY

Even before they enter school, young children have a rudimentary awareness of what makes a story. This understanding is called *concept of story* or *story schema.* Children's concept of story includes information about the elements of story structure, such as character, plot, and setting, as well as information about the conventions that authors use in stories. This knowledge is usually intuitive; that is, children are not conscious of what they know. Golden (1984) describes children's concept of story as part of their cognitive structure: "a mental representation of story structure, essentially an outline of the basic story elements and their organization" (p. 578).

Researchers have documented that children's concept of story begins in the preschool years, and that children as young as 2-1/2 years of age have a rudimentary sense of story (Applebee, 1978, 1980; Pitcher & Prelinger, 1963). Children acquire this concept of story gradually, through listening to stories read to them, later by reading stories themselves, and by telling and writing stories. Not surprisingly, older children have a better understanding of story structure and conventions than younger children do. Similarly, the stories that older children tell and write are increasingly more complex; the plot structures are more tightly organized, and the characters are more fully developed. Yet, Applebee (1980) found that by the time children begin kindergarten they have already developed a concept of what a story is, and these expectations guide them as they respond to stories and tell their own stories. For example, he found that kindergartners could use three story markers: the convention "Once upon a time . . ." to begin a story, the past tense consistently in telling a story, and formal endings such as "The End" or "they lived happily ever after."

Most of the research examining students' understanding of story structure and conventions has been applied to reading. Concept of story plays an important role in students' ability to comprehend and recall information from the stories they read (Mandler & Johnson, 1977; Rumelhart, 1975; Stein & Glenn, 1979). However, children's concept of story is just as important in writing (Golden, 1984). Just as they draw on their concept of story in reading stories, students use this knowledge in writing stories.

Developing Children's Concept of Story

Activities in elementary classrooms can help students develop and refine their concept of story, preparing them to better comprehend the stories they read and create the stories they write. Five different types of activities are reading stories, talking about stories, retelling stories, examining the structure of stories, and writing stories.

Reading Stories. Reading stories aloud and providing opportunities for children to read stories themselves is the most basic way to help children develop a concept of story. Reading to young children helps them internalize the structure of stories and to assimilate the sophisticated language structures that authors use. Reading aloud is also essential for elementary students even though many teachers mistakenly feel that after children have learned to read they no longer need to be read to (Hoskisson & Tompkins, 1987). However, reading aloud provides the opportunity to share literature with children that they might otherwise miss. After the shared reading experience, the teacher and students can talk about the story together.

Primary grade students often beg to have a familiar book reread. While it is important to share a wide variety of books with children, researchers have found that children benefit in specific ways from repeated readings. Through these repetitions, students gain control over the parts of a story and synthesize the story parts into a whole. The quality of children's responses to a repeated story also changes (Beaver, 1982).

Martinez and Roser (1985) examined young children's responses to stories and found that as stories become increasingly familiar, students' responses indicate a greater depth of understanding. They found that children talked almost twice as much about familiar books as about unfamiliar books that had been read only once or twice. The form and focus of children's talk changed, too. While children tended to ask questions about unfamiliar stories, they made comments about familiar stories. In unfamiliar stories, children's talk focused on characters; the focus changed to details and word meanings when children talked about familiar stories. Martinez and Roser also found that children's comments after repeated readings were more probing and more specific, suggesting that they had greater insights into the story.

Talking About Stories. In a survey of nursery schools and kindergartens, Morrow (1982) found that teachers typically neither preceded nor followed the stories they read aloud with questions or discussions. The few times that teachers asked questions about stories, they usually asked for factual details. They rarely asked questions that emphasized structural elements of a story, such as setting, theme, or plot or questions that elicited interpretive and critical thinking. Morrow concluded that the story-reading events showed little or no evidence that teachers provided children with organizational strategies for understanding the stories.

Teachers should encourage students to think about and talk about stories they have read. Asking questions is one way to stimulate that talk. According to the results of recent research, the questions that teachers ask should focus on the structure of stories because these questions are more effective for comprehension than traditional questions about main ideas and details. Stephanie McConaughy (1980) recommends that teachers ask questions about the plot, theme, and characters, and these questions should be tailored to students' developmental levels. Questions to primary grade students, for example, might focus on story events while questions to older students might deal with theme, characters, and the motivations behind the characters' actions. Similarly, Spiegel and Fitzgerald (1986) recommend a set of generic questions that can be adapted for particular stories. These questions are:

How did (character) feel?

What did (character) want (or decide)?

What did (character) do?

What did (character) do next?

How did it turn out?

How did (character) feel about this after it was all over? (p. 681)

Retelling Stories. Retelling a story provides interaction between teller and listener, opportunities for active engagement with literature, and the transfer of meaning from author/teller to reader/listener. Unfortunately, retelling stories has been seen by many teachers as a time-consuming frill; however, through a series of studies Lesley Morrow (1984, 1985a, 1985b, 1986) has documented the educational value of this activity.

In a series of three studies conducted with kindergarten students, Morrow examined the effect of retelling activities on students' comprehension of stories. In the first study, one group of kindergartners retold a story that had been read to them while another group drew pictures of the story. According to the results of a comprehension test that included both questions about story structure and "traditional" questions, students who participated in the retelling activity scored higher than students who drew pictures. Next, Morrow compared the value of "simple" retelling with guided retelling over an extended time period. Kindergartners in one group retold well-structured stories and were guided in their retellings by teachers who focused on the stories' structural framework while students in the other group retold the stories without any prompts from the teacher. She found that students who retold stories with guidance understood the stories better according to a comprehension test that included both "traditional" and story structure questions. Also, the children who retold stories with guidance used more structural elements and used them in a proper sequence during the retelling activities. In the third study, Morrow examined the effect of guided story retellings in preparing kindergartners to tell original stories. One group of students retold stories that had been read to them and the other group of students drew pictures about the stories. Morrow found that students who participated in retelling activities created more complex stories that included more information about setting and plot. She also found that the students who retold stories used more sophisticated language in their original stories. The results of these three studies suggest that, through retelling stories, children learn about story structure, comprehend stories better, and grow in their language ability.

Morrow (1985a, 1986) provides the following recommendations for classroom practice based on her research findings:

1. Encourage children to retell familiar stories to classmates and the teacher.
2. Guide students' retelling with prompts based on the story's structure.
3. When students need assistance, ask "Then what happened?" or "What comes next?"
4. Do not expect young children to provide a complete retelling of the story.

Examining the Structure of Stories. Stories are organized in predictable ways, and children who are aware of these organizational arrangements use this knowledge to know what to expect in a story (Gordon & Braun, 1982; McConaughy, 1980). Researchers have developed several different approaches for analyzing the structure of stories. Cognitive psychologists, for instance, have developed a story grammar that includes the following elements: a setting, an initiating event, an internal response, a goal, an attempt, an outcome, a consequence, and a reaction (Mandler & Johnson, 1977). In contrast, rhetoricians describe the structure of stories using these elements: plot, setting, characters, theme, and point of view. In this chapter, these elements will be used in teaching students about how authors organize their stories. This choice was made because the literary elements provide a general structure rather than a prescriptive formula for children's story-making, and they seem to better describe the more complex stories that children read and write.

Because research has demonstrated that knowlege of story structure improves students' comprehension and production of stories, many educators recommend that students be explicitly taught about the structure of stories. Several strategies for teaching students about the structure of stories have been recommended (Fitzgerald & Spiegel, 1983; Gordon & Braun, 1982; Hoskisson & Tompkins, 1987; Spiegel & Fitzgerald, 1986; Tompkins & McGee, 1989), and the common features of these strategies are:

1. An element of story structure (or story part) is presented, often using a chart to summarize important information.
2. Students read stories exemplifying this element.
3. Students discuss how the element was used in the stories they read.
4. Students participate in a variety of activities to reinforce their understanding of the element, including drawing diagrams of the story, comparing story versions, and retelling the story.
5. Students write stories incorporating the element being studied.

These common features involve both direct instruction about the elements of story structure and the integration of reading, writing, and oral language activities.

Writing Stories. Writing is a valuable way of learning (Emig, 1977), and by writing stories children apply their expanding knowledge of stories—of the structural elements as well as of the creative story ideas. For example, second-grade Micah wrote the following story about a snake with a problem.:

The Snake and His Blocked Door

Page 1: Once there was a long snake. He had a problem. His front door is blocked by a piece of thick wood.
Page 2: He tried to push it off but he was too small.
Page 3: So he went to the king, Bill Boa Constrictor.
Page 4: He said, "This is the work of humans. I think you should dig a new door." "I can't dig. I am too young" "Yes," said the Boa.
Page 5: So he got home and night came. So he burrowed in a hole for the night.
Page 6: The snake got up. He went to the Snake Store and got some breakfast.
Page 7: After breakfast he went home and tried to think how to get in.
Page 8: So he went to the king.
Page 9: He said, "King, I am locked out. Could I spend the night here?" "Of course!"
Page 10: That night he had a dream about the most wonderful things.
Page 11: The next day he went home and remembered about his back door!

In his story, Micah sets up a problem to solve and he heightens interest in the story as readers learn about how the snake struggles to solve the problem. First, he tries to push the block of wood away, but the snake is too small. Next, he asks his king for help, and the king suggests that he dig a new door. Third, after spending a miserable night burrowed in a hole and thinking hard and long (but unsuccessfully) he asks to stay with the king. Finally, after a wonderful dream he remembers about his back door! Micah cleverly combines what he has learned about the structure of stories with a creative story idea.

ELEMENTS OF STORY STRUCTURE

Stories have unique elements of structure that distinguish them from other forms of writing. In fact, the structure of stories is quite complex as authors manipulate the elements of characters, plot, setting, and other elements to produce an interesting story. Seven elements of story structure—beginning-middle-end, repetition, plot, setting, characters, theme, and point of view—will be discussed in this section, with familiar and award-winning tradebooks used to illustrate each element.

Beginning-Middle-End

The most basic element of story structure is the division of the main events of a story into three parts: the beginning, middle, and end.[1] In *Where the Wild Things Are* (Sendak, 1963), for instance, the three story parts can be picked out easily. As the story begins, Max plays a mischievous wolf and is sent to his room for misbehaving. In the middle, Max magically travels to the land of the wild things to become their king. Then Max feels lonely and returns home to find his supper waiting and still hot—the end of the story. A cluster for *Where the Wild Things Are* is presented in Figure 4-3.

Authors include specific types of information in each of the three story parts. In the beginning, they introduce the characters, describe the setting, and present a problem. The author uses the characters, setting, and events to develop the plot and sustain the theme through the story. In the middle, authors introduce conflict to the events presented in the beginning, with each event preparing readers for what will follow. Conflict heightens as the characters face roadblocks that keep them from solving their problems. How the characters tackle these problems adds suspense to keep readers interested. In the end, authors reconcile all that has happened in the story, and readers learn whether or not the characters' struggles are successful.

---

[1]Older students may substitute the terms introduction, development or complication, and resolution for beginning, middle, and end. No matter what these three parts are called, their function in a story remains the same.

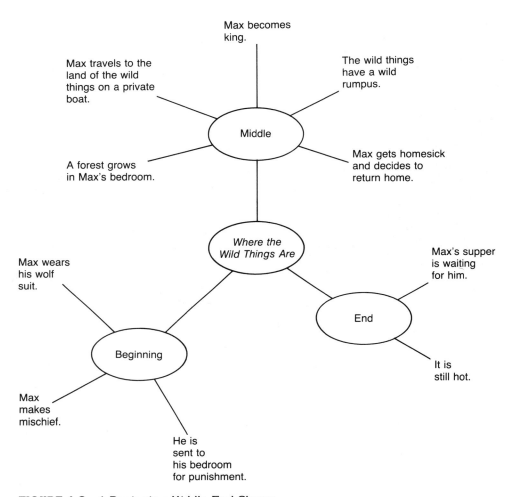

FIGURE 4-3 A Beginning-Middle-End Cluster

Almost any story can be divided into these three parts. The beginning, middle, and end parts of other short stories with clearly identifiable beginnings, middles, and ends are listed in Figure 4-4.

Repetition

Authors use repetition to make the plot more complex and the story more interesting. In Paul Galdone's retelling of *Henny Penny* (1968), for instance, Henny Penny meets a series of animals—Cocky Locky, Ducky Lucky, Goosey Loosey, Turkey Lurkey, and Foxy Loxy—who join her on her trip to the king's palace to tell the king that the sky is falling. In this story, the repetition involves presenting new characters, each with a rhyming name, and repeating the hen's warning that "The sky is falling." A variation of the beginning-middle-end cluster presented in Figure 4-3 can be used to chart repetition stories (Tompkins & McGee, 1989). A cluster for *Henny Penny* is presented in Figure 4-5. In this cluster, the middle ray is divided into two parts, one for repeated events and one for repeated dialogue.

Many traditional stories or folktales, such as *Henny Penny, The Gingerbread Boy* (Galdone, 1975), and *The Little Red Hen* (Galdone, 1973), have both repeated events and repeated dialogue. In other stories, either the events or the words are repeated. A list of stories using repetition is presented in Figure 4-6. Many of these traditional stories or folktales began as oral stories, retold by traveling minstrels. Just as repetition made the stories easier for storytellers to remember, this element of story structure is particularly effective for students in the primary grades because the repetition helps them predict the events and words in the stories they read and write (Blackburn, 1985; Tompkins & Webeler, 1983; Tompkins & McGee, 1989).

Plot

Plot is the sequence of events involving characters in conflict. It is based on the goals of one or more characters and the processes involved in attaining these

FIGURE 4-4   Short Stories Illustrating Beginning-Middle-End

Andersen, H. C. (1979). *The ugly duckling.* New York: Harcourt Brace Jovanovich. (P–M)

Gag, W. (1956). *Millions of cats.* New York: Coward. (P)

Gallo, D. R. (Ed.) (1984). *Sixteen short stories by outstanding writers for young adults.* New York: Dell. (U)

Hyman, T. S. (1983). *Little red riding hood.* New York: Holiday House. (P)

Kellogg, S. (1973). *The island of the skog.* New York: Dial. (P–M)

London, J. (1960). To build a fire. *The call of the wild and other selected stories.* New York: Signet. (U)

Mayer, M. (1987). *The pied piper of Hamelin.* New York: Macmillan. (M)

Potter, B. (1902). *The tale of Peter Rabbit.* New York: Warne. (P)

Rogasky, B. (1982). *Rapunzel.* New York: Holiday House. (M–U)

Schulevitz, U. (1978). *The treasure.* New York: Farrar. (M)

Sendak, M. (1963). *Where the wild things are.* New York: Harper and Row. (P)

Van Allsburg, C. (1981). *Jumanji.* Boston: Houghton Mifflin. (M)

Yorinks, A. (1986). *Hey, Al.* New York: Farrar. (P)

Zemach, H., & Zemach, M. (1973). *Duffy and the devil.* New York: Farrar. (P–M)

P = primary grades (K–2)
M = middle grades (3–5)
U = upper grades (6–8)

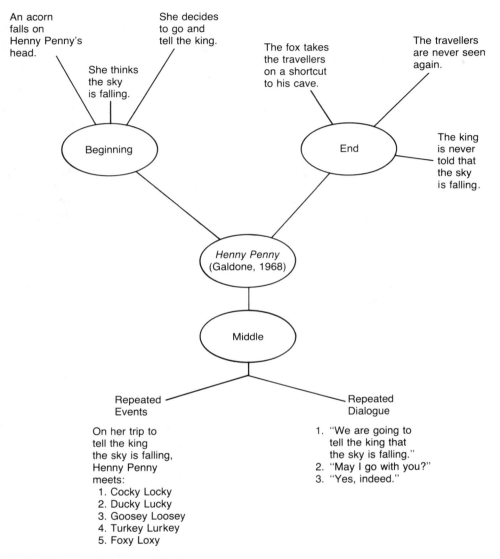

An acorn
falls on
Henny Penny's
head.

She decides
to go and
tell the king.

She thinks
the sky
is falling.

The fox takes
the travellers
on a shortcut
to his cave.

The travellers
are never seen
again.

Beginning

End

The king
is never
told that
the sky
is falling.

Henny Penny
(Galdone, 1968)

Middle

Repeated
Events

Repeated
Dialogue

On her trip to
tell the king
the sky is falling,
Henny Penny
meets:
 1. Cocky Locky
 2. Ducky Lucky
 3. Goosey Loosey
 4. Turkey Lurkey
 5. Foxy Loxy

1. "We are going to
 tell the king that
 the sky is falling."
2. "May I go with you?"
3. "Yes, indeed."

FIGURE 4-5 A Repetition Cluster

goals (Lukens, 1986). The main characters want to achieve a goal, and other characters are introduced to oppose or prevent the main characters from being successful. The story events are put in motion by characters as they attempt to overcome conflict, reach their goals, and solve their problems.

Conflict is the tension or opposition between forces in the plot, and it is introduced to interest readers enough to continue reading the story. Conflict usually takes one of four forms:

FIGURE 4-6 Stories with Repetition

Burningham, J. (1975). *Mr. Gumpy's outing*. New York: Holt. (P)

Ets, M. H. (1973). *Elephant in a well*. New York: Viking. (P)

Flack, M. (1958). *Ask Mr. Bear*. New York: Macmillan. (P)

Galdone, P. (1973). *The little red hen*. New York: Seabury. (P–M)

Galdone, P. (1973). *The three billy goats Gruff*. Boston: Houghton Mifflin. (P)

Galdone, P. (1975). *The gingerbread boy*. New York: Seabury. (P)

Hailey, G. E. (1970). *A story a story*. New York: Atheneum. (P–M)

Kent, J. (1971). *The fat cat*. New York: Scholastic. (P–M)

McGovern, A. (1967). *Too much noise*. New York: Scholastic. (P)

Plume, I. (1980). *The Bremen town musicians*. New York: Watts. (P–M)

Tolstoy, A. (1969). *The great big enormous turnip*. New York: Watts. (P–M)

Tresselt, A. (1964). *The mitten*. New York: Lothrop. (P)

Zemach, M. (1976). *It could always be worse*. New York: Farrar. (P–M)

1. Conflict between a character and nature
2. Conflict between a character and society
3. Conflict between characters
4. Conflict within a character (Lukens, 1986)

Conflict between a character and nature is represented in stories in which severe weather plays an important role, as in Jean Craighead George's *Julie of the Wolves* (1972), and in stories set in isolated geographic locations, such as Scott O'Dell's *Island of the Blue Dolphins* (1960) in which the Indian girl Karana struggles to survive alone on a Pacific island. In some stories, a character's activities and beliefs are different from those held by other members of the society, and these differences cause conflict. One example of this type of conflict is Elizabeth Speare's *The Witch of Blackbird Pond* (1958) in which Kit Tyler is accused of being a witch because she continues activities in a New England Puritan community that were acceptable in the Caribbean community where she grew up. Conflict between characters is commonly used in children's literature. In Judy Blume's *Tales of a Fourth Grade Nothing* (1972), for instance, the never-ending conflict between Peter and his little brother Fudge is what makes the story interesting. The fourth type of conflict is conflict within a character, and stories such as Bernard Waber's *Ira Sleeps Over* (1972) and Betsy Byars's *The Summer of the Swans* (1970) are examples. In *Ira Sleeps Over*, 6-year-old Ira must decide whether to take his teddy bear with him when he goes next door to spend the night with a friend. In *The Summer of the Swans,* Sara feels guilty when her mentally retarded brother wanders off and is lost. A list of stories representing the four types of conflict is presented in Figure 4-7.

Authors develop plot through the introduction, development, and resolution of the conflict. Plot development can be broken into four steps:

1. A problem that introduces conflict is presented in the beginning of a story.
2. Characters face roadblocks as they attempt to solve the problem in the middle of the story.
3. The high point in the action occurs when the problem is about to be solved. This high point separates the middle and end of the story.
4. The problem is solved and the roadblocks are overcome at the end of the story.

The problem is introduced at the beginning of the story, and the main character (or characters) is faced with trying to solve it. This problem determines the conflict. In *The Pied Piper of Hamelin* (Mayer, 1987), the problem is that the town of Hamelin is infested with rats, and conflict develops between the townspeople and the Pied Piper, who has been hired to rid the town of the rats. This conflict can be characterized as conflict between characters, the third of four types described above.

Once the problem has been introduced, authors use conflict to throw roadblocks in the way of an easy solution. As one roadblock is removed, another is devised to thwart the characters as they strive to reach their goal. Postponing the

FIGURE 4-7   Stories Illustrating the Four Types of Conflict

Conflict Between a Character and Nature

Ardizzone, E. (1971). *Little Tim and the brave sea captain.* New York: Scholastic. (P)

George, J. C. (1972). *Julie of the wolves.* New York: Harper and Row. (M–U)

O'Dell, S. (1960). *Island of the blue dolphins.* Boston: Houghton Mifflin. (M–U)

Sperry, A. (1968). *Call it courage.* New York: Macmillan. (U)

Conflict Between a Character and Society

Hickman, J. (1978). *Zoar blue.* New York: Macmillan. (U)

Kellogg, S. (1973). *The island of the skog.* New York: Dial. (P–M)

O'Brien, R. C. (1971). *Mrs. Frisby and the rats of NIMH.* New York: Atheneum. (M)

Speare, E. G. (1958). *The witch of Blackbird Pond.* Boston: Houghton Mifflin. (M–U)

Conflict Between Characters

Blume, J. (1972). *Tales of a fourth grade nothing.* New York: Dutton. (M)

Hoban, R. (1970). *A bargain for Frances.* New York: Scholastic. (P)

Raskin, E. (1978). *The westing game.* New York: Dutton. (U)

Zelinsky, P. O. (1986). *Rumpelstiltskin.* New York: Dutton. (P–M)

Conflict Within a Character

Byars, B. (1970). *The summer of the swans.* New York: Viking. (M)

Fritz, J. (1958). *The cabin faced west.* New York: Coward-McCann. (M)

Taylor, T. (1969). *The cay.* New York: Doubleday. (U)

Vaber, B. (1972). *Ira sleeps over.* Boston: Houghton Mifflin. (P)

solution by introducing roadblocks is the core of plot development. Stories may contain any number of roadblocks, but many children's stories contain three, four, or five roadblocks.

In *The Pied Piper of Hamelin,* the first conflict comes when the townspeople demand that the mayor get rid of the rats. The mayor promises to do something, but he doesn't know what to do. Next, the piper visits the mayor and offers to rid the town of the rats. The mayor promises to pay the piper 1,000 pieces of silver. Third, the piper gets rid of the rats. He plays a mesmerizing tune on his pipe, and the rats follow him out of town and are drowned in a nearby river. Fourth, it appears that the problem is solved, but the mayor belittles the piper's accomplishment and refuses to pay the agreed-upon reward. When the mayor refuses, the piper threatens terrible consequences if he is not paid.

The high point of the action is when the solution of the problem hangs in the balance. Tension is high, and readers continue reading to learn whether or not the main characters will solve the problem. In *The Pied Piper of Hamelin,* readers experience some relief because the town of Hamelin has been saved, but tension exists because of the disagreement between the mayor and the piper. The piper plays his pipe again, this time enticing all the children to follow him out of Hamelin. They follow him to a nearby mountain, which they enter through a magic door. The mayor and other townspeople are left with their money but without their children.

At the end of the story, the problem is solved and the goal is achieved. Only one little lame boy whom the piper cures returns to tell the story and remind everyone that "a promise is a promise" and "the piper must be paid."

The plot of a story can be diagrammed or charted. A basic plot diagram, shaped somewhat like a mountain, is presented in Figure 4-8, and the four steps of plot development—introduction of the problem, roadblocks, high point in the action, and solution of the problem—are marked on the diagram. Information about any story's plot can be added to this diagram. As an example, a plot diagram of *The Pied Piper of Hamelin* is presented in Figure 4-9.

Setting

In some stories the settings, called backdrop settings, are barely sketched. The setting in many folktales, for example, is relatively unimportant and may simply use the convention, "Once upon a time . . . " to set the stage. In other stories, however, the setting is elaborated and integral to the story's effectiveness. These settings are called integral settings (Lukens, 1986). Whether or not the setting is important to plot and character development determines how much attention writers give to describing the setting. Some stories could take place anywhere and require little description; in others, however, the setting must be specific and authors must take care to ensure the authenticity of the historical period or geographic location in which the story is set.

Of the elements of story structure, setting is the one most people feel comfortable with. For them, setting is where the story takes place. Certainly location is an important dimension of setting, but there are three other dimensions as well: weather, time, and time period.

Location. Location is a very important dimension of setting in many stories. The Boston Commons in *Make Way for Ducklings* (McCloskey, 1969), the Alaskan North Slope in *Julie of the Wolves* (George, 1972), and New York City's Metropolitan Museum of Art in *From the Mixed-up Files of Mrs. Basil E. Frankweiler* (Konigsburg, 1983) are integral to these stories' effectiveness. These settings are artfully described by the authors and add something unique to the story. In contrast, many stories take place in predictable settings that do not contribute to the story's effectiveness.

Weather. Weather is a second dimension of setting and, like location, it is crucial in some stories. For example, a rainstorm is essential to the plot development in both *Bridge to Terabithia* (Paterson, 1977) and *Sam, Bangs, and Moonshine* (Ness, 1966). At other times, the author may not even mention the weather because it does not impact on the story. Many stories take place on warm, sunny days. Think about the impact weather could have on a story; for example, what might have happened if a snow storm had prevented Little Red Riding Hood from reaching her grandmother's house?

Time. The third dimension, time, includes both time of day and the passage of time within a story. The time of day is ignored in most stories, except for Halloween or ghost stories, which typically take place after dark. In stories that take place at night, such as the folktale *The Teeny-Tiny Woman* (Galdone, 1984), time is a more important dimension than in stories that take place during the day because events that happen at night seem more scary than those that happen during the day.

Many short stories span a brief period of time, often less than a day, and sometimes less than an hour. In Chris Van Allsburg's *Jumanji* (1981), for instance, Peter and Judy's bizarre adventure in which their house is overtaken by an exotic jungle lasts only the several hours their parents are at the opera. Other stories,

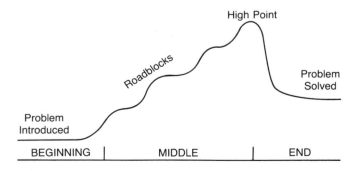

FIGURE 4-8 A Basic Plot Diagram

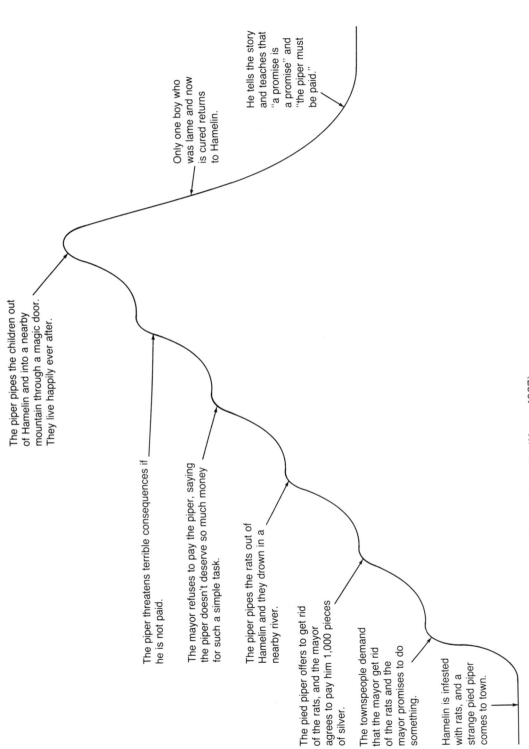

The piper pipes the children out of Hamelin and into a nearby mountain through a magic door. They live happily ever after.

Only one boy who was lame and now is cured returns to Hamelin.

He tells the story and teaches that "a promise is a promise" and "the piper must be paid."

The piper threatens terrible consequences if he is not paid.

The mayor refuses to pay the piper, saying the piper doesn't deserve so much money for such a simple task.

The piper pipes the rats out of Hamelin and they drown in a nearby river.

The pied piper offers to get rid of the rats, and the mayor agrees to pay him 1,000 pieces of silver.

The townspeople demand that the mayor get rid of the rats and the mayor promises to do something.

Hamelin is infested with rats, and a strange pied piper comes to town.

FIGURE 4-9 Plot diagram of *The Pied Piper of Hamelin* (Mayer, 1987)

such as *The Ugly Duckling* (Andersen, 1979), span a time period long enough for the main character to grow to maturity.

Time Period. The fourth dimension of setting is the time period in which a story is set. The time period is important in stories that are set in the past or in the future. If *The Witch of Blackbird Pond* (Speare, 1958) and *Beyond the Divide* (Lasky, 1983) were set in different eras, for example, they would lose much of their impact. Today, few people would believe that Kit Tyler is a witch, and travel across the United States would not be nearly so difficult today with modern conveniences. Other stories, such as *A Wrinkle in Time* (L'Engle, 1962), take place in the future where events occur that are not possible today. A list of stories with integral settings is presented in Figure 4-10. These stories illustrate the four dimensions of setting—location, weather, time, and time period.

Characters

Characters are the people or personified animals who are involved in the story. Often characters are the most important element of story structure because the experience the author creates for readers is centered around a character or group of characters. Usually , one fully rounded and two or three supporting characters are introduced and developed in a story. Fully developed main characters have all the characteristics of real people. A list of fully developed main characters in children's stories is presented in Figure 4-11.

The supporting characters may be individualized, but they will be portrayed much less vividly than the main character. The extent to which the supporting characters are developed depends on the author's purpose and the needs of the story. In *Queenie Peavy* (Burch, 1966), for instance, Queenie is the main character and we get to know her as a real person. She pretends that she is tough, as she does when the other children taunt her that her father is in the chain gang, but actually Queenie is a sensitive girl who wants a family to care for her. In contrast, Robert Burch tells us very little about the supporting characters in the story: Queenie's parents, her neighbors, her classmates, and her teachers. This story focuses on Queenie and how this lonely 13-year-old copes with times that have "turned off hard" in the 1930s.

Authors must determine how to develop and present characters to involve readers in the experiences they are writing about. They develop characters in four ways: (a) appearance, (b) action, (c) dialogue, and (d) monologue.

Appearance. Authors describe how their characters look as the story develops; however, they generally provide some physical description when characters are introduced. Readers learn about characters by the description of their facial features, body shapes, habits of dress, mannerisms, and gestures. For example, Roald Dahl vividly describes James' two wicked aunts in *James and the Giant Peach* (1961):

> Aunt Sponge was enormously fat and very short. She had small piggy eyes, a sunken mouth, and one of those white flabby faces that looked exactly as though it had been boiled. She was like a great white soggy overboiled cabbage. Aunt Spiker, on the other

FIGURE 4-10 Stories with Integral Settings

Andersen, H. C. (1979). *The ugly duckling.* New York: Harcourt Brace Jovanovich. (P–M)

Babbitt, N. (1975). *Tuck everlasting.* New York: Farrar. (M–U)

Cauley, L. B. (1984). *The town mouse and the country mouse.* New York: Putnam. (P–M)

Fritz, J. (1982). *Homesick: My own story.* New York: Putnam. (M–U)

Galdone, P. (1984). *The teeny-tiny woman.* New York: Clarion. (P)

George, J. C. (1972). *Julie of the wolves.* New York: Harper and Row. (M–U)

Hodges, Margaret. (1984). *Saint George and the dragon.* Boston: Little, Brown. (M–U)

Konigsburg, E. L. (1983). *From the mixed-up files of Mrs. Basil E. Frankweiler.* New York: Atheneum. (M)

Lasky, K. (1983). *Beyond the divide.* New York: Macmillan. (M–U)

L'Engle, M. (1962). *A wrinkle in time.* New York: Farrar. (U)

McCloskey, R. (1969). *Make way for ducklings.* New York: Viking. (P)

Ness, E. (1966). *Sam, Bangs and moonshine.* New York: Holt. (P)

Paterson, K. (1977). *Bridge to Terabithia.* New York: Crowell. (M–U)

Speare, E. (1958). *The witch of Blackbird Pond.* Boston: Houghton Mifflin. (M–U)

Van Allsburg, C. (1981). *Jumanji.* Boston: Houghton Mifflin. (P–M)

White, E. B. (1952). *Charlotte's web.* New York: Harper and Row. (M)

Wilder, L. I. (1971). *The long winter.* New York: Harper and Row. (M)

FIGURE 4-11 Fully Developed Characters in Children's Literature

Character	Story
Queenie	Burch, R. (1966). *Queenie Peavy.* New York: Viking. (U)
Leigh	Cleary, B. (1983). *Dear Mr. Henshaw.* New York: Morrow. (M)
Harriet	Fitzhugh, L. (1964). *Harriet the spy.* New York: Harper and Row. (M)
Sam	George, J. C. (1959). *My side of the mountain.* New York: Dutton. (U)
Frances	Hoban, R. (1976). *Best friends for Frances.* New York: Harper and Row. (P)
Anastasia	Lowry, L. (1979). *Anastasia Krupnik.* Boston: Houghton Mifflin. (M)
Karana	O'Dell, S. (1960). *Island of the blue dolphins.* Boston: Houghton Mifflin. (M–U)
Gilly	Paterson, K. (1978). *The great Gilly Hopkins.* New York: Crowell. (M–U)
Peter	Potter, B. (1902). *The tale of Peter Rabbit.* New York: Warne. (P)
Matt	Speare, E. (1983). *The sign of the beaver.* Boston: Houghton Mifflin. (M–U)
Mafatu	Sperry, A. (1968). *Call it courage.* New York: Macmillan. (U)
Cassie	Taylor, M. (1976). *Roll of thunder, hear my cry.* New York: Dial. (U)

hand, was lean and tall and bony, and she wore steel-rimmed spectacles that fixed onto the end of her nose with a clip. She had a screeching voice and long wet narrow lips, and whenever she got angry or excited, little flecks of spit would come shooting out of her mouth as she talked. (p. 7)

Dahl's descriptions bring these two despicable characters vividly to life. He has carefully chosen the specific details to influence readers to appreciate James' dismay in having to live with these two aunts.

Action. What a character does is the best way of knowing about that character. In Betsy Byars' story about three unwanted children, *The Pinballs* (1977), 15-year-old Carlie is described as "as hard to crack as a coconut" (p. 4), and her dialogue is harsh and sarcastic; however, Carlie's actions belie these other ways of knowing about her. She demonstrates through her actions that she cares about her two fellow-pinballs and the foster family who cares for them. For example, she gets Harvey a puppy as a birthday present and sneaks it into the hospital.

Dialogue. Another important technique that authors use to develop their characters is dialogue. What characters say is important, but so is the way they speak. The level of formality of the language that characters use is determined by the social situation. A character might speak less formally with friend than with respected elders or characters in positions of authority. The geographic location of the story and the socioeconomic status of the characters also determine the way the characters speak. For example, in *Roll of Thunder, Hear My Cry* (Taylor, 1976), Cassie and her family speak Black English, and in *Ida Early Comes over the Mountain* (Burch, 1980), Ida's speech is characteristic of rural Georgia, and she says, "Howdy-do?" and "Yes, sir-ee." Even in animal stories such as *Rabbit Hill* (Lawson, 1972), dialect is important. Uncle Analdas from Danbury speaks a rural dialect in contrast to the "proper" standard English spoken by the animals on the hill.

Monologue. Authors also provide insight into their characters by revealing the characters' thoughts. In *Anastasia Krupnik* (Lowry, 1979), for example, Lois Lowry shares 10-year-old Anastasia's thinking with us. Anastasia has enjoyed being an only child, and she is very upset that her mother is pregnant. To deal with Anastasia's feelings of sibling rivalry, her parents suggest that she choose a name for the new baby, and Anastasia agrees. Through monologue readers learn why Anastasia has agreed to choose the name: She will pick the most awful name she can think of for the baby. Lowry also has Anastasia keep a journal in which she lists things she likes and hates, another reflection of her thinking.

Theme

Theme is the underlying meaning of a story. Themes embody general truths about society or human nature and usually deal with the characters' emotions and values. Themes can be stated either explicitly or implicitly. Explicit themes are stated openly and clearly in the story, while implicit themes are implied in the story rather than explicitly stated in the text (Lukens, 1986).

Friendship is an important theme in many children's stories. In *Charlotte's Web* (White, 1952), Wilbur, who is grateful for Charlotte's encouragement and protection, remarks that "Friendship is one of the most satisfying things in the world" (cited in Lukens, 1986, p. 102). Wilbur's statement is an example of an explicitly stated theme. Friendship is also one theme in *Bridge to Terabithia* (Paterson, 1977), but it is implied through Jess and Leslie's enduring friendship rather than explicitly stated in the text.

Authors convey the theme through the characters' actions, dialogue, and monologue as they strive to resolve their problems, rather than by moralizing. A list of stories with explicit and implicit themes is presented in Figure 4-12.

Point of View

People see others and the world from different points of view. Listening to several people recount an event they have witnessed proves the impact of the viewpoint. The focus of the narrator determines to a great extent readers' understanding of the story—the characters, events—and whether or not readers will believe what they are being told. Student authors must decide who will tell their stories and follow that viewpoint consistently in the stories they write. Four points of view are first-person viewpoint, omniscient viewpoint, limited omniscient viewpoint, and objective viewpoint (Lukens, 1986). A list of stories written from each point of view is presented in Figure 4-13.

FIGURE 4-12   Stories with Implicit and Explicit Themes

Andersen, H. C. (1965). *The nightingale.* New York: Harper and Row. (M–U)

Cooney, B. (1958). *Chanticleer and the fox.* New York: Crowell. (P–M)

Galdone, P. (1968). *Henny Penny.* New York: Clarion. (P)

Greene, B. (1973). *Summer of my German soldier.* New York: Dial. (U)

Lawson, R. (1972). *Rabbit hill.* New York: Viking. (M)

L'Engle, M. (1962). *A wrinkle in time.* New York: Farrar. (U)

Lewis, C. S. (1981). *The lion, the witch and the wardrobe.* New York: Macmillan. (M–U)

Mayer, M. (1987). *The pied piper of Hamelin.* New York: Macmillan. (M)

Neville, E. (1963). *It's like this cat.* New York: Harper and Row. (U)

Piper, W. (1954). *The little engine that could.* New York: Platt and Munk. (P)

Steig, W. (1982). *Doctor De Soto.* New York: Farrar. (P)

Westcott, N. B. (1984). *The emperor's new clothes.* Boston: Little, Brown. (P–M)

White, E. B. (1952). *Charlotte's web.* New York: Harper and Row. (M)

Yep, L. (1977). *Child of the owl.* New York: Harper and Row. (M–U)

Yorinks, A. (1986). *Hey, Al.* New York: Farrar. (P)

First-person Viewpoint. Authors use the first-person viewpoint when they tell the story through the eyes of one character using the first person pronoun *I*. This point of view is used so the reader can live the story as the narrator tells it. The narrator, usually the main character, speaks as an eyewitness and a participant in the events. For example, in *The Slave Dancer* (Fox, 1973), Jessie tells the story of his kidnapping and frightful voyage on a slave ship, and in *Alexander and the Terrible, Horrible, No Good, Very Bad Day* (Viorst, 1977), Alexander tells about a day when everything seemed to go wrong for him. One limitation to this viewpoint is that the narrator must remain an eyewitness.

The Omniscient Viewpoint. Here the author is god-like, seeing all and knowing all. The author tells the readers about the thought processes of each character without worrying about how the information is obtained. William Steig's *Doctor De Soto* (1982), a story about a mouse dentist who outwits a fox with a toothache, is an example of a story written from the omniscient viewpoint. Steig lets readers

FIGURE 4-13 Stories Illustrating the Four Viewpoints

First-person Viewpoint

Greene, B. (1974). *Philip Hall likes me. I reckon maybe.* New York: Dial. (M–U)

Howe, D., & Howe, J. (1979). *Bunnicula.* New York: Atheneum. (M)

MacLachlan, P. (1985). *Sarah, plain and tall.* New York: Harper and Row. (M)

Viorst, J. (1977). *Alexander and the terrible, horrible, no good, very bad day.* New York: Atheneum. (P)

Omniscient Viewpoint

Babbitt, N. (1975). *Tuck everlasting.* New York: Farrar. (M–U)

Grahame, K. (1961). *The wind in the willows.* New York: Scribner. (M)

Lewis, C. S. (1981). *The lion, the witch and the wardrobe.* New York: Macmillan. (M–U)

Steig, William. (1982). *Doctor De Soto.* New York: Farrar. (P)

Limited Omniscient Viewpoint

Burch, R. (1966). *Queenie Peavy.* New York: Dell. (U)

Cleary, B. (1981). *Ramona Quimby, age 8.* New York: Random House. (M)

Lionni, L. (1969). *Alexander and the wind-up mouse.* New York: Pantheon. (P)

Lowry, L. (1979). *Anastasia Krupnik.* Boston: Houghton Mifflin. (M)

Objective Viewpoint

Brown, M. (1954). *Cinderella.* New York: Scribner. (P)

Lobel, A. (1972). *Frog and toad together.* New York: Harper and Row. (P)

Wells, R. (1973). *Benjamin and Tulip.* New York: Dial. (P)

Zemach, M. (1983). *The little red hen.* New York: Farrar. (P)

know that the fox is thinking about eating the dentist as soon as his toothache is cured and that the mouse dentist is aware of the fox's thoughts and plans a clever trick.

Limited Omniscient Viewpoint. Authors use this point of view to overhear the thoughts of one of the characters without being all-knowing and all-seeing. The story is told in third person and the author concentrates on the thoughts, feelings, and significant past experiences of the main character or another important character. Robert Burch used the limited omniscient viewpoint in *Queenie Peavy* (1966) and Queenie is the character Burch concentrates on, showing why she has a chip on her shoulder and how she overcomes it.

Objective Viewpoint. Authors use the objective viewpoint as though they were making a film of the story and can learn only what is visible and audible and what others say about the characters and situations. Readers are eyewitnesses to the story and are confined to the immediate scene. A limitation is that the author cannot probe very deeply into characters. Stories, such as *Cinderella* (Brown, 1954) and *The Little Red Hen* (Zemach, 1983), are examples of stories told from the objective viewpoint. In these stories, authors focus on recounting the events of the story rather than developing the personalities of the characters.

These seven elements are the building blocks of stories. With this structure, authors—both children and adults—can let their creativity flow and combine ideas with structure to craft a good story.

TEACHING STUDENTS TO WRITE STORIES

Children develop their concept of story through listening to stories read aloud and telling stories during the preschool years. With this introduction to narratives, elementary students are ready to learn more about how stories are organized and how authors use the elements of story structure to create stories. Students use this knowledge to compose the stories they write as well as to comprehend stories they read.

The instructional strategy presented in this section builds on students' concept of story by examining the elements of story structure—beginning-middle-end, repetition, plot, setting, characters, theme, and point of view—in connection with a reading or literature program and then having students apply these elements in writing stories. Rather than a collection of cookbook-like activities, this strategy is a holistic approach in which students read, talk, think, and write stories. The reader-writer connection is crucial: As readers, students consider how the author used a particular structure and consider its impact on themselves as readers; then, as writers, they experiment with the structure in the stories they write and consider the impact on their classmates who read the stories.

This instructional strategy has two components: preparing to teach and teaching students about the elements of story structure. Before introducing an element, teachers prepare by learning about the element, collecting stories that exemplify the element, and developing a set of instructional materials. Through this preparation, teachers gain valuable insights into how authors use the elements of story structure in constructing their stories.

In the second component, teachers introduce their students to an element of story structure using the stories they collected and the instructional materials they developed. Students read stories and analyze how authors use the element in the story. Next, they participate in activities, such as retelling stories and drawing clusters, in which they investigate how authors used the element in particular stories. With this background of experiences, students write collaborative and individual stories applying what they have learned about the element.

Part 1: Preparing to Teach

1. *Learn about the element.* Review the information about the element of story structure presented in this chapter and in other reference books, such as Rebecca Lukens' *A Critical Handbook of Children's Literature* (1986).
2. *Collect stories illustrating the element.* Collect as many stories illustrating the element as possible. Folktales, other short stories, and novels can be used as examples. It is helpful to collect multiple copies of books that students will read independently. Stories can also be tape-recorded for students to listen to at a listening center. Also identify stories in basal reading textbooks that illustrate specific elements of story structure. Lists of stories that illustrate specific elements were presented with the information about that element in this chapter.
3. *Analyze the element in stories.* Read the stories to learn how authors use the element in constructing their stories. Take notes about how authors use the element in particular stories to aid in teaching.
4. *Develop charts.* Develop one or more charts to present the information to students. The charts should define the element and list characteristics of the element. Figure 4-14 presents charts that can be developed for each element of story structure. Leave space on the charts for students to add information about the element in their own words. Develop and laminate the charts; then add children's words in grease pencil. In this way, the charts can be personalized for each group of students.

Part 2: Teaching an Element of Story Structure

1. *Introduce the element.* Introduce the element of story structure and display charts defining the element and/or listing the characteristics of the element. Next, read several stories illustrating the element to students or have students read the stories themselves. After reading, discuss the story to probe students' awareness of how the author used the element in constructing the story.

2. *Analyze the element in stories.* Have students read or listen to one or more stories read aloud that illustrates the element. After reading, students analyze how the author used the element in each story. They should tie their analyses to the definition and the characteristics of the element presented in the first step. Students can also make their own copies of the chart to put in their writer's notebooks.
3. *Participate in application activities.* Students participate in application activities in which they investigate how authors use the element in particular stories. Possible activities include retelling stories orally, with drawings, and in writing; dramatizing stories with puppets and with informal drama; and drawing clusters to graphically display the structure of stories. Here are 10 application activities:

Class Collaboration Retelling of Stories. Choose a favorite story that students have read or listened to several times and have each student draw or write a retelling of a page or short part of the story. Then collect each child's contribution and compile them to make a class book. Younger students can draw pictures and dictate their retellings, which the teacher prints in large type. Then these pictures and text can be attached to sheets of posterboard to make a big book that students can read together.

Retelling and Telling Stories. Students can retell familiar stories to small groups of classmates using simple hand or finger puppets or with pictures on a flannel board. Similarly, students can create their own stories to tell. A gingerbread boy might become a gingerbread bunny that runs away with a basket of Easter eggs or Max might make a second trip to visit the wild things.

Retelling Stories with Pictures. Students can retell a favorite story by drawing a series of pictures and compiling them to make a wordless picture book. Young children can make a booklet by folding one sheet of drawing paper in quarters like a greeting card. Then they write the title of the book on the front side; on the three remaining sides, they draw illustrations to represent the beginning, middle, and end of the story. A sample four-sided booklet is presented in Figure 4-15. Older students can produce a film of a favorite story by drawing a series of pictures on a long sheet of butcher paper and scrolling the pictures on a screen made out of a cardboard box. Students can also draw pictures to retell a story on a filmstrip. (Filmstrip kits with blank film and colored pens are available from school supply stores.)

Retelling Stories in Writing. Students can write retellings of favorite stories in their own words. Predictable books, stories with repetition, are often the easiest to retell. They don't copy the text out of a book; rather, they retell a story that they know well. Sixth-grade Ilya wrote the following retelling of "Little Red Riding Hood." Notice that her sentences are written in alphabetical order. The first sentence begins with A, the second with B, the third with C, and so on.

FIGURE 4-14 Charts About the Elements of Story Structure

Chart 1
Stories
Stories have three parts:

1. A beginning

2. A middle

3. An End

Chart 2
Beginnings of Stories
Writers put these things in the beginning of a story.

1.

2.

3.

Chart 3
Middles of Stories
Writers put these things in the middle of a story.

1.

2.

3.

4.

5.

Chart 4
Ends of Stories
Writers put these things in the end of a story.

1.

2.

3.

Chart 5
Repetition
Writers sometimes repeat words and events in stories:

1. Sometimes words are said over and over.

2. Some events happen over and over.

Chart 6
Conflict
Conflict is the problem that characters face in the story. There are four kinds of conflict:

1. Conflict between a character and nature

2. Conflict between a character and society

3. Conflict between characters

4. Conflict within a character

FIGURE 4-14 (continued)

Chart 7

Plot

Plot is the sequence of events in a story. It has four parts:

1. A problem: The problem introduces conflict at the beginning of the story.

2. Roadblocks: Characters face roadblocks as they try to solve the problem in the middle of the story.

3. The High Point: The high point in the action occurs when the problem is about to be solved. It separates the middle and the end.

4. The Solution: The problem is solved and the roadblocks are overcome at the end of the story.

Chart 8

Setting

The setting is where and when the story takes place.

1. Location: Stories can take place anywhere.

2. Weather: Stories take place in different kinds of weather.

3. Time of Day: Stories take place during the day or at night.

4. Time Period: Stories take place in the past, at the current time, or in the future.

Chart 9

Characters

Writers develop characters in four ways:

1. Appearance: How characters look

2. Action: What characters do

3. Dialogue: What characters say

4. Monologue: What characters think

Chart 10

Theme

Theme is the underlying meaning of a story.

1. Explicit themes are stated clearly in the story.

2. Implicit themes are suggested by the characters, action and monologue

Chart 11

Point of View

Writers tell the story according to one of four viewpoints:

1. First-Person Viewpoint: The writer tells the story through the eyes of one character using "I."

2. Omniscient Viewpoint: The writer sees all and knows all about each character.

3. Limited Omniscient Viewpoint: The writer focuses on one character and tells that character's thoughts and feelings.

4. Objective Viewpoint: The writer focuses on the events of the story without telling what the characters are thinking and feeling.

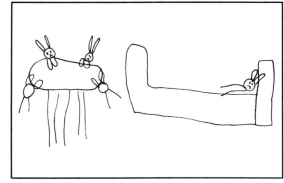

FIGURE 4-15 A Four-sided Booklet Retelling *The Tale of Peter Rabbit* (Potter, 1902) —Anonymous, grade 1

■ Little Red Riding Hood

"Another plain day," said Little Red Riding Hood. "Boy, oh boy, oh boy," she wondered. "Could I do something fun today?"

"Dear," called her mother to Little Red Riding Hood. "Eat your breakfast and then take these goodies to grandma's house."

"Fine, I'll do it. Great" said Little Red Riding Hood, "My first time I get to go through the forest."

"Hold it," said a wolf in the forest. "I want to look in that basket of yours."

"Just stay out of there, you wolf. Keep your hands off me! Let go of me, you wolf." Mighty and brave she slapped the wolf. Not knowing what to do, she ran down the path to grandma's house.

Open minded, the wolf ran to grandma's house. Putting his hands through the window, he climbed in and swallowed grandma. Quietly he jumped in her bed.

Running to grandma's house, still scared from the wolf, Little Red Riding Hood knocked on grandma's door. Silently the wolf came to meet her. Too late for Red Riding Hood to run, she panicked and yelled. Unaware she was. Very loudly her yell traveled through the forest. Wondering what it was, a woodsman heard it and came to grandma's house and killed the wolf. X-raying the body of the wolf, he saw grandma.

"Your help sure has paid off," said Little Red Riding Hood after the woodsman saved her. Zooming from grandma's house came Little Red Riding Hood, to tell her mom what had just happened.

After writing, students can point out how they used the element of story structure being studied in their retelling. They can point out the conflict situation, the point of view, repeated words, or the beginning-middle-end parts. This activity is a good confidence-builder for students who can't seem to continue a story to its conclusion. By using a story they are familiar with, they are more successful.

Dramatizing Stories. Students can dramatize favorite stories or use puppets to retell a story. These dramatizations should be informal; fancy props are unnecessary and students should not memorize or read dialogue.

Drawing Story Clusters and Other Diagrams. Students can draw beginning-middle-end story clusters, repetition clusters, and plot diagrams for stories they have read.

Comparing Different Versions of Stories. Students can compare different versions of folktales such as "The Hare and the Tortoise" and "The Gingerbread Boy." A list of various picturebook versions of familiar folktales is presented in Figure 4-16. Students can compare the beginning-middle-end of each version. In one version of "The Hare and the Tortoise," for example, the beginning is much longer as the author describes the elaborate plans for the race while in other versions the beginning is brief. Students can also compare the events in each story. The characters that the Gingerbread Boy runs past vary in different versions, and in one version of "Cinderella," the heroine attends the ball twice.

Creating Character Clusters. Students can complete a character cluster for a fully developed main character as shown in Figure 4-17. This character cluster describes Rumpelstiltskin from Paul O. Zelinsky's retelling of the Grimm's folktale of the same name (1986). Rumpelstiltskin, the name of the character, is the nucleus word for the cluster, and the four ways authors develop characters—*appearance, action, dialogue,* and *monologue*—are the main ideas for the rays. Details about the character are added to each main idea, as the cluster illustrates.

Writing Dialogue. Students can choose an excerpt from a favorite story and create a script with dialogue. Then students read the script to classmates as a readers theater presentation. Also, students can draw comic strips for an excerpt from a story and add dialogue. Students might try varying the register of the language, from informal to very formal, from standard to nonstandard English to appreciate the power of language.

Retelling Stories from Different Points of View. Students need to experiment with point of view to understand how the author's viewpoint can slant a story. To demonstrate how point of view changes according to the viewpoint of the person telling the story, read Judy Blume's *The Pain and the Great One* (1974) to students. In this book, the same brief story is told twice, first from the viewpoint of

FIGURE 4-16   Versions of Familiar Folktales

The Hare and the Tortoise

Castle, C. (1985). *The hare and the tortoise.* New York: Dutton.
Galdone, P. (1962). *The hare and the tortoise.* New York: McGraw-Hill.
Stevens, J. (1984). *The tortoise and the hare.* New York: Holiday House.
Wildsmith, B. (1966). *The hare and the tortoise.* Oxford: Oxford University Press.

Jack and the Beanstalk

Cauley, L. B. (1983). *Jack and the beanstalk.* New York: Putnam.
De Regniers, B. S. (1985). *Jack and the beanstalk.* New York: Atheneum.
Haley, G. (1986). *Jack and the bean tree.* New York: Crown.
Johnson, D. W. (1976). *Jack and the beanstalk.* Boston: Little, Brown.
Still, J. (1977). *Jack and the wonder beans.* New York: Putnam.

Cinderella

Brown, M. (1954). *Cinderella.* New York: Scribner.
Ehrlich, A. (1985). *Cinderella.* New York: Dial.
Galdone, P. (1978). *Cinderella.* New York: McGraw Hill.
Grimm, J. C. K. (1981). *Cinderella.* New York: Greenwillow.
Perrault, C. (1972). *Cinderella.* New York: Penguin.

The Gingerbread Boy

Asbjornsen, P. C., & Moe, J. (1980). *The runaway pancake.* New York: Larousse.
Brown, M. (1972). *The bun: A tale from Russia.* New York: Harcourt Brace Jovanovich.
Galdone, P. (1975). *The gingerbread boy.* New York: Seabury.
Jacobs, J. (n.d.). *Johnny-cake.* New York: Putnam.
Jarrell, R. (1964). *The gingerbread rabbit.* New York: Collier.
Lobel, A. (1978). *The pancake.* New York: Greenwillow.
Sawyer, R. (1953). *Journey cake, ho!* New York: Viking.

Little Red Riding Hood

Galdone, P. (1974). *Little red riding hood.* New York: McGraw Hill.
Grimm, J. (1983). *Little red cap.* New York: Morrow.
Goodall, J. (1988). *Little red riding hood.* New York: Macmillan.
Marshall, J. (1987). *Little red riding hood.* New York: Dial.

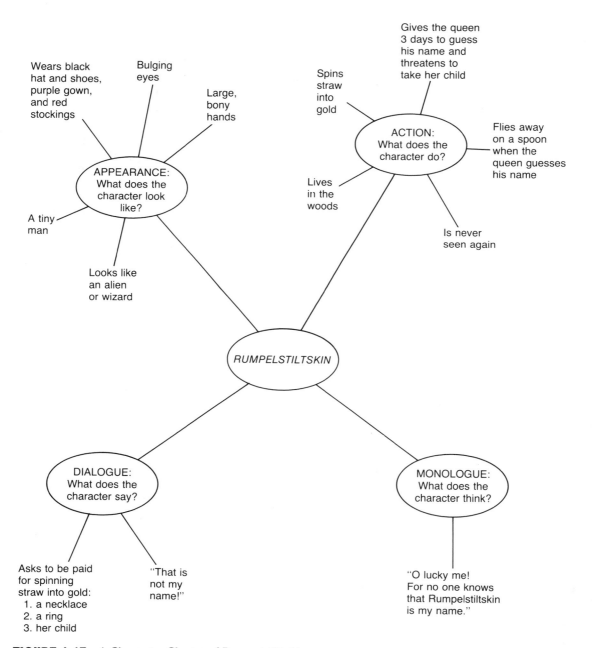

Wears black hat and shoes, purple gown, and red stockings

Bulging eyes

Large, bony hands

Spins straw into gold

Gives the queen 3 days to guess his name and threatens to take her child

ACTION: What does the character do?

Flies away on a spoon when the queen guesses his name

APPEARANCE: What does the character look like?

A tiny man

Lives in the woods

Is never seen again

Looks like an alien or wizard

RUMPELSTILTSKIN

DIALOGUE: What does the character say?

MONOLOGUE: What does the character think?

Asks to be paid for spinning straw into gold:
1. a necklace
2. a ring
3. her child

"That is not my name!"

"O lucky me! For no one knows that Rumpelstiltskin is my name."

FIGURE 4-17   A Character Cluster of Rumpelstiltskin

"the great one," an 8-year-old sister, and then from the viewpoint of "the pain," the 6-year-old brother. Even children in the primary grades are struck by how different the two versions are and how the narrator filters the information.

Another way to demonstrate the impact of different viewpoints is for students to retell or rewrite a familiar story, such as *Little Red Riding Hood,* (Galdone, 1974) from specific points of view—through the eyes of Little Red Riding Hood, her sick, old grandmother, the hungry wolf, or the woodsman.

As they shift the point of view, students learn that they can change some aspects of a story but not others. To help them appreciate how these changes affect a story, have them take a story such as C. S. Lewis' *The Lion, the Witch and the Wardrobe* (1981), which is told from the omniscient viewpoint, and retell short episodes from the viewpoints of each character as well as from the four viewpoints. The omniscient viewpoint is a good one to start with because, in this viewpoint, the readers learn all. As students shift to other points of view, they must decide what to leave out according to the new perspective. They must decide whether to tell the story in first or third person and what kinds of information about the characters they are permitted to share.

4. *Review the element.* Review the characteristics of the element being studied, using the charts introduced in the first step. Ask students to restate the definition and characteristics of the element in their own words, using one book they have read to illustrate the characteristics.

5. *Write a class collaboration story.* Have students apply what they have learned about the element of story structure by writing a class (or group) collaboration story. A collaborative story provides students with a rehearsal before they write stories independently. Review the element of story structure and refer to the chart presented in the first step as the story is being written. Encourage students to offer ideas for the story and explain how to incorporate the element into the story. Follow the writing process stages by writing a rough draft on the chalkboard, chart paper, or overhead projector. Then have students revise the story, working both to improve the content as well as to check that the element of story structure being studied has been incorporated in the story. Next, edit the story and make a final copy to be shared with all class members. Two collaborative stories written by a class of transitional students (students who have completed kindergarten but need additional experiences before first grade) are presented in Figure 4-18. The second story became necessary when students couldn't agree on the ending for the first story. As a compromise, the teacher promised the students who wanted a different ending that they could write a sequel.

6. *Write individual stories.* Have students write individual stories incorporating the element being studied and other elements of story structure that they have already learned. Students use the process approach to writing in which they move through the drafting, revising, editing, and publishing stages of the writing process. The activities involved in the first five steps of this instructional

strategy constitute the prewriting stage. In this step, students complete the remaining stages of the writing process. First, they write rough drafts of their stories and meet in writing groups to share their writing. Writing-group members focus their comments on both the content of the story and how effectively the writer has used the element of story structure being studied. Next, they revise using the feedback they receive. Before completing the revising stage, students can complete a "Revision Checklist" in which they doublecheck their story to be sure that they have applied the element being studied. A sample revision checklist for plot is presented in Figure 4-19. The first two questions in the checklist require students to focus on the type of conflict used in their story and their overall development of plot, the two most important components of plot. The third question focuses on a trouble spot for many students— roadblocks that complicate the plot—and asks students to count their roadblocks and to add more if they don't have at least three. After editing their stories and correcting as many mechanical errors as possible, students recopy the stories and share them with an appropriate audience.

Assessing Stories that Students Write

Assessing the stories that students write through this approach involves far more than simply judging the quality of the finished stories. Any assessment should also take into account students' activities and learning as they study the element of story structure as well as the activities students engage in as they write and refine their stories. These four components should be considered in assessing students' stories: (a) students' study of the element of story structure, (b) their knowledge about and application of the element in writing, (c) their use of the writing process, and (d) the quality of the finished stories.

The first component is students' participation in the study of the element of story structure. Assess students' participation in these ways:

- Did the student read stories illustrating the element?
- Did the student participate in discussions analyzing how the element was used in particular stories?
- Did the student participate in one or more application activities?

A second component is students' knowledge about the element of story structure and their application of the element in the stories they write. Determining whether students learned about the element and applied what they have learned in their stories is crucial in assessing students' stories. Consider the following points:

- Can the student define or identify the characteristics of the element?
- Can the student explain how the element being studied was used in a particular story?
- Did the student apply the element in the story he/she has written?

FIGURE 4-18 Class Collaboration Story

STORY 1: BILLY AND THE LEPRECHAUN

Once upon a time there was a little leprechaun named Fred. He had a miserable life because nobody would believe that he had a pot of gold. Also, Fred was always being teased because he was the smallest leprechaun. Fred did have a pot of gold that was hidden underground in a tunnel under a mushroom. This mushroom was Fred's home.

One afternoon a little boy named Billy was walking in the meadow. Suddenly, he heard the grass moving. Billy was startled by the noise, but he was brave and went over to see what it was. He found a little man that he recognized as a leprechaun.

Billy grabbed the leprechaun by the seat of his britches and said, "What is your name and where is your gold?"

"My name is Fred and my gold is hidden."

"Well, I won't let you go until you give me your gold," said Billy.

Then Fred said, "I will not give you my gold!"

"Well," said Billy, "You are not obeying fairy law and I will tell the fairies on you."

"So what, I don't care," said Fred.

So Billy thought to himself, "I will tease Fred and make him angry so he will accidently tell me where his gold is hidden."

So Billy said, "You are so little you haven't been alive long enough to earn some gold."

Fred said, "Yes, I have."

"No you haven't."

"Yes I have," said Fred.

"Then prove it," said Billy.

Fred said, "All right, I'll prove it. Just follow me."

In the mushroom was a trap door that led to a big tunnel. This tunnel was big enough for Billy and the leprechaun. It was dark and spooky in the tunnel with bats flying everywhere. They kept on sliding and crawling until they saw the sparkling gold.

Billy said, "There is so much gold. It is too heavy to carry all by myself. I will have to go get a wagon to carry it."

"Then, I'll stay here and guard it," said Fred.

"What if you are tricking me?" said Billy.

"Oh no, I wouldn't be tricking you."

"Then, I'll go get the wagon," said Billy.

Fred watched as Billy started to walk all the way back to town. As soon as Billy was out of sight, Fred went to get some more real mushrooms that looked just like his home. He stuck them all around the meadow and then went back to his tunnel.

Hours later, Billy came back and he saw all the mushrooms around the meadow. He knew it would take too long to find the right one so he gave up and went home. Fred the leprechaun lived happily ever after after counting his gold.

FIGURE 4-18 (continued)

STORY 2: BILLY'S REVENGE

It was Wednesday. Billy and his friends were thinking about how they could get Fred the leprechaun's gold. Billy had told his friends how he had met the leprechaun in the meadow under a mushroom and been tricked by him.

His friends believed him because they all knew that leprechauns were tricky. So they decided to help Billy get the gold back from Fred. Billy told them that if they helped him, they would split up all the gold. They knew that they would have to trick Fred and fight dirty to get the gold.

This was the plan. They decided that Billy's friend Spike who was little, fat, and wrinkly, would dress like a leprechaun and pretend to be Fred's long lost brother. They put a fake mustache and beard on him and then bought green clothes and a hat from the costume store for him to wear.

Billy, Spike, and all the other boys and girls rode down to the meadow on a wagon pulled by horses. There they saw only one mushroom. Fred had taken all the other mushrooms away because he didn't think that Billy would be back.

The boys and girls hid in the trees while Spike went to knock on the door. Fred the leprechaun opened the door and said, "Who are you?"

Spike said, "I am your long lost brother and I live in New Mexico. I have traveled a long way. Can I lie down somewhere?"

"Yes, you can brother," said Fred.

Spike lay down and began to talk to Fred.

Spike asked, "Fred, how much gold have you made during all these years?"

"Trillions and trillions and billions and millions and I used to hide it in the tunnel under my mushroom until this little pest named Billy came along and tried to steal it. Now I hide it inside the apple tree on the left side of my house," said Fred.

All this time, Billy and his friends were listening at the door that Fred had forgotten to close. As soon as they heard where the gold was hidden, they went to the apple tree on the left, took the chain saw that they had brought, and chopped down the tree. Fred never heard any noise outside because Spike liked rock and roll music and had turned the radio on full blast.

As the tree fell down, the gold flew out. All the girls and boys put the gold into the wagon and they rode home. In the meantime, Spike danced by the window and he saw his friends signal him to leave. As Spike saw the signal, he danced right out the door and ran as fast as he could to Billy's house. Fred didn't see him leave because he was dancing the other way.

Finally, Fred turned and noticed that Spike was gone. In a flash, he rushed out to check on his gold and he found that it was missing. All of it was gone except 20 pieces. Then Fred noticed a sign. The sign said:

Dear Fred,

I like you Fred, but you were so mean to me that I wanted to take revenge. I left you 20 pieces of gold. That should be enough and I know that you can make more.

Love,
Billy, Spike, and Friends

Fred felt a little bit better and started on a hunt to find more gold.

This time Billy lived happily ever after counting his half of the gold.

FIGURE 4-19 Sample Revision Checklist

REVISION CHECKLIST ON PLOT

Name _____

Story _____

1. Which type of conflict did you use in your story?

2. Draw a plot diagram of your story.

3. How many roadblocks are in your story? _____

   Circle each of the roadblocks on your plot diagram with a colored pencil.

REMEMBER!
YOU MUST HAVE AT LEAST 3 ROADBLOCKS IN YOUR STORY.

A third component is students' use of the process approach to write their stories. Learning about the element is prewriting, and after they learn about the element, students draft, revise, edit, and share their stories as they do with other types of writing. Assess students' use of the writing process by observing them as they write and asking these questions:

- Did the student write a rough draft?
- Did the student participate in a writing group?
- Did the student revise the story according to feedback received from the writing group?
- Did the student complete a revision checklist?

- Did the student proofread the story and correct as many mechanical errors as possible?
- Did the student share the story?

The fourth component is the quality of the story. Quality is difficult to measure, but it is often described as the creativeness or inventiveness. In addition, a second aspect of quality is organization. Students who write high quality and interesting stories use the elements of story structure to their advantage. Ask these questions to assess the quality of children's stories.

- Is the story interesting?
- Is the story well organized?

These four components and the questions listed under each can be used in assessing students' stories. Assessing or grading students' stories is more than simply evaluating the quality of the finished product, and any assessment should reflect all components of students' involvement with stories. For more information about assessing students' writing, see Chapter 10.

ANSWERING TEACHERS' QUESTIONS ABOUT NARRATIVE WRITING

1. It sounds as if this approach is very time-consuming, and I don't have any time to spend on teaching writing. What can I do?

Your concern is a common one. Many teachers are frustrated trying to squeeze writing instruction into an already full school day. One way to make time to teach students about the elements of story structure and have them write stories is to incorporate the activities discussed in this chapter into the reading program. Stories in basal reading texts illustrate many of the elements of story structure, and they can be supplemented with class sets of several stories suggested in this chapter, stories that you read aloud to the entire class, and library books that students read independently. As students read the stories in the basal readers or in trade-books, focus the discussion on the elements of story structure rather than other questions provided in teacher manuals. If you teach creatively, you can use a combination of basal readers and tradebooks to teach students about stories.

2. I told my sixth graders about plot and then they wrote stories. I was very disappointed with their stories. They weren't very good.

It sounds as if you explained plot to the students rather than helping the students analyze stories to see how authors use plot in their stories. It is important to follow the instructional strategy and allow time for students to examine and experiment with plot before they write stories. It isn't enough to explain an element of story structure to students and assume that they really understand it. Did students write a class collaboration story before they wrote individual stories? Writing a collaborative story is an important step because it gives you an opportunity to check that the students understand the element and how to apply it in their stories.

3. Is there a sequence I should follow in teaching the elements of story structure or can I teach them all together?

Each element of story structure should be taught separately, and it is best to teach the elements in the order presented in this chapter. Beginning-middle-end is the most basic element of story structure. And even if you teach older children, they need to understand this basic organization of stories before examining the other elements. Some upper grade teachers skip repetition, but older students enjoy rereading the folktales and can easily incorporate repetitive events and words into their more sophisticated narratives. Writing repetition stories is a good way for both older and younger children to feel success. If students haven't been taught about plot, setting, characters, theme, and point of view, they need to study each element and write stories incorporating each.

4. What should I do when Wilson can't write an individual story?

I'd recommend that you work with Wilson to find out *why* he can't write a story. Any one of several reasons is possible. First, check his understanding of the elements of story structure. Can he explain the element of story structure and give examples? If not, he is not prepared to write a story incorporating that element and should be involved in additional activities to examine the element. Second, check Wilson's ability to retell a story he has read that incorporates the element. Can he retell a story orally? If not, read a short story to him or have it read one himself and retell it to you. If he can retell a story successfully, you might want to have Wilson retell a story in writing instead of writing an original story. Third, check to see if he has an idea for his story. If he doesn't, talk to him about possible story ideas, ideas for writing a sequel to a story he has read, or if all else fails, suggest that he retell a favorite story. It is important the Wilson writes something so that he can overcome his writer's block.

REFERENCES

Andersen, H. C. (1979). *The ugly duckling.* New York: Harcourt Brace Jovanovich.

Applebee, A. N. (1978). *The child's concept of story: Ages 2 to 17.* Chicago: University of Chicago Press.

Applebee, A. N. (1980). Children's narratives: New directions. *The Reading Teacher, 34,* 137–142.

Beaver, J. M. (1982). *Say it! over and over.* Language Arts, 59, 143–148.

Blackburn, E. (1985). Stories never end. In J. Hansen, T. Newkirk, & D. Graves (Eds.), *Breaking ground: Teachers relate reading and writing in the elementary school* (pp. 3–13). Portsmouth, NH: Heinemann.

Blume, J. (1972). *Tales of a fourth grade nothing.* New York: Dutton.

Blume, J. (1974). *The pain and the great one.* New York: Bradbury.

Brown, M. (1954). *Cinderella.* New York: Scribner.

Burch, R. (1966). *Queenie Peavy.* New York: Viking.

Burch, R. (1980). *Ida Early comes over the mountain.* New York: Viking.

Byars, B. (1970). *The summer of the swans.* New York: Viking.

Byars, B. (1977). *The pinballs.* New York: Harper.

Dahl, R. (1961). *James and the giant peach.* New York: Knopf.

Dahl, R. (1978). *The enormous crocodile.* New York: Knopf.

Emig, J. (1977). Writing as a mode of learning. *College Composition and Communication, 28,* 122–128.

Fitzgerald, J. & Spiegel, D. L. (1983). Enhancing children's reading comprehension through instruction in narrative structure. *Journal of Reading Behavior, 15,* 1–17.

Fox, P. (1973). *The slave dancer.* New York: Bradbury.

Galdone, P. (1968). *Henny Penny.* New York: Seabury.

Galdone, P. (1973). *The little red hen.* New York: Seabury.

Galdone, P. (1974). *Little red riding hood.* New York: Seabury.

Galdone, P. (1975). *The gingerbread boy.* New York: Seabury.

Galdone, P. (1984). *The teeny-tiny woman.* New York: Clarion.

George, J. C. (1972). *Julie of the wolves.* New York: Harper and Row.

Golden, J. M. (1984). Children's concept of story in reading and writing. *The Reading Teacher, 37,* 578–584.

Gordon, C. J., & Braun, C. (1982). Story schemata: Metatextual aid to reading and writing. In J. A. Niles & L. A. Harris (Eds.), *New inquiries in reading: Research and instruction.* Rochester, NY: National Reading Conference.

Hoskisson, K., & Tompkins, G. E. (1987). *Language arts: Content and teaching strategies.* Columbus, OH: Merrill.

Konigsburg, E. L. (1983). *From the mixed up files of Mrs. Basil E. Frankweiler.* New York: Atheneum.

Lasky, K. (1983). *Beyond the divide.* New York: Macmillan.

Lawson, R. (1972). *Rabbit hill.* New York: Penguin.

L'Engle, M. (1962). *A wrinkle in time.* New York: Farrar.

Lewis, C. S. (1981). *The lion, the witch, and the wardrobe.* New York: Macmillan.

Lowry. L. (1979). *Anastasia Krupnik.* Boston: Houghton Mifflin.

Lukens, R. J. (1986). *A critical handbook of children's literature* (3rd ed.). Glenview, IL: Scott, Foresman.

Mandler, J. M., & Johnson, N. S. (1977). Remembrance of things parsed: Story structure and recall. *Cognitive Psychology, 9,* 111–115.

Martinez, M. & Roser, N. (1985). Read it again: The value of repeated readings during storytime. *The Reading Teacher, 38,* 782–786.

Mayer, M. (1987). *The pied piper of Hamelin.* New York: Macmillan.

McCloskey, R. (1969). *Make way for ducklings.* New York: Viking.

McConaughy, S. H. (1980). Using story structure in the classroom. *Language Arts, 57,* 157–165.

Morrow, L. M. (1982). Relationships between literature programs, library corner designs and children's use of literature. *Journal of Educational Research, 75,* 339–344.

Morrow, L. M. (1984). Effects of story retelling on young children's comprehension and sense of story structure. In J. A. Niles and L. A. Harris (Eds.), *Changing perspectives on research in reading/language processing and instruction* (pp. 96–100). Rochester, NY: National Reading Conference.

Morrow, L. M. (1985a). Reading and retelling stories: Strategies for emergent readers. *The Reading Teacher, 38,* 870–875.

Morrow, L. M. (1985b). Retelling stories: A strategy for improving young children's comprehension, concept of story structure, and oral language complexity. *Elementary School Journal, 85,* 647–661.

Morrow, L. M. (1986). Effects of structural guidance in story retellings on children's dictation of original stories. *Journal of Reading Behavior, 18,* 135–152.

Ness, E. (1966). *Sam, Bangs and moonshine.* New York: Holt.

O'Dell, S. (1960). *Island of the blue dolphins.* Boston: Houghton Mifflin.

Paterson, K. (1977). *Bridge to Terabithia.* New York: Crowell.

Pitcher, E. G., & Prelinger, E. (1963). *Children tell stories: An analysis of fantasy.* New York: International Universities Press.

Potter, B. (1902). *The tale of Peter Rabbit.* New York: Warne.

Rosen, H. (1986). The importance of story. *Language Arts, 63,* 226–237.

Rumelhart, D. (1975). Notes on a schema for stories. In D. G. Bobrow (Ed.), *Representation and understanding: Studies in cognitive science.* New York: Academic Press.

Sendak, M. (1963). *Where the wild things are.* New York: Harper and Row.

Speare, E. G. (1958). *Witch of Blackbird Pond.* Boston: Houghton Mifflin.

Spiegel, D. L. & Fitzgerald, J. (1986). Improving reading comprehension through instruction about story parts. *The Reading Teacher, 39,* 676–682.

Steig, W. (1982). *Doctor De Soto.* New York: Farrar.

Stein, N. L., & Glenn, C. G. (1979). An analysis of story comprehension in elementary school children. In R. O. Freedle (Ed.), *New Directions in Discourse Processing.* Norwood, NJ: Ablex.

Taylor, M. C. (1976). *Roll of thunder, hear my cry.* New York: Dial.

Tompkins, G. E., & McGee, L. M. (1989). In K. D. Muth (Ed.), *Children's comprehension of narrative and expository text: Research into practice, (pp. 59–78).* Newark, DE: International Reading Association.

Tompkins, G. E., & Webeler, M. B. (1983). What will happen next? Using predictable books with young children. *The Reading Teacher, 36,* 498–502.

Van Allsburg, C. (1981). *Jumanji.* Boston: Houghton Mifflin.

Viorst, J. (1977). *Alexander and the terrible, horrible, no good, very bad day.* New York: Atheneum.

Waber, B. (1972). *Ira sleeps over.* Boston: Houghton Mifflin.

White, E. B. (1952). *Charlotte's web.* New York: Harper and Row.

Zelinsky, P. O. (1986). *Rumpelstiltskin.* New York: Dutton.

Zemach, M. (1983). *The little red hen.* New York: Farrar.

5

Poetic Writing

"Hold your horses," says B.J. as he rushes to catch up with Josh who is walking down the hall from his fourth-grade classroom toward the cafeteria. "I can't! I can't," Josh responds, bending down and grunting as though he were trying to lift a heavy load. "They're too heavy. I can't hold them." Arm in arm, both boys laugh as they enter the cafeteria. These two students have been studying idioms, and their play with words doesn't stop at the classroom door.

B.J. and Josh's teacher, Mrs. Mayes, is teaching her fourth graders about idioms, words that have special figurative meanings. She begins by dropping some common idioms, such as "it's raining cats and dogs" and "I'm all ears," into her speech and commenting on her students' use of these everyday expressions. Then she shares Fred Gwynne's books of idioms, *The King Who Rained* (1970), *A Chocolate Moose for Dinner* (1976), *The Sixteen Hand Horse* (1980), and *A Little Pigeon Toad* (1988) as well as books of idioms her students have compiled in previous years. With this introduction, students begin to brainstorm a list of idioms on a large chart that they will add to over a 2-week period. Some students incorporate idioms into their journal entries and others simply choose idioms to explain in their journals. Next, each student chooses an idiom and designs a poster to illustrate the literal meaning of the phrase. A poster of "hold your horses" is presented in Figure 5-1. Later, Mrs. Mayes plans to have students make a class collaboration book of idioms.

Through these activities the fourth graders in Mrs. Mayes' class are playing with language, discriminating between literal and figurative meanings, and laughing with language. Too often children fear words; instead, they need to become wordsmiths, recognizing that words can be manipulated as easily as play-dough. Through playing with words, children learn that words have multiple meanings, invent new words, create word pictures, and play with rhyme. While these activities are not poetry, students gain a confidence and a flexibility in using words necessary when they write poetry.

A list of word play books that elementary students enjoy is presented in Figure 5-2.

The first section of this chapter will continue the discussion of word play activities. These types of activities provide experiences that children need to write poetry.

In the second section, five types of poems—formula poems, free-form poems, syllable- and word-count poems, rhymed verse poems, and model poems—will be described and sample poems written by elementary students will be shared. The instructional strategy for teaching children to write these five types of poems will be presented in the following section. The chapter concludes with information about poetic devices, such as alliteration and onomatopoeia, that students can incorporate in the poems they write.

FIGURE 5-1 A Fourth Grader's Idiom Poster

While elementary students who haven't been involved in writing poetry say that poetry is boring or too hard, it is important to remember that children are natural poets. Through their observations of children, the Opies (1959) have verified "that children have a natural affinity to verse songs, riddles, jokes, chants, and puns." Babies and preschoolers respond positively when their parents or other care-givers repeat Mother Goose rhymes, read A.A. Milne's Winnie-the-Pooh stories, and sing songs to them. Youngsters often create jump-rope rhymes and other ditties on the playground.

Sadly, many children seem to lose interest in poetry during the elementary grades. Poetry books sit unopened on library shelves and few children write poetry. However, students change their minds after they've written free-form poems with words collected through brainstorming and freewriting. They look at poetry in a new way after they've written short, two-word, rhyming hink-pinks that are similar to riddles, or concrete poems in which words and phrases are arranged to create a word-picture.

Through the activities presented in this chapter, students can gain confidence in their abilities as wordsmiths and word play will become a favorite activity.

Bancheck, L. (1976). *Snake in, snake out.* New York: Crowell. (M)

Barrett, J. (1983). *A snake is totally tail.* New York: Atheneum. (P–M)

Bayer, J. (1984). *A my name is Alice.* New York: Dial. (P–M)

Brown, M. (1983). *What do you call a dumb bunny? And other rabbit riddles, games, jokes, and cartoons.* Boston, Little, Brown. (P–M)

Cox, J. A. (1980). *Put your foot in your mouth and other silly sayings.* New York: Random House. (P–M)

Degen, B. (1983). *Jamberry.* New York: Harper and Row. (P)

Elting, M. & Folsom, M. (1980). *Q is for duck: An alphabet guessing game.* New York: Clarion. (P–M)

Esbensen, B. J. (1986). *Words with wrinkled knees.* New York: Crowell. (M–U)

Funk, C. E. (1948). *A hog on ice and other curious expressions.* New York: Harper and Row. (U)

Gwynne, F. (1970). *The king who rained.* New York: Dutton. (M–U)

Gwynne, F. (1976). *A chocolate moose for dinner.* New York: Dutton. (M–U)

Gwynne, F. (1980). *The sixteen hand horse.* New York: Prentice-Hall. (M–U)

Gwynne, F. (1988). *A little pigeon toad.* New York: Simon & Schuster. (M–U)

Hall, R. & Friends. *Sniglets for kids.* Yellow Springs, OH: Antioch. (M–U)

Hanson, J. (1972). *Homographs:* Bow *and* bow *and other words that look the same but sound as different as* sow *and* sow. Minneapolis: Lerner. (M)

Hanson, J. (1973). *Homographic homophones:* Fly *and* fly *and other words that look and sound the same but are as different in meaning as* bat *and* bat. Minneapolis: Lerner. (M)

P = primary grades (K–2)
M = middle grades (3–5)
U = upper grades (6–8)

FIGURE 5-2 Word Play Books

WORD PLAY

Learning the Meaning of Words

The meaning of words is crucial in word play. Many riddles, for instance, depend on words with multiple meanings. A familiar riddle asks, "How are children and fish alike?" and the answer is that "Both are in school." The word *school* is ambiguous, and understanding this riddle requires the the second meaning—a group of fish or aquatic animals traveling together—is known. While young children often assume a one-to-one relationship between words and their meanings, elementary students, as they gain more experience with language, learn that words have multiple meanings, that the sound of some words called homophones doesn't predict meaning, and that some words have both literal and figurative meanings. This ability to understand and even appreciate multiple meanings makes word play possible for children.

Houget, S. R. (1983). *I unpacked my grandmother's trunk: A picture book game.* New York: Dutton. (P–M)

Hunt, B. K. (1975). *Your ant is a which: Fun with homophones.* New York: Harcourt Brace Jovanovich. (P–M)

Juster, N. (1982). *Otter nonsense.* New York: Philomel. (P–M)

Kellogg, S. (1987). *Aster Aardvark's alphabet adventures.* New York: Morrow. (P–M)

Maestro, G. (1984). *What's a frank Frank? Tasty homograph riddles.* New York: Clarion. (P–M)

Perl, L. (1988). *Don't sing before breakfast, don't sing in the moonlight.* New York: Random House. (M–U)

Schwartz, A. (1973). *Tomfoolery: Trickery and foolery with words.* Philadelphia: Lippincott. (M–U)

Schwartz, A. (1982). *The cat's elbow and other secret languages.* New York: Farrar. (M–U)

Sterne, N. (1979). *Tyrannosaurus wrecks: A book of dinosaur riddles.* New York: Crowell. (M)

Tallon, R. (1979). *Zoophabets.* New York: Scholastic. (P–M)

Terban, M. (1982). *Eight ate: A feast of homonym riddles.* New York: Clarion. (P–M)

Terban, M. (1983). *In a pickle and other funny idioms.* New York: Clarion. (M)

Terban, M. (1985). *Too hot to hoot: Funny palindrome riddles.* New York: Clarion (M–U)

Tobias, H. & Baskin, L. (1972). *Hosie's alphabet.* New York: Viking. (M–U)

Van Allsburg, C. (1987). *The z was zapped.* Boston: Houghton Mifflin. (M)

Zalben, J. B. (1977). *Lewis Carroll's jabberwocky.* New York: Warne. (M–U)

FIGURE 5-2   (continued)

Words with Multiple Meanings.   One of the concepts that students learn about words during the elementary grades is that words have more than one meaning. The word *bank,* for example, may refer to:

- a piled-up mass of snow or clouds
- the slope of land beside a lake or river
- the slope of a road on a turn
- the lateral tilting of an airplane in a turn
- to cover a fire with ashes for slow burning
- a business establishment that receives and lends money
- a container in which money is saved
- a supply for use in emergencies (e.g., blood bank)
- a place of storage (e.g., computer's memory bank)
- to count on
- similar things arranged in a row (e.g., a bank of elevators)
- to arrange things in a row

You may be surprised that there are at least 12 meanings for the common word *bank*. Why does this happen? The meanings of *bank* in this example come from three different sources. The first five meanings came from an old Norse (or Viking) word, and you will note that they are related, all dealing with something slanted or making a slanted motion. Meanings 6 through 10 come from the Italian word *banca*, which originally meant a money changer's table. These meanings deal with financial banking except the 10th meaning, to count on, which requires a bit more thought. We use the saying "to bank on" figuratively to mean "to depend on," but it began more literally, from the actual counting of money on a table. The 11th and 12th meanings came from the Old French word *banc*, meaning "a bench." Words acquired multiple meanings as society became more complex and finer shades of meaning were necessary. For example, the 9th and 10th meanings of bank, "an emergency supply" and "a storage place" are fairly new. As with many words with multiple meanings, it is a linguistic accident that three original words from three languages with their related meanings came to be spelled the same way.

Words assume additional meanings when an affix is added or they are compounded (used together with another word). Consider the word *night,* and the variety of words and phrases that incorporate *night: night blindness, nightcap, nightclub, night crawler, nightfall, nightgown, nightingale, nightlife, nightly, nightmare, night owl, night school, nightstick,* and *nighttime.* Students can compile a list of these words or make a booklet illustrating the words. Figure 5-3 presents a list of more than 100 *down* words that a sixth grade class compiled.

Homophones. *Homophones* are words that sound alike but are spelled differently, such as *fairy* and *ferry.* In most cases, these homophones happen by chance; they develop from entirely different root words and even from words in two different languages (Tompkins & Yaden, 1986). In contrast, other homophones such as *flower* and *flour* and *flea* and *flee* are related etymologically; the first word in each pair is derived from the second. Homophones and other homonyms are confusing to kids because some sound alike and others are spelled alike or differ only by one letter.

As was true with the unit on idioms described at the beginning of this section, students can learn about homophones by noticing these words in their environment, reading books that play with homophones, and then making their own books in which students draw pictures to illustrate pairs of homophones and use the pairs of confusing words in sentences. A sample page from a second grader's homophone book is presented in Figure 5-4.

Idioms. Because *idioms* are figurative sayings, many children have difficulty learning them. Through the activities presented at the beginning of this section, children can move beyond the literal meanings of words, learning flexibility in using language.

FIGURE 5-3   A Sixth-Grade Class Collaboration List of "Down" Words

downtown	climb down	reach down	downward
touchdown	down payment	write down	hunt down
get down	sit down	settle down	knock down
chow down	throw down	down it	breakdown
shake down	cut down	goose down	sundown
squat down	downhill	hop down	fall down
showdown	low down	hands down	tear down
lie down	slow down	downfall	turn down
quiet down	down right	close down	push down
shut down	beam down	run down	downstairs
shot down	downy	pin down	look down
cool down	downer	come down	inside down
crackdown	downslope	slam down	zip down
countdown	kickdown	slap down	pour down
pass down	stare down	hoe down	down pour
pass me down	boogy down	lock down	tape down
burn down	put down	water down	downgrade
downbeat	wrestle down	downturn	downstream
down to earth	flop down	stuff down	mow down
shimmey down	hung down	downcast	downhearted
downtrodden	chase down	hurl down	beat down

Creating New Words[1]

New words continually appear in English, many created to describe new inventions and scientific projects. Some of the newest words come from computer science and the space program. They are created in a variety of ways, including compounding, adding affixes, coining, and clipping.

Compounding. *Compounding* means combining two existing words to create a new word. *Friendship* and *childhood* are two examples of words that were compounded by the Anglo-Saxons more than a thousand years ago. More recently created ones include *body language* and *software.* Compound words usually progress through three stages. They begin as separate words (e.g., *ice cream*), later are hyphenated (e.g., *baby-sit*), and finally are written as one word (e.g., *splashdown*). There are many exceptions to this rule, such as the compound words *post office* and *high school,* which have remained separate words. Other compound words use Greek and Latin elements. Scientific terms, such as *stethoscope* and *television,* were developed this way.

Adding Affixes. Vocabulary is created by adding prefixes and suffixes to existing words. For example, *pre-,* a Latin prefix meaning "before or in front of" was used

[1]Adapted from Tompkins & Yaden, 1986.

in creating these words: *precinct, prehistoric, preview, premonition,* and *pre-school.* Prefixes and suffixes used in English words come from English, Latin, and Greek. Children in the upper elementary grades typically study prefixes and suffixes, and to add word play, students can create new words using affixes. The students in one fifth-grade class coined the word *precess* for the recess before school. They used the word this way: "Do we have outside precess today?"

Coining. Creative people have always coined new words. Lewis Carroll, author of *Alice in Wonderland* and *Through the Looking Glass,* is perhaps the best-known inventor of words. He called his new words *portmanteau words,* borrowing from the British word for a suitcase that opens into two halves because his new words were created by blending two words into one. His best-known example, *chortle,* a blend of *snort* and *chuckle,* is from the poem "Jabberwocky." Jan Breskin Zalben's beautifully illustrated picturebook version of *Jabberwocky* (1977) is very popular with elementary students. Other examples of blended words include *brunch* (*breakfast* and *lunch*), *electrocute* (*electric* and *execute*), *guesstimate* (*guess* and *estimate*), and *smog* (*smoke* and *fog*).

Trademarks and Acronyms. Two other types of coined words are trademarks and acronyms. Examples of well-known trademarks and brand names include

FIGURE 5-4 A Page from a Second Grader's Homophone Book

Kleenex, Coca-Cola, Xerox, and *nylon.* Nylon, for instance, was invented by scientists working in New York and London, and they named their product by combining *ny,* the abbreviation for New York, with *lon,* the first three letters of London. *Acronyms,* words formed by combining the initial letters of several words, include *radar, laser,* and *scuba.* For example, *scuba* was formed by combining the initial letters of *self-contained underwater breathing apparatus.*

Clipping. *Clipping* is a process of shortening existing words. For instance, *zoo* is the shortened form of *zoological park* and *pants* comes from *pantaloons.* Most clipped words are only one syllable long and are used in informal conversation. For example, children may shorten a favorite teacher's name from Mrs. Edison to Mrs. E.

While it is unlikely that students in your class will create new words that will be added to the dictionary, students do create words to add pizzazz to their writing, and some terms created to fill a particular need may become part of the everyday jargon in your classroom. For example, a group of third graders created the word *crocket* (*croc* + *ket*) to describe the crocodile who became a rocket at the end of Roald Dahl's *The Enormous Crocodile* (1978).

Authors also create new words in the stories they write, and students should be alert to the possibility of finding a created word as they read or as they listen to stories read aloud. Adrienne Adams used *woggle* in *A Woggle of Witches* (1971), and Elinor Horwitz described the night as *bimulous* in *When the Sky is Like Lace* (1975).

A group of first graders created an ABC dinosaur book in which they created and described a mythical dinosaur beginning with each letter of the alphabet. Figure 5-5 presents the "D" page from the book, introducing a new plant-eater named the *Dandelionsaurus.* Taking words and word parts and combining them in new ways is fun for children who don't feel restricted to using words that have been already created.

Sniglets. A *sniglet* is a word that isn't in the dictionary, but should be. Once example is *beavo,* a pencil covered with teeth marks (Hall, 1985). This type of word play was created by Rich Hall on HBO's "Not Necessarily the News," and several books of sniglets have been published, including one especially for children, *Sniglets for Kids* (Hall, 1985). Elementary students enjoy reading these books and creating their own words. To create a sniglet, they use compounding, adding affixes, coining, and clipping. The sniglet *tappee,* created by a fifth grader, is presented in Figure 5-6. In this word, the student used the Latin suffix *-ee,* meaning "one who."

Laughing with Language

As children learn that words have the power to amuse, they enjoy reading, telling, and writing riddles and jokes. Linda Gibson Geller (1985) has researched children's humorous language and identified two stages of riddle play that elementary students move through. Primary grade children experiment with the riddle

Dandelionsaurus

He weighs 400000 pounds. And he likes to eat dandelions. He is very very strong. And he is the bigget plant eater on earth and the stronget to.

The end.

FIGURE 5-5 A Page from a First Grader's ABC Dinosaur Book

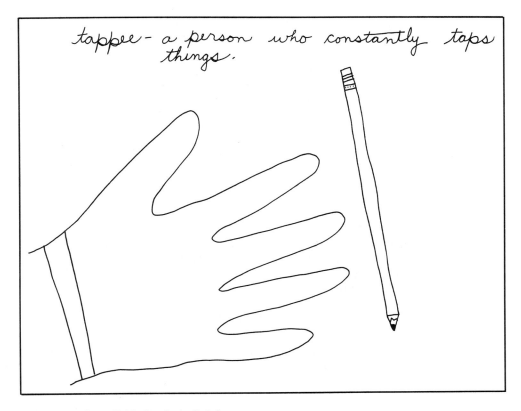

tappee — a person who constantly taps things.

FIGURE 5-6   A Fifth Grader's Sniglet

form and its content while middle and upper grade students explore the paradox-ical constructions in riddles. Riddles are written in a question-answer format, but at first young children may only ask questions or ask questions and offer unre-lated answers. With more experience, students provide both questions and re-lated answers, and their answers may be either descriptive or nonsensical. An example of the descriptive answer to the question *Why did the turtle go out of his shell?* is *Because he was getting too big for it.* An example of a nonsensical an-swer involving an invented word for the riddle *Why did the cat want to catch a snake?* is *Because he wanted to turn into a rattlecat* (Geller, 1981, p. 672). Many primary grade students' riddles seem foolish by adult standards, but this word play is an important precursor to creating true riddles.

Riddles depend on manipulating words with multiple meanings or similar sounds and using metaphors. The Opies (1959) identified five riddle strategies used by elementary students:

1. Using multiple referents for a noun: What has an eye but cannot see? (A needle).

2. Combining literal and figurative interpretations for a single phrase: Why did the moron throw the clock out the window? (Because he wanted to see time fly).
3. Shifting word boundaries to suggest another meaning: Why did the cookie cry? (Because its mother was a wafer/away for so long).
4. Separating a word into syllables to suggest another meaning: When is a door not a door? (When it's ajar/a jar).
5. Creating a metaphor: What are polka dots on your face? (Pimples).

Children begin riddle play by telling familiar riddles and reading riddles written by others. Several excellent books of riddles to share with elementary students are Noelle Sterne's *Tyrannosaurus Wrecks: A Book of Dinosaur Riddles* (1979), *What Do You Call a Dumb Bunny? And Other Rabbit Riddles, Games, Jokes, and Cartoons* by Marc Brown (1983), and Marvin Terban's *Eight Ate: A Feast of Homonym Riddles* (1982). Soon children are composing their own riddles by adapting riddles they have read and creating new ones. Others take jokes and turn them into riddles. An excellent book for helping children write riddles is *Fiddle with a Riddle: Write Your Own Riddles* by Joanne E. Bernstein (1979).

Larissa, a third grader, wrote this riddle using two meanings for Milky Way: *Why did the astronaut go to the Milky Way? Because he wanted a Milky Way Bar.* Terry, a fifth grader, wrote this riddle using the homophones *hair* and *hare: What is gray and jumpy and on your head? A gray hare!* The juxtaposition of words is important in many jokes and riddles. A sixth grader created the humorous cartoon presented in Figure 5-7, and this cartoon is funny because of the switch in word order from *sidekick* to *kick in the side.*

Creating Word Pictures

In the primary grades, children learn to place words in horizontal lines from left-to-right and top-to-bottom across a sheet of paper just as the lines on this page are printed; however, they can break this pattern and create word pictures by placing words as they would draw lines in a drawing. These word-pictures can be single-word pictures or a string of words or a sentence arranged in a picture. Four types of concrete word-pictures are described below and examples are presented in Figure 5-8.

Using Words to Draw a Picture. Children use words instead of lines to draw a picture as the *lamb, rabbit,* and *television* in Figure 5-8 illustrate. In these word pictures, the children first drew the picture using lines and then placed a second sheet of paper over the drawing and replaced all or most of the lines with repeated words.

Writing a Word to Illustrate Its Meaning. Students write descriptive words such as *falling, bite,* and *disappear* so that the arrangement, size, and intensity of the letters in the word illustrate the meaning. The words *explode* and *nervous* are written pictorially in Figure 5-8. Students might write the names of objects and ani-

FIGURE 5-7 A Sixth Grader's Word Play Cartoon

mals, such as *bird* and *cacti,* so that features of the item being named are illustrated in the name.

Writing Sentences to Create Word Pictures. Students can compose a descriptive phrase, sentence, or paragraph and write it in the shape of an object. A heart, pizza, and ice cream cone are presented in Figure 5-8. An asterisk indicates where to start reading each word picture.

Representing Words and Sayings in Pictures. In a more sophisticated form of word pictures, students can illustrate or represent a word or idiom with a picture. In Figure 5-8, the word *broken-hearted* is represented with a heart splitting in two and the saying *face the music* is represented by a face with a musical score in place of a mouth.

Playing with Rhyme

Through their experience with Dr. Seuss stories, fingerplays, and nursery rhymes, kindergartners and first graders enjoy creating rhymes. Unfortunately many children equate rhyme with poetry, and often their dependence on rhyme thwarts their attempts to write poetry. Nonetheless, rhyme is a special kind of word play, and one that children enjoy. A small group of first graders created their own version of *Oh, A-hunting We Will Go* (Langstaff, 1974). After reading the book, they identified the refrain (lines 1, 2, and 5) and added their own rhyming couplets. For example:

Oh, a-hunting we will go,
a-hunting we will go.
We'll catch a little bear
and curl his hair,
and never let him go.

Oh, a-hunting we will go,
a-hunting we will go.
We'll catch a little mole
and put him in a hole,
and never let him go.

FIGURE 5-8 Examples of Students' Word Pictures

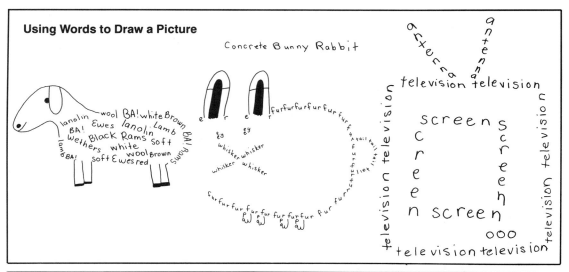

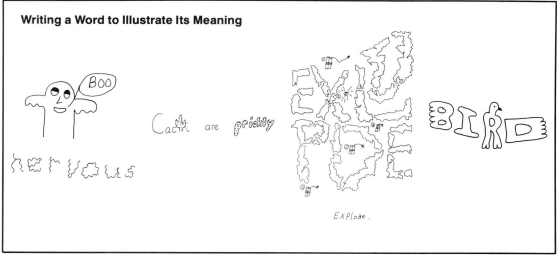

FIGURE 5-8 (continued)

Writing Sentences to Create Word Pictures

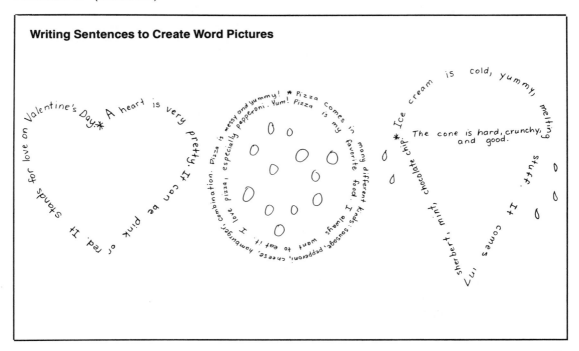

Representing Words and Sayings in Pictures

heart broken

face the music

Oh, a-hunting we will go,
a-hunting we will go.
We'll catch a little snake
and hit him with a rake,
and never let him go.

Oh, a-hunting we will go,
a-hunting we will go.
We'll catch a little bug
and give him a big hug
and never let him go.

Oh, a-hunting we will go,
a-hunting we will go.
We'll catch a little bunny
and fill her full of honey,
and never let her go.

Oh, we'll put them in a ring
and listen to them sing
and then we'll let them go.

The first graders wrote this collaboration with the teacher taking dictation on a large chart. After the rough draft was written, students reread it, checking the rhymes and changing a word here or there. Then each student chose one stanza to copy and illustrate. The pages were collected and compiled to make a book. Children shared the book with their classmates, with each student reading his or her "own" page.

Hink-pinks. Hink-pinks are short poems that either take the form of an answer to a riddle or describe something. Hink-pinks are composed with 2, one-syllable rhyming words, but they are hinky-pinkies when 2, two-syllable words are used, and hinkity-pinkities with 2, three-syllable words (Geller, 1981). Examples of these rhymes written by upper grade students include:

Gas Station
Car
Bar
Rachel, grade 7

What do you call an astronaut?
A sky guy
Tara, grade 6

POETIC FORMS

On St. Patrick's Day, Mrs. Garner hangs a large sheet of green paper on the wall and asks her second graders to help write a poem about the color green. The children eagerly suggest things that are green: caterpillars, apples, grasshoppers, frogs, leprechauns, alligators, aliens, and so on. Then Mrs. Garner explains that the list will become a poem, and while the children are skeptical, she chooses one of the items in the brainstormed list and writes: *Green is aliens from outer space.* Quickly Naomi suggests another line: *Green is the paper you're writing on for St. Patrick's Day.* Other children grasp the pattern and suggest additional lines for the poem. Mrs. Garner reads the poem in a dramatic voice, lengthening some words, softening others, but she ends the list abruptly. Spontaneously, Antoine adds: *And that's what is green!* The children clap their hands as Mrs. Garner adds the line to complete their green poem:

Too Much Green
Green is aliens from outer space.
Green is the paper you're writing on for St. Patrick's Day.
Green is a caterpillar climbing up the trunk of a tree.
Green is an inchworm measuring.
Green is a green hairdo.
Green is a fierce alligator.
Green is a shiny apple.
Green is kool-aid that you drink.
Green is a leaping grasshopper.
Green is a hopping frog.
Green is the grass that a leprechaun steps on.
And that's what is green!

Elementary students can successfully write poetry using poetic formulas. They can write formula poems by beginning each line with particular words (such as color poems), counting syllables for haiku, or creating word pictures in concrete poems. Because poems are written quickly and guidelines are provided, children can use the writing process to revise, edit, and share their writing without a time-consuming process of making changes, correcting errors, and recopying. Poetry also allows students more freedom in how they use the mechanics of writing—punctuation, capitalization, and page arrangement.

Many types of poetry that children write do not use rhyme. Rhyme is the sticking point for many would-be poets. In searching for a rhyming word, children often create inane verse such as:

I see a funny little goat
Wearing a blue sailor's coat
Sitting in an old motorboat.

This is not to suggest that children should not be allowed to write rhyming poetry, but rhyme should never be imposed as a criterion for acceptable poetry. Children may use rhyme when it fits naturally into their writing. As children write poetry during the elementary grades, they are searching for their own voices, and they need freedom to do that. Freed from the pressure to create rhyming poetry or other constraints, children create sensitive word pictures, vivid images, and unique comparisons in their poems, as the poems presented throughout this chapter illustrate.

Five types of poetic forms are presented in this section: formula poems, free-form poems, syllable- and word-count poems, rhymed poems, and model poems. Elementary students' poems illustrate each poetic form and additional examples are presented in Appendix A at the end of the book. The additional examples are included to provide model poems written by students in the primary, middle, and upper grades to use when teaching these poetic forms. The poems written by kindergartners and first graders may seem little more than lists of sentences compared to the more sophisticated poems written by older students. The range of poems, however, effectively shows how elementary and middle grade students grow in their ability to write poetry through these writing activities.

Formula Poems

These poetic forms may seem like recipes to be followed rigidly, but that is not how they are intended. Rather, they provide a scaffold, organization, or skeleton for students' poems. After collecting words, images, and comparisons through brainstorming, clustering, freewriting, or another prewriting strategy, students craft their poems, choosing words and arranging them to create a message. Meaning is always most important; form follows the search for meaning. Perhaps a better description is that children "dig for poems" (Valentine, 1986) through words, ideas, poetic forms, rhyme, rhythm, and conventions. Poet Kenneth Koch (1970) worked with students in the elementary grades and developed some simple formulas that make it easy for nearly every child to become a successful poet. Some of these forms may seem more like sentences than poems, but the dividing line between poetry and prose is blurry, and these poetry experiences help direct children toward poetic expression. Koch suggests a structure in which children begin every line the same way or insert a particular kind of word in every line. This structure involves the use of repetition, a stylistic device that can be much more effective for young poets than rhyme.

These poetic formulas provide a structure that is easy for students to follow and fun to do. Many teachers are at first skeptical about the effectiveness of formula poems. However, after they introduce their students to them, they often report that these poetry writing activities are among the most successful writing experiences their students have ever participated in.

"I wish . . ." Poems. Children begin each line of their poems with the words "I wish" and then complete the line with a wish (Koch, 1970). In this second-grade class collaboration, children simply listed their wishes:

Our Wishes
I wish I had all the money in the world.
I wish I was a star fallen down from Mars.
I wish I were a butterfly.
I wish I were a teddy bear.
I wish I had a cat.
I wish I were a pink rose.
I wish it wouldn't rain today.
I wish I didn't have to wash a dish.
I wish I had a flying carpet.
I wish I could go to Disney World.
I wish school was out.
I wish I could go outside and play.

After this first experience, students choose one of their wishes and expand on the idea in several more lines. Seven-year-old Brandi chose her wish, "I wish I were a teddy bear," and wrote:

I Wish

I wish I were a teddy bear
Who sat on a beautiful bed
Who got a hug every night
By a little girl or boy.
Maybe tonight I'll get my wish
And wake up on a little girl's bed
And then I'll be as happy as can be.

Color Poems. Students begin each line of their poems with a color. The same color may be repeated in each line, or a different color may be used (Koch, 1970). For example, second-grade Cheyenne describes yellow in this color poem:

Yellow

Yellow is bright,
Yellow is light.
Yellow glows in the dark,
Yellow likes to lark.
Yellow is an autumn tree,
Yellow is giving to you and me.

In her poem, Cheyenne uses rhyming words effectively, and in searching for a rhyming word for *dark,* she creates a particularly powerful line, "Yellow likes to lark." Older students, like seventh-grade Nancy in the following poem "Black," expand each of their ideas into a stanza:

Black

Black is a deep hole
sitting in the ground
waiting for animals
that live inside.

Black is a beautiful horse
standing on a high hill
with the wind
swirling its mane.

Black is a winter night sky
without stars
to keep it
company.

> Black is a panther
> creeping around a jungle
> searching for
> its prey.

Mary O'Neill's book of color poems, *Hailstones and Halibut Bones: Adventures in Color* (1961) may also be shared with students; however, O'Neill uses rhyme as an important poetic device, and it is important to emphasize that students' poems need not rhyme.

Writing color poems can be coordinated with teaching young children to read and write the color words. Instead of having kindergartners and first graders read color words on worksheets and then color pictures with the designated colors, students can create color poems in booklets of paper stapled together. They write and illustrate one line of the poem on each page.

Five Senses Poems. Children write about a topic by describing it with each of the five senses. These poems are usually five lines long, with one line for each sense, as the following poem written by a seventh grader demonstrates:

> Winter
> Winter smells like chimney smoke.
> Winter tastes like ice.
> Winter looks like heaven.
> Winter feels like a deepfreeze.
> Winter sounds like a howling wolf.

Sometimes students add an additional line at the beginning or at the end of a poem, as sixth-grade Amy did in this Valentine's Day poem:

> Valentine's Day
> Smells like chocolate candy
> Looks like a flower garden
> Tastes like sugar
> Feels like silk
> Sounds like a symphony orchestra
> Too bad it comes only once a year!

It is often helpful to have students develop a five senses cluster and collect ideas for each sense. From the cluster, students select the most vivid or strongest idea for each sense to use in a line of the poem.

"If I were . . ." Poems. Children write about how they would feel and what they would do if they were something else—a Tyrannosaurus Rex, a hamburger, or the sunshine (Koch, 1970). They begin each poem with "If I were" and tell what it would be like to be that thing. For example, 8-year-old Jeff writes about what he would do if he were a giant:

> If I were a giant
> I would drink up the seas
> And I would touch the sun.
> I would eat the world
> And stick my head in space.

Students use personification in composing "If I were . . ." poems, explore ideas and feelings, and consider the world from a different vantage point.

"I used to . . . /But now . . ." Poems. In these contrast poems, students begin the first line (and every odd-numbered line) with "I used to" and the second line (and every even-numbered line) with "But now" (Koch, 1970). Using this formula, students can explore ways in which they have changed as well as how things change. Eighth-grade Sondra writes from the point of view of piece of gold ore:

> I used to be a hunk of gold sitting in
> A mine having no worries
> Or responsibilities.
> Now I'm a wedding band bonding
> Two people together, with all
> The worries in the world.

A third-grade teacher adapted this formula for her social studies class, and her students wrote a class collaboration "I used to think . . . /But now I know . . ." poem using the information they had learned during a unit on the Plains Indians. Here is their poem:

> But Now I Know about the Plains Indians
> I used to think that Indians always wore beads,
> but now I know they didn't until the white men came.
> I used to think that Indians used pouches to carry their babies,
> but now I know that they used cradle boards, too.
> I used to think that Indians didn't paint their teepees,
> but now I know that they did.
> I used to think that one chief ruled all the tribes,
> but now I know that there are different chiefs for each tribe.
> I used to think that Indians had guns,
> but now I know that Indians didn't before the white men came.
> I used to think that Indians burned wood,
> but now I know they burned buffalo chips.
> I used to think that Indians caught their horses,
> but now I know they got them from the Spaniards.

Lie Poems. Children write a poem in which nothing is true or with a lie in each line (Koch, 1970). It is important to explain that these "lies" are imaginary or make-believe, such as "I live on Pluto," rather than a real lie, such as whether or not a child has set the table for dinner. A group of fifth graders collaborated on this lie poem:

> I am an owl who sleeps during the night
> and is awake all day.
> My favorite food is fuzzy caterpillar knees
> and I eat a gallon of them every day.
> My home is in a cabin
> at the top of Mt. Everest.
> I get younger as I get older
> and when I'm 50, I'll be a owlet.
> I can fly across the Atlantic Ocean
> in five minutes or maybe less.
> I talk a secret language
> that only kids and owls understand.

Lie poems are more appropriate for older students who understand the difference between lies they aren't supposed to tell and the imaginary lies in these poems.

"_____ is" Poems. In these description or definition poems, students describe what something is or what something or someone means to them. To begin, the teacher or students identify a topic to fill-in the blank, such as *anger, a friend, liberty,* or *fear.* Then students start each line with "_____ is" and describe or define that thing. Ryan, a sixth grader, wrote the following poem in which he described fear:

> Fear is not knowing what's around the next corner.
> Fear is strange noises scratching on my window at night.
> Fear is a cold hand touching you in an old, dusty hallway.
> Fear is being in a jet that's losing altitude at 50,000 feet.
> Fear is the earth blowing up.

Ryan evoked strong, concrete images of fear in his poem, and students often write very powerful poems using this formula when they move beyond "Happiness is . . . " and "Love is. . . . "

Preposition Poems. Students begin each line of preposition poems with a preposition, and a delightful poetic rewording of lines often results as children attempt to place a preposition at the beginning of each line. A fourth grader wrote this preposition poem about a race with a friend:

> We Ran Forever
> About noon one day
> Along came my friend
> To say, "Want to go for a run?"
> Below the stairs my mom said, "Go!"

> Without waiting, I flew out the door,
> Down the steps,
> Across the lawn, and
> Past the world we ran, forever.

It is helpful for children to brainstorm a list of prepositions to refer to when they write preposition poems. As they write, students may find that they need to drop the formula for a line or two to give the content of their poems top priority or they may mistakenly begin a line with an infinitive verb (e.g., *to say*) rather than a preposition, as was done in the "We Ran Forever" poem. The forms presented in this section provide a structure or skeleton for students' writing that should be adapted as needed.

Free-form Poems

In *free-form* poems, children put words and phrases together to express a thought or tell a story without concern for rhyme or other arrangements. The number of words on a line and use of punctuation varies. In the following poem "Loneliness," eighth-grade Bobby poignantly describes his topic concisely, using only 15 well-chosen words:

> Loneliness
> A lifetime
> Of broken dreams
> And promises
> Lost love
> Hurt
> My heart
> Cries
> In silence

In contrast, Don, a sixth grader, writes a humorous free-form poem about misplaced homework:

> Excuse for Not Having Homework
> Oh no, my English homework
> Cannot be found—
> Nor my science book.
> Did my dog eat it?
> Or maybe I dropped my mitt on it.
> Possibly, Martians took it away,
> Or it fell deep down in the hay.
> Maybe it's lost or shut in the door.
> Oh no, I broke my rule—
> I forgot and left it at school!

Students can use one of several methods for writing free-form poems. First, they can select words and phrases from brainstormed lists and clusters they have written and compile them to create a free-form poem. As an alternative, they write a paragraph and then "unwrite" to create the poem by deleting unnecessary words. The remaining words are arranged to look like a poem. Eighth-grade Craig wrote his poem this way:

A Step Back in Time
It is late evening
On a river bank.
The sky has clouds
That seem to be moving
Towards the moon.
The only light is my lantern,
Which gives enough glare to see
A few feet in front of me.
Several sounds are heard
In the distance: an owl
Hooting in the trees,
A deer crossing the river.
Life overflows around me
Like many different colored bugs.
The wind is chilly,
Making the large pines dance.
The sand is damp.
It's like the beginning of time,
Before man existed,
Just animals and plants.

Concrete Poems. Students create concrete poems by arranging words on a page and by combining art and writing. Words, phrases, and sentences can be written in the shape of an object, or word pictures can be inserted within poems that are written left-to-right and top-to-bottom on a sheet of paper. These concrete poems are extensions of the word pictures discussed in the section on "Word Play." Three examples of concrete poems are presented in Figure 5-9. In the "Washington Monument" poem, fourth graders brainstormed a list of facts about the monument and then combined their ideas to form the sentence that was written in the shape of the Washington, DC landmark. In the "Key" and "Lightbulb" poems, seventh graders used the same approach to create their concrete poems. Several books of concrete poems that will give students ideas for their poems include *Concrete is Not Always Hard* (Pilon, 1972), *Seeing Things* (Froman, 1974), and *Walking Talking Words* (Sherman, 1980).

Found Poems. Students create poems by culling words from other sources, such as newspaper articles, songs, and stories. Seventh-grade Eric found this poem in an article about racecar driver Richard Petty:

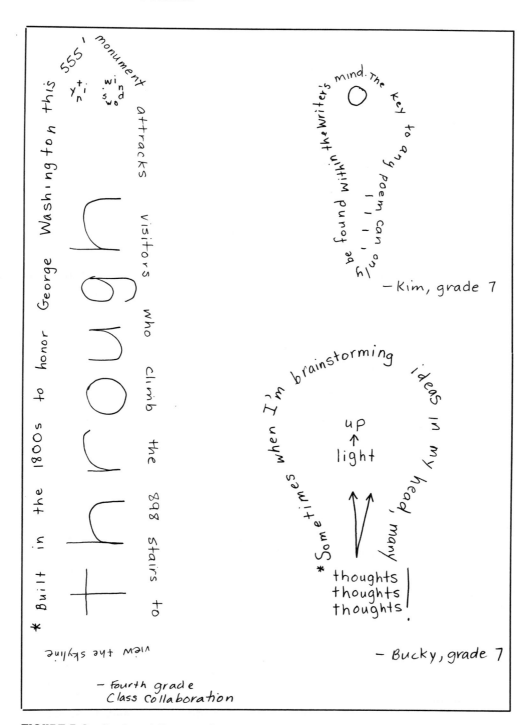

FIGURE 5-9 Students' Concrete Poems

Fast Moving
Moving down the track,
faster than fast, is Richard Petty
seven-time winner of
the crowned jewel
Daytona 500.
At 210 mph—dangerous—
pushing his engine to the limit.
Other NASCARs running fast
but Richard Petty takes the lead
at last.
Running across the line
with good time.

Eric developed his poem by circling powerful words and phrases in the 33-line newspaper article and then writing the words in a poetic arrangement. After reading over the draft, he deleted two words and added three other words not included in the newspaper article that were needed for transitions in the poem. By writing found poems, students have the opportunity to manipulate words and sentence structures they don't write themselves.

Syllable- and Word-count Poems

Haiku and other syllable- and word-count poems provide a structure that helps students succeed in writing; however, the need to adhere to the formula in these poems may restrict students' freedom of expression. In other words, the structure of these poems may both help and hinder students. The exact syllable counts force students to search for just the right words to express their ideas and feelings and provide a valuable opportunity for students to use a thesaurus and dictionary.

Haiku. The best known syllable-counting poem is *haiku* (high KOO), a Japanese poetic form consisting of 17 syllables arranged in 3 lines, 5–7–5. Haiku poems deal with nature and present a single clear image. It is a concise form, much like a telegram. Ten-year-old Shawn wrote this haiku poem about the feeling of mud swishing between his toes:

The mud feels slimy
As it splashes through my toes
Making them vanish.

Books of haiku poems to share with students include *My Own Rhythm: An Approach to Haiku* (Atwood, 1973), *Haiku: The Mood of the Earth* (Atwood, 1971), *In a Spring Garden* (Lewis, 1965), *Cricket Songs* (Behn, 1964), and *More Cricket Songs* (Behn, 1971). The photographs and art work used in these tradebooks may provide students with ideas for illustrating their haiku poems. Richard Lewis (1968, 1970) has written about the lives of two of the greatest Japanese haiku poets, Issa and Basho. He provides biographical information as well as a collection of poems in these books.

Tanka. *Tanka* (TANK ah) is a Japanese verse form containing 31 syllables arranged in 5 lines, 5–7–5–7–7. This form is very similar to haiku except that two additional lines of 7 syllables each are added to the haiku form. Quenton, age 14, wrote this tanka poem about spring that was published in his middle school anthology:

> Trees are budding out;
> Grass is sprouting everywhere
> Birds chirping again,
> They are signs of happiness
> Spring is coming once again.

Students may "unwrite" parts of their poems, if the lines are too long, by deleting one or more words. For example, in the spring poem, if the fourth line had been too long, Quenton could have unwritten *They are* and shortened it to *signs of happiness.*

Cinquain. A *cinquain* (SIN cane) is a 5-line poem containing 22 syllables in a 2–4–6–8–2 syllable pattern. Cinquain poems usually describe something but they may also tell a story. Encourage students to search for words and phrases that are precise, vivid, and sensual. Have students ask themselves what their subject looks like, smells like, sounds like, and tastes like and record their ideas using a five senses cluster. The formula is:

Line 1: a one-word subject with two syllables

Line 2: four syllables describing the subject

Line 3: six syllables showing action

Line 4: four syllables expressing a feeling or observation about the subject

Line 5: two syllables describing and renaming the subject

This cinquain poem was written by sixth-grade Kevin:

> Wrestling
> skinny, fat
> coaching, arguing, pinning
> trying hard to win
> tournament

If you compare Kevin's poem to the cinquain formula, you'll notice that some lines are short a syllable or two. Kevin bent some of the guidelines in choosing words to create a powerful image of wrestling. The message of the poem is always more important than adhering to the formula.

An alternative cinquain form contains five lines but does not follow the syllable count. Instead, each line contains a specified number of words rather than syllables. Thus, the first line contains a one-word title, the second line has two words that describe the title, the third line has three words that express action, the fourth line has four words that express feelings, and the fifth line contains a two-word synonym for the title.

Diamante. Iris Tiedt (1970) invented the *diamante* (dee ah MAHN tay), a seven-line contrast poem written in the shape of a diamond. In this poetic form, students apply their knowledge of opposites and parts of speech. The formula is:

Line 1: one noun as the subject

Line 2: two adjectives describing the subject

Line 3: three participles (ending in -*ing*) telling about the subject

Line 4: four nouns (the first two related to the subject and the second two related to the opposite)

Line 5: three participles telling about the opposite

Line 6: two adjectives describing the opposite

Line 7: one noun that is the opposite of the subject

When the poem is written, it is arranged in a diamond shape:

```
                     noun
            adjective      adjective
      participle    participle    participle
noun        noun         noun         noun
      participle    participle    participle
            adjective      adjective
                     noun
```

Sixth-grade Shelley wrote the following diamante poem about heaven and hell:

```
                    HEAVEN
                  happy, love
          laughing, hunting, everlasting
    pearly gates, Zion, Satan, netherworld
             burning, blazing, yelling
                   pain, fire
                     HELL
```

Notice that Shelley created a contrast between *heaven,* the subject represented by the noun in the first line, and *hell,* the opposite in the last line. Creating the contrast gives students the opportunity to play with words and extend their understanding of opposites. The third word *Satan* in the fourth line begins the transition from *heaven* to its opposite, *hell.*

Rhymed Verse Forms

Several rhymed verse forms such as limericks and clerihews can be used effectively with middle and upper grade students. In using these forms, it is important that teachers try to prevent these forms and rhyme schemes from restricting students' creative and imaginative expression.

Limericks. The *limerick* is a form of light verse that uses both rhyme and rhythm. The poem consists of five lines, and the first, second, and fifth lines rhyme, while the third and fourth lines rhyme with each other and are shorter than the other three lines. The rhyme scheme is a–a–b–b–a, and a limerick is arranged this way:

Line		Rhyme
1	_____	a
2	_____	a
3	_____	b
4	_____	b
5	_____	a

Often the last line contains a funny or surprise ending as shown in the following limerick written by eighth-grade Angela:

> There once was a frog named Pete
> Who did nothing but sit and eat.
> He examined each fly
> With so careful an eye
> And then said, "You're dead meat."

Writing limericks can be a challenging assignment for many upper grade students, but middle grade students can also be successful with this poetic form, especially when they work together and write a class collaboration. This class collaboration limerick was written by fourth graders:

> Leprechaun
> There once was a luck leprechaun
> That rode on a big, fat fawn.
> He ate a cat,
> And got so fat,
> To lose some weight he had to mow the lawn.

Limericks are believed to have originated in the city of Limerick, Ireland and were first popularized over a century ago by Edward Lear (1812–1888). Poet X. J. Kennedy (1982) described limericks as the most popular type of poem in the

English language today. Introduce students to limericks by reading aloud some of Lear's verses so that students can appreciate the rhythm (stressed and unstressed syllables) of the verse. One fine edition of Lear's limericks is *How Pleasant to Know Mr. Lear!* (Livingston, 1982). Another book of limericks that students will enjoy is *They've Discovered a Head in the Box of Bread and Other Laughable Limericks* (Brewton & Blackburn, 1978). Arnold Lobel has also written a book of unique pig limericks, *Pigericks* (1983). After sharing Lobel's pigericks, students will want to write "birdericks" or "fishericks."

Clerihews. A *clerihew* (KLER i hyoo) is a four-line rhymed verse that describes a person. The form is named for Edmund Clerihew Bentley (1875–1956), a British detective writer who invented it. The formula is:

Line 1: the person's name

Line 2: the last word rhymes with the last word in the first line

Lines 3 and 4: the last words in these lines rhyme with each other

Clerihews can be written about anyone—historical figures, characters in stories, and even the students themselves. The following clerihew was written by an eighth-grader named Johnny about another John:

> John Wayne
> Is in the Cowboy Hall of fame.
> In movies he shot his gun the best,
> And that's how he won the west.

Model Poems

Students can write poems that are modeled on poems composed by adult poets. Kenneth Koch suggested this approach in *Rose, Where Did You Get That Red* (1973). According to this approach, students read a poem and write their own poems using the same theme expressed in the model poem.

Apologies. Using William Carlos Williams' poem, "This is Just to Say," as the model poem, children write a poem in which they apologize for something they are secretly glad they did (Koch, 1973). Middle and upper grade students are very familiar with offering apologies, and they enjoy writing humorous apologies to inanimate things. For example, fifth-grade Clay wrote an apology to his eraser:

> Dear Eraser,
> This is just to say
> I'm so sorry
> for
> biting you off
> my pencil
> and
> eating you
> and
> putting you
> in
> my digestive
> system.
> Forgive me!
> Forgive me
> p-l-e-e-e-a-s-e-e-e.

Apology poems don't have to be humorous; they may be sensitive, genuine apologies as this poem written by seventh-grade Angela demonstrates:

> Open Up
>
> | I didn't | a death |
> | open my | had caused. |
> | immature eyes | Forgive me, |
> | to see | I misunderstood |
> | the pain | your anguished |
> | within you | broken heart. |

Invitations. Students write poems in which they invite someone to a magical, beautiful place full of sounds and colors and where all kinds of marvelous things happen. The model poem is William Shakespeare's poem, "Come Unto These Yellow Sands" (Koch, 1973). The guidelines for writing an invitation poem are that it must be an invitation to a magical place and include sound or color words. The following example of an invitation poem written by seventh-grade Nikki follows these two guidelines:

> The Golden Shore
> Come unto the golden shore
> Where days are filled with laughter,
> And nights filled with whispering winds.
> Where sunflowers and sun
> Are filled with love.
> Come take my hand
> As we walk into the sun.

Prayers from the Ark. Students write a poem or prayer from the viewpoint of an animal, following the model poems in Carmen Bernos de Gasztold's *Prayers from the Ark* (1965). Gasztold was a French nun during World War II and, in her poems, she assumed the persona of the animals on Noah's ark as they prayed to God, questioning their existence and thanking Him for His mercies. Children can write similar poems, in which they assume the persona of an animal. Second-grade Candice assumes the persona of the Easter Bunny for her prayer:

> Dear Lord,
> I am the bunny.
> Why did you make me so fluffy?
> I thank you for keeping the carrots
> sweet and orange so I can be strong.
> Thank you for making me the Easter Bunny.
> Oh, I almost forgot, bless you
> for last month's big crop of carrots.

If I Were in Charge of the World. Students write poems in which they describe what they would do if they were in charge of the world. Judith Viorst's poem, "If I Were in Charge of the World" (1981) is the model for this poetic form. Children are eager to share ideas about how they would change the world, as this fourth-grade collaborative poem illustrates:

If I Were In Charge of the World

If I were in charge of the world
School would be for one month,
Movies and videogames would be free, and
Foods would be McCalorieless at McDonalds.
Poor people would have a home,
Bubble gum would cost a penny, and
Kids would have cars to drive.
Parents wouldn't argue,
Christmas would be in July and December, and
We would never have bedtimes.
A kid would be president,
I'd meet my long lost cousin, and
Candybars would be vegetables.
I would own the mall,
People would have as much money as they wanted, and
There would be no drugs.

TEACHING STUDENTS TO WRITE POEMS

Before writing their first poems, students should be presented with an "enlightened" view of what poetry is. Too often children have misconceptions about poetry that interfere with their ability to write poems. Many students think poems must rhyme and, in their search for rhymes, they create inane verse. This instructional strategy for teaching poetry is divided into three parts. First, an approach to introduce students to poetry is explained. Next, the strategy for teaching each poetic form is outlined, and, third, information about how to assess students' poetry writing experiences is presented.

Introducing Students to Poetry

Many children have misconceptions about what poetry is and how to write it. Too often they think poetry must rhyme or they are unsure about what it should look like on a page. Children need to have a concept of poetry before beginning to write poems. One way to expand students' knowledge about poetry is to share a variety of poems written by children and adults. Choose from poems included in this chapter as well as poems written by well-known poets who write for children, such as Karla Kuskin (1975, 1980), David McCord (1962, 1967, 1977), Jack Prelutsky (1976, 1977, 1983), and Shel Silverstein (1974, 1981). Include poems that do not rhyme and concrete poems with creative page arrangements.

Another way to introduce poetry is to read excerpts from the first chapter of Lois Lowry's *Anastasia Krupnik* (1979). In this book, 10-year-old Anastasia, the main character of the story, is excited about fourth grade when her teacher, Mrs. Westvessel, announces that the class will write poems. Anastasia works at home for eight nights to write a poem. Lowry does an excellent job of describing how writers search long and hard for words to express meaning and the delight that comes when writers realize their poems are finished. On the appointed day, Anastasia and her classmates bring their poems to class to read aloud. One student reads his four-line rhymed verse aloud:

> I have a dog whose name is Spot.
> He likes to eat and drink a lot.
> When I put water in his dish,
> He laps it up just like a fish. (p. 10)

Anastasia is not impressed. She knows that the child who wrote the poem has a dog named Sputnik, not Spot! But Mrs. Westvessel gives it an A, and hangs it on the bulletin board. Soon it is Anastasia's turn and she is nervous because her poem is very different. She reads her poem about tiny creatures that move about in tidepools at night:

> hush hush the sea-soft night is aswim
> with wrinklesquirm creatures
> listen(!)
> to them move smooth in the moistly dark
> here in the whisperwarm wet. (pp. 11–12)

In this free-form poem without rhyme or capital letters, Anastasia has created a marvelous word-picture with invented words such as *whisperwarm* and *wrinklesquirm*. Regrettably, Mrs. Westvessel has an antiquated view that poems should be about serious subjects only, be composed with rhyming sentences, and use conventional capitalization and punctuation. Mrs. Westvessel doesn't understand Anastasia's poem and gives Anastasia an F because she didn't follow directions.

While this first example presents a depressing picture of elementary teachers and their lack of knowledge about poetry, it is a dramatic introduction about what poetry is and what it is not. After reading excerpts from this first chapter of *Anastasia Krupnik,* develop a chart with your students comparing what poetry is in Mrs. Westvessel's class and what poetry is in your class. A class of upper grade students developed the chart in Figure 5-10. Expanding children's understanding of poetry is a crucial first step because, although most children have some knowledge about poetry, many of their notions are more like Mrs. Westvessel's than like Anastasia's.

FIGURE 5-10 Guidelines for Writing Poems

Rules About Writing Poetry

Mrs. Westvessel's Rules
1. Poems must rhyme.
2. The first letter in each line must be capitalized.
3. Each line must start at the left margin.
4. Poems must have a certain rhythm.

5. Poems should be written about serious things.
6. Poems should be punctuated like other types of writing.

7. Poems are failures if they don't follow these rules.

Our Rules
1. Poems do not have to rhyme.
2. The first letter in each line does not have to be capitalized.
3. Poems can take different shapes and be anywhere on a page.
4. You hear the writer's voice in a poem—with or without rhythm.
5. Poems can be about anything—serious or silly things.
6. Poems can be punctuated in different ways or not be punctuated at all.
7. There are no real rules for poems and no poem is a failure.

Teaching Students to Write Poems Following a Poetic Form

After being introduced to an "enlightened" view of poetry, children are ready to write poetry. Beginning with formula poems (e.g., "I wish . . . " poems and color poems) will probably make the writing easier for young children or for students who have had little or no experiences with poetry. The steps for writing any type of poetry are:

1. *Explain the poetic form.* The teacher describes the poetic form and explains what is included in each line or stanza. Displaying a chart that describes the form or having students write a brief description of the poetic form in their writers' notebooks will help them remember it.
2. *Share examples written by children.* The teacher reads poems adhering to the poetic form written by children. Poems included in this chapter may be shared, as well as additional poems written by your students. Point out how the writer of each poem used the form. Examples written by adults that adhere to the form may also be shared.
3. *Review the poetic form.* After explaining the poetic form and sharing poems, review the form with students and read one or two more poems that follow the form. Have students explain how the poems fit the form or have them freewrite about the poetic form to check their understanding. In the following freewrite, Eric, a seventh grader, writes about his assignment to write a concrete poem:

I don't know what I'm going to do about my concrete poem but I'm sure I will come up with something sooner or later. I have to write a poem in the shape of some object. Maybe I'll do one on a shape of a horse. Hey, that sounds good to me. I think I'll do that. Oh wait, how about a car? Ya, even better. All right, this freewriting stuff really works. Know what? I have nothing to say so I hope my five minutes are about up cause my arm is getting tired of writing. I'm lost for words.

---

4. *Write class collaboration poems.* Have children write a class collaboration poem before writing individual poems. Students can each contribute a line for a class collaboration "I wish . . . " Poem or a couplet for an "I used to/But now" Poem. For other types of poems, such as apology or concrete poems, students can work together by suggesting ideas and words to create the poem. They dictate the poem to the teacher who records it on the chalkboard or on chart paper. Older students can work in small groups to create their poems. Through writing a class collaboration poem, students review the form and gather ideas that they might later use in writing their own poems. The teacher should compliment students when they use word play or poetic devices. As always, encourage students to be creative with language. Students also need to know how to arrange the poem on the page, how to use capital letters and punctuation marks, and why it may be necessary to unwrite and delete unnecessary words.

   Children in a fourth-fifth grade remedial reading class composed the class collaboration poem, "If I Were a Tornado," presented in Figure 5-11. The class began by clustering ideas about tornadoes, and then students used the words in the cluster in dictating a rough draft of their "If I were . . . " poem. After reading the draft aloud, one child commented that the poem looked "too full of words" and counted 52 words in the poem. The children decided to "unwrite" some of the unnecessary words (e.g., the repetitious *I'd* at the beginning of four lines) and reduced the number of words in the poem to 39. After making the changes and reading the revised poem aloud, the children declared the poem finished. It was then copied on a sheet of paper and copies were made for each student.

5. *Write individual poems using the writing process.* The four steps listed above are prewriting, and with this background of experiences, students are prepared to write their own poems following the poetic form they have been taught. Students prewrite to gather and organize ideas, write rough drafts, meet in writing groups to receive feedback, make revisions based on this feedback, and then edit their poems with a classmate and with the teacher. Students then share their poems in any of a variety of ways. Often students keep their poems in a poetry notebook. Other possibilities include filmstrips and oral presentations.

FIGURE 5-11 Steps in Writing a Class Collaboration Poem

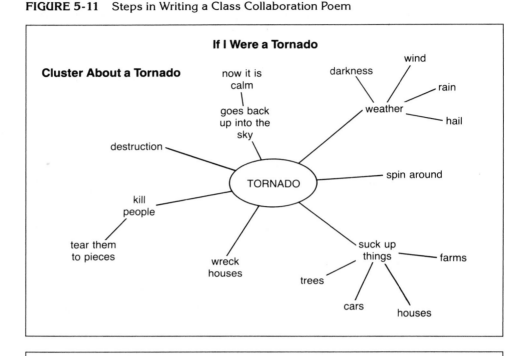

Rough Draft
If I were a tornado,
I'd bring darkness, wind, rain and hail
I'd spin around fl-rr-sss
I'd suck things like houses and cars up
   into me
I'd wreck up houses
I'd kill people—tear them to pieces
And then I'd go back up into the sky
Leaving behind destruction
And everything calm.

Final Draft
If I were a tornado,
I'd bring darkness, wind, rain
Spin around fl-rr-sss
Suck houses up into the sky
Drop the wrecked houses
Kill people—tear them to pieces
Then go back up into the sky
Leaving behind death and destruction.

Too often teachers will simply explain several poetic forms and then allow students to choose any form they like and write poems. This approach ignores the teaching component; it's back to the "assign and do" syndrome. Instead, students need to learn and experiment with each poetic form. After these preliminary experiences, they can apply what they have learned and write poems adhering to any of the poetic forms they have learned. Class collaborations are a crucial component because they provide a practice run for children who are not sure what to do. The 5 minutes it takes to write a class collaboration poem are sometimes the difference between success and failure for many would-be poets.

Assessing Students' Poems

A variety of poetic formulas have been presented in this chapter, and these formulas provide options for students to experiment with different ways to express their thoughts. Although children should experiment with a variety of forms during the elementary grades, they should not be tested on their knowledge of particular forms. Knowing that a haiku is a Japanese form composed of 17 syllables arranged in 3 lines will not make a child a poet. Instead, the forms should be posted in the classroom or added to students' writing notebooks to refer to as they write.

Assessing the quality of students' poems is especially difficult because poems are creative combinations of word play, poetic forms, and poetic devices. Instead of trying to give a grade for quality, student writing may be assessed on three other criteria:

- Has the student written the poem following the formula presented in class?
- Has the student used the process approach in writing, revising, and editing the poem?
- Has the student used word play or a poetic device in the poem?

Teachers might also ask students to assess their own progress in writing poems. Students should keep copies of the poems they write in their writing folders or poetry booklets so they can review and assess their work. If a grade for quality is absolutely necessary, students should be permitted to choose several of the poems in their writing folders to be evaluated.

POETIC DEVICES

Seventh-grade Joe rereads the final copy of his poem "Eagle" before turning it in for the class literary magazine:

Eagle

Eagle, is it the color
you see from the sky,
or is it the movement
that catches your eye?

Eagle, at what moment do you know
as you dive from the sky,
precisely when something will die?

> Eagle, do you have fear
> while you dive and peal,
> or might your nerves be made of steel?
>
> Eagle, what are your thoughts,
> as your claws and beak
> prepare the main course?
>
> Eagle, do you know,
> as you perch majestically on the tree,
> that you represent our country's liberty?

It's one of the best poems he has ever written, and with a slight smile on his lips, he turns it in. Returning to his desk, he thumps a classmate from his writing group on the arm and gives the thumbs-up sign.

His writing group had suggested that Joe begin each stanza with the word *Eagle* and end each stanza with a question mark. Those ideas strengthened his writing.

Good poets choose words carefully. They create powerful images when they use unexpected comparisons, repeat sounds within a line or stanza, imitate sounds, repeat words and phrases, and choose rhyming words. These techniques, called *poetic devices,* are comparison, alliteration, onomatopoeia, repetition, and rhyme. Children need to be aware of these devices so that they can use them in their writing. Knowledge of this terminology will also be helpful in writing discussion groups, when students compliment classmates on their use of a device or suggest that they try a particular device.

Comparison

One way to describe something is to compare it to something else. Students can compare images, feelings, and actions to other things using two types of comparisons, similes and metaphors. A *simile* is an explicit comparison of one thing to another by stating that one thing is like something else. Similies are signalled by the use of *like* or *as . . . as.* In contrast, a metaphor compares two things by implying that one is something else, without using *like* or *as.* Differentiating between the two terms is less important than using comparisons to make writing more vivid. For example, children can compare anger to a thunderstorm. Using a simile, they might say: *Anger is like a thunderstorm, screaming with thunder-feelings and lightning-words.* Or, as a metaphor, they might say: *Anger is a volcano, erupting with poisonous words and hot-lava actions.*

There are many stale comparisons, such as "high as a kite," "butterflies in your stomach," and "soft as a feather." Students begin by learning traditional comparisons and idioms, and then invent fresh, unexpected comparisons. Sixth-grade Amanda uses a combination of expected and unexpected comparisons in the following poem:

                              People
          People are like birds
          who are constantly getting their feathers ruffled.
          People are like alligators
          who find pleasure in evil cleverness.
          People are like bees
          who are always busy.
          People are like penguins
          who want to have fun.
          People are like platypuses—
                    unexplainable!

Alliteration

Alliteration is the repetition of the same initial consonant sound in consecutive words or in words in close proximity to one another. Repeating the same initial sound makes poetry fun to read, and children enjoy reading and reciting alliterative books such as Jane Bayer's *A My Name is Alice* (1984) and Chris Van Allsburg's *The Z Was Zapped* (1987). After reading one of these books, children can create their own versions. A fourth-grade class created their own version of Van Allsburg's book which they called "The Z was Zipped." Students divided into pairs and each pair composed two pages for the class book. On the front of the sheet of paper, students illustrated their letter and on the back wrote the sentence to describe their illustration, following Van Allsburg's pattern. Four pages from the book are presented in Figure 5-12. The alliterative sentences for each page are presented below, but before reading the sentences, examine the illustrations and try to guess the sentences.

    D The D got dunked by the duck.
    O The O was occupied oddly by the ox.
    T The T was totally terrified.
    Y The Y was yachting on the Yangtze.

Tongue twisters are an exaggerated form of alliteration in which every word (or almost every word) in the twister begins with the same letter. Dr. Seuss has compiled an easy-to-read collection of tongue twisters in *Oh Say Can You Say?* (1979) for primary grade students. Alvin Schwartz's *A Twister of Twists, a Tangler of Tongues* (1972) and Steven Kellogg's *Aster Aardvark's Alphabet Adventures* (1987) are two good books of tongue twisters that are available for middle and upper grade students.

Practice with tongue twisters and alliterative books increases children's awareness of the repetition of words with the same initial sounds in the poems they read and write. Few students consciously think about adding alliteration to a poem they are writing, but they get high praise in writing groups when classmates note an alliteration and compliment the writer on it.

FIGURE 5-12 Four Pages from "The Z was Zipped"

Onomatopoeia

Onomatopoeia is a device in which poets use sound words to make their writing more sensory and more vivid. These sound words (e.g., *crash, slurp, varoom, me-e-e-ow*) sound like their meanings. Students can compile a list of sound words found in stories and poems they read. The list can be displayed on a classroom chart or entered in their writer's journals to be referred to when students write their own poems.

Peter Spier has compiled two books of sound words. *Gobble Growl Grunt* (1971) is about animal sounds, and *Crash! Bang! Boom!* (1972) is about the sounds people and machines make. Students can use these books in selecting sound words to use in their writing. Comic strips are another good source of sound words. Children collect frames from comic strips with sound words and add them to a classroom chart. Collecting these words naturally leads to a discussion of the spelling of sound words, one area of spelling in which children have a great deal of freedom. Sounds can be stretched out by repeating letters in words, such as *sl-i-i-i-de.*

In his book *Wishes, Lies and Dreams* (1970) Kenneth Koch recommends having children write noise poems in which they include a noise or sound word in each line. These first poems often sound contrived (e.g., *A dog barks "bow-wow"*), but through these experiences children learn to use onomatopoeia. This poem, written by seventh-grade Brian, illustrates onomatopoeia:

> Greyhound
> Fast and slick
> Out of the dogbox—
> ZOOM, ZOOM, ZOOM
> Burst into the air
> Then they smoothly touch the ground.

Repetition of Words

Repetition of words and phrases is another device that writers of stories and poems can use effectively to structure their writing and add interest. Edgar Allen Poe's effective use of the fearful word *nevermore* in "The Raven" is one poetic example, as is the gingerbread boy's boastful refrain in "The Gingerbread Boy."

An easy way to introduce repetition of words in poetry is through a class collaboration poem. In this collaborative poem, a first grader's comment "Gee, it's fun wishing!" is repeated after every three wishes:

> Wishing Time
> I wish I could go to the moon.
> I wish I had a pony.
> I wish I was a professional baseball player
> Gee, it's fun wishing!

> I wish I had a million dollars.
> I wish I could go to Disneyland.
> I wish I could be a movie star.
> Gee, it's fun wishing!
> I wish I owned a toy store.
> I wish I was the smartest kid in the world.
> I wish I could never stop wishing.
> Gee, it's fun wishing!

This repetition adds structure and enjoyment. As students read the poem aloud, the teacher reads each stanza and the students chant each refrain. In the following poem, a fifth grader writes about a piece of chocolate and uses the refrain "Here it comes" to heighten anticipation and to structure the poem:

> Chocolate
> I drool.
> Here it comes.
> The golden brown covering never looked
> so scrumptious, so tempting, so addicting.
> Here it comes.
> I don't know anything that's going on around me.
> All I can concentrate on is chocolate.
> Here it comes.
> I can feel the sweet, rich, thick chocolate
> on the roof of my mouth. A-a-a-ah-h!
> And the chocolate is gone.

One way to suggest an improvement in a child's poem is to suggest that the child repeat a particularly effective phrase throughout the poem.

Rhyme

It is unfortunate that rhyme has been considered almost synonymous with poetry. While rhyme is an important part of many types of poetry, it can dominate the poetry of many young children. When rhyme comes naturally, it adds a delightful quality to children's writing, but when it *equals* poetry, it gets in the way of word play and vivid images. In the following Halloween poem, a fifth grader describes a witch's brew using rhyming words and an invented magical word—*allakaboo*:

> Bats, spiders, and lizards, too
> Rats, snakes—Allakaboo!
> Eggs and spiderwebs, a-choo
> Wings of a bug—Allakaboo—
> a witch's brew!

■ *ANSWERING TEACHERS' QUESTIONS ABOUT POETIC WRITING*

1. Isn't it true that children either have poetic ability or they don't?

Perhaps it is true that great poets are born, not made, but every child can write poems and enjoy the experience. Children benefit from experiences with poems by developing a sensitivity to language and learning to play with words and evoke fresh images with words. The poetic forms presented in this chapter have been field-tested with students in kindergarten through eighth grade, and both teachers and students find these poetry writing activities valuable learning experiences.

2. My students think that poems must rhyme. How can I convince them that poems don't have to rhyme?

Many children think that poems must rhyme. Reading the excerpt from Lowry's *Anastasia Krupnik* (1979) and developing the list of poetry rules for your class described in the section on "Teaching Students to Write Poems" will introduce the concept that poems are more than strings of rhyming words. Teaching students about concrete poems, haiku, and other forms that don't use rhyme will help them understand that they have options other than rhyming poetry. Also read aloud to students some poetry that does not rhyme.

3. My students' poems look more like paragraphs that poems. What can I do?

Have students examine the poems written in books to see how they are arranged on the page. Also, write class poems and discuss with students the various options that poets have for arranging their poems on the page. To demonstrate some of the options, have students, working in small groups, each design a different arrangement for a class collaboration poem. If you have access to a word processor, have students type their poems on the computer and arrange the poem in various ways. For example:

> Words
> written
> up
> and
> down
> and
> centered
> SMACK
> in the middle
> of
> the
> page—
> That's a poem
> to me!

If the poems also sound like a paragraph, some "unwriting" might be necessary in which children delete unnecessary and repetitive function words. For example, this paragraph was unwritten to create the poem printed above:

> In a poem you can write words up and down on a page. They are centered right in the middle of the page. They are fun to write. That's what a poem is to me.

4. How can I teach poetry when I've never liked it or been any good at writing poetry myself?

Teachers often ask this question and I tell them that this is a new way of writing poetry. The emphasis has changed from rhyming verse to word play and expressing feelings and word pictures. Children's enthusiasm for this type of poetry is contagious; even the most skeptical teacher quickly becomes a convert.

■ *REFERENCES*

Adams, A. (1971). *A woggle of witches.* New York: Scribner.

Atwood, S. (1971). *Haiku: The mood of the Earth.* New York: Scribner.

Atwood, S. (1973). *My own rhythm: An approach to haiku.* New York: Scribner.

Bayer, J. (1984). *A my name is Alice.* New York: Dial.

Behn, H. (1964). *Cricket songs.* New York: Harcourt Brace Jovanovich.

Behn, H. (1971). *More cricket songs.* New York: Harcourt Brace Jovanovich.

Bernstein, J. E. (1979). *Fiddle with a riddle: Write your own riddles.* New York: Dutton.

Brewton, J. E., & Blackburn, L. A. (1978). *They've discovered a head in the box of bread and other laughable limericks.* New York: Crowell.

Brown, M. (1983). *What do you call a dumb bunny? And other rabbit riddles, games, jokes, and cartoons.* Boston: Little, Brown.

Dahl, R. (1976). *The enormous crocodile.* New York: Knopf

de Gasztold, C. B. (1965). *Prayers from the ark.* New York: Penguin Books.

Froman, R. (1974). *Seeing things: A book of poems.* New York: Crowell.

Geller, L. G. (1981). Riddling: A playful way to explore language. *Language Arts, 58,* pp. 669–674.

Geller, L. G. (1985). *Word play and language learning for children.* Urbana, IL: National Council of Teachers of English.

Gwynne, F. (1970). *The king who rained.* New York: Windmill Books.

Gwynne, F. (1976). *A chocolate moose for dinner.* New York: Windmill Books.

Gwynne, F. (1980). *The sixteen hand horse.* New York: Prentice-Hall.

Gwynne, F. (1988). *A little pigeon toad.* New York: Simon & Schuster.

Hall, R., & Friends. (1985). *Sniglets for kids.* Yellow Springs, OH: Antioch.

Horwitz, E. L. (1975). *When the sky is like lace.* Philadelphia: Lippincott.

Kellogg, S. (1987). *Aster Aardvark's alphabet adventures.* New York: Morrow.

Kennedy, X. J., & Kennedy, D. M. (1982). *Knock at a star: A child's introduction to poetry.* Boston: Little, Brown.

Koch, K. (1970). *Wishes, lies, and dreams.* New York: Vintage.

Koch, K. (1973). *Rose, where did you get that red.* New York: Vintage.

Kuskin, K. (1980). *Dogs and dragons, trees and dreams.* New York: Harper and Row.

Kuskin, K. (1975). *Near the window tree.* New York: Harper and Row.

Langstaff, J. (1974). *Oh, a-hunting we will go.* New York: Atheneum.

Lewis, R. (Ed.) (1965). *In a spring garden.* New York: Dial.

Lewis, R. (1968). *Of this world: A poet's life in poetry.* New York: Dial.

Lewis, R. (1970). *The way of silence: The prose and poetry of Basho.* New York: Dial.

Livingston, M. C. (Ed.) (1982). *How pleasant to know Mr. Lear!* New York: Holiday House.

Lobel, A. (1983). *Pigericks: A book of pig limericks.* New York: Harper and Row.

Lowry, L. (1979). *Anastasia Krupnik.* Boston: Houghton Mifflin.

McCord, D. (1962). *Take sky.* Boston: Little, Brown.

McCord, D. (1967). *Everytime I climb a tree.* Boston: Little, Brown.

McCord, D. (1977). *One at a time: Collected poems for the young.* Boston: Little, Brown.

O'Neill M. (1961). *Hailstones and halibut bones: Adventures in color.* Garden City, NJ: Doubleday.

Opie, I., & Opie, P. (1959). *The lore and language of school children.* Oxford, England: Oxford University Press.

Pilon, B. (1972). *Concrete is not always hard.* Middletown, CT; Xerox Educational Publications.

Prelutsky, J. (1976). *Nightmares: Poems to trouble your sleep.* New York: Greenwillow.

Prelutsky, J. (1977). *The snopp on the sidewalk and other poems.* New York: Greenwillow.

Prelutsky, J. (1983). *The Random House book of poetry for children.* New York: Random House.

Schwartz, A. (1972). *A twister of twists, a tangler of tongues.* New York: Harper and Row.

Seuss, Dr. (1979). *Oh say can you say?* New York: Random House.

Sherman, I. (1980). *Walking talking words.* New York: Harcourt Brace Jovanovich.

Silverstein, S. (1974). *Where the sidewalk ends.* New York: Harper and Row.

Silverstein, S. (1981). *The light in the attic.* New York: Harper and Row.

Spier, P. (1971). *Gobble growl grunt.* New York: Doubleday.

Spier, P. (1972). *Crash! Bang! Boom!* New York: Doubleday.

Sterne, N. (1979). *Tyrannosaurus wrecks: A book of dinosaur riddles.* New York: Crowell.

Terban, M. (1982). *Eight ate: A feast of homonym riddles.* New York: Clarion.

Tiedt, I. (1970). Exploring poetry patterns. *Elementary English, 45,* 1082–1084.

Tompkins, G. E., & Yaden, D. B., Jr. (1986). *Answering students' questions about words.* Urbana, IL: ERIC Clearinghouse on Reading and Communication Skills and National Council of Teachers of English.

Valentine, S. L. (1986). Beginning poets dig for poems. *Language Arts, 63,* 246–252.

Van Allsburg, C. (1987). *The z was zapped.* Boston: Houghton Mifflin.

Viorst, J. (1981). *If I were in charge of the world and other worries.* New York: Atheneum.

Zalben, J. B. (1977). *Lewis Carroll's jabberwocky.* New York: Warne.

Zolotow, C. (1980). *Say it!* New York: Harper and Row.

6

Expository Writing

The sixth graders in Ms. Hardy's classroom have taken a computerized test to determine which occupations they are most suited for. On the computer printout, Matt discovers he has aptitude for several different careers, but the one that catches his interest is petrologist. A petrologist? To help Matt and the other students explore careers, Ms. Hardy suggests that they research one of the careers identified by the computer, and then compile what they learn in a report.

They begin by brainstorming a list of questions about careers:

- How much money can you make in this career?
- What kinds of work do you do in this career?
- What kind of schooling is needed to prepare for this career?
- What are the working conditions?
- Would you travel in this career?
- What type of person would be happy in this career?

The students decide that the questions about kinds of work and working conditions are the most basic, and they all agree to research these two questions for their reports. They also decide to choose at least two additional questions from the list to investigate.

Next, students draw a cluster with their career as the nucleus word in the middle circle and with four rays, each listing one of the questions to be investigated. Matt chooses these four questions to research: (a) How much money do you make in this career? (b) What kind of work do you do in this career? (c) What kind of schooling is needed for this career?, and (d) What are the working conditions in this career? Matt uses library books to find answers to his questions, and he will consult at least three sources which he will list in the bibliography at the end of his report. If he locates a petrologist in his community, he can interview this person as one of his resources. He adds the information he collects to complete his cluster as shown in Figure 6-1.

Ms. Hardy reminds the students that their reports will include an introduction to attract the readers' attention, at least four questions in the body of the report with one paragraph to answer each question, and a brief conclusion. Matt uses the information in his cluster to write a rough draft. First, he writes the four paragraphs for the body of the report. He puts each on a separate sheet of paper after deciding to postpone determining the order of the paragraphs until later. As he adds the information from the cluster to his paragraphs, he checks it off on the cluster. He marks *ROUGH DRAFT* on the top of each page and double spaces the text so that there will be space for revising and editing.

Next, he turns to Eric for advice about writing the introduction and conclusion. Eric also seems unsure about how to proceed. Ms. Hardy notices that a number of students are confused about these two parts, and she invites interested students to meet together for a mini-lesson. They discuss the purpose of introductions and conclusions and suggest ways to word these two parts. Students at the mini-lesson who have already drafted these two parts share their writing. Now Matt returns to his desk and quickly drafts his introduction and conclusion.

The next day Matt rereads his report, adding a word in several places and one additional sentence. He sequences his paragraphs one way and reads it again but

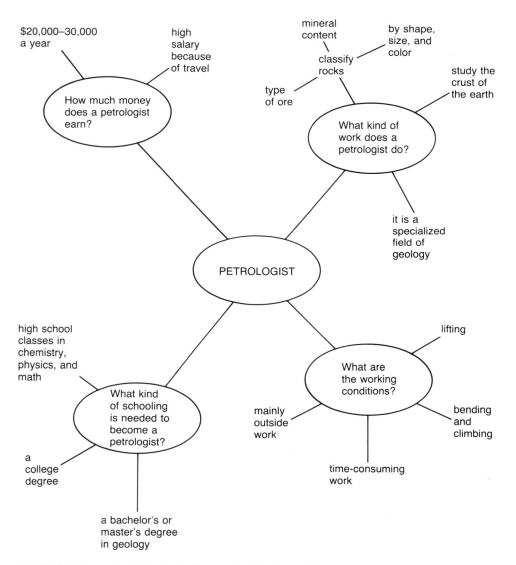

FIGURE 6-1 A Sixth Grader's Cluster for His Career Report

isn't satisfied with the arrangement so he reorders them. Then he rereads the report and seems satisfied.

Several days later after most of the students have completed their rough drafts, they meet in writing groups to share their writing. Matt's group calls themselves "The Awesome Authors." The four boys in this group pull chairs into a circle, ready to critique each other's writing. Matt reads his report first and receives the following compliments:

"You had good facts, lots of information about petrologists in your report. It sounds like a pretty interesting career."

"I like your introduction. It caught my attention."

"You wrote good paragraphs. I could pick out your topic sentences, and I think you stuck to one question in each paragraph."

He asks for suggestions on how to improve his report, and Eric suggests that he list a petrologist's salary by month as well as by year. The boys discuss how to translate a yearly salary of $20,000 to $30,000 to a monthly rate but do not reach a conclusion. Matt asks for other suggestions and Micha asks for clarification about the type of outside work that petrologists do. Then it is Robert's turn to read his report.

After the writing group, Matt makes the two recommended changes. Then Eric and Matt work together to edit their reports using an editing checklist that they staple on top of their rough drafts. They check for spelling errors, punctuation marks, capital letters at the beginning of sentences and in proper nouns, topic sentences in paragraphs, and correct bibliographic form in the bibliography. After editing, Matt shows his report to Ms. Hardy who reads it quickly, spotting two additional mechanical errors. She also peruses the bibliography on the last page, checking that Matt included at least three sources and used the correct bibliographic format. Then she gives Matt permission to write the final copy of his report. Here is Matt's report:

■
Petrologists: What Do They Do?

Petrology is an interesting career. If you like the earth and rocks you would probably enjoy this career.

Petrology is the study of rocks and the ground. If you were a petrologist you would classify and determine the rocks you found by their shape, size, and color. You would also classify according to the mineral and types of ore the rock came from. You would study the crust of the earth, and the earth itself. Petrology is a specialized field of geology.

The salary of a petrologist ranges anywhere from $20,000 to $30,000 a year or $2,000 to $3,000 a month. Part of the reason for these wages is because you go to different places a lot and you also travel a lot. You don't stay in the same place very often.

If you want to be a petrologist you will have to go to school about as long as any other career. The most essential classes to take in high school to help you prepare for petrology are chemistry, physics, and math. Petrology also requires at least four years of college. You can either get a bachelor's degree or a master's degree in geology.

The kind of working conditions you will experience in petrology are mainly outside work but some inside work. There is a lot of medium lifting. It also requires a lot of bending and climbing. Being a petrologist is very hard and time-consuming work.

Petrology is a career for people who like studying the ground and the many things it contains.

Bibliography

Fodor, R. V. *What Does a Geologist Do?* New York: Dodd, 1977.

Goldreich, Gloria and Esther. *What Can She Be? A Geologist.* New York: Lothrop, 1976.

no author. *Growing Up with Science.* Westport, CT: Suttman, 1984.

Robinson, H. Alan. "Career Guidance." *Collier's Encyclopedia,* vol. 5, pp. 421–444. New York: Macmillan, 1981.

Matt and his classmates wrote reports for a specific purpose—to learn about a career and to share the information they have learned. They designed their own research questions and pursued the study because of genuine interest. This project might better be called a "search," not "research," project because the students are searching for answers to questions they posed, not just satisfying a teacher's assignment for library research (Macrorie, 1984).

Expository writing is writing to share information. James Britton (1970) describes this type as writing used "to interact with people and things and to make the wheels of the world, for good or ill, go round" (p. 8).

In addition to research reports, I will discuss two types of expository writing in this chapter. Autobiographies and biographies are special types of expository writing in which writers combine information with narration in writing life stories about themselves and others. Letters are another type of expository writing with a specialized audience. In contrast to research reports and life stories, which are often shared with large and unknown audiences, letters are usually written to specific people. When students write letters, they share information, experiences, and feelings in personal letters and share or seek information in business letters.

RESEARCH REPORTS

Too often students are not exposed to research reports until they must write a term paper in high school. Then they become overwhelmed with learning how to take notes on notecards, how to organize and write the paper, and how to compile a bibliography. There is no reason to postpone report writing until students reach high school. Students in the elementary grades can search for answers to questions that interest them and write both class collaboration and individual reports (Krogness, 1987; Queenan, 1986). Through early, successful experiences with report writing, students not only learn how to write research reports but they also learn about content areas.

Young Children's Reports

Contrary to the popular assumption that young children's first writing is narrative, educators have found that kindergartners and first graders write many nonnarrative compositions in which they provide information about familiar topics including "Signs of Fall" or directions for familiar activities such as "How to Feed

Your Pet" (Bonin, 1988; Sowers, 1985). Many of these writings might be termed "All About _____ " books, and others are informational pieces that children dictate for the teacher to record. These two types introduce young children to expository writing.

"All About _____ " Books. In young children's "All About _____ " books, they write an entire booklet on a single topic. Usually one piece of information and an illustration are presented on each page. First-grade David wrote an "All About _____ " book, "The Sea Animals" (presented in Figure 6-2) as a part of a unit on the sea. You will notice that David numbered each page of his book, 1 through 4, in the upper right corner of the page. Then he added a cover, and after a minute of confusion he added a zero to the cover so that each page would be numbered. David used invented spelling to spell many words in his report, but the information can be deciphered easily. Also, on page 1, David was experimenting with word boundaries and chose to use a dot to mark the division between words that he recognized as separate words. He considered *The dolphin* and *swim fast* as single units. When he wrote other pages, David's attention changed and he focused on other dimensions of writing.

"All About _____ " books can be collaborative production in which each child contributes one page for the book. For example, as a part of the unit on insects, the students in a primary level class for emotionally disturbed children each contributed one page to a class book about ladybugs. After collecting some ladybugs to observe in the classroom and reading a book or two about the distinctive insects, the teacher and children brainstormed a list of things they had learned about ladybugs. Then the six children each chose one thing from the list or any other information, if they preferred, for their page. They wrote the information on a sheet of paper and added an illustration. Their teacher collected the pages, included a sheet at the end of the book called "How We Learned about Ladybugs," and then added construction paper cover. Here is their report:

All about Ladybugs

Page 1: There are about 600 kinds of ladybugs.
Page 2: Ladybugs are supposed to bring you good luck.
Page 3: Ladybugs pretend to be dead when frightened.
Page 4: Ladybugs like the rain.
Page 5: Ladybugs spend the winter in pinecones, cracks, under leaves, and even in houses sleeping and waiting for spring.
Page 6: Ladybugs don't bite!
Page 7: How We Learned about Ladybugs:
    1. We watched three ladybugs that we kept in a jar in our classroom.
    2. We read these books:
       Insects by Illa Podendorf, 1981.
       Ladybug, Ladybug, Fly Away Home by Judy Hawes, 1967.

Dictated Reports. Young children can dictate reports to their teacher who serves as scribe to record them. After listening to a guest speaker, viewing a film, or reading several books about a particular topic, kindergartners and first graders can dictate brief reports. A class of kindergartners compiled the book-length report on police officers presented in Figure 6-3. The teacher read two books aloud to the students and Officer Jerry, a police officer, visited the classroom and talked to the students about his job. The students also took a field trip to visit the police station. The teacher took photos of Officer Jerry, his police car, and the police station to illustrate the report. With this background, the students and the teacher together developed a cluster with these five main ideas: what police officers do, what equipment police officers have, how police officers travel, where police officers work, and how police officers can be your friends. The students added details and developed each main idea to fill one page of the report. The background of experiences and the clustering activity prepared students to compose their report. After students completed their report, included a bibliography called "How We Learned About Police Officers for Our Report," and inserted the photographs, it was ceremoniously presented to the school library to be enjoyed by all students in the school. The proud authors were the students who borrowed it most frequently because it was "our best book ever!"

Collaborative Reports

A successful first report writing experience for middle and upper grade students is a class collaboration research report. Small groups of students work together to write sections of the work and then compile their sections to form the report. Students benefit from writing a group report first because they learn the steps in writing a research report using the group as a scaffold or support system before tackling individual reports. Also, by working in groups, the laborious parts of the work are shared.

A group of 4 fourth graders wrote a collaborative report on hermit crabs. These students sat together at one table and watched the hermit crabs that lived in the terrarium on their table. They cared for these crustaceans for 2 weeks and made notes of their observations in learning logs. After this period, these students were bursting with questions about the hermit crabs and were eager for answers. They wanted to know where the crabs' real habitat was, what the best habitat was for them in the classroom, how they breathed air, why they lived in "borrowed" shells, why one pincher was bigger than the other, and so on. Their teacher provided some answers and directed them to books that would provide additional information. As they collected information, they created a cluster that they taped to their table next to the terrarium. Soon the cluster wasn't an adequate way to report information so they decided to share their knowledge by writing a book which they called "The Encyclopedia About Hermit Crabs." This book and the cluster used in gather information for it is presented in Figure 6-4 (pp. 210–211).

The students decided to share the work of writing the book, and they chose four main ideas, one for each student to write. The four main ideas were what hermit crabs look like, how they act, where they live, and what they eat. A different student wrote each section and then returned to the group to share the rough

FIGURE 6-2 A First Grader's "All About _____" Book

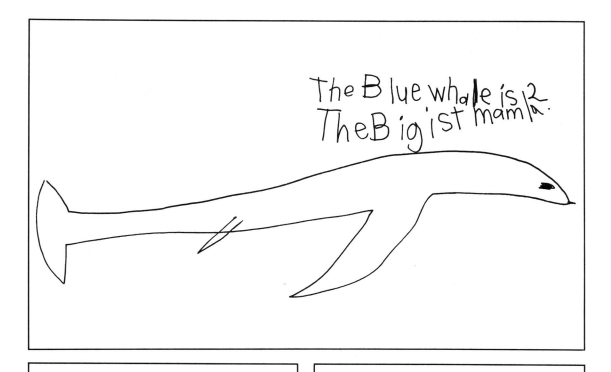

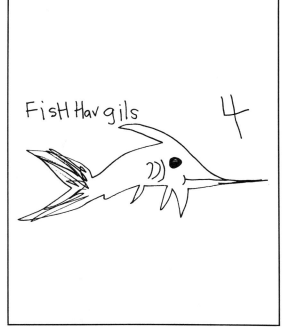

FIGURE 6-2 (continued)

FIGURE 6-3   Kindergartners' Report About Police Officers

Our Report about Police Officers

Page 1: Police officers help people who are in trouble. They are nice to kids. They are only mean to robbers and bad people. Police officers make people obey the laws. They give tickets to people who drive cars too fast.

Page 2: Men and women can be police officers. They wear blue uniforms like Officer Jerry's. But sometimes police officers wear regular clothes when they work undercover. They wear badges on their uniforms and on their hats. Officer Jerry's badge number is 3407. Police officers have guns, handcuffs, whistles, sticks, and two-way radios. They have to carry all these things.

Page 3: Police officers drive police cars with flashing lights and loud sirens. The cars have radios so the officers can talk to other police officers at the police station. Sometimes they ride on police motorcycles or on police horses or in police helicopters or in police boats.

Page 4: Police officers work at police stations. The jail for the bad people that they catch is right next door. One police officer sits at the radio to talk to the police officers who are driving their cars. The police chief works at the police station, too.

Page 5: Police officers are your friends. They want to help you so you shouldn't be afraid of them. You can ask them if you need some help.

Page 6: How We Learned About Police Officers for Our Report
1. We read these books:
   Police by Ray Broekel
   What Do They Do? Policemen and Firemen by Carla Greene
2. We interviewed Officer Jerry.
3. We visited the police station.

Kindergarten class

draft. The students gave each other suggestions for revisions. Next they edited their report with the teacher and added an introduction, conclusion, and bibliography. Finally, they recopied their report and added illustrations in a cloth-bound book that they read to each class in the school before adding it to the school library.

Individual Reports

Toby Fulwiler (1985) recommends that students do "authentic" research in which they explore topics that interest them or hunt for answers to questions that puzzle them. As students become immersed in content area study, questions arise that students want to explore. Students in a fourth-grade class were studying dinosaurs and they quickly asked more questions than the teacher could answer. She encouraged them to search for answers in the books they had checked out of the school and community public libraries. As they located answers to their questions, the students were eager to share their new knowledge and decided to write reports and publish them as books.

Fourth-grade Dustin's "The World of the Dinosaurs" is presented in Figure 6-5. His report is divided into three chapters plus a table of contents, a bibliography, and an "All About the Author" page at the end. (Only the three chapters are presented in the figure.) Each chapter focuses on a question he examined. The first chapter, "The Death Star," was written to answer his question about how the dinosaurs died. Dustin wrote the second chapter on the three periods to answer his question about whether or not the dinosaurs all lived at the same time. In the third chapter, Dustin wrote a description of the pterodactyl, an unusual flying lizard that lived when the dinosaurs did. He chose this topic after locating an interesting book about these flying lizards.

Formats for Research Reports. Students can organize their reports in a variety of formats—formats that they have seen used in informational books. One possibility is a question-answer format, and another possibility is an alphabet book. A second-grade class chose to organize their report on insects as an alphabet book, with one page for each letter of the alphabet. The "G" page is presented in Figure 6-6.

Students can also vary the genre they use to present the information they have gathered (Wilde, 1988). For example, after gathering information, students can present the information in a story, letter, or a poem format rather than as a report. Seventh-grade Chris has woven the information he learned about eagles' mating habits into this report that is written in a narrative format:

Lord Eagle

One morning Lord Eagle woke up. Lady Eagle was still asleep. Lord Eagle flew out of their four foot deep nest. Then he flew to a perch in their tree. Lord Eagle stands three feet tall and with a wing span of eight feet. Lord Eagle flew to a perch in a tree beside a nearby river and waited for a careless fish to swim near the surface. When one did, Lord Eagle swooped down and dipped his talons just below the surface of the river, grabbing the fish! He flew to the ground. With his sharp curved beak, he tore strips of the fish off and swallowed it.

Once Lady Eagle has had her breakfast, the Lord and Lady fly through the sky. Today is different. It is about time for Lord Eagle to fertilize the eggs. Eagles usually lay two eggs at a time. This is the second year Lord and Lady Eagle have flown together. Eagles stay together until one dies.

Lord and Lady Eagle soar in the sky, going upward until just small dots in the sky are seen from earth. Since this is their mating period, they lock claws and close their wings. They plummet earthward, tumbling. Falling a couple of hundred feet. Then opening their wings and releasing each other's claws, they soar upward again. This is repeated.

It is time to add to the nest. Lord Eagle found a good tree branch still attached to the tree. He flies up and swoops down. With his strong wings and claws, he tears the branch off. Then he adds it to the nest.

The day is over for the eagles so they settle into the nest.

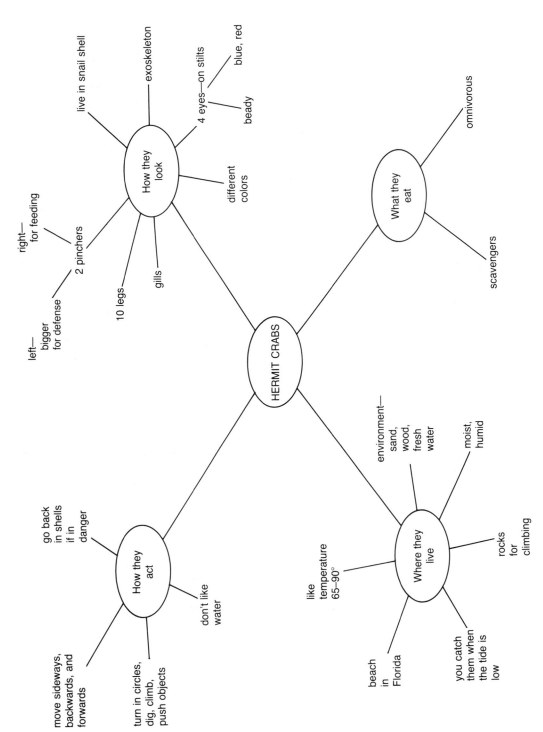

FIGURE 6-4 Fourth Graders' Cluster and Collaborative Report on Hermit Crabs

The Encyclopedia About Hermit Crabs

HOW THEY LOOK

Hermit crabs are very much like regular crabs but hermit crabs transfer shells. They have gills. Why? Because they are born in water and when they mature they come to land and kill snails so they can have a shell. They have two beady eyes that look like they are on stilts. Their body is a sight! Their shell looks like a rock. Really it is an exoskeleton which means the skeleton is on the outside. They have two pinchers. The left one is bigger so it is used for defense. The right one is for feeding. They also have ten legs.

WHERE THEY LIVE

Hermit crabs live mostly on beaches in Florida where the weather is 65°–90°. They live in fresh water. They like humid weather and places that have sand, wood, and rocks (for climbing on). The best time to catch hermit crabs is a low tide.

WHAT THEY EAT

Hermit crabs are ominorous scavengers which means they eat just about anything. They even eat leftovers.

HOW THEY ACT

Hermit crabs are very unusual. They go back into their shell if they think there is danger. They are funny because they walk sideways, forwards, and backwards. They can go in circles. They can also get up when they get upside down. And that's how they act.

FIGURE 6-4 (continued)

FIGURE 6-5 A Fourth Grader's Dinosaur Report

The World of the Dinosaurs

Chapter 1
The Death Star

Over the years, scientists have noticed that almost all stars have a sister star. But what about the sun? Scientists have found out that the sun does have a sister star. It's darker than the sun, and it takes 28 million years to orbit around our solar system. They named it Nemesis after the Greek god of revenge. When Nemesis reaches its closest point to the sun, it makes the asteroid belt go beserk! Asteroids and comets were flying everywhere! The earth was a disaster! Scientists have studied and found out that if a comet or an asteroid hit the earth it would be like dropping an atomic bomb (or a thousand billion tons of dynamite) on the earth. Whenever that happens, almost everything on the face of the earth is destroyed. The next time Nemesis reaches its closest point to the sun will be in about fifteen million years.

Chapter 2
The Three Periods: Triassic, Jurassic, and Cretaceous

There were three periods when the dinosaurs came, and then they were just wiped off the face of the earth. It may have been the Death Star. Whatever the reason, nobody knows. The three periods were the Triassic, Jurassic, and the Cretaceous.

Most of the smaller animals like Orniholestes and Hysilophodon came in the Triassic Period. They were mostly plant eaters.

Most of the flying dinosaurs like Pteradactyl and Pteranadon came in the Jurassic Period. A number of the big plant eaters like Brontosaurus and Brachiosaurus also came in that period. A lot of sea reptiles came in that time, too.

The bigger dinosaurs like Tyrannosaurus Rex and Trachodon came in the Cretaceous Period. Most of these were meat eaters.

Chapter 3
Pterodactyl: The Flying Lizard

The Pterodactyl is a flying lizard that lived millions of years ago when the dinosaurs lived. Pterodactyl means "flying lizard." It was huge animal. It had skin stretched between the hind limb and a long digit of the forelimb. It didn't have any feathers. Some had a wingspan of 20 feet. Some paleontologists think Pterodactyl slept like a bat, upside down, because of the shape of its wings. It had a long beak and very sharp teeth. When it would hunt for food, it would fly close to the water and look for fish. When it saw one, it would dive in and get it. It also had sharp claws that helped it grab things. The Pterodactyl had a strange looking tail. It was long with a ball shape at the end. Some people say it really looked like a flying lizard.

Dustin, grade 4

G is for grasshopper. It sings by rubbing its hind legs against its wings.

FIGURE 6-6 One Page from an ABC Book on Insects

Teaching Students to Write Research Reports

In writing a research report—either as a class collaboration or individually—students use a process approach to writing. They search for answers to questions about a topic and then compose a report to share what they have learned. Designing questions and gathering information is the prewriting stage and as they draft, revise, edit, and publish their reports they complete the stages.

Writing Class Collaboration Reports. The process approach for writing class collaboration reports involves six steps:

1. *Choose a topic.* The first step in writing class collaboration research reports is to choose a topic, one that students are studying or want to study. Almost any topic in social studies, science, or current events that can be subdivided into 4 to 10 parts works well for class collaboration reports. Possible general topics

include oceans, dinosaurs, the solar system, the human body, continents, life in the Middle Ages, and transportation.

From these general topics, students choose specific topics that small groups or pairs of students research. For example, for a report on the continents, students choose which continent they will research, or for a unit on the solar system they choose which planet to research. For other units, such as dinosaurs or the Middle Ages, students may not be able to identify the specific topic they will research until they have learned more and designed research questions.

2. *Design research questions.* As students study the topic, research questions emerge. They brainstorm a list of questions on a chart posted in the classroom and add to the list as other questions arise. In a report on the human body, for example, small groups of students studying each organ may decide to research the same three, four, or five questions, such as these: "What does the organ look like?" "What job does the organ do?" "Where is the organ located in the human body?" Interestingly, elementary students who research the human body often want to include a question on whether or not a person can live without the organ. This interest probably reflects the current attention in the news media to organ transplants.

Students studying a unit such as the Middle Ages might brainstorm the following questions about life in that era: "What did the people wear?" "What did they eat?" "What were their communities like?" "What kind of entertainment did people enjoy?" "What kinds of occupations?" "How did people protect themselves?" "What kinds of transportation did people use?" Each small group selects one of these questions as the specific topic for its report and chooses questions related to the specific topic.

To rehearse the process before students research and write their section of the report, the teacher and students may work through the procedure using one of the research questions the students did not choose. Together as a class, students gather information, organize it, and then write the section of the report using the drafting, revising, and editing stages of the writing process.

3. *Gather and organize information.* Students work in small groups or in pairs to search for answers to their research questions. These questions provide the structure for data collection because students are seeking answers to specific questions, not just randomly writing information. Students can use clusters or data charts (McKenzie, 1979) to record the information they gather. An example of a cluster and data chart for the report on the human body is presented in Figure 6-7. The research questions are the same for each data collection instrument. On a cluster, students add information as details to each main idea ray, and on data charts, they record information from the first source in the first row under the appropriate questions, from the second source in the second row, and so on. These two instruments are effective because they organize data collection question by question and limit the amount of information that can be gathered from any source. For both clusters and

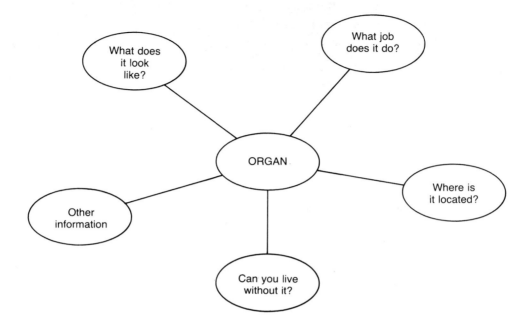

FIGURE 6-7   A Cluster and a Data Chart on the Human Body

data charts, students list their sources of information on the back of the sheet of paper.

Students gather information from a variety of reference materials, including tradebooks, textbooks, encyclopedias, magazines, films, videotapes, film-strips, field trips, interviews, demonstrations, and observations. Teachers often require that students consult two or three different sources and that no more than one source be an encyclopedia.

Too often, report writing has been equated with copying facts out of an en-cyclopedia. Elementary students are not too young to understand what pla-giarism is and why it is wrong. Even primary grade students realize that they should not "borrow" items belonging to classmates and pretend the items are theirs. Similarly, students should not "borrow" someone else's words, espe-cially without giving credit in the composition. The format of clusters and data charts makes it easier for students to take notes without plagiarizing.

After students gather information, they read over it to check that they have answered their research questions fully and delete any unnecessary or redun-dant information. Next, they consider how they will sequence the information in their rough drafts. Some students tentatively number the research ques-tions in the order they plan to use them in their composition. They also identify a piece of information that is especially interesting to use as the lead-in to their section.

4. *Draft the sections of the report.* With this preparation, students write their sec-tions using the process approach to writing. They write the rough draft, skip-ping every other line to allow space for revising and editing. Because students are working in pairs or small groups, one student can be the scribe to write the draft while the other students in the group dictate the sentences using infor-mation from a cluster or data chart. Next, they share their draft with students from other small groups and revise it on the basis of feedback they receive. Last, students proofread and correct mechanical errors.

5. *Compile the sections.* Students bring their completed sections for the research report and compile them. As a class, they write the introduction, conclusion, and bibliography and add them to the report. A list should also be added at the end, identifying the authors of each section. After all the parts are compiled, the entire report is read aloud so that students can catch any inconsistencies or redundant passages.

6. *Publish the report.* The last step in writing a class collaboration research re-port is to publish it. A final copy with all of the parts of the report in the correct sequence is made. If the report has been written on a microcomputer, it is easy to print out the final copy. Otherwise, the report can be typed or recopied by hand. Copies are made for each student, and special bound copies can be constructed for the class or school library.

Writing Individual Reports. Writing an individual report is similar to writing a collaborative report. Students continue to design research questions, gather information to answer the questions, and then report what they have learned. Writing individually makes two significant changes necessary. Students must narrow their topics and then assume the entire responsibility for writing the report. The steps in writing individual research reports are:

1. *Choose and narrow a topic.* Students choose topics for research reports from content area units, hobbies, or other interests. After choosing a general topic, such as cats or the human body, they need to narrow their topic so that it is manageable. The broad topic of *cats* might be narrowed to pet cats or tigers and the human body to one organ or system.
2. *Design research questions.* Students design research questions by brainstorming a list of questions that they want to find answers to in a learning log. Then they review their list, combine some questions, delete others, and finally arrive at four to six questions that are worthy of answering. As they begin their search, new questions may be added and others deleted if they reach a dead end.
3. *Gather and organize information.* As in collaborative reports, students use clusters or data charts to gather and organize information. For upper grade students, data charts with their rectangular spaces for writing information serve as a transition between cluster and notecards.
4. *Draft the report.* Students write a rough draft using the information they have gathered in the previous step. Each research question can become a paragraph, a section, or a chapter in the report.
5. *Revise and edit the report.* Students meet in writing groups to share their rough drafts, and they make revisions based on the feedback they receive from their classmates. After they make the needed revisions, students use an editing checklist to proofread their reports and identify and correct the mechanical errors.
6. *Publish the report.* Students recopy their reports in books and add bibliographic information. Research reports can also be published in several other ways. For example, students can produce filmstrip or video presentations, create a series of illustrated charts or dioramas, or they can dramatize the information presented in the report.

Assessing Students' Research Reports

Students need to know what the requirements are for the research project and how they will be assessed or graded. Many teachers develop a checklist with the requirements for the project and distribute this to students before they begin working. In this way, students know what is expected of them and they assume responsibility for completing each step of the assignment. For an individual research report, the checklist might include these observable behaviors and products:

- Choose a narrow topic.
- Identify four or five research questions.
- Use a cluster to gather information to answer the questions.
- Write a rough draft with a section (or chapter) to answer each question.
- Meet in writing groups to share your report.
- Make at least three changes in your rough draft.
- Complete an editing checklist with a partner.
- Add a bibliography.
- Write the final copy of the report.
- Share the report with someone.

This checklist can be made simpler or more complex depending on the age and experiences of the students.

Students staple the checklist to the inside cover of the folder in which they keep all the work for the project. As each requirement is completed, they check it off. In this way, students monitor their own work and learn that writing is a process, not just a final product.

When the project is completed, students submit their entire folders to the teacher to be assessed. All of the requirements listed on the checklist are considered in determining the student's grade. If the checklist has 10 requirements, each requirement might be worth 10 points and the grading can be done objectively on an 100-point scale. Thus, if the student's project is complete with all required materials, the student scores 100 or a grade of A. Points can be subtracted for work that is sloppy or incomplete. If additional grades are necessary, each item on the checklist can be graded separately. If a subjective assessment of the quality of the final copy of the research report is needed, then a second grade can be awarded. For more information on grading and assessing students' writing, see Chapter 10.

LIFE STORIES

Elementary students enjoy sharing information about their lives and learning about the lives of well-known personalities. When students write about their own life stories, they are writing autobiographies. When they write about the lives of others, they are writing biographies. As they read life stories written for young people, students examine their structure and use the books as models for their own writing. In writing life stories, writers combine expository writing with some elements of narration.

Authors use several different approaches in writing autobiographies and biographies (Fleming & McGinnis, 1985). The most commonly used approach is historical. In this approach, the writer focuses on the dates and events of the person's life and presents them in chronological order. Many autobiographies and biographies that span the person's entire life follow this pattern.

A second approach is the sociological approach. Here the writer describes what life was like during a historical period, providing information about family life, food, clothing, education, economics, transportation, and so on. For instance, in *Worlds Apart: The Autobiography of a Dancer from Brooklyn* (1980), Robert Maiorano describes his childhood in an impoverished New York City neighborhood and how he escapes it through a career with the Metropolitan Opera Company.

A third approach is psychological, and the writer focuses on the conflicts that the person faces. These conflicts may be with oneself, others, nature, or society. (For more information about conflict, see Chapter 4 on Narrative Writing.) This approach has many elements in common with stories and is most often used in shorter, event or phase autobiographies and biographies. One example is Jean Fritz's single-event biography, *And Then What Happened, Paul Revere?* (1973), in which Paul Revere faces a conflict with the British army.

Autobiography

An *autobiography* is the story of a person's life narrated by that person. In writing an autobiography, students relive and document their lives, usually in chronological order. They describe memorable events, the ones that are necessary to know their personality. A second grader's autobiography is presented in Figure 6-8. In this autobiography, you learn about Eddie through six chapters in which he describes himself and his family, his pets, his "favorites" and hobbies, and vacations to a Texas town.

Autobiographical writing grows out of children's personal narratives and "All About Me" books that they write in kindergarten and first grade. Children's greatest source of information for writing is their own experiences, and when they write autobiographies, they draw from this wealth of experiences.

"All About Me" Books. Children in kindergarten and first grade often compile "All About Me" books. These first autobiographies usually contain information such as the child's birthday, family members, friends, and favorite activities with drawings as well as text used to present the information. Four pages from a first grader's "All About Me" book is presented in Figure 6-9. In these books, the children and the teacher decide on the topic for each page and after brainstorming possible ideas for the topic, children draw a picture and write about the topic. Children may also need to ask their parents for information about their birth and events during their preschool years. In Figure 6-9, for example, first-grade Jana reports that it was her father who told her that she was choosy about the clothes she wore when she was five.

Biography

A *biography* is an account of a person's life written by someone else, and writers try to make this account as accurate and authentic as possible. In researching biographies, writers consult a variety of sources of information. The best source of information, of course, is the person himself or herself, and through an interview, writers can learn many things about the person. Other primary sources include

A

Story About

Me

Written

By

Eddie Heck

1

FIGURE 6-8 A Second Grader's Autobiography

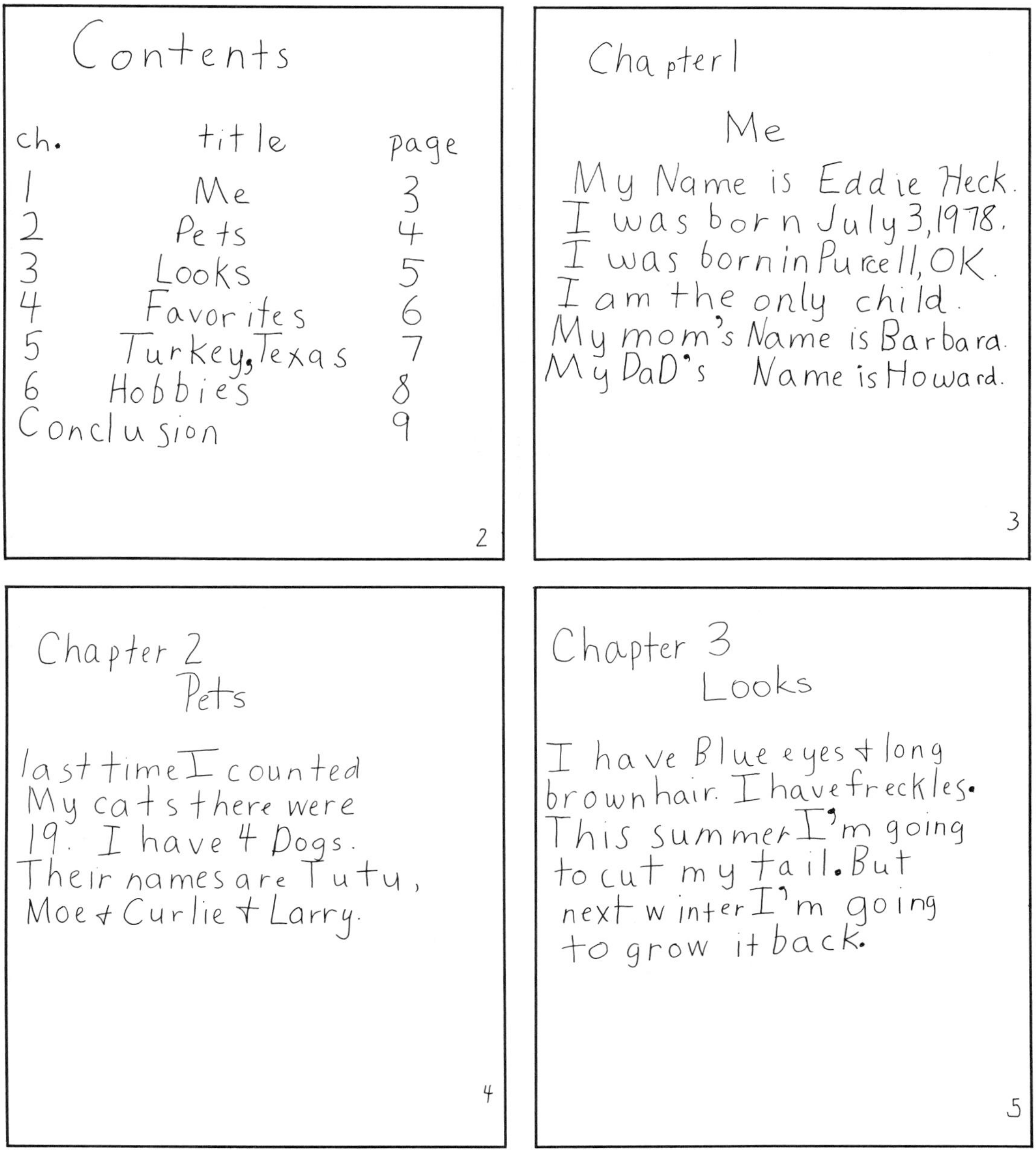

Contents

2

Chapter 1

Me

My Name is Eddie Heck.
I was born July 3, 1978.
I was born in Purcell, OK.
I am the only child.
My mom's Name is Barbara.
My DaD's Name is Howard.

3

Chapter 2
Pets

last time I counted
My cats there were
19. I have 4 Dogs.
Their names are Tutu,
Moe & Curlie & Larry.

4

Chapter 3
Looks

I have Blue eyes & long
brown hair. I have freckles.
This summer I'm going
to cut my tail. But
next winter I'm going
to grow it back.

5

FIGURE 6-8 (continued)

Chapter 4
   Favorites
My favorite president
is Georrge Washington.
My favorite pet is a
Dog. My favorite
thing is my Bike.
My favorite toy
is GI. LoE.
My favorite color
is black. My favorite
Game is NINJA.

6

Chapter 5
   Turkey, Texas
I went to Turkey, Texas
for My first time at
2½ yrs. old. I liked
it so much we have gone
ever since. I went to
see BoB Wills and his
Texas Play Boys but
BoB Wills is dead now.

7

Chapter 6
   Hobbies
My favorite hobbies
are inventing games.
I've invented these
games: NINJA & Goldtar
defender of The
Universe. These are Games
that sometimes I play
by my self and some
times I play with my
friends.

8

   Conclusion
The day after school
is out I'm going to Dog-
Patch, Arkansas to see
Daisy Mae and Mammy
Yoakum. I may go to
   Six Flags this summer.
I may also go to Frontier
City. I will be looking
forward to school
starting.

9

FIGURE 6-8 (continued)

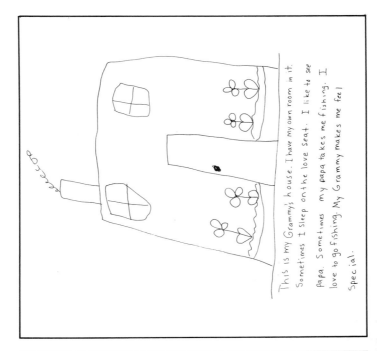

This is my Grammy's house. I have my own room in it. Sometimes I sleep on the love seat. I like to see papa. Sometimes my papa takes me fishing. I love to go fishing. My Grammy makes me feel special.

Kasey   Randy   Kimberly

I have 3 best friends. they are very nice to do things with me. My friends names are Randy, Kasey, and Kimberly. I go to Randy's house every morning. Her mom baby sits me.

FIGURE 6-9 Four Pages from a First Grader's "All About Me" Book

I went to Six Flags. I ate eggs before I got on the roller coaster and wen we went down my stomach strted to hurt.

This is me wen I'm five. I'm reading a book. My mom comes in and puts out my cloths for me to wear but I didn't, wah t to wear them. I became very picky about my cloths my dad said.

FIGURE 6-9 (continued)

diaries and letters written by the person, photographs, mementos, historical records, and recollections of people who know that person. Secondary sources are
books, newspapers, and films about the person written by someone else.

Biographies may be categorized as contemporary or historical. Contemporary
biographies are written about a living person, especially a person that the writer
can interview. In contrast, historical biographies are written about persons who
are no longer alive, and the information must come from secondary sources.

Contemporary Biographies. Students write biographies about living people
they know personally as well as about well-known living personalities, such as the
President of the United States or a children's author. Although there are many primary sources of information available for researching local people, students may
have to depend on secondary sources of information (e.g., books, newspapers,
letters) to research well-known and geographically more distant persons. However, it is usually possible for students to write letters to these well-known personalities or, sometimes, to arrange conference telephone calls.

Mrs. Comeau's second-grade class interviewed their principal Mrs. Reno and
compiled a biography that became the most popular book in the school. Before
the interview, the students brainstormed questions, and each child selected a
question to ask. Then Mrs. Reno came to the classroom and answered the children's questions. After the interview, the students compiled a book of their questions and Mrs. Reno's answers. A page from the in class collaboration biography
is presented in Figure 6-10. You will also notice that the students practiced using
quotation marks in their report.

Historical Biographies. While biographies are based on the facts known about
a person's life, some parts of historical biographies must be fictionalized out of
necessity. Moreover, dialogue and other details about daily life must often be invented after careful research of the period. In *The Double Life of Pocahontas* by
Jean Fritz (1983), for instance, the author had to take what sketchy facts are
known about Pocahontas and make some reasonable guesses to fill in the missing ones. To give one example, historians know that Pocahontas was a young
woman when she died in 1617, but they are not sure how old she was when John
Smith and the other English settlers arrived in Virginia in 1607. Fritz chose to
make her 11 years old when the settlers arrived.

When children write historical biographies, they will have make some of the
same types of reasonable guesses that Jean Fritz did. In the following biography
of Daniel Boone, third-grade Charles added details and dialogue to complete his
report.

■ Daniel Boone was born in 1734 in Omley, Pennsylvania. When Daniel grew up,
he hunted a lot. He began his journey to Kentucky to hunt for game.

Every day, Daniel tried to hunt for game in Kentucky. In the morning, he
would catch two or three deers. At night, he wouldn't hunt because all the
animals would be hiding. Daniel wouldn't give up hunting for game in Kentucky.

Finally, he decided to travel through Kentucky. Soon Indians took their meat
and furs away. Would Daniel and his family survive?

FIGURE 6-10 A Page from a Second-grade Collaborative Biography of Their Principal

One day when Daniel was walking to his fellow friend's fort, he looked all around. Indians were surrounding him. One Indian called Chief Blackfish said, "Take me to your men. If you do, I will not hurt you or them. If you don't, I will kill you and your friends." Daniel was trapped. When they were walking to the fort, Daniel ran inside. Just then, gunshots were fired. They were at war. Soon the war was over. Daniel's people had won.

Daniel died in 1820 at the age of 85. Daniel Boone is remembered for opening the land of Kentucky for white men to hunt in and fighting for Kentucky.

Engaging Students in Biographical Study. When students study someone else's life to prepare for writing a biography, they need to become personally involved in the project (Zarnowski, 1988). There are several ways to engage students in biographical study; that is, to help students walk in the footsteps of the other person. For contemporary biographies, meeting and interviewing the person is the best way. For other biography projects, students read books about the person, view films and videos, dramatize events from the person's life, and write about the persons they are studying. An especially valuable activity is simulated journals in which students assume the persona of the person they are studying and write journal entries just as that person might have. (See Chapter 2 for more information about simulated journals.)

Teaching Students to Write Life Stories

Students learn to write through a process approach. While this instructional strategy includes similar steps for writing autobiographies and biographies, these two writing forms are different and should be taught separately. The steps are:

1. *Read to learn about the format and unique conventions.* Autobiographies and biographies written by others can serve as models for the life stories that students write. Many autobiographies of scientists, entertainers, sports figures, and others are available for upper grade students, but, unfortunately, only a few autobiographies have been written for younger children. A list of suggested autobiographies is presented in Figure 6-11. These books provide examples of both entire-life and shorter event autobiography forms. As students read autobiographies, they can note which events the narrator focuses on, how the narrator presents information and feelings, and what the narrator's viewpoint is.

   Biographies of well-known people such as explorers, kings, queens, scientists, sports figures, artists, and movie stars, as well as "common" people who have endured hardship and shown exceptional courage, are available for elementary students to read. A list of recommended biographies is also presented in Figure 6-11. Biographers Jean Fritz and the D'Aulaires have written many excellent biographies for primary- and middle-grade students, some of which are included in the list, and numerous authors have written biographies for older students.

   The autobiographies and biographies that students have written in previous years are another source of books for your students to read. While life stories become prized possessions, some students can often be persuaded to bring their life stories back the following year to share with your students.

2. *Gather information for the life story.* Students gather information about themselves or about the person they will write about in several different ways. For autobiographical writing, students are the best source of information about their life, but they may need to get information from parents and other family members. Often parents will share information from baby books and photo al-

FIGURE 6-11 A List of Recommended Life Stories for Elementary Students

---

AUTOBIOGRAPHIES

Ali, M. (with R. Durham). (1976). *The greatest: Muhammad Ali.* New York: Ballantine. (M–U)

Begley, K. A. (1977). *Deadline.* New York: Putnam. (U)

Bulla, C. R. (1985). *A grain of wheat: A writer begins.* New York: Godine. (U)

Chukosky, K. (1976). *The silver crest: My Russian boyhood* (B. Stillman, Trans.). New York: Holt. (U)

Collins, M. (1976). *Flying to the moon and other strange places.* New York: Farrar. (M–U)

de Paola, T. (1989). *The art lesson.* New York: Putnam. (P–M).

Fisher, L. E. (1972). *The death of evening star: Diary of a young New England whaler.* New York: Doubleday. (U)

Fritz, J. (1982). *Homesick: My own story.* New York: Putnam. (M–U)

Gish, L. (1988). *An actor's life for me.* New York: Viking. (U)

Goodall, J. (1988). *My life with the chimpanzees.* New York: Simon and Schuster.

Hamill, D. (with E. Clairmont). (1983). *Dorothy Hamill: On and off the ice.* New York: Knopf. (M)

James, N. (1979). *Alone around the world.* New York: Coward. (U)

Jenner, B. (with R. S. Kiliper). (1980). *The Olympics and me.* New York: Doubleday. (M)

Keller, H. (1980). *The story of my life.* New York: Watermill Press. (M–U)

Maiorano, R. (1980). *Worlds apart: The autobiography of a dancer from Brooklyn.* New York: Coward. (U)

Huynh, Q. N. (1982). *The land I lost: Adventures of a boy in Vietnam.* New York: Harper and Row. (M–U)

North, S. (1963). *Rascal.* New York: Dutton. (M–U)

O'Kelley, M. L. (1983). *From the hills of Georgia: An autobiography in paintings.* Boston: Little, Brown. (P–M–U)

Rudolph, W. (1977). *Wilma. The story of Wilma Rudolph.* New York: New American Library. (U)

Schulz, C. M. (with R. S. Kiliper). (1980). *Charlie Brown, Snoopy and me: And all the other Peanuts characters.* New York: Doubleday. (M–U)

Singer, I. B. (1969. *A day of pleasure: Stories of a boy growing up in Warsaw.* New York: Farrar. (U)

Sullivan, T., & Gill, D. (1975). *If you could see what I hear.* New York: Harper and Row. (U)

---

bums. Also, older brothers and sisters can share their remembrances. Another strategy students can use to gather information before writing an autobiography is to collect some objects that symbolize their life and hang them on a "lifeline" clothesline or put them in a "life box" made from a shoebox (Flem-

FIGURE 6-11   (continued)

BIOGRAPHIES

Adler, D. A. (1989). *A picture book of Martin Luther King.* New York: Holiday House. (See other biographies by the same author.) (P–M)

Blassingame, W. (1979). *Thor Heyerdahl: Viking scientist.* New York: Elsevier/Nelson. (M–U)

Brandenberg, A. (1965). *A weed is a flower: The life of George Washington Carver.* Englewood Cliffs, NJ: Prentice-Hall. (M) (See other biographies by the same author.)

Burleigh, R. (1985). *A man named Thoreau.* New York: Atheneum. (U)

D'Aulaire, I. & D'Aulaire, E. P. (1936). *George Washington.* New York: Doubleday. (See other biographies by the same authors.) (P–M)

Dobrin, A. (1975). *I am a stranger on Earth: The story of Vincent Van Gogh.* New York: Warne. (M–U)

Felton, H. W. (1976). *Deborah Sampson: Soldier of the revolution.* New York: Dodd, Mead. (M)

Freedman, R. (1987). *Lincoln: A photobiography.* New York: Clarion. (M–U)

Fritz, J. (1973). *And then what happened, Paul Revere?* New York: Coward. (See other biographies by the same author.) (P–M)

Giff, P. R. (1987). *Laura Ingalls Wilder.* New York: Viking. (M)

Greenberg, K. E. (1986). *Michael J. Fox.* Minneapolis: Lerner (M)

Greenfield, E. (1977). *Mary McLeod Bethune.* New York: Crowell. (P–M)

Hamilton, V. (1974). *Paul Robeson: The life and times of a free black man.* New York: Harper and Row. (U)

Jakes, J. (1986). *Susanna of the Alamo: A true story.* New York: Harcourt Brace Jovanovich. (M)

Mitchell, B. (1986). *Click: A story about George Eastman.* Minneapolis: Carolrhoda Books. (M)

Monjo, F. N. (1973). *Me and Willie and Pa: The story of Abraham Lincoln and his son Tad.* New York: Simon & Schuster. (M)

Peterson, H. S. (1967). *Abigail Adams: "Dear partner."* Champaign, IL: Garrard. (M)

Provensen, A., & Provensen, M. (1984). *Leonardo da Vinci.* New York: Viking. (A moveable book) (M–U)

Quackenbush, R. (1981). *Ahoy! Ahoy! are you there? A story of Alexander Graham Bell.* Englewood Cliffs, NJ: Prentice-Hall. (See other biographies by the same author.) (P–M)

Stanley, D. (1986). *Peter the great.* New York: Four Winds. (P–M)

P = primary grades (K–2)
M = middle grades (3–5)
U = upper grades (6–8)

ming, 1985). Then students write briefly about each object, explaining what the object is and how it relates to their lives. Students can also decorate the box with words and pictures clipped from magazines to create an autobiographical collage.

For biographical writing, students interview living persons to gather information about their lives. For persons living in the community, students can interview the person. Telephone interviews and letters are other possibilities for persons who live a distance from the community. For historical biographies, students read books to learn about the person and the time period in which he or she lived. Other sources of information are films, videotapes, and newspaper and magazine articles. Students also need to keep a record of the sources they consult for the bibliography they will include with their biographies.

Lifelines. Students sequence the information they have gathered, either about their life or someone else's, on a lifeline or timeline. This activity helps students to identify and sequence the milestones and other events in the person's life. A lifeline for Benjamin Franklin is presented in Figure 6-12. Students can use the information included on the lifeline to identify topics for the life story. Three important events in Franklin's life, for example, were writing *Poor Richard's Almanac,* proving that lightning was electricity, and helping to write the Declaration of Independence. These could become the topics that a student writes about in a biography of Franklin.

3. *Organize the information for the life story.* Students select the topics from their lifelines that they will write about for their autobiography and biography and develop a cluster with each topic as a main idea. They add details from the information they have gathered, and if they do not have a four or five details for each topic, they can search for additional information. When students aren't sure if they have enough information, they can cluster the topic using the "5Ws plus one" questions (who, what, when, where, why, and how) and try to answer the six questions. If they can complete the cluster, students are ready to write, but if they cannot, then they need to gather additional information. The cluster that fourth-grade Brian developed before writing his autobiography is presented in Figure 6-13 with his autobiography. After developing the cluster, students make decisions about the sequence topics will be presented in—often in chapters—and add an introduction and conclusion.

4. *Write the life story using the writing process.* Students use the clusters they developed in the previous step to write their rough drafts. The main ideas become topic sentences and details are expanded into sentences. After they write the rough draft, students meet in writing groups to get feedback on their writing, then they make revisions. Next, they edit their writing and recopy it. They add drawings, photographs, or other memorabilia. For biographies, students also add a bibliography, listing the sources of information they consulted.

Besides making the final copy of their life stories, students can share what they have learned in other ways. Based on what they have learned through writing a biography, they can dress up as that person and tell the person's story to their classmates, or come as that person to be interviewed by their classmates. For example, Matt could have dressed as Ben Franklin and come to class to be interviewed. Through researching and writing about Ben Franklin's life, he

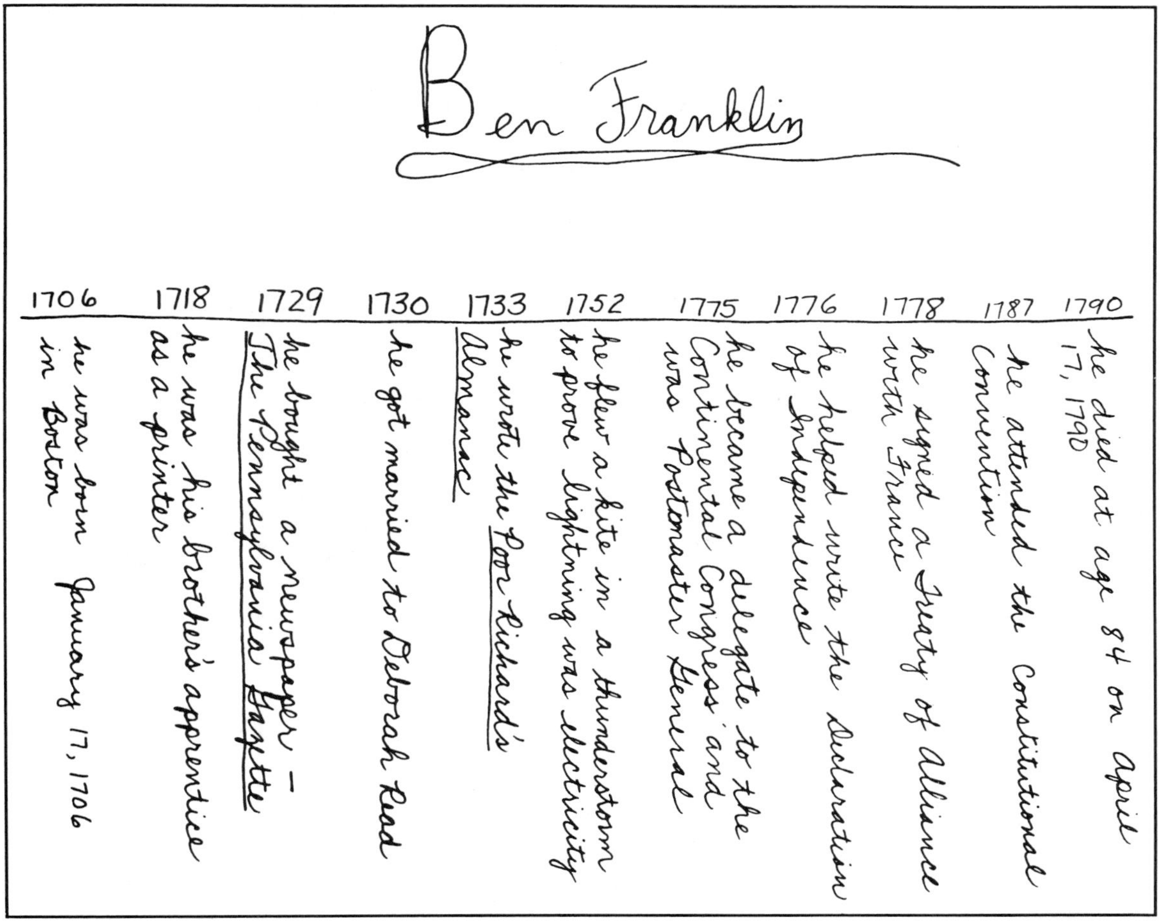

The lifeline reads (years across the top, entries written vertically beneath each):

- **1706** — he was born January 17, 1706 in Boston
- **1718** — he was his brother's apprentice as a printer
- **1729** — he bought a newspaper — The Pennsylvania Gazette
- **1730** — he got married to Deborah Read
- **1733** — he wrote the Poor Richard's Almanac
- **1752** — he flew a kite in a thunderstorm to prove lightning was electricity
- **1775** — he became a delegate to the Continental Congress and was Postmaster General
- **1776** — he helped write the Declaration of Independence
- **1778** — he signed a Treaty of Alliance with France
- **1787** — he attended the Constitutional Convention
- **1790** — he died at age 84 on April 17, 1790

FIGURE 6-12 A Fourth Grader's Lifeline of Benjamin Franklin

could have become knowledgeable enough to answer questions about Ben's life, his accomplishments, and his role in colonial and revolutionary times.

Assessing Students' Life Stories

Students need to know what the requirements are for their autobiography or biography project and how they will be assessed or graded. A checklist approach similar to the one described for research reports in the previous section is recommended. For an autobiography, the checklist might require the following components:

- Make a lifeline with at least one important event listed for each year of your life.
- Draw a cluster with at least three main-idea topics and at least five details for each topic.
- Write a rough draft with an introduction, three chapters (or more), and a conclusion.
- Meet in a writing group to share your autobiography.
- Make at least three changes in your rough draft.

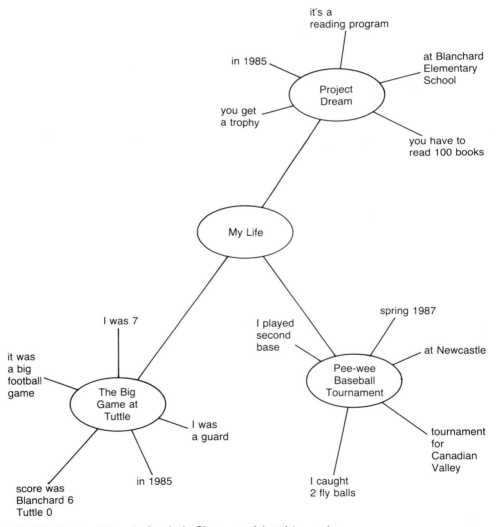

FIGURE 6-13 A Fourth Grader's Cluster and Autobiography

Introduction

I, Brian Spencer, being of sound mind and body, a healthy young boy about 4 ft. 6, with brown eyes and blond hair, do write this autobiography. My nickname is Snake because I am sneaky. At ten years of age, I have managed to survive my 16-year-old brother and my mom and dad!

Chapter 1: The Big Win

There was a big football game between Blanchard and Tuttle in 1985. And Blanchard was ahead. The score was Blanchard six and Tuttle nothing. My position was guard. The guard's position is to block other players. The uniforms are maroon and white. All the round robin games were played at the Blanchard High School field and we won them all. Pretty good for a seven-year-old! HA!

Chapter 2: Round Robin Victory

In the spring of 1987 on a bright sunny Saturday, my pee-wee team and I went to Newcastle to play our big pre-season tournament baseball game. We were all excited and hoping to win. I played second base. I caught two fly balls, but that didn't win the game but I would like to think it did. Anyway we won the round robin tournament for Canadian Valley and I sure was happy!

Chapter 3: Project Dream

In the year 1985 there was a big program called Project Dream. It was a reading program for the elementary students at Blanchard Elementary School. We are supposed to read 100 books a year. At the end of the school year the students that completed their 100 books got a trophy for first place. Anyone that reads a smaller amount of books gets a T-shirt. You could also win other prizes, for example, buttons, posters, and ribbons. I won a T-shirt, a trophy, and ribbons. So encourage your kids to read for Project Dream!

Conclusion

I am in the fourth grade at Blanchard Elementary School. My favorite subject is science. I like science because you get to do a lot of experiments. What I am going to do when I graduate is be a bass guide. A bass guide is to take people to fish.

FIGURE 6-13 (continued)

- Complete an editing checklist with a partner.
- Write a final copy with photos or drawings as illustrations.
- Add an "All About the Author" page.
- Compile your autobiography as a book.
- Decorate the cover of your book.

For a biography, the checklist might require the following components:

- Learn about the person's life from at least three sources (and no more than one encyclopedia).
- Make a lifeline of person's life with at least 10 important events listed.
- Write a least 10 simulated journal entries as the person you are studying.
- Make a cluster with at least three main idea topics and at least five details for each topic.
- Write a rough draft with at least three chapters and a bibliography.
- Meet in a writing group to share your biography.
- Make at least three changes in your rough draft.
- Complete an editing checklist with a partner.
- Recopy the biography.
- Add an "All About the Author" page.

Students keep the checklist in their project folders and they check off each item as it is completed. At the end of the project, students submit their entire folders to be assessed or graded. Teachers can award credit for each item on the checklist as described in the section on research reports. Through this approach, students assume a greater responsibility for their own learning, and they can better understand why they received a particular grade.

LETTER WRITING

A few minutes after morning recess, 10-year-old Travis thoughtfully folds the note he has written and gives it to Mr. Wyatt. As his teacher reads the note, Travis walks backward to his desk, never taking his eyes off him. Mr. Wyatt reads:

Dear Mr. W.,
I am sorry. Real sorry. It's bad to kick soccer balls on the blacktop and it hurts when a soccer ball hits you. They are hard. I won't do it no more. A good punishment is to have to write to Erica and Christy and tell them I am sorry. Ok?
Travis

After he reads the note and gives Travis a long, probing look, Mr. Wyatt takes a pencil and writes the following note:

Dear Travis,
It is a good idea for you to write to Christy and Erica and tell them that you are sorry that the soccer ball you kicked hit them. Why don't you write the

letters during afternoon recess. If you finish the letters today, you can come outside with us for recess again tomorrow morning. Thank you for writing to me. I know that you are very sorry that you kicked the ball on the blacktop so that it hit Christy and Erica.

Mr. W.

Mr. Wyatt gives his note to Travis and then he moves over to work with a group of students. Travis reads his teacher's note and with a sigh of relief he folds it up and puts it in his pocket.

Writing notes is a common activity in many elementary classrooms, but too often this activity is discouraged rather than encouraged. In Mr. Wyatt's class, students write notes to classmates, the teacher, and parents. These notes are not graded; rather, they serve genuine communicative purposes: Students write notes to ask permission, to solve problems, to plan activities, to apologize, to ask questions, to remind, and to sustain friendships (Karelitz, 1988). Mr. Wyatt also uses notes as a disciplinary technique. When a child misbehaves as Travis did, he or she writes to Mr. Wyatt to explain what happened and to decide on disciplinary measures. Then Mr. Wyatt writes back, and sometimes the exchange of letters is repeated several times before the problem is resolved.

Reta Boyd (1985) is a firm believer in the value of note writing and she encourages her elementary students to write notes and post them on a special message board in the classroom. The children write notes for a variety of purposes but Boyd emphasizes their educational value: Children practice reading and writing skills, and they recognize the functional and social nature of writing. An added benefit is that through note writing Boyd stays in touch with all students even though she may be working with a small group.

Letter writing is the logical extension of these informal notes. As with note writing, audience and function are important considerations, but form is also important in letter writing. While letters may be personal, they involve a genuine audience of one or more persons. Not only do students have the opportunity to sharpen their writing skills through letter writing, but they also increase their awareness of audience. Because letters are written to communicate with a specific and important audience, students think more carefully about what they want to say; are more inclined to use spelling, capitalization, and punctuation conventions correctly; and write more legibly.

Letters written by elementary students are typically classified as friendly or business letters. The forms for friendly and business letters are presented in Figure 6-14, and the choice of format depends on the function of the letter. When students write informal, chatty letters to pen pals or thank you notes to a television newscaster who has come to the classroom to be interviewed, they write friendly letters. When they write letters to General Mills requesting information about the nutritional content of breakfast cereals or letters to the President expressing an opinion about current events, they use the more formal, business letter form. Be-

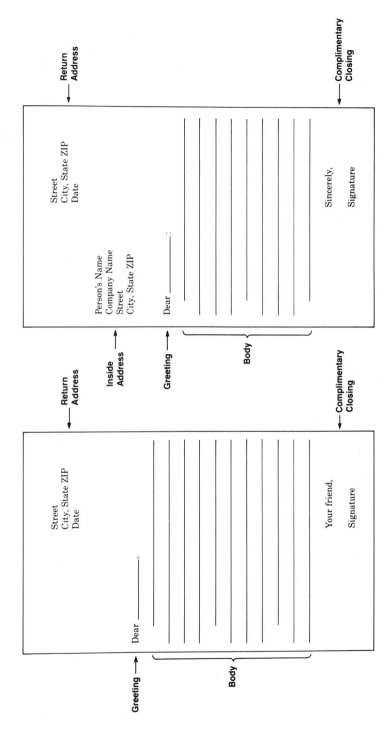

FIGURE 6-14 Forms of Friendly and Business Letters

fore students write either type of letters, they need to learn how to format their letters.

Friendly and business letter formats are accepted writing conventions, and most teachers simply explain the formats to students and prepare a set of charts to illustrate them. This attention to format should not suggest that form is more important than content; rather, it highlights the fact that elementary students are typically unfamiliar with the formatting considerations of letter writing.

Friendly Letters

Children write friendly letters to classmates, friends who live out of town, relatives, and pen pals. Students may want to list addresses of people to whom they can write friendly letters to on a special page in their journals or in address booklets. In these casual letters, they share news about events in their lives and ask questions to learn more about the person to whom they are writing and to encourage that person to write back. Receiving mail is the real reward for letter writing!

After being introduced to the friendly letter format, students need to choose a "real" someone to write to. Writing authentic letters that are delivered is much more valuable than writing practice letters to be graded by the teacher. Students may draw names and write letters to classmates, to pen pals by exchanging with students in another class in the same school or in a school in another town, or to friends and relatives.

Students use the writing process in letter writing, In the prewriting stage of the writing process, they decide what to include in their letters. Brainstorming and clustering are effective strategies to help students choose types of information to include and questions to ask in their letters. A cluster with four rays developed by a third-grade class for pen pal letters they were writing is presented in Figure 6-15. As a class, the students brainstormed a list of possible topics and finally decided on the four main idea rays (me and my family, my school, my hobbies, and questions for my pen pal). Then students each completed their clusters by adding details to each main idea. As they wrote their rough drafts, students incorporated the information from one ray in the first paragraph, information from a second ray in the second paragraph, and so on for the body of their letters. After writing their rough drafts, students met in writing groups to revise the content of their letters, and they edited their letters to correct mechanical errors with a classmate and later with the teacher. Next, they recopied the final draft of their letters, addressed envelopes, and mailed them. A sample letter is also presented in Figure 6-15. Compare each paragraph of the letter with the cluster, and you will notice that by using the cluster, the student wrote a well-organized and interesting letter that was packed with information.

Pen Pal Letters. Teachers can arrange for their students to write and exchange pen pal letters with students in another class by contacting a teacher in a nearby school, through local educational associations, or by answering advertisements in educational magazines.

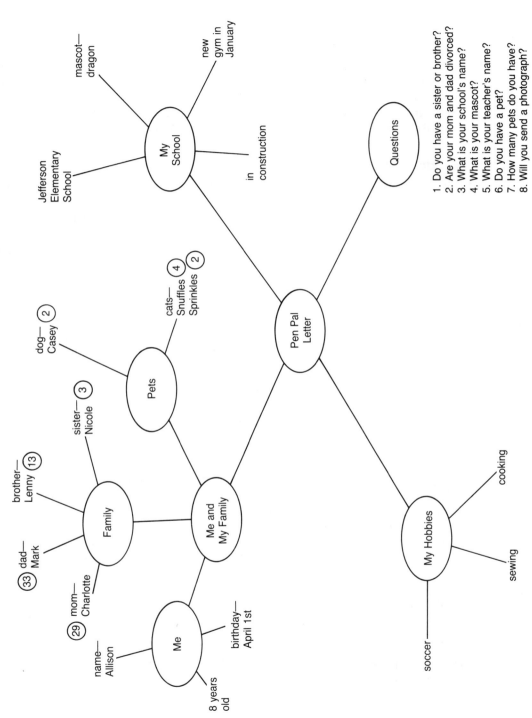

FIGURE 6-15 A Third Grader's Cluster and Pen Pal Letter

My School
- mascot—dragon
- new gym in January
- Jefferson Elementary School
- in construction

Questions

1. Do you have a sister or brother?
2. Are your mom and dad divorced?
3. What is your school's name?
4. What is your mascot?
5. What is your teacher's name?
6. Do you have a pet?
7. How many pets do you have?
8. Will you send a photograph?

Pets
- dog—Casey ②
- cats—Snuffles ④ Sprinkles ②

Pen Pal Letter

Family
- brother—Lenny ⑬
- sister—Nicole ③
- ㉝ dad—Mark
- ㉙ mom—Charlotte

Me and My Family

Me
- name—Allison
- birthday—April 1st
- 8 years old

My Hobbies
- cooking
- sewing
- soccer

December 10

Dear Annie,

I'm your pen pal now. My name is Allison and I'm 8 years old. My birthday is on April 1st.

I go to Jefferson Elementary School. Our mascot is a dragon. We are in construction because we're going to have a new gym in January.

My hobbies are soccer, sewing, and cooking. I play soccer, sewing I do in free time, and I cook dinner sometimes.

My pets are two cats and a dog. The dog's name is Casey and he's a boy. He is two years old. The cat is a girl and her name is Snuffles. She is four years old. The kitten is a girl and her name is Sprinkles. She is two months old.

My dad's name is Mark and my mon's name is Charlotte. Her birthday is the day after Mother's Day. My brother's name is Lenny. He is 13 years old. My sister's name is Nicole. She is 3 years old.

I have some questions for you. Do you have a sister or a brother? Are your mom and dad divorced? Mine aren't. What is your school's name? What is your mascot? What is your teacher's name? Do you have a pet? How many pets do you have? Will you send me a photograph of yourself?

Your friend,
Allison

FIGURE 6-15 (continued)

Individual students can also arrange for pen pals by contacting one of the following organizations:

- International Friendship League, 22 Batterymarch, Boston, MA 02109
- League of Friendship, PO Box 509, Mt. Vernon, OH 43050
- Student Letter Exchange, 910 Fourth Street SE, Austin, MN 55912
- World Pen Pals, 1690 Como Avenue, St. Paul, MN 55108

Students should write to one of the organizations, describing their interests and including their name, address, age, and sex. Also, they should inquire if a fee is required and enclose a self-addressed, stamped envelope (identified by the acronym SASE) for a reply.

Another pen pal arrangement is for a class of elementary students to become pen pals with college students in a language arts methods class. Over a semester, the elementary students and preservice teachers write to each other four, five, or six times, and perhaps they can even meet each other at the end of the semester. The children have the opportunity to be pen pals over a semester with college students, and the college students have the opportunity to get to know an elementary student and examine the student's writing. In a recent study (Greenlee, Hiebert, Bridge, & Winograd, 1986), a class of second graders became pen pals with a class of college students who are majoring in elementary education. The researchers investigated whether having a genuine audience would influence the quality of the letters these students wrote. Second graders' letters were compared with letters written by a control group of students who wrote letters to imaginary audiences and received traditional teacher comments on their letters. The researchers found that the students who wrote pen pal letters wrote longer and more complex letters once they received responses to their letters. The results of this study emphasize the importance of providing real audiences for student writing.

Courtesy Letters. Invitations and thank you notes are two other types of friendly letters that elementary students write. They may write to parents to invite them to an after school program, to the class across the hall to visit a classroom exhibit, or to a community person to be interviewed as part of a content area unit. Similarly, children write letters to thank persons who have been helpful.

Mrs. LoBaugh's sixth-grade social studies class developed a multimedia presentation about the United States Constitution and shared their presentation with a fourth-grade class. The fourth graders wrote a thank you note to each sixth grader, and they included a question in their letters so that the sixth graders would write back. One of the thank you notes is presented in Figure 6-16 together with the sixth grader's response.

Letters to Authors and Illustrators. Students write letters to favorite authors and illustrators to share their ideas and feelings about the books they read. They ask questions about how a particular character was developed or why the illustrator used a certain art medium. Students also describe the books they have written. A first grader's letter to Dr. Seuss is presented in Figure 6-17. Most authors and

Dear Marci,

You did a good job in the play that we watched. Can you tell me what union means please? Also what does tranquility mean? Well I just wanted to write you to ask you questions and tell you that you did good. Well got to go now. Bye.

Your friend,
Amy

Dear Amy,
Thank you for telling me I was good. Union means when all states get together and tranquility means peace!

Your friend,
Marci

FIGURE 6-16 A Fourth Grader's Thank You Note and Response by a Sixth Grader

illustrators will reply to children's letters; however, they receive thousands of letters from children every year and cannot be pen pals with students.

Beverly Cleary's award-winning book, *Dear Mr. Henshaw* (1983), provides a worthwhile lesson about what students (and their teachers) can realistically expect from authors and illustrators. The following guidelines are suggested when writing to authors and illustrators:

- Follow the correct letter format with return address, greeting, body, closing, and signature.
- Use the process approach to write, revise, and edit the letter. Be sure to proofread the letter and correct errors.
- Recopy the letter as a courtesy to the reader so that it will be neat and easy to read.
- Write the return address on the envelope and on the letter.
- Include a stamped, self-addressed envelope for a reply.
- Be polite in the letter, and as a courtesy, use the words *please* and *thank you.*
- Write genuine letters to share thoughts and feelings about the author's writing or the illustrator's artwork. Students should write only to authors and illustrators with whose work they are familiar.

Avoid these pitfalls:

- Do not include a long list of questions to be answered.
- Do not ask personal questions, such as how much money he or she earns.
- Do not ask for advice on how to become a better writer or artist.
- Do not send stories for the author or artwork for the illustrator to critique.
- Do not ask for free books because authors/illustrators do not have copies of their books to give away.
- Send letters to the author/illustrator in care of the publisher.

Publishers' names are listed on the book's title page and addresses are usually located on the copyright page, the page following the title page. If the complete mailing address is not listed, check *Books in Print* or *Literary Market Place,* reference books which are available in most public libraries. The suggestions in this list were adapted from Cleary (1983, 1985).

Young Children's Letters. Young children can write individual letters as the first grader's letter to Dr. Seuss presented in Figure 6-17 illustrates. They prewrite as older students do, by brainstorming or clustering possible ideas before writing. A quick review of how to begin and end letters is also helpful. In contrast to older children's letters, kindergartners and first graders' letters may involve only a single draft, since invented spellings and the artwork may carry much of the message.

Primary grade students also compose class collaboration letters. The children brainstorm ideas that the teacher records on a large chart. After the letter is finished, children add their signatures. They might write these collaborative letters to thank community persons who have visited the class, to invite another class to

Dear Dr. Seuss,
I like the SLEEP Book
Becos it is contagus
Amd the illustrations
Are the best of all.
I hav fourde Books
of yours and I have
rede them all.
Love, Sara

FIGURE 6-17 A First Grader's Letter to Dr. Seuss

attend a puppet show, or to a favorite author. Class collaboration letters can also be used as pen pal letters to another class.

Two books have been published that are very useful in introducing young children to letter writing. The Ahlbergs' *The Jolly Postman or Other People's Letters* (1986) is a fantastic story-like introduction to reasons why people write letters, and Lillian Hoban's story *Arthur's Pen Pal* (1982) is a delightful way to explain what it means to be a pen pal. In this way, kindergartners and other young children are introduced to the format of and the types of information included in a letter.

Business Letters

Students write business letters to seek information, to complain and compliment, and to transact business. These more formal letters are used to communicate with businesses, local newspapers, and governmental agencies. Students write to businesses to order products, ask questions, and complain about or compliment specific products. Students write letters to the editors of local newspapers and magazines to comment on recent articles and to express their opinions on a particular issue. It is important that students support their comments and opinions with facts if they hope to have their letters published. Students can also write to local, state, and national government leaders to express their concerns, make suggestions, or seek information.

Addresses of local elected officials are listed in the telephone directory. Addresses of state officials are available in the reference section of the public library, and the addresses of the President and United States senators and representatives are listed here:

- President's name, The White House, Washington, DC 20500
- Senator's name, Senate Office Building, Washington, DC 20510
- Representative's name, House of Representatives Office Building, Washington, DC 20515

Students may also write other types of business letters to request information and free materials. One source of free materials is *Free Stuff for Kids* (Lansky, 1989), which lists more than 250 free or inexpensive materials that elementary students can write for. This book is updated yearly. In addition, children can write to NASA, the National Wildlife Federation, publishers, state tourism bureaus, and other businesses to request materials.

As part of a literature unit on Laura Ingalls Wilder and her series of *Little House* books, a fourth-grade class decided to write a letter to the Laura Ingalls Wilder-Rose Wilder Lane Memorial Museum and Home in Missouri to request some information about the author and the museum. The class discussed what information needed to be included in the letter, and one child was selected to write the letter. A copy of this business letter is presented in Figure 6-18.

Simulated Letters

Students can also write simulated letters—letters in which students assume the identity of an historical or literary figure. They can write letters as though they were Davy Crockett or another of the men defending the Alamo or Thomas Edison, inventor of the electric light. Students can write from one book character to another. For example, after reading Patricia MacLachlan's *Sarah Plain and Tall* (1985), students can assume the persona of Sarah and write a letter to her brother William as third-grade Adam did in this letter:

FIGURE 6-18 A Fourth-Grade Class Letter to the Laura Ingalls Wilder-Rose Wilder Lane Memorial Museum and Home

Horace Mann Elementary
School
1201 Whisenant Street
Duncan, Oklahoma 73533
February 23, 1989

Ms. Irene V. Lichty, Director
Laura Ingalls Wilder-Rose Wilder Lane
   Memorial Museum and Home
Mansfield, Missouri 65704

Dear Ms. Lichty:

My fourth grade class has been studying about Laura Ingalls Wilder because February is the month of her birthday. We even have a learning center about her. Our teacher has put a few chapters on tape of *The Little House in the Big Woods.* It is a very good book.

We'd like to learn more about Laura. If you wouldn't mind, could you please send our class some brochures about the museum and any other information about her?

Thank you.

Sincerely,

Kyle Johnson and
Mrs. Wilkins' Class

■ Dear William,
   I'm having fun here. There was a very big storm here. It was so big it looked like the sea. Sometimes I am very lonesome for home but sometimes it is very fun here in Ohio. We swam in the cow pond and I taught Caleb how to swim. They were afraid I would leave. Maggie and Matthew brought some chickens.
   Love,
   Sarah

Even though these letters are never mailed, they give students an opportunity to focus on a specific audience as they write. After students write the original letters, they can exchange letters with a classmate, who then assumes the role of the respondent and replies to the letter.

Teaching Students to Write Letters

Students use the process approach to write both friendly and business letters. The steps in writing letters are:

1. *Gather and organize information for the letter.* Students participate in prewriting activities, such as brainstorming or clustering, to decide what kinds of information to include in their letters. For friendly letters and pen pal letters in particular, they also identify several questions to include in their letters.
2. *Review the friendly or business letter form.* Before writing the rough drafts of their letters, students review the friendly or business letter form.
3. *Write the letters using a process approach.* Students write a rough draft, incorporating the information developed during prewriting and following either the friendly or business letter form. Next, students meet in a writing group to share their rough drafts, receive compliments, and get feedback about how to improve their letters. Then they make changes in their letters based on the feedback they have received. Students edit their letters with a partner, proofread to identify errors, and then correct as many errors as possible. They also check that they have used the appropriate letter format. After all mechanical corrections have been made, students recopy their letters and address envelopes for mailing their letters. As the crucial last step, students mail their letters.

Assessing Student's Letters

Traditionally, students wrote letters that were turned in to the teacher to be graded. After they were graded, the letters were returned to the students but they were never mailed. Educators now recognize the importance of having an audience for student writing, and research suggests that students will write better when they know their writing will be read by people other than the teacher. While it is often necessary to assess student writing, it seems unimaginable for the teacher to place a grade at the top of the letter, next to the return address, before mailing it. Instead of placing a grade on students' letters before mailing them, teachers can develop a checklist to use in evaluating students' letters without marking on them.

The third-grade teacher whose students wrote the pen pal letters mentioned earlier developed the checklist presented in Figure 6-19. This checklist identifies specific behaviors and products that are measurable. These checklists are shared with students before they begin to write so they understand what is expected of them and how they will be graded. At an evaluation conference before the letters were mailed, the teacher reviewed the checklist with each student. Then the letters were mailed without any evaluative comments or grades written on them, but the completed checklist is placed in student's writing folders. A grading scale can be developed from the checklist. For example, points can be awarded for each checkmark in the *yes* column or five checkmarks can be determined to equal a grade of A, four checkmarks a B, and so on.

■ ANSWERING TEACHERS' QUESTIONS ABOUT EXPOSITORY WRITING

1. You must be kidding. My second graders can't write research reports. They still need to learn basic reading and writing skills.

The writing samples in this chapter show that second graders *can* write research reports. The question you seem to be asking is why should second graders write reports. Writing collaborative and individual research reports is not frivolous! Children learn basic reading and writing skills as they develop research questions, read to find answers, and then write a report to share what they have learned. What is more basic than having students read to find answers to research questions? They apply decoding and comprehension skills as they read, searching for answers to their questions. What is more basic than having students share their findings through writ-

ing? They use the writing process to write their reports. Report writing is authentic and meaningful, the kind of activity that promotes basic reading and writing skills.

2. When do I teach outlining?

Outlining is a sticking point for many writers. Because the format of an outline seems so formidable, students often write it *after* the report. I recommend that outlining not be taught to elementary students because it is unnecessary. Instead, have students use clusters and data charts to organize their writing. These forms are more effective and flexible than outlining. If you do teach outlining, have students make a cluster first and then transfer the information from the cluster to the outline. Each main idea item from the cluster becomes a main idea in the out-

FIGURE 6-19 A Checklist for Assessing Students' Pen Pal Letters

PEN PAL LETTER CHECKLIST		
Name _____		
	Yes	No
1. Did you complete the cluster?	☐	☐
2. Did you include questions in your letter?	☐	☐
3. Did you put your letter in the friendly letter form? _____ return address _____ greeting _____ 3 or more paragraphs in the body _____ closing _____ salutation and name	☐	☐
4. Did you write a rough draft of your letter?	☐	☐
5. Did you revise your letter with suggestions from people in your writing group?	☐	☐
6. Did you proofread your letter and correct as many errors as possible?	☐	☐

line and is marked with a Roman numeral. The details are listed under the main ideas and are marked with uppercase letters. If additional details have been added, they are marked with lowercase letters and written under the particular detail. For example, the main idea "How they act" section of the cluster on hermit crabs presented in Figure 6-4 can be rewritten this way as an outline:

1. How They Act
   A. Move sideways, backwards, and forwards
   B. Turn in circles, dig, climb, push objects
   C. Go back in shells if in danger
   D. Don't like water

3. Why do you insist that students—even first graders—should add a bibliography to their reports?

Students should give credit to the sources they used in their reports because adding a bibliography lends credibility that the information in their reports is accurate. Adding a bibliography to a report is not a complicated matter even though some junior and senior high school students who have never written a report before seem overwhelmed when asked to write a bibliography—a word they often confuse with biography. In contrast, elementary students accept the responsibility easily when it has been a natural part of report writing since kindergarten. Young children simply add a page at the end of their reports to tell everyone who reads it how they became experts about the subject and found answers to their research questions. It is sufficient if kindergartners and first graders list only the name and author of the book. Students at each grade level gradually add more information so that upper grade students include author, title, city of publication, publisher, and copyright date for the books they reference.

Another benefit is that middle graders begin to note that the authors of the informational books they read have references, too, and they become more critical readers when they look for verification of the accuracy of information they are reading.

4. Don't my students need to write practice letters before they write "real" pen pal letters that we mail?

Writing practice letters is a waste of time because the activity is artificial. When writing just for practice or for a grade, students feel little impetus to do their best work, but when they are writing to an authentic audience—their pen pals—they are careful about their writing because they want to communicate effectively. The instructional strategy for letter writing presented in this chapter provides the opportunity for teachers to introduce or review the friendly letter format during the prewriting stage, to help students revise the content of letters after meeting in writing groups, and for students to identify and correct mechanical or formatting errors during the editing stage. With these activities built into the instructional strategy, students can eliminate most errors before they mail their letters so that writing practice letters is unnecessary.

■ REFERENCES

Ahlberg, J., & Ahlberg, A. (1986). *The jolly postman or other people's letters.* Boston: Little, Brown.

Bonin, S. (1988). Beyond storyland: Young writers can tell it other ways. In T. Newkirk & N. Atwell (Eds.), *Understanding writing* (2nd ed.). (pp. 47–51). Portsmouth, NH: Heinemann.

Boyd, R. (1985). The message board: Language comes alive. In J. M. Newman (Ed.), *Whole language: Theory in use* (pp. 91–98). Portsmouth, NH: Heinemann.

Britton, J. (1970). *Language and learning.* New York: Penguin Books.

Cleary, B. (1983). *Dear Mr. Henshaw.* New York: Morrow.

Cleary, B. (1985). Dear author, answer this letter now . . . *Instructor, 95,* 22–23, 25.

Fleming, M. (1985). Writing assignments focusing on autobiographical and biographical topics. In Fleming, M., & McGinnis, J. (Eds.), *Portraits: Biography and autobiography in the secondary school* (pp. 95–97). Urbana, IL: National Council of Teachers of English.

Fleming, M., & McGinnis, J. (Eds.). (1985). *Portraits: Biography and autobiography in the secondary school.* Urbana, IL: National Council of Teachers of English.

Fritz, J. (1973). *And then what happened, Paul Revere?* New York: Putnam.

Fritz, J. (1983). *The double life of Pocahontas.* New York: Putnam.

Fulwiler, T. (1985). Research writing. In M. Schwartz (Ed.), *Writing for many roles* (pp. 207–230). Upper Montclair, NJ: Boynton/Cook.

Greenlee, M. E., Hiebert, E. H., Bridge, C. A., & Winograd, P. N. (1986). The effects of different audiences on young writers' letter writing. In J. A. Niles & R. V. Lalik (Eds.), *Solving problems in literacy: Learners, teachers, and researchers* (pp. 281–289). Rochester, NY: National Reading Conference.

Hoban, L. (1982). *Arthur's pen pal.* New York: Harper and Row.

Karelitz, E. B. (1988). Notewriting: A neglected genre. In T. Newkirk & N. Atwell (Eds.), *Understanding writing* (2nd ed.). (pp. 88–113). Portsmouth, NH: Heinemann.

Krogness, M. M. (1987). Folklore: A matter of the heart and the heart of the matter. *Language Arts, 64,* 808–818.

Lansky, B. (1989). *Free stuff for kids.* New York: Simon and Schuster.

MacLachlan, P. (1985). *Sarah plain and tall.* New York: Harper.

Macrorie, K. (1984). *Searching writing: A context book.* Upper Montclair, NJ: Boynton/Cook.

Maiorano, R. (1980). *Worlds apart: The autobiography of a dancer from Brooklyn.* New York: Coward.

McKenzie, G. R. (1979). Data charts: A crutch for helping pupils organize reports. *Language Arts, 56,* 784–788.

Queenan, M. (1986). Finding grain in the marble. *Language Arts, 63,* 666–673.

Sowers, S. (1985). The story and the 'all about' book. In J. Hansen, T. Newkirk, & D. Graves (Eds.), *Breaking ground: Teachers relate reading and writing in the elementary school* (pp. 73–82). Portsmouth, NH: Heinemann.

Wilde, J. (1988). The written report: Old wine in new bottles. In T. Newkirk & N. Atwell (Eds.), *Understanding writing* (2nd ed.). (pp. 179–190).

Zarnowski, M. (1988, February). The middle school student as biographer. *Middle School Journal, 19,* 25–27.

7

Persuasive Writing

One Tuesday morning, first-grade Linda wrote this letter to her teacher:

Miss McDonell,
I haf to go to heBrow skoll on tosday for 2 owr's and then eat bener that taks 1 ower and then I uwshulle have 1/2 un oher and I usulle ken not bo my Hom work on time so pleas gev me not as muj home work
Linda

(*Translation*: I have to go to Hebrew school on Tuesday for 2 hours and then eat dinner that takes 1 hour and then I usually have one-half hour and I usually cannot do my homework on time so please give me not as much homework.)

Parents have little doubt that children are effective persuaders as they argue to stay up beyond their bedtimes or plead to keep as a pet the stray puppy they have found. First-grade Linda's letter to her teacher shows that primary grade students can write persuasively even though researchers have found that children's persuasive writing abilities develop more slowly than their abilities in any other genre (Hidi & Hildyard, 1983).

Writers' sense of audience and ability to tailor writing to fit the audience is perhaps strongest in persuasive writing because they can judge how effective their persuasion is by readers' reactions. If Linda has less homework on Tuesdays, her letter was effective. While an audience's enjoyment of a story or poem or the information learned from a research report is hard to gauge, the effect of persuasion on others is not.

Researchers have examined audience adaption (Crowhurst & Piché, 1979; Kroll, 1978; Rubin & Piché, 1979) and found that upper-grade students were unable to decenter their writing and focus on the needs of their audience. More recently, Barry Kroll (1984) found that sixth graders could adapt to their audience in writing persuasive letters. He concluded that when students have a clear purpose and plausible reason for writing, they can adapt their writing to meet the needs of their readers.

Topics for persuasive writing come through at-home and in-school activities as well as through content area study. At home, children might try to persuade their parents to let them go to bed later, play on a football team, go to a slumber party, buy new clothes or shoes, join Boy or Girl Scouts, increase their allowance, buy a new toy, or have a pet. At school, children might try to persuade their teachers to let them have less homework, have outside recess in cold weather, change lunchroom rules, or sponsor a student council election. Through content area study, students can use writing to persuade others to stop smoking, avoid drugs, save the world from the destruction of a nuclear war, stop polluting our environment, endorse particular political candidates, critique books, movies, or support community, state, or national issues.

Persuasive arguments can be written as essays or as letters. Students write essays arguing against the use of drugs or book reports to recommend a book they have read. In these essays, students present a point of view and then defend the position by citing several supporting reasons or examples. Another type of persuasive writing is letters. Students write letters to legislators or letters to the editor of the local newspaper to express their opinions about community, state, or national issues and to try to persuade others to endorse their viewpoint.

Persuasive writing can also take other forms. Advertisements are a third type of persuasive writing. Through print advertisements on posters and scripted video commercials, students use both persuasion and propaganda to influence people to "buy" ideas, products, and services.

PERSUASION AND PROPAGANDA

To persuade is to convince or to win someone over to your viewpoint or cause. Persuasion involves reasoned or logical appeal in contrast to propaganda, which has a more sinister connotation. Propaganda can be deceptive, hyped, emotion-laden, or one-sided. While the purpose of both is to influence, there are ethical differences.

Persuasion

People may be persuaded in three basic ways. The first appeal is reason. People seek logical generalizations and cause-and-effect conclusions, whether from absolute facts or from strong possibilities. For example, people can be persuaded to practice more healthful living as the result of medical research. It is, of course, necessary to distinguish between reasonable arguments and unreasonable appeals. For example, the use of diet pills that promise exaggerated weight loss is an unreasonable appeal.

A second way to persuade is through an appeal to character. Other people are important to us, and we can be persuaded by what another person recommends—if we trust that person. Trust comes from personal knowledge of the person or the reputation of the person who is trying to persuade: Can we believe the persuader? Does the persuader have the expertise or personal experience necessary to endorse a product or a cause? For example, can we believe what scientists say about the dangers of nuclear energy? Can we believe what a sports personality says about the effectiveness of a particular sports shoe?

The third way people may be persuaded is by an appeal to their emotions. Emotional appeals can be as strong as intellectual appeals because people have strong feelings and concern for themselves and the human rights of others. We support or reject arguments according to our strong feelings about what is ethical and socially responsible. At the same time, fear and the need for peer acceptance are strong feelings that also influence our opinions and beliefs.

Any of the three appeals can be used to try to persuade another person. For example, when a child tries to persuade her parents that her bedtime should be delayed by 30 minutes, she might argue that neighbors allow their children to stay up later; this is an appeal to character. It is an appeal to reason when the argument focuses on the amount of sleep that a 10-year-old needs. When the child finally announces that she has the earliest bedtime of anyone in her fourth-grade class and it makes her feel like a baby, the appeal is to the emotions.

These same three types of appeal are used in in-school persuasion. When trying to persuade classmates to read a particular book in a "book selling" poster project, for example, students might argue that the book should be read because it is short and interesting (reason), because it is hilarious and you'll laugh (emotion), or because it is the most popular book in the second grade and everyone else is reading it (character).

Propaganda

The word *propaganda* suggests something shady or underhanded. While propaganda, like persuasion, is designed to influence people's beliefs and actions, propagandists may use underhanded techniques to distort, conceal, and exaggerate. Two of these techniques are deceptive language and propaganda devices.

People seeking to influence us often use words that evoke a variety of responses. For example, they claim something is "improved," "more natural," or "50% better." These words, called loaded words, are deceptive because they have positive connotations, but perhaps no basis in fact. For example, when a product is advertised as 50% better, consumers need to ask, "50% better than what?" That question is rarely answered in advertisements.

Doublespeak is another type of deceptive language. It is characterized as evasive, euphemistic, confusing, and self-contradictory. For example, janitors may be called "maintenance engineers," and repeats of television shows are termed "encore telecasts." William Lutz (1984) cited a number of kinds of doublespeak. Elementary students can easily understand two kinds, euphemisms and inflated language. Other kinds of doublespeak, such as jargon specific to particular groups, overwhelming an audience with words, and language that pretends to communicate but does not, are more appropriate for older students.

Euphemisms are words or phrases, such as "passed away," that are used to avoid a harsh or distasteful reality. They are often used out of concern for someone's feeling's, rather than to deceive. Inflated language includes words designed to make the ordinary seem extraordinary. For example, car mechanics become "automotive internists" and used cars become "pre-owned" or "experienced cars." Examples of deceptive language are listed in Figure 7-1. Children need to learn that people sometimes use words that only pretend to communicate; at other times they use words to intentionally misrepresent. For instance, a wallet advertised as genuine imitation leather is a vinyl wallet and a faux diamond ring is made of glass. The word *faux* is French, meaning false. Children need to be able to interpret this decceptive language and to avoid using it themselves.

Advertisers use propaganda devices, such as testimonials, bandwagon effect, and rewards, to sell their products. Nine devices that elementary students can identify are listed in Figure 7-2. Students can locate examples of each propaganda device in advertisements and discuss the effects the device has on them. They can also investigate how the same devices are used in advertisements directed to youngsters, teenagers, and adults. For instance, while a snack food ad-

FIGURE 7-1 Examples of Deceptive Language

Loaded Words	
best buy	longer lasting
better than	lowest
carefree	maximum
discount	more natural
easier	more powerful
extra strong	new/newer
fortified	plus
fresh	stronger
guaranteed	ultra
improved	virtually

Doublespeak	Translations
bathroom tissue	toilet paper
civil disorder	riot
correctional facility	jail, prison
dentures	false teeth
disadvantaged	poor
encore telecast	re-run
funeral director	undertaker
genuine imitation leather	vinyl
inner city	slum, ghetto
inoperative statement or misspeak	lie
memorial park	cemetery
mobile home	house trailer
nervous wetness	sweat
occasional irregularity	constipation
passed away	died
people expressways	sidewalks
personal preservation flotation device	life preserver
pre-owned or experienced	used
pupil station	student's desk
senior citizen	old person
terminal living	dying
urban transportation specialist	cab driver, bus driver

Lutz, n.d.

vertisement with a sticker or toy in the package will appeal to a youngster, an appliance advertisement with a factory rebate will appeal to an adult. The propaganda device for both ads is the same: a reward! These devices can be used to sell ideas as well as products. Public service announcements about quitting smoking or wearing seat belts as well as political advertisements, endorsements, and speeches use these same devices.

FIGURE 7-2 Propaganda Devices

1. Glittering Generality

Generalities such as "motherhood," "justice," and "The American Way" are used to enhance the quality of a product or the character of a political figure. Propagandists select a generality so attractive that listeners do not challenge the speakers' real point. If a candidate for public office happens to be a mother, for example, the speaker may say, "Our civilization could not survive without mothers." The generalization is true, of course, and listeners may—if they are not careful—accept the candidate without asking these questions: Is she a mother? Is she a good mother? Does being a mother have anything to do with being a good candidate?

2. Testimonial

To convince people to purchase a product, an advertiser associates it with a popular personality such as an athlete or film star. For example, "Bozo Cereal must be good because Joe Footballstar eats it every morning." Similarly, film stars endorse candidates for political office and telethons to raise money for medical research and other causes. Consider these questions: Is the person familiar with the product being advertised? Does the person offering the testimonial have the expertise necessary to judge the quality of the product, event, or candidate?

3. Transfer

In this device, which is similar to the testimonial technique, the persuader tries to transfer the authority and prestige of some person or object to another person or object that will then be accepted. Good examples are found regularly in advertising: A film star is shown using Super Soap, and viewers are supposed to believe that they too may have healthy, youthful skin if they use the same soap. Likewise, politicians like to be seen with famous athletes or entertainers in hopes that the luster of the stars will rub off on them. This technique is also known as guilt or glory by association. Questions to determine the effect of this device are the same as for the testimonial technique.

4. Name-calling

Here advertisers try to pin a bad label on something they want listeners to dislike so that it will automatically be rejected or condemned. In a discussion of health insurance, for example, an opponent may call the sponsor of a bill a socialist. Whether or not the sponsor is a socialist does not matter to the name-caller; the purpose is to have any unpleasant associations of the term rub off on the victim. Listeners should ask themselves whether or not the label has any effect on the product.

5. Plain Folks

Assuming that most listeners favor common, ordinary people (rather than elitish, stuffed shirts), many politicians like to assume the appearance of common folk. One candidate, who really went to Harvard and wore $400 suits, campaigned in clothes from J. C. Penney's and spoke backcountry dialect. "Look at me, folks," the candidate wanted to say, "I'm just a regular country boy like you; I wouldn't sell you a bill of goods!" To determine the effect of this device, listeners should ask these questions: Is the person really the type of person he or she is portraying? Does the person really share the ideas of the people with whom he or she professes to identify?

6. Card Stacking

In presenting complex issues, the unscrupulous persuader often chooses only those items that favor one side of an issue. Any unfavorable facts are suppressed. To consider the argument objectively, listeners must seek additional information about other viewpoints.

7. Bandwagon

This technique appeals to many people's need to be a part of a group. Advertisers claim that everyone is using this product and you should, too. For example, "more physicians recommend this pill than any other." (Notice that the advertisement doesn't specify what "any other" is.) Questions to consider include the following: Does everyone really use this product? What is it better than? Why should I jump on the bandwagon?

8. Snob Appeal

In contrast to the plain folks device, persuaders use snob appeal to try to appeal to the people who want to become part of an elite or exclusive group. Advertisements for expensive clothes, cosmetics, and gourmet foods often use this technique. Listeners should consider these questions in evaluating the commercials and advertisements using this device: Is the product of high quality or does it have an expensive nametag? Is the product of higher quality than other non-snobbish brands?

9. Rewards

Increasingly, advertisers offer rewards for buying their products. For many years, snack food and cereal products offered toys and other gimmicks in their product packages. More often, adults are being lured by this device, too. Free gifts, rebates from manufacturers, low-cost financing, and other rewards are being offered for the purchase of expensive items such as appliances and automobiles. Listeners should consider the value of these rewards and whether they increase the cost of the product.

Techniques 1–6 adapted from Devine, 1982, pp. 39–40.

When students locate advertisements and commercials that they believe are misleading or deceptive, they can write letters of complaint to the following watchdog agencies:

Action for Children's
Television
46 Austin Street
Newtonville, MA 02160

Children's Advertising
Review Unit
Council of Better
Business Bureaus
845 Third Avenue
New York, NY 10022

Federal Trade
Commission
Pennsylvania Avenue at
Sixth Street NW
Washington, DC 20580

Penny Power Ad
Complaints
256 Washington Street
Mt. Vernon, NY 10553

In their letters, students should carefully describe the advertisement and explain what bothers them about it. They should also tell where they saw the advertisement (name of magazine and issue) or the commercial (date, time, and channel) seen on television or heard on the radio.

PERSUASIVE ESSAYS

Persuasion is a part of everyday life. Children and adults frequently try to convince others to do or believe what they want. Andrew Wilkinson and his colleagues (1980) investigated children's ability (ages 7–13) to write persuasively. They found that children at all ages could state an opinion and, not surprisingly, as they grew older, they were better able to provide a logical justification for their opinions. Younger children were very egocentric in their reasoning and often failed to consider others' viewpoints. Furthermore, they found that children aged 10 and older often wrote self-contradictory essays. In these essays, students started with a definite position but through writing a justification for that position they concluded with a position which was opposite of the one made in the beginning. However, it should be noted that these students wrote single draft compositions and did not participate in writing groups to critique and revise their writing.

When persuasion is oral, it is informally presented, loosely constructed, and often underdeveloped. In contrast, when people want to present an argument in writing and try to persuade other people to act or believe as they want them to, the form and organization become more important.

Organization of a Persuasive Essay

A persuasive essay has a beginning, middle, and end, much like a story does. In the beginning, writers state their position, argument, or opinion clearly. In the middle, as in any story, the opinion is developed. In persuasive essays, writers select and present three or more reasons or pieces of evidence to support their position. These reasons may appeal to reason, character, or emotions. Writers sequence the evidence in a logical order and use concrete examples whenever possible. They often use cue words such as *first, second,* and *third* to alert readers to the organization. In the end, writers lead their readers to draw the conclusion that they intend using one or more of these techniques: giving a personal statement, making a prediction, or summarizing the major points. The organization of the persuasive essay is illustrated schematically in Figure 7-3.

Elementary Students' Persuasive Essays

Students write persuasive essays in which they argue on topics they have strong beliefs and opinions about. For example, sixth-grade Michael wrote the following essay about drinking soft drinks during class:

■ I think we, the students of Deer Creek School, should be allowed to drink refreshments during class. One reason is that it seems to speed the passing of the day. Secondly, I feel it is unfair and rude for teachers to drink coffee and soft drinks in front of the students. Finally, I think if the students were not worried about making trips to the water fountain, they would concentrate more on school work. Being allowed to drink refreshments would be a wonderful addition to the school day.

Michael's essay is well organized with a well-articulated beginning, middle, and end. He begins by clearly stating his position in the first sentence. Next, he lists three reasons and cues readers to the reasons using the words *one reason, secondly,* and *finally.* In the last sentence, Michael concludes the argument by making a prediction.

On another topic, girls' right to play sports, sixth-grade Amy writes:

■ I think there should be more sports for girls. Girls are capable of playing sports such as soccer and football. Some girls dislike basketball, but they want to participate in other sports. If girls could participate in other sports, they could learn to coordinate as a team. Everyone needs exercise and alternative activities would keep all females physically fit. Girls should have the chance to participate and excel in other sports.

Amy's essay also follows the three-part organizational structure, but she does not cue readers to her reasons in the middle using cue words as Michael did. She begins with a clear statement of her position, and at the end she uses a summary or generalization to conclude her appeal.

As a Letter. Students' persuasive essays can also be written as letters by adding a greeting and a closing to the essay. As with other types of letters, these letters are written to real audiences and are mailed. As part of a unit on drugs, students in a fifth-grade class each chose a family member or a friend to write a persuasive letter to. Some children wrote to parents or grandparents, arguing that they should stop smoking, or they wrote to siblings or friends urging them to avoid taking drugs or not to drink and drive. Fifth-grade Tom wrote this letter to his friend, Mike:

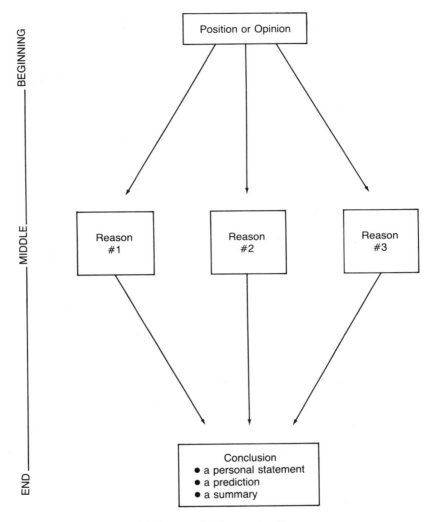

FIGURE 7-3 Organizational Scheme of a Persuasive Essay

■ Dear Mike,

I think drugs are very bad. They hurt people a lot and they can cost money. Mike, I know you're 15 and you don't think drugs can hurt you, but you can get addicted to drugs just the same as everybody else.

You can get hurt taking drugs, Mike. Some of the possible consequences are that you may get hurt dealing drugs, you may get AIDS by sharing infected needles or the pressure may become so great you just commit suicide. You might hurt others, too. You could rob a bank, hurt people in an auto accident, or just get violent and hurt someone. Michael, you might lose a friend and get into fights, be unpopular, or just be sad.

Drugs are out and it's the truth. More people are saying no to drugs. It isn't worth it, so be smart, not stupid, and don't get into trouble. Don't waste your time, and it costs lots of money to do drugs and you will be depressed a lot.

Many people say drugs are only as bad a cigarettes. That is not so. See Mike, you could go from $1 a day on cigarettes to $100 a day on heroin. Money and health problems arise from drugs. Each year, 200,000 are hurt by drugs and 25,000 people die from drug related accidents. Half a million people are arrested for drugs each year.

So, doing drugs is wrong. This evidence that you should not take any kind of drugs, Mike. I hope you make the right decision.

Your friend,
Tom

In his letter, Tom uses all three appeals—reason, character, and emotion. He uses statistics and cause-and-effect arguments in his rational appeal to persuade Michael to not use drugs. He says in his appeal to character that people who take drugs are stupid, and he evokes our universal fear of contracting AIDS in his appeal to emotion. Tom tells Michael that he might die or hurt other people if he takes drugs.

Persuasive letters can also be sent to newspapers. A letter sent to the editor of a local newspaper is presented in Figure 7-4. In this letter, seventh-grade Becky argues that the adult admission prices that teens pay at movies are unfair considering that they are not allowed to see "adult" movies.

Writing Persuasively in Content Area Classes

Mrs. Williams' fifth-grade class was studying the American Revolution. She asked students to think about whether or not the American Revolution was a good or necessary thing. Did they favor the patriot or loyalist position? The students brainstormed a list of reasons in support of the Revolution and a list of reasons in opposition. Then Mrs. Williams asked students to pick one side or the other and write an essay articulating their position. They were to begin by stating their position, providing a least three reasons to support their view, and then conclude the essay. Fifth-grade Marshall wrote:

■ I am in favor of the American Revolution and here are three of my reasons. First, after the colonists won the war, they could believe in God how they wanted. Next, if we didn't win the war, we would probably be British and not American. Third, after the war, the colonists could speak their mind without being tortured or killed. That is why I am for the American Revolution.

Tim took the opposing point of view and wrote:

■ I'm against the American Revolution. I think it was a bad war and unnecessary for several reasons. The first reason is that the colonists were already pretty much free, and they didn't need to have a war. The second reason is that there was way too much suffering, fighting, and loss of life. The last reason was that it

Editor, The Transcript:
I am a student at Longfellow Middle School. I am writing to express my feelings on the price teenagers pay to get into the movie theater. In most movie theaters at the age of 13, they consider you an adult, so you have to pay full price. But you pay the adult price to see a children's movie. They say we aren't old enough to see these movies, yet they consider us adult enough to pay the adult price. Why is this? I strongly urge the movie theaters to think this through and change the price, so if you are an adult you pay the adult price to see an adult movie and if you are a child you pay to see a children's movie. I am not saying that at the age of 13 you should be able to see "R" rated movies, but I'm saying don't make us pay for them. Let us pay for what we see.

REBECCA PIERCE
Norman

The Norman (Okla.) *Transcript,* Sunday, February 28, 1988

FIGURE 7-4   A Seventh Grader's Letter to the Editor

was a tremendous loss of lots of money. These are three reasons why I'm against the Revolutionary War.

Teaching Students to Write Persuasive Essays

Students use a process approach in which they investigate persuasion and then apply what they have learned in writing their own persuasive essays. The steps in the instructional strategy are described in the following paragraphs.

1. *Examine how persuasion is used in everyday life.* Talk with students about the points of view and positions people take on various issues. Also, share a chil-

dren's book such as *Molly's Pilgrim* (Cohen, 1983), *Oliver Button Is a Sissy* (de Paola, 1979), or *William's Doll* (Zolotow, 1972) in which the authors try to persuade readers to their viewpoint. In *Molly's Pilgrim,* for example, Barbara Cohen argues that there are modern-day Pilgrims like Molly's mother who emigrated from Russia and came to America for religious freedom. Read one or more of these books and discuss the argument with students.

After reading and discussing the story, teachers and students work together to develop a persuasive essay scheme or organizer similar to the one presented in Figure 7-3 to map out the persuasion used in the story and then write a collaborative summary of the argument. A class of fourth graders created a scheme after reading and discussing *Molly's Pilgrim* and then they wrote a class collaboration summary which is presented in Figure 7-5.

2. *Identify a topic and develop a list of reasons to support the position.* Students identify a topic for their essays and as a prewriting activity create a scheme to plan their essay as shown in Figure 7-3. Through this activity, students gather and organize their ideas before beginning to write. Fifth-grade Lance wrote a letter to his Uncle Bobby to try to persuade him to stop smoking and his scheme is presented in Figure 7-6.

Betty Jane Wagner (1986) found that middle and upper grade students wrote significantly better persuasive letters after role playing. In particular, Wagner reported that students who had participated in informal drama tailored their persuasion to their audience more effectively than students who did not. Role playing before writing the rough draft may help students to write better persuasive essays.

3. *Write the rough draft.* Students write rough drafts of their essays using the scheme developed during prewriting. As with other types of rough drafts, students label their papers as *rough drafts* and write on every other line to leave space for revision.

4. *Revise and edit the essay.* After writing their rough drafts, students revise and edit them. Before meeting in a writing group, students may first revise their own papers, reviewing to make sure that they have developed the beginning, middle, and end of their essays. Students can use a "Writer's Revision Checklist" as shown in Figure 7-7 to revise their essays. After completing the checklist, they make any needed changes before sharing their compositions in writing groups.

When students share their compositions in writing groups, they may ask their classmates to complete a "Reader's Revision Checklist" as shown in Figure 7-8. After classmates complete this form, writers compare their own responses with their classmates'. If readers' comments differ significantly from the writer's, then students should conclude that they are not communicating effectively and that additional revision is necessary. Discussing these revision checklists can be the major activity of the writing group or group members may offer compliments, have the writer ask clarifying questions, and then offer suggestions for improvement.

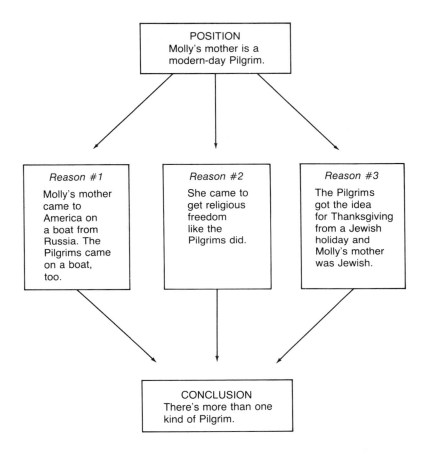

Summary

   Molly's mother is a Pilgrim, but she's not a Pilgrim from the first Thanksgiving in 1621. She's a modern-day Pilgrim. Here are three reasons why we believe this. First, Molly's mother came to America on a boat from Russia and the first Pilgrims came on a boat, too. It was named the Mayflower. Second, Molly's mother came to America for religious freedom. She was Jewish and in Russia, people weren't nice to Jews. The first Pilgrims came to America for religious freedom, too, because they couldn't worship God like they wanted in England. Third, the Pilgrims got the idea for Thanksgiving from a Jewish holiday called Tabernacles and Molly's mother was Jewish so it was her holiday, too. There's more than one kind of Pilgrim and even though Molly's mother wasn't a Pilgrim in 1621, she is one now.

FIGURE 7-5   An Organizational Scheme and Summary of *Molly's Pilgrim*

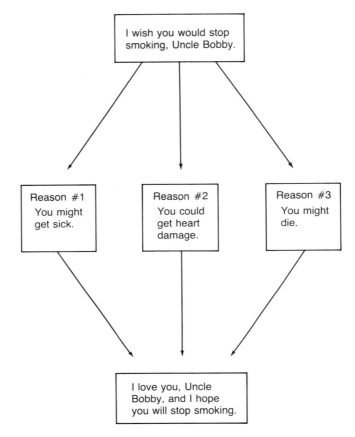

FIGURE 7-6 A Fifth Grader's Scheme and Final Copy of his Persuasive Letter

Lance and his writing group members completed the revision checklists illustrated in Figures 7-7 and 7-8, and their responses were very similar, suggesting to Lance that his readers were understanding his argument. Then Lance received compliments from writing-group members about the number and quality of pieces of evidence he used in the essay. Lance asked his writing-group members if he needed to resequence his pieces of evidence and his classmates responded that the order was fine. Finally, his classmates suggested that he elaborate on the second and fourth pieces of evidence, and he decided to expand the second argument about emphysema.

Then students proofread their essays, hunting for mechanical errors, and later they correct these errors. Lance and a classmate proofread his paper and located some of his spelling, capitalization, and punctuation errors. Then Lance met with his teacher for a final proofreading. After most of the errors had been corrected, Lance recopied his letter to Uncle Bobby and a copy of his

---

Final Copy

Dear Uncle Bobby,

Please listen to me. I wish you would stop smoking. If you don't stop smoking, you will get sick and you might die. You could get heart damage and that means you might die. I don't want you to die.

There is a disease called emphysema. If you smoke long enough, you will get it. Then if you try to walk a mile, it would seem like you walked fifty miles. Emphysema is a deadly disease.

When I hang around you and you smoke it is hurting my health as well as yours. You're polluting the air in your own house. That means you are hurting your own family.

I think smoking can kill you. If I get to be president, I will take them cigarettes and burn them. I think smoking is down right ridiculous.

If you stop smoking now, your heart will probably slow down and your lungs will be healthy again. Your whole body will shape up.

I love you Uncle Bobby and I hope you will think about what I said and stop smoking.

Love,
Lance

FIGURE 7-6 (continued)

final paper is presented together with his scheme and rough draft in Figure 7-6.

5. *Share the essay.* As with other types of writing, persuasive essays should be shared with a real audience. Essays may be shared by being read aloud, on posters, greeting cards, or in a bulletin board display. They can also be published in the school newspaper. Letters should be sent to the person to whom they are addressed, or letters to the editor can be published in school and local newspapers. Lance sent the final copy of his letter to his Uncle Bobby.

Assessing Students' Persuasive Essays

The process that students use to plan and write their persuasive essays is at least as important as the quality of their arguments, and a process approach to assessment is recommended. The assessment instrument should include the steps that students move through as they develop their essays, such as the following:

- Students create a plan for their essays using a scheme or cluster.
- Students write a rough draft of their essays.
- Students complete a "Writer's Revision Checklist."

- Students meet in writing groups to share their essays.
- Students have classmates complete a "Reader's Revision Checklist."
- Students compare the revision checklists.
- Students make one or two revisions based on the revision checklists and suggestions made in writing groups.
- Students proofread their essays and correct as many mechanical errors as possible.
- Students make a final copy of their essays.
- Students share their essays with an appropriate audience.

A checklist can be developed from these steps and be used in assessing students' essays. This checklist should be distributed to students before beginning the essay project so that they can keep track of their progress.

When an assessment of the quality of students' essays is necessary, the three items included in the revision checklists (see Figures 7-7 and 7-8) may be used as criteria. It is important that the criteria that students use in revising their essays are the same ones that teachers use in judging the quality of their compositions.

FIGURE 7-7   Writer's Revision Checklist for Persuasive Essays

Name _____   Yes   No

1. At the beginning, did you state your position or opinion   ☐   ☐
   clearly?

   Write your position here:

   _____

   _____

   _____

2. In the middle, did you present three pieces of evidence   ☐   ☐
   to support your position?

   Write your pieces of evidence here:

   1. _____

   2. _____

   3. _____

3. At the end, did you lead your readers to the conclusion?   ☐   ☐

   How did you lead them?
   ☐ Gave a personal statement.
   ☐ Made a prediction.
   ☐ Summarized the three main points.

ADVERTISEMENTS

Children, even primary grade students, are exposed to advertising as they watch television, view billboard posters, and read magazines. Because so many advertisements are directed to children, it is essential that they learn to judge their claims critically. For example, do the sports shoes being advertised actually help you to run faster? Will the breakfast cereal make you a better football player? Will a toy make you more popular?

Children need to learn how to be critical consumers of advertisements (Rudasill, 1986; Tutolo, 1981). Advertisers use appeals to reason, character, and emotion, just as writers of other types of persuasive language do, to promote products, ideas, and services. However, advertisers may also use propaganda as they attempt to influence our beliefs and actions.

Two types of advertisements that elementary students can examine and compose are print advertisements and commercials. Students read print advertisements in magazines, as posters on bulletin boards, and as billboards. They view some commercials on television and listen to others on the radio.

FIGURE 7-8 Reader's Revision Checklist for Persuasive Essays

	Yes	No
Name _____		
1. At the beginning, did the writer state his/her position or opinion clearly?	☐	☐
Write the position here:		
_____		
_____		
_____		
2. In the middle, did the writer present three pieces of evidence to support the position?	☐	☐
Write the pieces of evidence here:		
1. _____		
2. _____		
3. _____		
3. At the end, did the lead you to the conclusion?	☐	☐
How did he/she lead you? ☐ Gave a personal statement. ☐ Made a prediction. ☐ Summarized the three main points.		

Print Advertisements

As a part of a unit on drugs, a class of sixth graders designed posters to display in their community to warn youngsters about the dangers of drugs. In the poster presented in Figure 7-9, Steve used a logical cause-and-effect appeal to warn of the dangers of driving under the influence of alcohol or drugs. The loaded words are *gamble* and *the odds are,* and card stacking is the propaganda device used in this ad.

Students can also design lost and found advertisements. After reading Mercer Mayer's *Liverwurst Is Missing* (1981), fourth-grade Kyle designed the poster illustrated in Figure 7-10 to help locate Liverwurst, the baby rhinosterwurst who is missing from the circus. In the story, Liverwurst is finally found and saved from a terrible fate: becoming the world's first rhino-burger. Kyle's poster has the important, logical appeal information and picture typically found on lost and found posters as well as a "reward." Liverwurst's tears in the picture also add an emotional appeal.

Commercials

A small group of fifth graders created a commercial for a dating service they created called "Dream Date." In their commercial, students used testimonials and rewards as the propaganda devices. The students portrayed young women who met their husbands through the service and were living happily ever after. The rewards were a honeymoon for one young woman and becoming pregnant for another.

The storyboard for the "Dream Date" commercial is presented in Figure 7-11. This storyboard was developed from the script and includes camera directions in the left column, a sketch of the scene in the middle column, and the script in the right column. After completing the storyboard, students rehearse the commercial, add music and sound effects, and then present the skit. Students enjoy having their commercial videotaped so that they can view it themselves.

Teaching Students to Write Advertisements

Students use a process approach as they write print advertisements and video-commercials, in which they learn about the persuasive appeals and propaganda techniques that writers use and then use what they have learned in creating an advertisement for an idea or for a product or service they have created.

1. *Examine advertisements.* Students look for different types of advertisements on television, radio, billboards, newspapers, magazines, and even on T-shirts. They collect copies of these advertisements to examine, including television commercials that have been videotaped. Working in small groups, students examine the advertisements and use the following questions to detect propaganda:

FIGURE 7-9 A Sixth Grader's Advertisement About Drugs

FIGURE 7-10 A Fourth Grader's Lost and Found Poster for Liverwurst

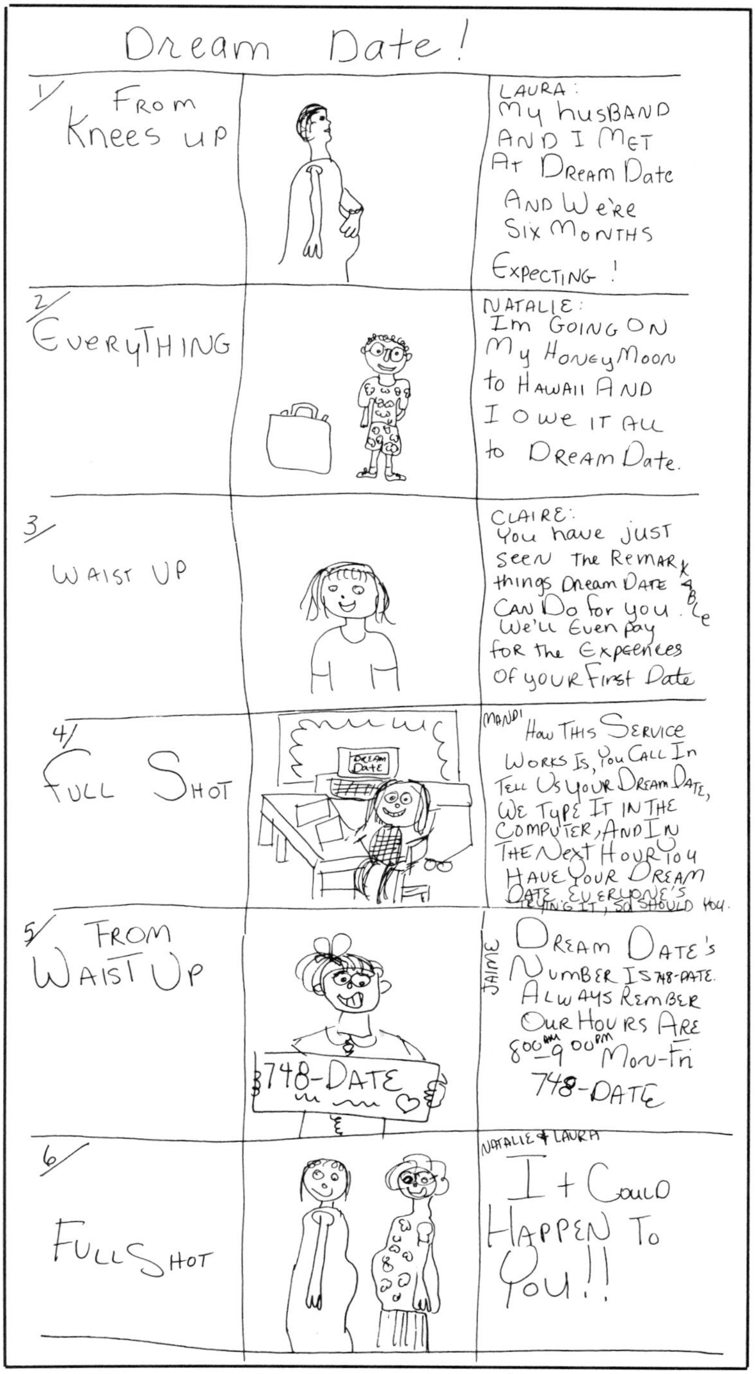

FIGURE 7-11 A Fifth Grader's "Dream Date" Commercial

1. What is the speaker's purpose?
2. What are the speaker's credentials?
3. Is there evidence of bias?
4. Does the speaker use persuasive language?
5. Does the speaker make sweeping genalizations or unsupported inferences?
6. Do opinions predominate the talk?
7. Does the speaker use any propaganda devices?
8. Do I accept the message? (Devine, 1982, pp. 41–42)

Students examine advertisements and then decide how the writer is trying to persuade them to support the idea, use the service, or purchase the product. They can also compare the amount of text to the amount of picture space. Appeals based on logic typically allocate more space to text than appeals based on character or emotions.

2. *Create a product or service to advertise.* Working in small groups or individually, students create a product or service to advertise. Possible products include breakfast cereals, toys, beauty and diet products, and sports equipment. Students might create homework services and housesitting services to advertise. They can also choose community or environmental issues to advertise.

3. *Design the advertisement.* Students design a print advertisement on a poster, using art and text to present the message or write a script for a commercial. As they create their rough drafts of the advertisement, students use specific types of persuasive language and propaganda devices to "sell" their idea, product, or service. They choose the type or types of persuasion that are most effective for the audience they want to reach.

4. *Use the writing process to refine and polish the advertisement.* Students complete the writing process by meeting in writing groups to refine their advertisements. Writing-group members focus their compliments on the use of persuasive language and propaganda devices in the advertisement. Their suggestions should deal with the most effective ways to "sell" the idea, product, or service. Writers should also be prepared to tell writing-group members which propaganda techniques they used and why. Students will take special care to edit print advertisements before making the final copy. For commercials, less attention is placed on editing because students will present the commercial in a skit. Instead, students will develop a storyboard in which they coordinate camera and stage directions with the script. A storyboard was illustrated in the "Dream Date" commercial presented in Figure 7-11.

5. *Present the advertisement.* Students share their advertisements with an appropriate audience. The ads students developed can be shared with classmates and with students in other classes. They can display poster advertisements related to community and environmental issues around the community. Students can also share commercials through live presentations and videotaped presentations with classmates and students in other classes.

6. *Critique the use of persuasion and propaganda.* As a last step, students assess their advertisements. In their critiques, they list the persuasive techniques and propaganda devices used in their print ads, and for commercials, they explain the techniques they used in the production.

Assessing Students' Advertisements

Teachers can assess students' advertisements according to the process that students use in creating the ads. Students should be able to identify and explain why they used particular persuasive techniques and propaganda devices. The steps in the process are subdivided into specific activities, and a checklist for assessing students' advertisements is presented in Figure 7-12. Two columns are included on the right side of the checklist, one for students to track their progress and one for the teacher to use. As with other types of process assessment checklists, students should receive a copy of the checklist *before* beginning the advertisement project. In this way, students understand how they will be assessed so they can monitor their own progress. The checklist can be easily adapted from print advertisements to commercials.

FIGURE 7-12   A Checklist for Assessing Students' Advertisements

Checklist for Assessing Students' Advertisements	Student's Check	Teacher's Check
Name _____		
1. Student examines advertisements and detects propaganda.	☐	☐
2. Student creates a product or service to advertise.	☐	☐
3. Student designs a print advertisement on a chart, using art and text to present the message.	☐	☐
4. Student meets in a writing group to share the advertisement.	☐	☐
5. Student revises the ad and makes at least one change.	☐	☐
6. Student and a partner edit the advertisement.	☐	☐
7. Student meets with the teacher for a final editing.	☐	☐
8. Student prepares a final copy of the advertisement.	☐	☐
9. Student shares the advertisement with an appropriate audience.	☐	☐
10. Student critiques the use of persuasion and propaganda in the advertisement.	☐	☐

■ ANSWERING TEACHERS' QUESTIONS ABOUT TEACHING PERSUASIVE WRITING

1. You must be kidding. My students can't write persuasive essays.

Even kindergartners and first graders use persuasion in their everyday talk. With guidance and encouragement, they can use the same kinds of persuasion in their writing. For example, a class of first graders used persuasion to compose Mother's Day cards. They began by talking about what kind of message to put in their cards and they decided to write about why their mothers were the best moms in the world. Their teacher, Mrs. Carson, asked them to draw a cluster and include at least three reasons their moms were best. Then they used the reasons in writing the message on the inside of their cards. John's cluster and Mother's Day message are presented in Figure 7-13. This message includes the same three parts that older students who write more complex essays use: the beginning, in which the position is stated; the middle, with at least three supporting reasons; and the end, in which the position is summarized.

2. I'm confused. What's the difference between persuasion and propaganda?

That's a good question. People use both persuasion and propaganda to influence someone to do or believe something. In both, people use appeals to reason, character, and feelings. The difference is that propagandists may use deceptive language and propaganda devices that distort, conceal, or exaggerate. The line between persuasion and propaganda is thin. Because it is so easy

to cross back and forth between the two, children must learn to detect propaganda in order not to be swayed by it. One of the best ways for children to learn this is through writing persuasive essays and advertisements themselves.

3. Writing advertisements seems awfully time-consuming.

Yes, it does take time to teach students about persuasive language and propaganda devices. It also takes time for students to create products or services and write ads or commercials. However, these activities teach students so much about oral and written language and consumer issues that I believe it is worth the time. As students are examining ads, they use critical thinking skills and learn to be more careful consumers as well as to read and write.

4. Can I tie persuasive writing to content areas?

Yes, students can write persuasively about topics they are learning in science and social studies. For example they can argue about historical events and even about contributions of various historical figures. They can investigate current issues about quotas for immigrants, English as the official language of the United States, or the rights of Native Americans. They can clarify positions on scientific concepts and consider topical issues such as nuclear energy, acid rain, pollution, and conservation efforts. For more information about writing across the curriculum, check Chapter 9.

■ REFERENCES

Cohen, B. (1983). *Molly's pilgrim*. New York: Lothrop.

Crowhurst, M., & Piché, G. L. (1979). Audience and mode of discourse effects on syntactic complexity in writing at two grade levels. *Research in the Teaching of English, 13,* 109–109.

de Paola, T. (1979). *Oliver Button is a Sissy*. New York: Harcourt.

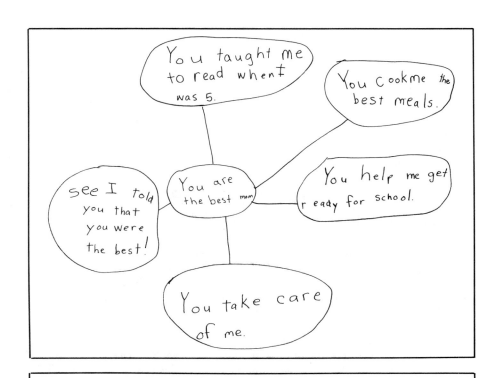

FIGURE 7-13 A First Grader's Cluster and Mother's Day Message

Devine, T. G. (1982). *Listening skills schoolwide: Activities and programs.* Urbana, IL: ERIC Clearinghouse on Reading and Communication Skills and the National Council to Teachers of English.

Hidi, S., & Hildyard, A. (1983). The comparison of oral and written productions in two discourse modes. *Discourse Processes, 6,* 91–105.

Kroll, B. M. (1978). Cognitive egocentrism and the problem of audience awareness in written discourse. *Research in the Teaching of English, 12,* 269–281.

Kroll, B. M. (1984). Audience adaption in children's persuasive letters. *Written Communication, 1,* 407–427.

Lutz, W. (1984). Notes toward a description of doublespeak. *Quarterly Review of Doublespeak, 10* 1–2.

Lutz, W. (n.d.). *Some examples of doublespeak.* Unpublished manuscript. National Council of Teachers of English Committee on Public Doublespeak.

Mayer, M. (1981). *Liverwurst is missing.* New York: Four Winds Press.

Rubin, D. L., & Piché, G. L. (1979). Development in syntactic and strategic aspects of audience adaption skills in written persuasive communication. *Research in the Teaching of English, 13,* 293–316.

Rudasill, L. (1986). Advertising gimmicks: Teaching critical thinking. In J. Golub (Ed.), *Activities to promote critical thinking* (Classroom practices in teaching English, 1986) (pp. 127–129). Urbana, IL: National Council of Teachers of English.

Tutolo, D. (1981). Critical listening/reading of advertisements. *Language Arts, 58,* 679–683.

Wagner, B. J. (1986). The effects of role-playing on written persuasion: An age and channel comparison of fourth and eighth graders. Unpublished doctoral dissertation, University of Illinois at Chicago. (University Microfilms No. 8705196)

Wilkinson, A., Barnsley, G., Hanna, P., & Swan, M. (1980). *Assessing language development.* Oxford: Oxford University Press.

Zolotow, C. (1972). *William's doll.* New York: Harper and Row.

8

Writers' Tools

Fourth-grade Stephanie pulls her chair over to Danielle's desk, and they trade rough drafts of their pen pal letters. A copy of Stephanie's letter with the spelling errors corrected appears in Figure 8-1. Each girl reads through the draft, checking for spelling errors. They point at each word with a green pen and pronounce the word softly, using pronounciation as an aid to spelling whenever they can. Danielle circles the word *anser* on Stephanie's letter because she thinks it might be misspelled. She mumbles that it just doesn't look right. Then they continue reading.

When they finish reading their two-page letters, each girl has circled 5 to 10 words. They share the errors with each other, agree or disagree about misspellings, write known correct spellings above circled spelling words. Then they ask Katrina who happens to walk by Danielle's desk, for advice about spelling several remaining words. She can't help with these words, but she does note one other spelling error she sees on Danielle's paper. Finally they resort to the dictionary to locate the correct spelling for *colet* (collect), *awile* (awhile), *Chrismas* (Christ-

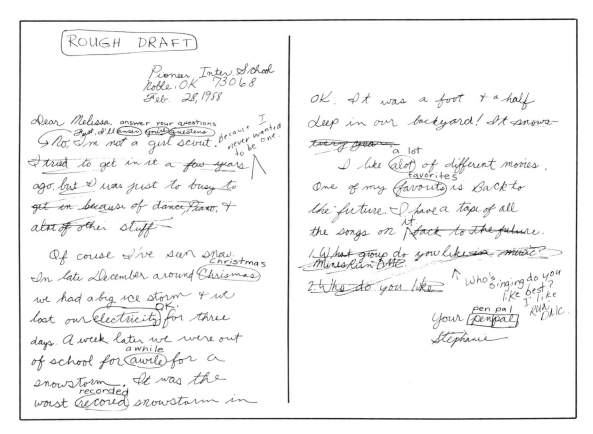

FIGURE 8-1 The Rough Draft of a Fourth Grader's Pen Pal Letter

mas), achemet (acheivement), and favorit (favorite), words that neither girl is sure how to spell. Then they add a checkmark to the spelling box in the editor's column on their editing checklists.

This editing checklist has a second spelling requirement. A copy of the editing checklist is in Figure 8-2. The girls are to reread the pen pal letters checking specifically for the following words that their teacher, Mrs. Jacks, has noticed were used and frequently misspelled in their previous pen pal letters. Her students check specifically for these words and correct them if they are misspelled. The words are: *friend, school, their-there-they're*, and *a lot*. They find *a lot* spelled as one word in Stephanie's letter, and they make the correction. None of these words are misspelled in Danielle's letter.

Tomorrow the girls will finish checking for punctuation, capitalization, and friendly letter format errors, which are the remaining three categories included on their editing checklists. For today, the rough drafts are returned to their writing folders.

FIGURE 8-2   An Editing Checklist for a Pen Pal Letter

	Author	Editor
1. I have circled misspelled words.	☐	☐
2. I have checked for these spelling monsters:	☐	☐
☐ friend ☐ school ☐ their-there-they're ☐ a lot		
3. I have checked that proper nouns and adjectives begin with capital letters.	☐	☐
Pioneer Intermediate School American flag		
4. I have added commas to separate items in a series.	☐	☐
5. I have checked for the friendly letter format:	☐	☐
☐ return address ☐ date ☐ greeting ☐ closing		

Signatures: _____   _____
                              Author   Editor

Students should understand that spelling is merely a tool for writers, a tool that allows writers to communicate effectively and efficiently with readers. Donald Graves (1983) explains:

> Spelling is for writing. Children may achieve high scores on phonic inventories, or weekly spelling tests. But the ultimate test is what the child does under "game" conditions, within the process of moving toward meaning. (pp. 193–194)

This chapter focuses on four writers' tools: spelling, grammar, handwriting, and microcomputers. Like spelling, good grammar and legible handwriting are courtesies to readers that writers must attend to in the revising, editing, and sharing stages of the writing process. They are important when the writing will be made public; they are of far less concern when the writing is private—for the writer alone.

In contrast to the other writers' tools, microcomputers are mechanical tools. As microcomputers become familiar tools in elementary classrooms, children will find that writing, revising, and editing are simplified through word processing software. Each writing tool is discussed separately, and suggestions are offered about teaching the tool in conjunction with writing activities.

SPELLING

There are 26 letters in our alphabet, and the alphabetic principle suggests that there should be a one-to-one correspondence between graphemes (the letters) and phonemes (the sounds) so that each letter consistently represents one sound. English does not have this correspondence. Twenty-six letters, used singly or in combination, represent approximately 44 phonemes. Moreover, three letters—*c, q,* and *x*—are superfluous because they do not represent unique phonemes. The letter *c,* for instance, can be used either to represent /k/ as in *cat* or /s/ as in *decide.* The letter *c* can also be combined with *h* to represent the digraph /ch/. To further complicate the situation, there are more than 500 spellings (and perhaps as many as 2,000) to represent these 44 phonemes. For example, the long *e,* according to Ernest Horn (1957), is spelled 14 ways in English words! This situation is known as a "lack of fit." A list of common spelling options for long *e* and other phonemes is presented in Figure 8-3.

The reasons for this lack of fit can be found by examining events in the history of the English language. Approximately 75% of English words have been borrowed from other languages, and many of these words, especially the more recently acquired words (e.g., *cul-de-sac,* which was borrowed from French in the early 1700s and literally means bottom of a sack), have retained their native spellings. The spellings of other words have been tinkered with by linguists. More than 400 years ago, for instance, in an effort to relate the word *island* to its supposed French or Latin origin, the unnecessary and unpronounced *s* was added. However, *island* (spelled *ilond* in the Middle Ages) is a native English word, and the current spelling sends a false message about the word's etymology.

FIGURE 8-3 Common Spelling Options

Common Spelling Options

Sound	Spellings	Examples
ā	a-e a ai ay	date angel aid day
ē	ea ee e e-e ea-e	each feel evil these breathe
ĕ	e ea	end head
ō	o o-e ow oa	go note own load
ô	o a au aw	office all author saw
o͝o	oo u ou o	book put could woman
o͞o	u oo u-e o-e ue o ou	cruel noon rule lose blue to group

Common Spelling Options

Sound	Spellings	Examples
ŭ	u o ou	ugly company country
stressed syllabic r	er ur ir or ear our	her church first world heard courage
unstressed syllabic r	er or ure ar	better favor picture dollar
oi	oi oy	oil boy
ou	ou ow	out cow
ū	u u-e ue ew	union use value few
syllabic l	le al el il	able animal cancel civil
syllabic n	en on an in contractions ain	written lesson important cousin didn't certain

Note. From "Common Spelling Options" by E. Horn, 1957, *Elementary School Journal, 57,* pp. 426–428. Copyright 1957 by The University of Chicago Press. Reprinted by permission.

The controversy about whether English is a phonetic language has been waged for years, and will not likely be settled soon. Yet, the fact remains that spelling is a problem for many children. Because of the lack of fit between phonemes and graphemes, it is unlikely that children will learn to spell simply by sounding out words, even though that is the strategy that they are often advised to use by well-meaning teachers and parents. Instead, it is necessary to examine how children actually learn to spell and how their spelling development relates to writing.

Invented Spelling

Charles Read (1971, 1975, 1986) studied preschoolers' efforts to spell words and found that they used their knowledge of the alphabet and the English spelling system to invent spellings for words. These children used letter names to spell words, such as *U* (*you*), *ME* (*me*), and *R* (*are*), and they used consonant sounds rather consistently: *GRL* (*girl*), *TIGR* (*tiger*), and *NIT* (*night*). The preschoolers used several unusual but phonetically based spelling patterns to represent affricates. They spelled *tr* with *chr* (e.g., *CHRIBLES* for *troubles*), spelled *dr* with *jr* (e.g., *JRAGIN* for *dragon*) and substituted *d* for *t* (e.g., *PREDE* for *pretty*). Words with long vowels were spelled using letter names: *MI* (*my*), *LADE* (*lady*), and *FEL* (*feel*). The children used several ingenious strategies to spell words with short vowels. These 3-, 4-, and 5-year-olds rather consistently selected letters to represent short vowels on the basis of place of articulation in the mouth. Short *i* was represented with *e* as in *FES* (*fish*), short *e* with *a* as in *LAFFT* (*left*), and short *o* with *i* as in *CLIK* (*clock*). Although these spellings may seem odd to adults, they are based on phonetic relationships. The children often omitted nasals within words (e.g., *ED* for *end*) and substituted *-eg* or *-ig* for *-ing* (e.g., *CUMIG* for *coming* and *GOWEG* for *going*). Also they often ignored the vowel in unaccented syllables as illustrated in *AFTR* (after) and *MUTHR* (mother).

These children developed strategies for their spellings based on their knowledge of phonology, their knowledge of letter names, their judgments of phonetic similarities and differences, and their ability to abstract phonetic information from letter names. Read suggested that from among the many components in the phonological system, children abstract out certain phonetic details and preserve other phonetic details in their invented spellings.

Based on Charles Read's seminal work, other researchers began to systematically study the development of young children's spelling abilities. Henderson and his colleagues (Beers & Henderson, 1977; Gentry, 1978, 1981; Templeton, 1979; Zutell, 1979) have studied the manner in which children proceed developmentally from invented spelling to correct spelling.

Researchers have found that not all children do invent spellings in exactly the same way or at the same speed, but they do develop spelling strategies in roughly the same sequence (Henderson, 1980a). The five stages that children move through as they become conventional spellers are (a) precommunicative spelling, (b) semiphonetic spelling, (c) phonetic spelling, (d) transitional spelling, and (e) correct spelling (Gentry, 1978, 1981, 1982a, 1982b). The characteristics of each of the five stages of invented spelling are summarized in Figure 8-4.

Stage 1: Precommuncative Spelling. In this stage, children string scribbles, letters, and letter-like forms together but they do not associate the marks they make with any specific phonemes. Precommunicative spelling represents children's natural, early expression of the alphabet and other concepts about writing. They may write from left-to-right, right-to-left, top-to-bottom, or randomly across the page. Some precommunicative spellers have a large repertoire of letter forms to use in writing while others repeat a small number of letters over and over. Children may use both upper- and lowercase letters, but they show a distinct preference for uppercase letters. At this stage, children have not discovered the alphabetic principle—that graphemes represent phonemes in words. This stage is typical of preschoolers, ages 3 through 5.

Stage 2: Semiphonetic Spelling. At this stage, children begin to represent some phonemes in words with the correct graphemes, indicating that they are acquiring a rudimentary understanding of the alphabetic principle, that a link exists between letters and sounds. The spellings are very abbreviated, often using only one, two, or three letters to represent an entire word. Examples of stage 2 spelling include: *ET* (*eat*), *KLZ* (*closed*), and *LF* (*laugh*). As these examples illustrate, semiphonetic spellers use a letter-name strategy to determine which letters to use in spelling a word, and their spellings represent some sound features of words while ignoring other equally important features. Semiphonetic spellers include 5- and 6-year-old children.

Stage 3: Phonetic Spelling. In this stage, children's understanding of the alphabetic principle is further refined. They continue to use letter names to represent sounds but they also use consonant and short vowel sounds. Examples of stage 3 spelling include: *LIV* (*live*), *DRAS* (*dress*), and *PEKT* (*peeked*). As these examples show, children choose letter on the basis of sound alone without considering acceptable English letter sequences (e.g., using -*T* rather than -*ed* as a past tense marker in *peeked*) or other spelling conventions. These spellings do not resemble English words, and although children's spelling in this stage does not look like adult spelling, it usually can be deciphered. The major achievement of this stage is that for the first time children represent all essential sound features in the words being spelled. Henderson (1980b) explains that words are "bewilderingly homographic" at this stage because children spell on the basis of sound alone. For example, *bat, bet,* and *bait* might all be spelled *BAT* at this stage (Read, 1971). Phonetic spellers are typically 6-year-old children.

Stage 4: Transitional Spelling. Transitional spellers come close to the correct spellings of English words. They spell many words correctly, but words with irregular spellings continue to be misspelled. Examples of stage four spelling include *HUOSE* (*house*), *TRUBAL* (*trouble*), *EAGEL* (*eagle*), and *AFTERNEWN* (*afternoon*). This stage is characterized by children's increased ability to represent the features of English orthography. They have internalized information about spelling patterns and the underlying rules of English spelling. First, they include a vowel in every syllable as the *trouble* and *eagle* spellings show. Next, they demonstrate knowledge of vowel patterns even though they might make a

FIGURE 8-4   Characteristics of the Invented Spelling Stages

Stage 1: Precommunicative Spelling

The child:

Uses scribbles, letter-like forms, letters, and sometimes numbers to represent a message.

Writes from left-to-right, right-to-left, top-to-bottom, or randomly on the page.

Shows no understanding of phoneme-grapheme correspondence.

Repeats a few letters again and again or uses most of the letters of the alphabet.

Mixes upper- and lowercase letters but shows a preference for uppercase letters.

Stage 2: Semiphonetic Spelling

The child:

Becomes aware of the alphabetic principle that letters are used to represent sounds.

Uses abbreviated one-, two-, or three-letter spelling to represent an entire word.

Uses letter-name strategy to spell words.

Stage 3: Phonetic Spelling

The child:

Represents all essential sound features of a word in spelling.

Develops particular spellings for long and short vowels, plural and past tense markers, and other aspects of spelling.

Chooses letters on the basis of sound without regard for English letter sequences or other conventions.

faulty decision about which marker to use. For example, *toad* is often spelled *TODE* when children choose the wrong vowel marker or *TAOD* when the two vowels are reversed. Also, transitional spellers use common letter patterns in their spelling, such as *YOUNIGHTED* for *united* and *HIGHCKED* for *hiked*. In this stage, children use conventional alternatives for representing sounds, and, although they continue to misspell words according to adult standards, transitional spelling is closer to adult spelling. It resembles English orthography and can easily be read. As the preceding examples show, children stop relying entirely on phonological information and begin to use visual clues and morphological (word parts) information as well. Morphological information includes knowledge about plurals, possessives, past tense, and compounding. Transitional spellers generally include 7- and 8-year-old children.

Stage 5: Correct Spelling. As the name implies, children spell many, many words correctly at this stage, but not all words. Children have mastered the basic principles of English orthography, and this achievement indicates their prepara-

FIGURE 8-4 (continued)

Stage 4: Transitional Spelling

The child:

Adheres to basic conventions of English orthography.

Begins to use morphological and visual information in addition to phonetic information.

May include all appropriate letters in a word but reverse some of them.

Uses alternate spellings for the same sound in different words, but only partially understands the conditions governing their use.

Spells many words correctly.

Stage 5: Correct Spelling

The child:

Applies the basic rules of the English orthographic system.

Extends knowledge of word structure including the spelling of affixes, contractions, compound words, and homonyms.

Demonstrates growing accuracy in using silent consonants and doubling consonants before adding suffixes.

Recognizes when a word doesn't "look right" and can consider alternate spellings for the same sound.

Learns irregular spelling patterns.

Learns consonant and vowel alternations and other morphological structures.

Spells most words correctly.

Adapted from Gentry, 1982a, pp. 192–200.

tion for formal spelling instruction (Gentry, 1981, 1982a). Children typically reach this stage and are ready for formal spelling instruction by age 8 or 9. During the next four or five years, they learn to control homonyms (e.g., *road-rode*), contractions, consonant doubling and adding affixes (e.g., *runing/running*), and vowel and consonant alternations (e.g., *nation-national*). They also learn to spell most common irregularly spelled words and become familiar with spelling alternatives—different ways to spell the same sound.

Researchers are continuing to study children's spelling development beyond age 8. Much of the research has focused on the relationship between reading and spelling (Anderson, 1985). Researchers have examined the spelling strategies that poor readers in fourth through sixth grade use and found that these students were likely to use a sounding-out strategy. Good readers used a variety of spelling strategies, including using visual information, knowledge about root words and affixes, and analogy to known words, in spelling (Barron, 1980; Marsh et al., 1980). Uta Firth (1980) concluded that older students who are good readers and spellers made spelling errors that are characteristic of the transitional stage, while students who are poor readers and spellers made spelling errors that are characteristic of the semiphonetic and phonetic stages. With further research, it seems reasonable that several additional stages beyond 5 will be identified to more accurately describe children's spelling development through eighth grade.

Children's movement through these stages depends on immersion in a written language environment with daily opportunities to read and write. Also, teachers should de-emphasize standard spelling during this period and be tolerant of children's invented spelling, even celebrating students' nonstandard spellings. By analyzing spelling errors, teachers can determine when children have reached the fifth stage and are ready for formal spelling instruction.

Analyzing Children's Spelling Errors

Teachers can analyze the spelling errors in children's compositions by classifying the errors according to the five stages of spelling development. This analysis will provide information about the student's current level of spelling development and the kinds of spelling errors that child makes. Also, knowing the stage of a student's spelling development will suggest an appropriate type of spelling instruction. Children who are not yet at the correct stage of spelling development—that is, students who do not spell approximately 90% of spelling words correctly and whose errors are not mostly at the transitional level—do not benefit from formal spelling instruction. Instead, early instruction interferes with spelling development because children move from phonetic spelling to memorizing spelling words without learning visual and morphological strategies.

A composition written by Marc, a first grader, is presented in Figure 8-5. You will note that he reverses *b* and *s* and these two reversals make his writing more difficult to decipher. Here's a translation of Marc's composition:

■ Today a person at home called us and said that a bomb was in our school and made us go outside and made us wait a half of an hour and it made us waste our time on learning. The end.

Marc was writing about a traumatic event, and it was appropriate that he used invented spelling in his composition. Primary grade students need to feel free to write using invented spelling, and correct spelling needs to be added only if the composition will "go public" or if for some specific reason "adult" spelling is needed. Differentiating between "child" and "adult" spelling prematurely interferes with children's natural spelling development and makes children dependent on adults to supply "adult" spelling.

The words in students' writing can be categorized using a chart as illustrated in Figure 8-6 to gauge students' stage of spelling development and to anticipate upcoming changes in their spelling strategies. On the chart, write the stages of spelling development across the top and list each word in the student's composition under one of the categories, ignoring proper nouns, capitalization errors, and poorly formed or reversed letters. Because a quick review of Marc's writing revealed no precommunicative spellings, this category was not included in the analysis.

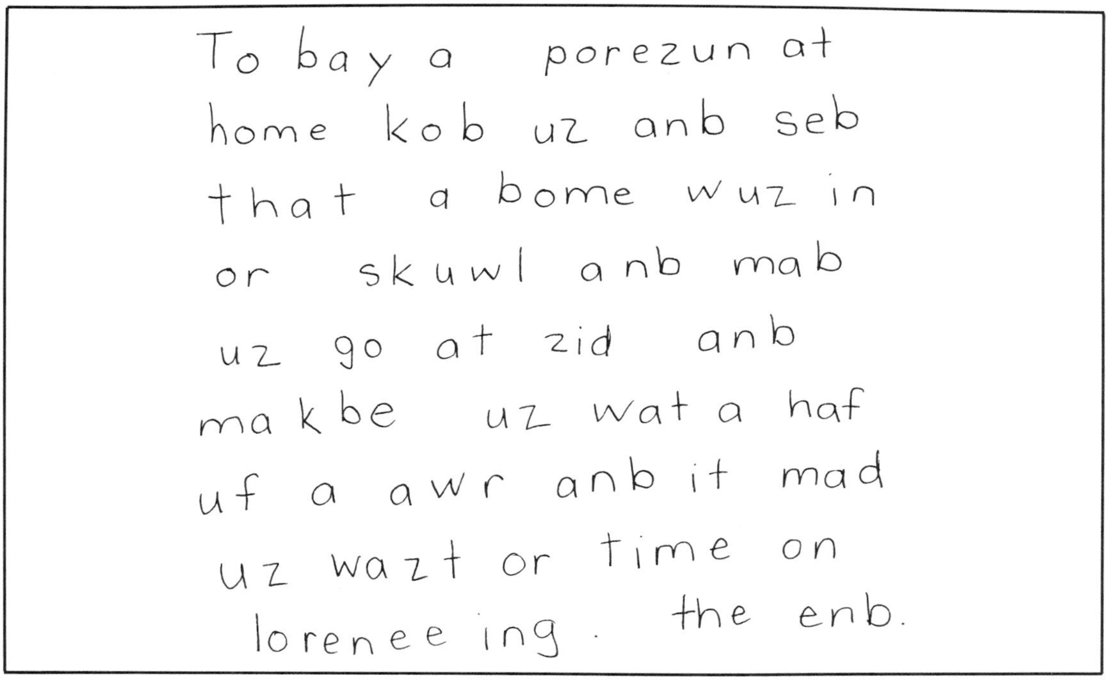

To bay a porezun at
home kob uz anb seb
that a bome wuz in
or skuwl anb mab
uz go at zid anb
makbe uz wat a haf
uf a awr anb it mad
uz wazt or time on
lorenee ing . the enb.

FIGURE 8-5 A First Grader's Composition Using Invented Spelling

Perhaps the most interesting thing about Marc's writing is that he spelled 56% of the words correctly. Only one word *kod* (*called*) is categorized as semiphonetic, and it was classified this way because the spelling is very abbreviated, with only the first and last sounds represented. The 12 words that were categorized as phonetic are words in which it appears his spelling represents only the sounds heard. Unpronounced letters, such as the final *e* in *made* and the *i* in *wait*, are not represented in the spelling. Marc pronounces *our* as though it were a homophone for *or*, so *or* is a reasonable phonetic spelling. Homophone errors are phonological because the child focuses on sound, not meaning.

The words categorized as transitional illustrate the use of some type of spelling strategy other than sound. In *BOME* (*bomb*), for example, Marc applies the final *e* rule which he recently learned even though it isn't appropriate in this word. In time he will learn to spell the word with an unpronounced *b* and that this *b* is needed because the word *bomb* is a newer, shortened form of *bombard* in which the *b* in the middle of the word is pronounced. The *b* remains in *bomb* to show the etymology of the word. The word *MAKDE* is especially interesting. Marc pronounced the word *maked* and the *DE* is a reversal of letters, a common characteristic of transitional spelling. Transitional spellers often spell *girl* as *gril* and *friend* as *freind*. That *made*, not *maked*, is the past tense of *make* is a grammatical error and unimportant in determining the stage of spelling development. *LORE-*

FIGURE 8-6 An Analysis of a First Grader's Invented Spelling

	Semiphonetic	Phonetic	Transitional	Correct
	kod	sed	poresun	today
		wus	bome	a
		or	skuwl	at
		mad	makde	home
		at sid	loreneeing	us
		wat		and
		haf		that
		uf		a
		awr		in
		mad		and
		wast		us
		or		go
				and
				us
				a
				a
				and
				it
				us
				time
				on
				the
				end
Total Words	1	12	5	23
Percent	3	29	12	56

NEEING (*learning*) is categorized as transitional because Marc added long vowel markers (an *e* after *lor* and *ee* after *n*). Since the spelling is based on his pronunciation of *learning*, the long vowel markers and the correct spelling of the suffix *-ing* signal a transitional spelling. Categorizing spelling errors in a child's composition and computing the percentage of errors in each category is a useful tool for diagnosing the child's level of spelling development and readiness for spelling instruction. From the spelling in Marc's composition, he might be classified as a phonetic speller who is moving toward the transitional stage. Marc's paper in Figure 8-6 was written in January of his first-grade year, and he is making expected progress in spelling. During the next few months, he will begin to notice that his spelling doesn't look right (e.g., *SED* for *said, UF* for *of*) and will note visual features of words. He will apply the vowel rules he is learning more effectively, particularly the final *e* (*MAD* will become *made, SID* will become *side,* and *WAST* will become *waste*).

Marc is not ready for formal spelling instruction in which he memorizes the correct spelling of words because he has not yet internalized the visual and morphological spelling strategies of the transitional stage. Also, Marc will probably self-correct the two letter reversals through daily writing experiences and as long as he is not placed under great pressure to form the letters correctly.

Teaching Spelling Using Writing Errors

Spelling is a writer's tool, and it is best learned through writing. Students who write daily and are encouraged in kindergarten and first grade to use invented spellings will move naturally toward correct spelling. As they begin to write, children guess at how words are spelled using their knowledge of letter names and sounds. Through reading and writing, they gradually recognize that the words they are reading and writing are spelled the same way each time. When students recognize that words have consistent spellings, they are ready to be helped in a direct way. Teachers begin to point out the conventions of the spelling system, but children continue to develop their basic knowledge about English orthography through writing, not through weekly spelling tests. Formal spelling instruction should begin when children reach the correct stage of spelling development, not at a particular grade level.

Choosing Spelling Words. Once children move from transitional spelling to correct spelling, they are ready for formal spelling instruction. Children's spelling words should come from their writing because these are the words that they want and need to be able to spell. A master list of these words can be compiled from several sources. Teachers can keep a list of words that have been misspelled in students' rough drafts, words that students ask how to spell, and words related to literature and other content area units. Students can suggest words that they want to learn to spell.

Taking a Pretest to Identify Spelling Words. Students take a pretest in which they attempt to spell the words on the master list. Then from among their misspelled words, they identify approximately 10 words to learn that week. Children take responsibility for accurately evaluating their own pretests, identifying the words they will study, and then making two lists of these identified words, one for themselves and one for the teacher to keep on file. Students who do not miss many words on the pretest can select other words to learn or not participate in spelling activities that week.

Practice Activities. Students don't need a wide variety of fill-in-the-blank or put-your-spelling-words-in-sentences activities to learn to spell words. Instead, they use a simple approach to practice words that takes only about 5 minutes a day. Time saved by this approach can be devoted to more meaningful reading and writing activities. The strategy is:

1. Look at the word and say it.
2. Read each letter in the word.
3. Close your eyes and spell the word to yourself.

4. Look at the word. Did you spell it correctly?
5. Copy the word from your list.
6. Cover the word and write it again.
7. Look at the word. Did you write it correctly?
8. If you made any mistakes, repeat the steps. (Cook et al., 1984, p. 1)

This is the only type of practice activity that is necessary. No busy-work activities such as writing spelling words in sentences or identifying the opposites or rhyming partners of the spelling words are needed.

Final Test. After several days of practice, students take a final test in which words are dictated and spelled. Students should not write the word in dictated sentences because this is a spelling test, not a secretary's dictation test. The teacher can read the entire spelling list and students write only the words they studied, or students can divide into pairs and test each other using the copy of their spelling words given to the teacher previously. If the teacher reads the entire spelling list aloud, students need to prepare in advance by identifying the numbers of their personal spelling words so that they will spell their own words rather than the entire list. Any words that the students misspell should become a part of their spelling list for the following week.

Modifying the Textbook Spelling Program. Textbook spelling programs are a less effective way to teach spelling because the words in the textbook are often classified by phonetic or spelling pattern similarities and involve a variety of unnecessary practice activities. However, words that children need to learn to spell for their writing can be added to the spelling textbook words to replace the words on the master list that students spelled correctly on the pretest.

The Spelling-Writing Connection

Elementary students make spelling errors in their writing because of the English orthographic system. Sometimes these errors need to be corrected; sometimes they do not. When children are writing informally in journals, as in a prewriting activity, or on their rough drafts, invented spellings and other spelling errors should be ignored. Similarly, young children's invented spellings should not be corrected. However, when students want to make their compositions public, standard spelling is a courtesy to readers. Through a process approach to writing, students who are planning to make their compositions public, as Stephanie and Danielle will with their pen pal letters, use the editing stage of the writing process to identify and correct misspelled words.

In addition to dealing with spelling errors in the editing stage of the writing process, there are three other components in the spelling-writing connection: learning to use a dictionary, keeping spelling logs, and developing a spelling conscience.

Learning to Use a Dictionary. While it is relatively easy to find a "known" word in the dictionary, it is much harder to locate an unfamiliar word, and students need to learn what to do when they do not know how to spell a word. They should consider spelling options and predict possible spellings for unknown words and then check their predicted spellings by consulting a dictionary. This strategy involves six steps:

1. Identify root words and affixes.
2. Consider related words (e.g., *medicine-medical*).
3. Determine the sounds in the word.
4. Generate a list of spelling options for each sound.
5. Select the most likely alternative.
6. Consult a dictionary to check the correct spelling.

The fourth step is undoubtedly the most difficult one in the strategy. Using both their knowledge of phonology and morphology, students develop a list of possible spellings. For some words, phoneme-grapheme relationships may rate primary consideration in generating spelling options, while for others root words and affixes or related words may be more important in determining how the word is spelled.

Keeping a Spelling Log. One strategy for helping upper grade students deal with their spelling errors is a spelling log (VanDeWeghe, 1982). Students keep a personal spelling notebook in which they list their misspellings and the correct spellings. They also consider why the spelling confuses them and design a mnemonic device to remember the correct spelling of the word. A sample spelling log is presented in Figure 8-7.

This strategy is important because researchers have found that words rarely have only one possible misspelling. Instead, many words have a number of trou-

FIGURE 8-7 An Upper Grade Student's Spelling Log

My Spelling Log			
Correct Spelling	My Misspelling	Why the Word Confuses Me	Helps to Remember the Correct Spelling
demonstrate	demenstrate	I use *e* instead of *o*.	A demo is used to demonstrate.
coarse	course	I get it mixed up with course as a class.	a = coarse is hard.
meant	ment	I spell it like I think it sounds.	It's the past of *mean*.

VanDeWeghe, 1982, p. 102.

ble spots and what is a trouble spot for one student may not be for another. There-fore, students must individualize the analysis of their own spelling errors and design their own mnemonic devices. While this is a strategy that many good spellers use intuitively, formalizing the strategy will help less strongly motivated students.

Developing a Spelling Conscience. Spelling involves more than just learning to spell specific words, whether they are drawn from children's writing or from words listed in spelling textbooks. Robert Hillerich (1977) believes that students need to develop a spelling conscience, or a positive attitude toward spelling and a concern for using standard spelling. He lists two dimensions of a spelling con-science: understanding that standard spelling is a courtesy to readers and devel-oping the ability to proofread to spot and correct misspellings.

Students in the middle and upper grades need to learn that is it unrealistic to expect readers to decipher numerous misspelled words as they read a piece of writing. This first dimension, understanding that standard spelling is a courtesy for readers, develops as students write frequently and for varied audiences. By writing for a variety of audiences, students acquire a concept of audience and re-alize that there are readers to read their writing. As students move from writing for themselves to writing that communicates, they internalize this concept. Teachers help students to recognize the purpose of standard spelling by providing mean-ingful writing activities directed to a variety of genuine audiences.

The second dimension, proofreading for spelling errors, is an essential part of the writing process. As discussed in Chapter 3, proofreading is part of the editing stage, and it should be introduced in kindergarten and first grade rather than postponing it until the middle grades. Young children and their teachers can proofread class collaboration stories together, and students can be encouraged to read over their own compositions and make necessary changes as soon as they begin writing. With this beginning, students will accept proofreading as a natural part of both spelling and writing, and together with their growing aware-ness of audience, students will appreciate the importance of proofreading to cor-rect misspellings and other mechanical errors.

GRAMMAR AND USAGE

■ Me and him brung them two little kittens home.
Nothing don't scare that monster.
George Washington who was the first president.
Then my mom and dad done got divorced.
He cry but he say, "I ain't hurt."
Elvis Presley he was a real good singer.

These sentences were extracted from elementary students' rough drafts. Each sentence contains one or more errors, but only one sentence (the one about George Washington) contains a grammatical error; the others are usage errors. Grammar is the description of the structure of a language, and it involves principles of word and sentence formation. In contrast, usage is "correctness" or the appropriate word in a sentence. It is the socially preferred way of using language within a dialect. Fraser and Hodson (1978) explain the distinction between grammar and usage this way: "Grammar is the rationale of language; usage is its etiquette" (p. 52).

Dealing with Grammar and Usage Errors

Whether these errors are classified as grammar or usage errors, the question of what to do about them remains. Only one error was grammatical, so teaching grammar will not help students correct the usage errors. In fact, teaching either grammar or usage to elementary students will probably not help to eliminate these errors in their speech or writing because the concepts are abstract. Educators have recommended for many years that this type of instruction be postponed at least until junior high school when students are more likely to be able to think abstractly (Fraser & Hodson, 1978; Haley-James, 1981).

Children learn English grammar intuitively as they learn to speak. They have almost completed learning the process by the time they enter kindergarten. The purpose of grammar instruction, then, is to make this intuitive knowledge about the English language explicit and to provide labels for sentence types, parts of sentences, and words within sentences. Children speak the dialect that their parents and community members speak. This dialect, whether standard or nonstandard, is informal and differs to some degree from written standard English that students will read and write in elementary school (Pooley, 1974).

Because children's knowledge of grammar and usage depends on language spoken in their homes and neighborhoods, some primary grade students do not recognize any difference between *me and him* and *he and I*. When this error is brought to these children's attention, they do not understand because semantically, the two versions are identical. Moreover, *me and him* sounds "right" to these students because they hear this construction at home. When other corrections are pointed out to middle and upper grade students, they repeat the correct form, shake their heads, and say that it doesn't sound right. *Real* sounds better to some students than *really* because it is more familiar to them. An explanation that adverbs, not adjectives, modify adjectives is not useful either, even if students have had grammar instruction. Too often the correction of usage errors is a repudiation of the language spoken in children's homes rather than an explanation that written language requires a more formal language dialect or register.

A better way to correct grammar and usage errors is to use a problem-solving approach during the editing stage of the writing process. Locating and correcting errors in student's writing is not as threatening as correcting their talk because it is not as personal. During editing, students are error-hunting, trying to make their papers "optimally readable" (Smith, 1982). They recognize that it is a courtesy to readers to make their papers as correct as possible. Classmates note errors and correct each other, and teachers point out other errors. Sometimes teachers explain the correction, (e.g., the past tense of *bring* is *brought*, not *brung*), and at other times they simply mark the correction, saying that "When we write, we usually write it this way." Also, some errors should be ignored, especially young children's errors. Correcting too many errors will only teach students that their language is inferior or inadequate. Guidelines for correcting students' grammar and usage errors are summarized in Figure 8-8.

Sentence Building Activities

Students experiment with grammatical structures as they revise their writing. As students manipulate sentences by adding, deleting, substituting, and moving words within a sentence, they become more aware of the structure of sentences (Hutson, 1980). Three types of sentence-building activities that children can participate in using sentences taken from their compositions are sentence slotting, sentence expansion and sentence combining. Through sentence slotting activities, students experiment with the functions of words and phrases in a sentence. Students learn about the effect of adding modifiers through sentence expansion activities, and in sentence combining, they combine short, choppy sentences to build more complex sentences.

Sentence Slotting. Students learn how words and phrases function in sentences when they brainstorm a list of alternatives for an ineffective word. One way to use the activity is to give students a sentence with a slot or blank, for example, *A horse _____ across the field.* Students brainstorm words or phrases that can be used to complete the sentence. The purpose of this activity is to demonstrate the function of words in sentences.

For example, in a writing group, students are sharing dinosaur reports, and a classmate may suggest that a vivid verb is needed to replace *ate* in this sentence: *The Tyrannosaurus Rex ate plant eaters.* Another classmate may recognize that

FIGURE 8-8 Guidelines for Correcting Students' Grammar and Usage Errors in Compositions

1. Use a problem-solving approach to correct grammar and usage errors.
2. Correct errors in the editing stage of the writing process.
3. Consider the function, audience, and form of the composition when determining whether to correct errors or which errors to correct.
4. Let student know that correcting grammatical and usage errors is a courtesy to readers.
5. Keep explanations for the corrections brief.
6. Sometimes simply make the change and say that in writing it is written this way.
7. Don't ask students if the correction makes the writing "sound better."
8. Use sentence building activities to rid the composition of lackluster and repetitious words and short, choppy sentence.
9. Ignore some errors, especially young children's.
10. Respect the language of children's home and community, and introduce standard written English as "book language."

a writer has begun each sentence about Tyrannosaurus Rex with *he*. The writer agrees that the problem exists and asks for help in thinking of alternatives. Writing-group members suggest:

_____was a meat eater.

(He)

It

Tyrannosaurus Rex

The dinosaur

This ancient reptile

The thunder-lizard

This carnivore

The king of the dinosaurs

The writer can replace *he* with some of these alternatives to make the paragraph about Tyrannosaurus Rex more interesting.

Sentence Expansion. Students take basic sentences, such as *Brontosaurus walked* or *Pteranodon flew*, and expand them by adding descriptive words, comparisons, and other modifiers. The "5 Ws plus one" strategy helps students focus on expanding particular aspects of the sentence. For example:

Basic sentence:	A Pteranodon flies.
What kind?	huge
Where?	past a tar pit where a Tyrannosaurus Rex is stuck
Why?	to see why the terrible lizard is howling.
How?	with its leathery wings outstretched
Expanded sentence:	A huge Pteranodon flies with its leathery wings outstretched past a tar pit where a Tyrannosaurus Rex is stuck to see why the terrible lizard is howling.

Depending on the questions asked and the answers given, many other expanded sentences are possible from the same basic sentence. Students enjoy working in small groups to expand the same basic sentence so that they can compare the expanded versions each group produces. Instead of using the "5 Ws plus one" to expand sentences, upper grade students can supply a specific part of speech for each expansion.

    This strategy can also be used in revision. For example, Nikki wrote this sentence in a chapter of her report about dinosaur nests: *Dinosaur moms lays eggs in nests*. Writing-group members asked Nikki to tell more about the eggs and the nests. They asked these questions and Nikki jotted down these answers:

Where do they build nests?	in sandy and rocky places covered with sand to hide the eggs
What do they look like?	big and kind of flat
How big are they?	big enough for five or six large eggs
Does the dinosaur mom stay with the nest like ducks do?	some do and some don't

Later Nikki wrote this revision in which she added the information her classmates asked about:

■ Dinosaur moms lay eggs in nests they build in sandy and rocky places. They lay five or six large eggs in the big nests. Next they cover the nests with sand to hide the eggs from other dinosaurs that like to eat eggs. Some dinosaur moms stay with the nests like ducks do and some don't.

Sentence Combining. Sentence combining is a strategy in which two or more short sentences are combined. They can be joined or embedded in a variety of ways. For example, the two sentences *Triceratops was a plant eater* and *Triceratops had three horns on its head* can be combined in several ways:

Triceratops was a plant eater and had three horns on its head.

Triceratops, a plant eater, had three horns on its head.

Triceratops, with three horns on its head, was a plant eater.

In the first combined sentence, the two short sentences were joined with *and* to make a compound sentence; in the second and third combined sentences, the short sentences were embedded.

Sentence combining was the focus of a study by Mellon (1969). His work suggested that sentence combining activities might be a profitable way to increase the rate of students' syntactic development. Work by Hunt and O'Donnell (1970) and by O'Hare (1973) showed that students could improve their writing when sentence combining exercises were taught. As a result of these studies, many teachers have introduced sentence combining activities to their students.

In writing groups, students often suggest sentence combining for descriptive paragraphs that are essentially lists of characteristics. For example, Brady shared this description of Tyrannosaurus Rex with his classmates:

■ He is called the king. He was a meat eater or carnivore. He was as tall as a telephone pole. He walked on two legs. He was 50 feet long. His teeth were six inches long. He was a terrible lizard.

As soon as he read this paragraph aloud, Brady realized he had used *he* too often and prepared to make some changes. Writing-group members mentioned that his sentences seemed short and choppy and suggested he could combine some of them. They suggested combining the tall and long sentences, the king and terrible lizard sentences, and the meat eater and teeth sentences. The children worked with Brady to help him draft the new sentences. Here is his revision:

■ Tyrannosaurus Rex was called the king of the dinosaurs. He was a meat eater or carnivore with six-inch long teeth. This dinosaur was as tall as a telephone pole and he was 50 feet long. He walked on two legs. He was a really, really terrible lizard.

Sentence combining activities give students opportunities to manipulate sentence structures; however, the activities are rather artificial unless they come from children's own writing or are connected with writing assignments (Lawlor, 1983; Strong, 1986). Weaver (1979) cautions that "sentence combining activities are only an adjunct to the writing program and should never be used as a substitute for actual writing" (pp. 83–84).

The Grammar and Usage-Writing Connection

Conventional wisdom is that knowledge about grammar and usage should improve students' writing, but research since the beginning of this century has not confirmed this assumption. Based on their review of research studies conducted before 1963, Braddock, Lloyd-Jones, and Schoer (1963) concluded that:

> The teaching of formal grammar has a negligible or, because it usually displaces some instruction and practice in actual composition, even a harmful effect on the improvement of writing. (pp. 37–38)

Since that time, other studies have reached the same conclusion (c.f., Elley, et al., 1976).

While there is much controversy about teaching grammar and its value for elementary students, grammar is part of the elementary language arts curriculum and will undoubtedly remain so for some time to come. Given this fact, it is only reasonable to suggest that grammar should be taught in the most beneficial manner possible. Some researchers suggest that integrating grammar study with writing may produce the best results (Noyce & Christie, 1983). Also, Peter Elbow (1973) and Shirley Haley-James (1981) view grammar as a tool for writers and recommend integrating grammar instruction with the revising and editing stages of the writing process.

HANDWRITING

Like spelling and grammar, handwriting is a functional tool for writers. Donald Graves (1983) explains:

> Children win prizes for fine script, parents and teachers nod approval for a crisp, well-crafted page, a good impression is made on a job application blank . . . all important elements, but they pale next to the *substance* they carry. (p. 171)

It is important to distinguish between writing and handwriting. Writing is the content of a composition, while handwriting is the formation of alphabetic symbols on paper.

The Goal of Handwriting

Too often, teachers insist that students demonstrate their best handwriting every time they pick up a pencil or a pen. This requirement is very unrealistic; certainly, there are times when handwriting is important, but sometimes speed or other considerations outweigh neatness. Even though a few students take great pleasure in flawless handwriting skills, most students feel that excessive attention to handwriting is boring and unnecessary. Instead, the goal should be for students to develop and use legible handwriting to communicate effectively through writing.

Students need to develop a legible and fluent style of handwriting to fully participate in all writing activities. Legibility means that the writing can be easily and quickly read, and fluency that the writing can be easily and quickly written. When students are writing for public display, legibility is more important than when they are doing private writing, but fluency is always important. Whether students are writing for themselves or others, they need to be able to write quickly and easily.

The best way to help students develop fluency and legibility is to use handwriting for genuine and functional public writing activities. A letter sent to a favorite author that is returned by the post office because the address on the envelope is not decipherable, or a child's published, hardcover book that sits unread on the library shelf because the handwriting is illegible makes clear the importance of legibility. Illegible writing means a failure to communicate, a harsh lesson for a writer!

Teaching Handwriting Through Writing

Teaching handwriting through writing is an incidental approach to handwriting instruction. This approach supplements the formal instructional program in the primary grades when students are learning the correct formation of each letter in manuscript and cursive forms. In the middle and upper grades, this approach is the more efficient approach because it is individualized. As teachers observe students writing, they identify letters that are formed incorrectly or other handwriting problems which they can work with students to remedy.

Elements of Fluency and Legibility. The goal of handwriting instruction is for students to develop fluent and legible handwriting. To reach this goal, students must first understand what qualities constitute fluency and legibility and then analyze their own handwriting according to these qualities and work to solve problems. There are six characteristics of fluent and legible handwriting according to the Zaner-Bloser handwriting program (Barbe et al., 1984).

1. *Letter Formation.* Each letter is formed with specific strokes. In manuscript handwriting, letters are composed of vertical, horizontal, and slanted lines plus circles or parts of circles. Cursive letters are composed of slanted lines, loops, and curved lines.
2. *Size and Proportion.* The size of students' handwriting decreases during the elementary grades, and the proportional size between upper- and lowercase letters increases.

3. *Spacing.* Students leave adequate space between letters in words and between words and sentences so their handwriting can be read easily.
4. *Slant.* Letters are consistently parallel. In the manuscript form, letters are vertical. In cursive handwriting, letters slant slightly to the right for right-handed students and are vertical to 45 degrees to the left of vertical for left-handed students.
5. *Alignment.* For proper alignment in both handwriting forms, all letters are uniform in size and consistently touch the baseline.
6. *Line Quality.* Students write at a consistent speed and hold their writing instruments correctly and in a relaxed manner to make steady, unwavering lines of even thickness. These characteristics are summarized in Figure 8-9.

Teachers teach fluency by making sure that students write easily and quickly without excessive muscular discomfort. Some children stop writing periodically, put down their pens or pencils, and shake their arms to relax their muscles. Others complain that their arms hurt when they write. Often these students squeeze their pens or pencils too tightly, causing unnecessary tension. Teachers can talk to students about the problem and ask them to monitor themselves, periodically stopping and removing their writing instruments from their hands. Students should hold the pencil or pen loosely enough that they can easily pull it out of their

FIGURE 8-9   Characteristics of Fluent and Legible Handwriting

1. Letter Formation
   • Letters are formed with specific strokes.
   • Cursive letters are joined carefully.
2. Size and Proportion
   • Letter size decreases for middle- and upper-grade students.
   • Proportion of upper- to lowercase manuscript letters is 2:1.
   • Proportion of upper- to lowercase cursive letters increases from 2:1 to 3:1.
3. Spacing
   • Adequate space is left between letters.
   • Adequate space is left between words and sentences.
   • Spacing is consistent.
4. Slant
   • Letters are consistently parallel.
   • Manuscript letters are vertical.
   • Cursive letters are slanted slightly to the right.
5. Alignment
   • Letters are uniform in size.
   • Letters consistently touch the baseline.
6. Line Quality
   • Lines are steady and unwavering.
   • Lines are of consistent thickness.

hands. Also, students who haven't written very much will benefit from daily journal writing or freewriting to exercise their arm muscles.

Correct letter formation and spacing receive the major focus in handwriting instruction during the elementary grades. While the other four elements usually receive less attention, they too, are important in developing legible and fluent handwriting.

Assessing Handwriting Skills. Students can use the characteristics of the six elements of fluency and legibility in assessing their handwriting skills. Primary grade students, for example, can check to see if they have formed a particular letter correctly, if the round parts of letters are joined neatly, or if slanted letters are joined in sharp points. Older students can examine a piece of handwriting and check to see if their letters were consistently parallel or if the letters touched the baseline consistently.

Checklists for students to use in assessing their own handwriting on final copies of their compositions can be developed from the characteristics of the six elements of legibility and fluency. A sample checklist for assessing manuscript handwriting is presented in Figure 8-10. Checklists can also be developed for cursive handwriting. It is important to involve students in developing the checklists

FIGURE 8-10   A Checklist for Assessing Manuscript Handwriting

HANDWRITING CHECKLIST

Name _____

	Never	Sometimes	Always
1. Do I form my letters correctly?	☐	☐	☐
☐ Do I start my line letters at the top?			
☐ Do I start my circle letters at 1:00?			
☐ Do I join the round parts of letters neatly?			
☐ Do I join the slanted strokes in sharp points?			
2. Do my lines touch the midline or top line neatly?	☐	☐	☐
3. Do I space evenly between letters?	☐	☐	☐
4. Do I leave enough space between words?	☐	☐	☐
5. Do I make my letters straight up and down?	☐	☐	☐
6. Do I make all my letters sit on the baseline?	☐	☐	☐

so they can appreciate the need to make their handwriting more legible and fluent.

Handwriting Mini-lessons. Handwriting can be tied to writing through mini-lessons in which the teacher introduces or reviews a specific handwriting skill. Students practice the skill in their writing, and one item on the evaluation checklist for that writing project will be whether or not the specific handwriting skill was used correctly on the final copy. For example, to review the formation of lowercase cursive *b*, the teacher might demonstrate how to form the letter and how to connect it to other letters such as *br, ba, bl* in the mini-lesson. Students need to write that letter a number of times, and in the old approach, would copy a number of perhaps unknown words out of a handwriting textbook. Instead, students can practice the letter and perhaps write a tongue twister as a class collaboration. To gain further practice, students could individually compose a tongue twister using another letter.

Left-handed Writers. Left-handed students have unique handwriting problems, and special adaptations of procedures used for teaching right-handed students are necessary (Howell, 1978). In fact, many of the problems that left-handed students have can be made worse by using the procedures designed for right-handed writers (Harrison, 1981). These special adjustments are necessary to allow left-handed students to write legibly, fluently, and with less fatigue.

The basic difference between right- and left-handed writers is physical orientation. Right-handed students pull their hands and arms toward their bodies as they write while left-handed writers must push away. As left-handed students write, they move their left hand across what has just been written, often covering it. Many children adopt a "hook" position to avoid covering and smudging what they have just written.

Because of this different physical orientation, left-handed writers need to make three major adjustments (Howell, 1978). First, left-handed writers should hold pencils or pens an inch or more farther back from the tip than right-handed writers do. This change will help them to see what they have just written and to avoid smearing their writing. Left-handed writers need to work to avoid "hooking" their wrists. They should keep their wrists straight and elbows close to their bodies to avoid the awkward hooked position.

Second, left-handed students should tilt their writing papers slightly to the right, in contrast to right-handed students who tilt their papers to the left. Sometimes it is helpful to place a piece of masking tape on the student's desk to indicate the proper amount to tilt.

Third, right-handed students are encouraged to slant their cursive letters to the right, but left-handed writers often write vertically or even slant their letters slightly backward. The Zaner-Bloser handwriting program (Barbe et al., 1984) recommends that left-handed writers slant cursive letters slightly to the right, as right-handed students do. Other educators, such as Harrison (1981), advise teachers to permit any slant between vertical and 45 degrees to the left of the vertical.

The Handwriting-Writing Connection

Most students use handwriting to record their ideas, and this makes an undeniable connection between handwriting and writing, although this may change as microcomputers with word processing programs become standard equipment in homes and elementary classrooms. This connection raises a number of questions about handwriting and writing: Should young children who have not learned to form the letters of the alphabet be permitted to write? Should students use manuscript or cursive handwriting for writing? Which writing instruments and paper are best? Does handwriting influence teachers' assessment of students' writing?

Young Children's Handwriting. Preschool children begin writing before they have been taught how to form the letters, and they often develop their own unique ways to form letters in much the same way adults might if they were trying to figure out how to form Chinese or Japanese symbols. Fluency is important and children should not be stopped from using letters they don't form correctly. Instead, children should be allowed to experiment with writing and gain confidence with using marks on paper to express meaning. Parents and preschool teachers can demonstrate "simpler" ways to form letters when children inhibit fluency by making letter formation more difficult than it needs to be. It is adequate to simply demonstrate the formation of the letter for the child; handwriting practice sheets are unnecessary. Rather, through experience with writing and by modeling adults' writing, children will learn to form most of the letters. Any problematic letters can be taught in kindergarten or first grade.

Young children's writing often reveals reversed letters such as *d* for *b* and *z* for *s*. These reversals are quite common for children who are learning the alphabet. In fact, it is amazing that more reversals are not made. Also, most reversals are left-right reversals, not top-bottom reversals. Most reversals take care of themselves by the end of first grade, especially if children are not continually reminded of their errors.

Manuscript Versus Cursive Handwriting. Upper grade students are often faced with a decision when they write: whether they should use manuscript or cursive writing. Teachers may require students to use a particular form of handwriting—manuscript or cursive—for writing when they are teaching or reviewing the form, but in general, students should write in whatever form they are more comfortable. Handwriting should not interfere with getting ideas down on paper during the drafting stage or preparing a legible final copy to share.

Writing Instruments and Paper. Students use all sorts of writing instruments on both lined and unlined paper as they write. Special pencils and handwriting paper are often provided for writing activities in the primary grades. Kindergartners and first graders commonly use "fat" beginner pencils, 13/32 inch in diameter, because it has been assumed that these pencils are easier for young children to hold. However, most children prefer to use regular size, 10/32 inch, pencils that older students and adults use. Moreover, regular pencils have erasers! Research now indicates that beginner pencils are not better than regular-sized pencils for young children (Lamme & Ayris, 1983). Likewise, there is no evidence that specially shaped pencils and little writing aids that slip onto pencils to improve children's grip are effective.

Many types of paper, both lined and unlined, are used in elementary classrooms. The few research studies that have examined the value of lined paper in general, and paper lined at specific intervals for particular grade levels, offer conflicting results. One study suggests that young children's handwriting is more legible using unlined paper while older children's handwriting is better using lined paper (Lindsay & McLennan, 1983). Most teachers seem to prefer that students use lined paper for most writing activities, but students easily adjust to whichever type of writing paper is available. Students often use rulers to line their paper when they are given unlined paper, and likewise, they may ignore the lines on lined paper if the lines interfere with their drawing or writing.

Impact of Handwriting on Writing. The quality of students' handwriting has been found to influence how teachers assess and grade compositions. Markham (1976) found that both student teachers and experienced elementary classroom teachers consistently graded papers with better handwriting higher than papers with poor handwriting, regardless of the quality of the content. Students in the elementary grades are not too young to learn that poor quality or illegible handwriting may lead to lower grades, and teachers must recognize that it is likely that they also have this bias.

MICROCOMPUTERS*

Microcomputers are another valuable tool for student writers, and word processing is one of the most important classroom applications for these computers (Daiute, 1985; Hoot & Silvern, 1988; Knapp, 1986; Rodrigues & Rodrigues, 1986; Wrench, 1987). Teachers and researchers have found that students write more and that both their writing and their attitude toward writing improves when they compose on microcomputers. Several reasons for these improvements seem obvious. First of all, it is fun to use a computer. Students can experiment with writing and easily correct errors, thus encouraging risk-taking and problem-solving. Next, microcomputers allow students to revise and refine their writing without the chore of having to recopy the final draft. In addition, writing looks professional after it is printed out on a printer.

Word processing is a method of producing written compositions using a computer to facilitate revising and formatting the text. Using a computer for word processing is much like using an electric typewriter: Writers plan their compositions, sit at a keyboard and type in words, and then revise and edit their work. Instead of seeing their words appear first on a piece of paper, writers using computers see their words appear on a video screen.

---

*Adapted from Smith & Tompkins, 1983

Word Processing Capabilities

Computers have several capabilities that make the tasks of formatting, revising, and editing mechanically easier.

Typeover. Word processing programs allow writers to back up and type over mistakes. This process is like using a self-correcting electric typewriter. Undesired letters are simply replaced by the new letters typed during the correcting.

Insert and Delete. Word processing programs allow writers to insert or delete letters, words, sentences, and paragraphs within the body of the text. These changes require only a few keystrokes. The remainder of the text automatically adjusts to the changes by shifting lines up, down, or over.

Block Move. The block function allows writers to define a block of text and move it from one location in the text to another. The more sophisticated the program, the larger the amount of text that can be moved in this manner. Usually the program allows writers to move their block of text back to its original location if they regret the move. Some word processing programs even allow writers to leave the text in its current location and move a copy of the block of text or portions of text to another location.

Search and Replace. Sometimes authors wish to locate every occurrence of a certain word within the text and to replace it with a more appropriate word. For example, writers who find that a word has been consistently misspelled throughout the composition can use the search and replace function to correct the misspelling. Most word processing programs have an option that allows writers to specify a particular word to be searched for throughout the composition and to identify a word or phrase to replace it.

Word Processing Programs

Many of the word processing programs currently available for use by adults have been simplified for use by elementary students. A list of some of these programs is presented in Figure 8-11. Several features have been specifically designed to make these programs easier for children to use. These features include:

1. *The Menu on the Screen.* The menu is usually displayed across the top of the monitor screen and shows the functions available for students to use.
2. *Commands on the Screen.* Commands should continually appear on the screen and be simple, one-keystroke commands. Placing the commands on the screen makes it unnecesary for students memorize lists of commands or to refer to instruction booklets.
3. *Pictures to Depict Word Processing Concepts.* Pictures (called icons) depict word processing concepts graphically. These pictures are easy for students to remember.
4. *Safeguards from Accidental Erasures.* Word processing programs should have safeguards to help prevent students from accidentally erasing text. A

FIGURE 8-11   Word Processing Programs Designed for Elementary Students

Title	Publisher	Grade Levels
Bank Street Writer	Scholastic 730 Broadway New York, NY 10003	Primary Middle Upper
Magic Slate	Sunburst Communications 39 Washington Street Pleasantville, NY 10570	Primary Middle Upper
MECC Writer	MECC 3490 Lexington Ave. North St. Paul, MN 55112	Middle Upper
Quill	DC Heath 125 Spring Street Lexington, MA 02173	Middle Upper
Writing Workshop	Milliken 1100 Research Blvd. PO Box 21579 St. Louis, MO 63132	Middle Upper

P = Primary (grades K–2)
M = Middle (grades 3–5)
U = Upper (grades 6–8)

question or warning should appear on the screen before the text can be deleted.

5. *Software Tutorials.* Students should be able to learn to use the word processing program on the microcomputer using a tutorial, not from reading the manual.

A checklist for evaluating word processing programs for both children and adults is presented in Figure 8-12. Specific requirements are included for each stage of the writing process. For example the revising stage requires that the software has space for reader comments; sentence and paragraph length check; the capacity to insert, delete, and move text; and search and replace features.

Auxiliary programs related to word processing include spelling checkers, keyboarding programs, text and graphics programs, and electronic mail. Students use these programs in conjunction with word processing programs.

Spelling Checkers. Spelling checkers are available for use with some word processing programs. After students have completed a piece of writing, a spelling checker program is used to search through the composition for misspelled words. A dictionary included in the computer disk usually holds 50,000 words or more, and the words in the student's composition are compared against the

FIGURE 8-12   A Checklist for Evaluating Word Processing Programs

Name of software _____
Software publisher _____
Address _____
Cost _____   Grade level _____
Type of computer required _____
Type of printer required _____
Number of disk drives needed _____   Recommended _____
Necessary memory capability required for program _____
Extra hardware needed _____

	Excellent	Adequate	Poor
1. Basic Requirements			
The software has:			
• Cataloging capability	_____	_____	_____
• Option to rename files	_____	_____	_____
• Disks that can be copied	_____	_____	_____
• Option to undo previous action	_____	_____	_____
• Familiar terms	_____	_____	_____
• Automatic updating of existing material	_____	_____	_____
• Directions on screen at all times	_____	_____	_____
• Help or aid key	_____	_____	_____
• Mnemonic commands that are logical and easy to use	_____	_____	_____
• Two key commands (control plus one other)	_____	_____	_____
• Displayed characters sufficiently readable for intended audience (40/80 column)	_____	_____	_____
• Easy change from one function to another	_____	_____	_____
• Instructional manual	_____	_____	_____
• Backup disks and manuals available at reduced cost	_____	_____	_____
• Glossary and illustrations in manual	_____	_____	_____
2. Prewriting Requirements			
The software has:			
• Tutorials	_____	_____	_____
• Data disk to accompany tutorial	_____	_____	_____
• Prewriting activities such as brainstorming, prompting, classifying	_____	_____	_____
3. Drafting Requirements			
The software has:			
• Screen warnings before deleting, saving, or quitting	_____	_____	_____
• Single-key capitalization	_____	_____	_____

Oklahoma Writing Project, 1986.

FIGURE 8-12 (continued)

4. **Revising Requirements**
   The software has:
   - Cursor movement using standard keys and rapid scrolling   _____ _____ _____
   - Choice of word wrap or hyphenation at end of line   _____ _____ _____
   - Upper- and lowercase printing and display   _____ _____ _____
   - Maximum length of document information   _____ _____ _____

4. **Revising Requirements**
   The software has:
   - Space for reader comments   _____ _____ _____
   - Sentence and paragraph length check   _____ _____ _____
   - Capability to insert, delete, and move text   _____ _____ _____
   - Search and replace features   _____ _____ _____

5. **Editing Requirements**
   The software has:
   - Spelling check   _____ _____ _____
   - Mechanics check   _____ _____ _____
   - Supplemental editing software available   _____ _____ _____

6. **Publishing Requirements**
   The software has:
   - Page number indicators   _____ _____ _____
   - Screen display truly representative of printed copy   _____ _____ _____
   - Integration of graphics with text   _____ _____ _____
   - Print options
       boldface type   _____ _____ _____
       underlining   _____ _____ _____
       subscript/superscript   _____ _____ _____
       centering   _____ _____ _____
       justified margins   _____ _____ _____
       multiple line spacing   _____ _____ _____
       interrupt or cancel printing process   _____ _____ _____
       variety of print fonts and sizes   _____ _____ _____
       foreign symbols   _____ _____ _____
       page break   _____ _____ _____
       prints specified text   _____ _____ _____
       single or continuous paper feed   _____ _____ _____

Comments:

words in the dictionary. The two greatest drawbacks of spelling checkers is that they do not recognize inflectional endings of words and homonym errors. For instance, a student may write *their* and spell it correctly, but if the word should be *they're* a spelling checker will not catch the error. Most spelling checkers allow users to add other words to the dictionary, including classmates' names, content area vocabulary, and slang.

Betza (1987) lists five suggestions for selecting and using a spelling checker with elementary students:

- Find the best spelling checker available for your computer and have students experiment with it and add words to make it better.
- Use spelling checkers to involve students with editing.
- Keep records of students' spelling progress.
- Use spelling checkers selectively.
- Reserve the spelling checker for the final draft.

Thesaurus and grammar programs are also available that allow students to highlight specific problems in their compositions and request the computer to supply options.

Keyboarding Tutorials. Keyboarding tutorial programs are designed to teach typing skills to children so they can use word processing more effectively. There are two types of tutorials. Comprehensive tutorials teach the correct fingering on the keyboard and include these features:

- Students are introduced to the home row of keys first.
- Students practice the keys using meaningful letter and word combinations.
- Students receive frequent feedback about accuracy and speed.
- Students can correct errors while typing.
- The program displays upper- and lowercase letters. (Knapp, 1986)

One of the best-known comprehensive tutorials is *Microtype, The Wonderful World of Paws* (South-Western Publishing). Other tutorials are presented in a game format, such as *Kids on Keys* (Spinnaker) and *Type Attack* (Sirus Software), and these drill programs are better suited for increasing children's typing speed than introducing them to keyboarding. One program, *Type to Learn* (Sunburst Communication), integrates keyboarding with reading and writing.

When students begin to use the microcomputer for word processing, the question of keyboarding arises because familiarity with the location of letters on the keyboard allows students to enter words easier and faster. Students who don't know the locations of keys on the keyboard use the hunt-and-peck technique to arduously produce their compositions. This ties up the use of the computer longer than necessary, and teachers worry that children learn bad keyboarding habits that may be hard to break later. The fact is that word processing will become a standard method of writing in the future, and keyboarding will become a basic literacy skill. Many educators recommend teaching students basic keyboarding skills as soon as they begin to use microcomputers, while others suggest postponing keyboarding instruction until third or fourth grade, after students have learned manuscript and cursive handwriting skills. Whether or not they have learned the correct fingering on the keyboard, children should not be discouraged from using a computer.

Text and Graphics Programs. Students can use text and graphics programs such as *Newsroom* (Springboard), *Newspaper Maker* (Scholastic), and *Print Shop* (Broderbund) to create class newspapers, literary magazines, signs, and greeting cards. These programs allow students to publish their writing in very professional-looking publications.

Electronic Mail. Students can use the word processor to write notes and letters to classmates, pen pals, and the teacher using an electronic mail program. They write letters on the computer, revise and edit the messages, and then transmit them to another computer using a modem hooked up to the sending and receiving computers. Teachers can also write messages back and forth to students and send announcements and reminders to students through electronic mail (Newman, 1986). A real advantage of this communication system is that students develop an increased sense of audience (Bruce, Michaels, & Watson-Gegeo, 1985). One word processing program that includes an electronic mail system, called the "Mailbag," for exchanging messages is D.C. Heath's *QUILL*.

Word Processing in the Elementary Classroom

The first step in using computers for word processing with elementary students is to introduce students to the computer using the tutorial lessons that accompany most word processing programs. Students work through the tutorial lesson in groups of two or three, and then they summarize what they have learned by making word processing reference charts that include general directions on operating the word processing program (e.g., how to access a file, save a file, and print out a hard copy) and a list of commands (e.g., insert, delete, move, search, and replace) and keystrokes that allow students to execute these commands. Students can use their charts for quick reference as they work at the computers.

It is a good idea for the teacher to complete the first writing assignment with the students as a large-group collaboration so all students can review the word processing procedures. A large screen is especially useful for class collaborations and group teaching sessions, but a regular monitor can be used. The next several writing assignments should be short, generally no longer than a paragraph or two. In this way, students can concentrate on working through the word processing procedure rather than having to focus on the demands of the writing assignments at the same time they are learning to use the computer.

One or two students in each classroom quickly assume an important new status as "computer expert," either because a special interest or expertise with computers. These experts help other students with word processing, mastering commands, and using the printer. Cochran-Smith and her colleagues (1988) found that the "experts" were often not the smartest or best behaved students, but they approached the computer more systematically than other children.

Word Processing with Young Children. Computers with word processing programs can be used very effectively to record young children's language experience stories (Barber, 1982; Smith 1985). Teachers may want to sit children on their laps or stand between them and the computer to model keyboarding. Teachers take children's dictation as they do in traditional language experience activities, using a computer rather than paper and pencil. After entering the child's dictation, the child and the teacher read the text and make any needed revisions. Next, the text is printed out and the child can add a drawing. If the child has already drawn a picture, the printout can be cut and taped onto the drawing. The microcomputer simplifies the process of taking children's dictation because teachers can record dictation on a computer more quickly than they can write, the dictation can be revised and edited easily, and a clean copy of the revised writing can be printed out.

Salinger (1988) recommends that language experience be used to introduce young children to word processing, and other educators suggest that young children can use computers themselves for word processing. Daiute (1985) reports that children as young as 6 years old can learn the positions of the keys on the keyboard. They can also use a graphic tablet (a device that attaches to the computer) to draw and handwrite letters and words that appear directly on the monitor screen.

In first and second grade, students can write their own compositions on the word processor. For an interesting report of first graders writing on a computer, check Phenix and Hannan's article, "Word Processing in the Grade One Classroom" (1984). These two teachers describe how their first graders wrote and revised a variety of compositions on computers and "learned that writing does not have to come out right the first time" and "that revising is a normal way writing is done" (p. 812). These are the same process approach generalizations that teachers work toward with students at all grade levels.

The Microcomputer-Writing Connection

In the process approach to writing, students write by developing and refining their compositions. The microcomputer with a word processing program is a useful tool in each of the five stages of the writing process. In prewriting, students use word processing to take notes, to freewrite, to brainstorm, and for other rehearsal activities. As students pour out and shape their ideas in the drafting stage, the computer is a more efficient tool than pen and paper. Students who have good typing skills can input text or make changes more quickly than they can write by hand. Even students who have not learned to type very well prefer to write using the word processor (Kane, 1983).

In the revising stage, students print out copies of their rough drafts to use in conferences. After reading and discussing their compositions during a conference, students return to the computer to make substantive revisions that reflect the reactions and suggestions received in the conference. Word processing allows students to revise easily, without cutting and pasting changes in their rough drafts.

Microcomputers are especially useful during editing when students correct mechanical errors in their compositions. Students have "clean" texts to proofread, whether they read them on the monitor screen or on printed copies. After proofreading and editing, students return again to the computer to make their corrections quickly and easily.

After students have completed all corrections, they decide about formatting their compositions (e.g., margins, types of print, spacing, numbering) and print out the final copy to share with an audience. Using word processing relieves students from the tedium of recopying their final copies by hand. The professional-looking final copies often boost students' feeling of accomplishment, especially students with poor handwriting skills.

Typically, two or three students work together in a buddy system and take turns using the microcomputer. Although this system is often necessitated by the small number of computers available for student use, there is an added benefit. Students working together are more inclined to collaborate with each other, providing support, assistance, and feedback to each other as they compose.

Cochran-Smith and her colleagues (1988) researched the methods used to introduce word processing to students in kindergarten through fourth grade over a 2-year period. They found that students had conceptual "bugs" about word processing and these misconceptions caused problems as they were learning to use word processing programs. One problem was equating keyboard-and-screen with paper-and-pencil. They did not recognize and appreciate the unique capabilities of a microcomputer for formatting, revising, or editing text. A second problem was their inexperience with keyboarding and locating letters on the keyboard.

Many teachers have expressed the hope that microcomputers will encourage students to use a process approach and write and revise a series of drafts. However, Kane (1983) found that students in her study composed the same way on the computer that they composed with pen and paper. In other words, students who normally write single-draft papers or who limit revisions to making minor changes are likely to continue to do so. This finding reinforces the idea that the computer is only a tool, and that good teaching is required for students to learn to write well.

■ ANSWERING TEACHER'S QUESTIONS ABOUT WRITERS' TOOLS

1. I'm concerned that if my students misspell words on rough drafts, they will learn to spell them incorrectly.

In a single composition—and sometimes in a single sentence—children spell an unfamiliar word several different ways as they problem-solve for the "best" spelling. Research studies have shown that allowing children to use invented spelling leads to increased achievement in spelling, not the other way around. Since learning to spell a word involves much more than simply writing it once or twice, there is little chance that children will internalize the incorrect spelling.

Seeing misspelled words on a composition bothers me, too. I think children's misspellings are a teacher problem, not a student problem. One way to solve the problem is to not look too closely while students are writing rough drafts and sharing them in writing groups. Instead of reading the drafts yourself, ask students to read their rough drafts to you, and you won't see the misspelled words. An overemphasis on correct spelling during writing, moreover, distracts students from their real purpose in writing—communicating! The time to express concern about student's spelling is during editing.

2. My students' parents have complained when their children misspell words on work I've sent home. What should I do?

It is crucial to explain to parents about the role of spelling in the writing process and the emphasis you will place on spelling in your classroom. It is helpful to have a rubber stamp marked ROUGH DRAFT for students to stamp on their papers to identify papers in which content counts more than mechanics. Also, even with careful editing, it is likely that children will continue to misspell a few words on their final copies. Spelling is a writer's tool and it needs to be put in proper perspective.

3. Many questions deal with grammar on the achievement tests that I am required to administer to my school district. You say that teaching grammar does little good, but I have to prepare students for the tests. What should I do?

Of course, you should prepare them for the tests, but don't confuse teaching grammar to prepare students for the achievement test with teaching grammar to improve writing skills. If grammar must be taught, it is probably more effective to have students manipulate sentences taken from their compositions rather than sentences in text-books. When using their own writing, students are more interested in learning how to combine words into sentences.

4. I don't want my students to learn bad habits so I always expect them to use their best handwriting skills. Are you suggesting that it is all right for them to be messy?

No one always uses his or her best handwriting skills. Think about the last time you scribbled a grocery list or a note to a neighbor. There are two types of handwriting activities—public and private. Adults know this and vary their own handwriting to fit the purpose. There's no reason to suppose that students aren't aware of these two types. In the past, students have assumed that all writing in school is public and that "genuine" writing at home may be either public or private depending on its purpose. This becomes a question of whether school is different than life.

5. I only have one microcomputer in my classroom. How can I use it to teach writing?

While an ideal situation would be to have a computer available on each student's desk, it is, unfortunately, not yet realistic. When you have only one or two computers in the classroom, students will probably prewrite and write rough drafts with paper and pencil, and then type their compositions into the word processor before revising them. A schedule is needed so that all students can have access to the computer. Expect students to volunteer to collaborate on compositions so that they can have more time on the computer, and this collaboration will also benefit their writing.

6. I don't know enough about computer programming to teach my students about word processing.

It isn't necessary for teachers or students to know computer programming to use word processing programs. These programs are "user friendly," and you and your students can learn to use them with several hours of practice and a few basic commands. The programs designed for elementary students are even easier to use than programs for adults. Many word processing programs have tutorials on disks accompanying the program to teach students (and their teachers) how to use it. Also, in almost every class one or two children will be familiar with computers and word processing programs, and they will quickly become the resident "computer experts".

■ REFERENCES

Anderson, K. F. (1985). The development of spelling ability and linguistic strategies. *The Reading Teacher, 39*, pp. 140–147.

Barbe, W. B., Wasylyk, T. M., Hackney, C. S. & Braun, L. A. (1984). *Zaner-Bloser creative growth in handwriting* (Grades K-8). Columbus, OH: Zaner-Bloser.

Barber, B. (1982). Creating BYTES of language. *Language Arts, 59*, 472–475.

Barron, R. W. (1980). Visual and phonological strategies in reading and spelling. In U. Frith (Ed.), *Cognitive processes in learning to spell.* London: Academic Press.

Beers, J. W., & Henderson, E. H. (1977). A study of developing orthographic concepts among first graders. *Research in the Teaching of English, 11*, 133–148.

Betza, R. E. (1987). Online: Computerized spelling checkers: Freinds (sic) or foes? *Language Arts, 64*, 438–443.

Braddock, R., Lloyd-Jones, R., & Schoer, L. (1963). *Research in written compostion.* Champaign, IL: National Council of Teachers of English.

Bruce, B., Michaels, S., & Watson-Gegeo, K. (1985). How computers can change the writing process. *Language Arts., 62*, 143–149.

Cochran-Smith, M., Kahan, J., & Pares, C. L. (1988). When word processors come into the classroom, In J. L. Hoot and S. B. Silver (Eds.), *Writing with computers in the early grades* (pp. 43–74). New York: Teachers College Press.

Cook, G. E., Esposito, M., Gabrielson, T., & Turner, G. (1984). *Spelling for word mastery.* Columbus, OH: Merrill.

Daiute, C. (1985). *Writing and computers.* Reading, MA: Addison-Wesley.

Elbow, P. (1973). *Writing without teachers.* New York: Oxford University Press.

Elley, W. B., Barham, I. H., Lamb, H., & Wyllie, M. (1976). The role of grammar in a secondary school English curriculum. *Research in the Teaching of English, 10*, 5–21.

Fraser, I. S., & Hodson, L. M. (1978). Twenty-one kicks at the grammar horse. *English Journal, 67*, 49–53.

Frith, U. (1980). Unexpected spelling problems. In U. Frith (Ed.), *Cognitive processes in learning to spell.* London: Academic Press.

Gentry, J. R. (1978). Early spelling strategies. *Elementary School Journal, 79*, 88–92.

Gentry, J. R. (1981). Learning to spell developmentally. *The Reading Teacher, 34*, 378–381.

Gentry, J. R. (1982a). An analysis of developmental spellings in *Gyns at wrk. The Reading Teacher, 36*, 192–200.

Gentry, J. R. (1982b). Developmental spelling: Assessment. *Diagnostique, 8*, 52–61.

Graves, D. H. (1983). *Writing: Teachers and writers at work.* Portsmouth, NH: Heinemann.

Haley-James, S. (Ed.). (1981). *Perspectives on writing in grades 1–8.* Urbana, IL: National Council of Teachers of English.

Harrison, S. (1981). Open letter from a left-handed teacher: Some sinistral ideas on the teaching of handwriting. *Teaching Exceptional Children, 13*, 116–120.

Henderson, E. H. (1980a). Developmental concepts of word. In E. H. Henderson & J. W. Beers (Eds.), *Developmental and cognitive aspects* of learning to spell: A reflection of word knowledge (pp. 1–14). Newark, DE: International Reading Association.

Henderson, E. H. (1980b). Word knowledge and reading disability. In E. H. Henderson & J. W. Beers (Eds.), *Developmental and cognitive aspects of learning to spell: A reflection of word knowledge* (pp. 138–148). Newark, DE: International Reading Association.

Hillerich, R. L. (1977). Let's teach spelling—Not phonetic misspelling. *Language Arts, 54,* 301–307.

Hoot, J. L., & Silvern, S. B. (Eds.). (1988). *Writing with computers in the early grades*. New York: Teachers College Press.

Horn, E. (1957). Phonetics and spelling. *Elementary School Journal, 57,* 424–432.

Howell, H. (1978). Write on, you sinistrals! *Language Arts, 55,* 852–856.

Hunt, K. W., & O'Donnell, R. C. (1970). *An elementary school curriculum to develop better writing skills*. Washington, DC: US Government Printing Office.

Hutson, B. A. (1980). Moving language around: Helping students become aware of language structure. *Language Arts, 57,* 614–620.

Kane, J. H. (1983). Computers for composing. In *Chameleon in the classroom: Developing roles for computers* (Technical Report No. 22). New York: Bank Street College of Education.

Knapp, L. R. (1986). *The word processor and the writing teacher*. Englewood Cliffs, NJ: Prentice-Hall.

Lamme, L. L., & Ayris, B. M. (1983). Is the handwriting of beginning writers influenced by writing tools? *Journal of Research and Development in Education, 17,* 32–38.

Lawlor, J. (1983). Sentence combining: A sequence for instruction. *The Elementary School Journal, 84,* 53–62.

Lindsay, G. A., & McLennan, D. (1983). Lined paper: its effects on the legibility and creativitiy of young children's writings. *British Journal of Educational Psychology, 53,* 364–368.

Markham, L. R. (1976). Influences of handwriting quality on teacher evaluation of written work. *American Educational Research Journal, 13,* 277–283.

Marsh, G., Friedman, M., Desberg, P., & Welsh, V. (1980). The development of strategies in spelling. In U. Frith (Ed.), *Cognitive processes in learning to spell*. London: Academic Press.

Mellon, J. C. (1969). *Transformational sentence combining: A method of enhancing the development of syntactic fluency in English compositions* (NCTE Research Report No. 10). Urbana, IL: National Council of Teachers of English.

Newman, J. M. (1986), Online: Electronic mail and newspapers. *Language Arts, 63,* 736–741.

Noyce, R. M., & Christie, J. F. (1983). Effects of an integrated approach to grammar instruction on third graders' reading and writing. *Elementary School Journal, 84,* 63–69.

O'Hare, F. (1973). *Sentence combining: Improving student writing without formal grammar instruction* (NCTE Research Report No. 15). Urbana, IL: National Council of Teachers of English.

Oklahoma Writing Project. (1986). *Checklist for evaluating word processing software*. Unpublished manuscript. Norman, OK: University of Oklahoma.

Phenix, J., & Hannan, E. (1984). Word processing in the grade one classroom. *Language Arts, 61,* 804–812.

Pooley, R. C. (1974). *The teaching of English usage*. Urbana, IL: National Council of Teachers of English.

Read, C. (1971). Preschool children's knowledge of English phonology. *Harvard Educational Review, 41,* 1–34.

Read, C. (1975). *Children's categorization of speech sounds in English* (NCTE Research Report No. 17). Urbana, IL: National Council of Teachers of English.

Read, C. (1986). *Children's creative spelling*. London: Routledge & Kegan Paul.

Rodrigues, D., & Rodrigues, R. J. (1986). *Teaching writing with a word processor, grades 7–13*. Urbana, IL: ERIC Clearinghouse on Reading and Communication Skills and National Council of Teachers of English.

Salinger, T. S. (1988). Language experience as an introduction to word processing. In J. L. Hoot & S. B. Silvern (Eds.), *Writing with computers in the early grades* (pp. 90–104). New York: Teachers College Press.

Smith, F. (1982). *Writing and the writer*. New York: Holt.

Smith, J. J. (1985). The word processing approach to language experience. *The Reading Teacher, 38*, 556–559.

Smith, P. L., & Tompkins, G. E. (1983). *Computers and writing*. Unpublished manuscript. Norman, OK: University of Oklahoma.

Strong, W. (1986). *Creative approaches to sentence combining*. Urbana, IL: ERIC Clearinghouse on Reading and Communication Skills and National Council of Teachers of English.

Templeton, S. (1979). Spelling first, sound later: The relationship between orthography and higher order phonological knowledge in older students. *Research in the Teaching of English, 13*, 255–265.

VanDeWeghe, R. (1982). Spelling and grammar logs. In C. Carter (Ed.), *Nonnative and nonstandard dialect students: Classroom practices in teaching English, 1982–1983* (pp. 101–105). Urbana, IL: National Council of Teachers of English.

Weaver, C. (1979). *Grammar for teachers: Perspectives and definitions*. Urbana, IL: National Council of Teachers of English.

Wrench, W. (1987). *A practical guide to computer uses in the English/language arts classroom*. Englewood Cliffs, NJ: Prentice-Hall.

Zutell, J. (1979). Spelling strategies of primary grade school children and their relationship to Piaget's concept of decentration. *Research in the Teaching of English, 13*, 69–79.

9

Writing Across the Curriculum

As part of a social studies unit on the Constitution of the United States, Mrs. Wilkins's fourth-grade class compose their own constitution, shown in Figure 9–1. In creating their class document, students discuss their rights and responsibilities as class members, choose the format of the constitution, and worry about how to amend the document if it proves unworkable. Through this activity, students learn more about composing a constitution, and what James Madison, George Washington, and the other founding fathers did in Philadelphia during the hot summer of 1787, than they would have by memorizing names, dates, and events.

This chapter extends the teaching of writing from language arts class across the curriculum. Writing is a powerful learning tool, and informal and formal writing activities are valuable in all content areas. A list of writing across the curriculum activities is presented in Figure 9–2. In these activities, students use writing to learn or to demonstrate learning. Mrs. Wilkins' class constitution, for example, is a formal writing activity. Students use a process approach to write a rough draft, revise, and edit the document much like the founders of the United States did. Then it is recopied and students sign their names and proudly display it in their classroom. These students were learning about the Constitution of the United States as they wrote their own. Their finished document demonstrates their learning, but it is the learning rather than the documentation of learning that really matters (Gere, 1985; Zinsser, 1988).

Writing across the curriculum has at least three significant benefits for elementary students (Hembrow, 1986; Myers, 1984). It encourages learning of content area information, develops writing fluency and skills, and activates critical thinking skills. Writing is a powerful learning tool that makes a significant contribution to learning because through writing, students develop their own knowledge of the subject. As students write in content areas, they develop writing fluency and also practice language skills. Writing makes thinking concrete. As they write, students discover, organize, classify, connect, and evaluate information.

In Mrs. Wilkins' class, students learned about the writing of the United States Constitution as they wrote their own. They played with the language and format of the document. Writing skills were important as they collaborated on the writing of the document and discussed the best way to state and punctuate a rule. Also, they used critical thinking as they decided to end their constitution with a statement about how to amend it, if necessary.

Writing to Learn

As she begins a unit on Thanksgiving with her first-grade class, Mrs. Jarvis hangs two large sheets of chart paper on the wall. On one chart she prints "Things We Know About Thanksgiving" and on the second "Things We Want to Learn About Thanksgiving." She asks students to brainstorm things they already know about Thanksgiving (e.g., "The Pilgrims and Indians had the first Thanksgiving."), which she records on the first chart. Questions arise as students offer conflicting information and these become the first items on the second list. Then children

FIGURE 9–1   A Fourth-grade Class Constitution

Our Class Constitution

We the students of Mrs. Wilkins's fourth-grade class, in order to have a good year, agree to work, learn, and play together in a cooperative way. These rules will help us to do that:

1. Put name on all assignments.

2. Be seated and quiet while teacher is speaking.

3. Raise hand before talking.

4. Take care of materials.

5. No talking or running in the hall.

6. No running in the classroom.

7. Respect the rights and property of others.

8. Six feet on the floor at all times (2 or yours; 4 of the chair's!)

9. Heads down on desks upon entering the room after recess, etc.

10. No pencil-sharpening during reading or writing groups.

11. No more than 2 people on the floor at a time.

12. Don't go to the restroom without a pass. (We'll make exceptions for emergencies.)

13. Turn in all assignments on time.

The members of this class, the students and the teacher, shall have the responsibility of seeing that these rules are followed. The teacher shall make the final decision as to whether or not the rules have been obeyed.

If we need to change these rules or add to them as the year goes on, we will discuss the problem and do what is necessary.

Mrs. Wilkins   Brian   Keith
Devon   Chad   Brandi   Manuel
John   Jeff   Kyle   Eric
Azurdé   allison
Justin   Carrie   Evan
Kimberly
Roy   Jamie   Trisha
Ben   Michelle   Stephanie

FIGURE 9–2 A List of Writing-Across-the-Curriculum Activities

simulated journals	memos	lab notebooks
biographies	pen pal letters	poems
scripts	collaborative reports	dictionaries
maps	stories	myths and legends
puzzles	learning logs	ABC books
newspaper articles	summaries	freewrites
cartoons	advertisements	posters
directions	math story problems	"All About _____"
wordless picture books	individual reports	books
brainstormed lists	cubing	clusters
book/film reviews	directions	telegrams
dialogues	raps/songs	comparisons
five senses clusters	rules	interviews
photos and captions	observations	predictions
reading logs	diagrams	business letters
charts	persuasive essays	lifelines/timelines
collages	word searches	simulated newspapers
		friendly letters

identify additional things they want to learn, for example, "Why do we eat turkey for Thanksgiving?" and "Why is Thanksgiving always in November?" Periodically during the unit, the first graders review the two charts and begin listing information on a third chart, "Things We've Learned About Thanksgiving."

Through this activity, first graders become engaged in learning. They think about what they know about a topic, what they want to learn, and later, what they have learned. Students' prior knowledge is activated by brainstorming the list for the first chart, and they set their own purposes for learning when they identify what they want to learn for the second chart. They use the third chart to monitor their learning. Older students can use a similar approach and make and update lists in their learning logs. This strategy is adapted from Ogle's (1986) K-W-L strategy for reading expository texts.

Writing is a powerful—even unique—learning strategy (Britton et al., 1975; Emig, 1977; Moffett 1968). It is a valuable strategy because it fosters critical thinking through a language scaffold. In the Thanksgiving unit example, the three charts served as a scaffold. Similarly, when students write learning logs after reading or cluster information after viewing a film, writing is a scaffold. Learning becomes interactive, not passive, as students become engaged and personally involved in what they are learning through writing.

Anne Gere (1985) describes writing to learn as a strategy that students need for lifelong learning; it allows students to assume responsibility for and ownership of their own learning. She describes these characteristics of writing to learn: the strategy fosters critical thinking; the writing is informal; the learning that comes from writing, rather than the writing itself, is what matters; teachers become guides, not information givers; and there are a variety of ways to use this learning strategy.

Brainstorming, clustering, freewriting, and cubing are used in writing to learn. The first graders in Mrs. Jarvis' classroom used brainstorming in making classroom charts. This informal writing strategy might be used in making a variety of lists: for example, steps in solving a math problem, knowledge about a social studies unit at the beginning and end of the unit, or words related to the theme before reading a story. Students may make clusters from their notes as they read a textbook or tradebook to gather and organize information before writing reports. Freewriting helps students explore their knowledge about a topic, reflect on a film after viewing it, respond to a novel as they read it, record observations in science, and clarify information presented in class by writing at the end of the class period. They can also assume the role of another person and freewrite in simulated journals. Students use cubing to analyze a multidimensional social studies or science topic they are studying.

Some of these writing to learn activities can be done in small groups or with the entire class. Brainstorming and cubing are especially valuable as group activities. Others such as learning logs, simulated journals, and freewriting are individual writing activities.

Learning Logs. Learning logs have become nearly synonymous with writing to learn because as they write in logs in content area classes, students brainstorm, cluster, freewrite, and cube. For example, in learning logs, students:

- Take notes.
- List vocabulary words.
- Write questions.
- Compare two topics.
- Make observations.
- Write reactions.
- List steps in a demonstration.
- Cluster main ideas.
- Draw diagrams and maps.
- Freewrite.

When teachers have students write after viewing a film or use the last 5 minutes of class to reflect on what they have learned, they can freewrite on these topics:

- What did I learn?
- What confused me?
- What questions do I have?
- What connections can I make? (Proett & Gill, 1986)

The writing in logs is informal and sometimes messy. The focus is on thinking, on exploring what students know. Betsy Sanford (1988) encourages her fourth graders to write reflectively about what they are learning. One of her students writes, "Understanding is what counts for you. These log entries help me a lot" (p. 53). Fulwiler (1987) has noted five characteristics of learning logs: informal word choice, frequent use of *I,* informal punctuation, tone of everyday speech, and experimentation with form, style, voice, and persona.

Simulated Journals. Another way to use learning logs in writing to learn is through simulated journals in which students assume the persona of another person and write from that person's viewpoint. For example, as they read a novel, students can assume the persona of a character and write a journal as though they were the person. In *Sam, Bangs, and Moonshine* (Ness, 1966), for instance, Samantha's entries would reflect her awareness (and perhaps guilt) that lies called "moonshine" cause great harm to her friends and pets. As they read biographies, students can also keep simulated journals in which they become the person they are reading about and through the journals "live" in another time period. When they read about Alexander Graham Bell and keep a journal as though they were Mr. Bell, students understand his lifelong interest in transmitting speech, and they appreciate what the inventor was feeling on March 10, 1876 when he successfully spoke on the telephone, "Mr. Watson, come here. I want you!"

EXPOSITORY TEXT STRUCTURES

Fourth-grade Russell wrote this chapter as a part of his report on dinosaurs:

■
    Digging Up Dinosaurs
    After the dinosaurs turned to fossils and after millions of years, paleontologists dig them up. It is not an easy task. You can't dig them up in an hour or two. It takes weeks, months, and years.
    I'm going to tell you how they find and put them together. Well, first they find the dinosaur and then they sand blast it or drill it out. Once they get it out, the workers chip all of the pieces of the rock off them. Then they put shellac on the fossils with a paint brush. Then they number the fossils and put tissue paper around them and dip them in a plaster cast. Then they put them in crates and ship them to the museum.
    There they study the fossils to see how old they are. Then they put them together. Then everybody pours in to see the dinosaurs.

Russell's chapter is easy to read because it is carefully organized. Sequence is the organizing pattern that Russell used as he described the activities involved in digging up dinosaurs. He stated his purpose (*"I'm going to tell you how they find and put them together"*) and then listed the activities step-by-step. He even used transition words—*first* and *then*—to cue readers to the sequence pattern.

When students write in science, social studies, and other content areas, they organize their writing, as Russell did, according to specific organizational patterns, called expository text structures. Five of the most commonly used patterns are description, sequence, comparison, cause and effect, and problem and solution (Meyer & Freedle, 1984; Niles, 1974).

Description. In this organizational pattern, the writer describes a topic by listing characteristics, features, and examples. Phrases such as *for example* and *characteristics are* cue this structure. When students delineate any topic, such as cobras, Jupiter or another planet, or Russia, they use description.

Sequence. The writer lists items or events in numerical or chronological order. Cue words include *first, second, third, next, then,* and *finally.* Directions for completing a math problem, steps in the life cycle of a plant or animal, and events in a biography are often written using the sequence pattern.

Comparison. The writer explains how two or more things are alike or how they are different. *Different, in contrast, alike, same as,* and *on the other hand* are cue words and phrases that signal this structure. When students compare and contrast book and movie versions of a story, insects with spiders, or life in colonial America with life today, they use this organizational pattern.

Cause and Effect. The writer explains one or more causes and the resulting effect or effects. *Reasons why, if . . . then, as a result, therefore,* and *because* are words and phrases that cue this structure. Explanations of why the dinosaurs died, the effects of pollution on the environment, or the causes of the American Revolution are written using the cause and effect pattern.

Problem and Solution. In this expository structure, the writer states a problem and provides one or more solutions to the problem. A variation is the question and answer format in which the writer poses a question and then answers it. Cue words and phrases include *the problem is, the puzzle is, solve,* and *question . . . answer.* When students write about why money was invented, saving endangered animals, and building dams to stop flooding, they use this structure. Also, students often use the problem and solution pattern in writing advertisements and other persuasive writing. In Figure 9–3, these patterns are summarized.

These organizational patterns correspond to the traditional organization of main ideas (or topic sentences) and details within paragraphs. The main idea is embodied in the organizational pattern and the details are the elaboration. For example, in the sample passage for the comparison pattern presented in Figure 9-3, the main idea is that the modern Olympic games are very different from the ancient Olympic games. The details are the specific comparisons and contrasts. The main idea and details for the comparison are illustrated in this diagram:

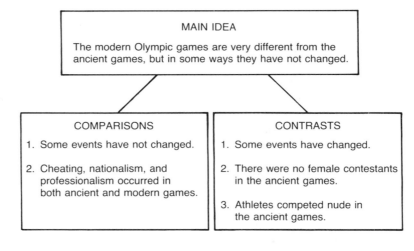

MAIN IDEA

The modern Olympic games are very different from the ancient games, but in some ways they have not changed.

COMPARISONS	CONTRASTS
1. Some events have not changed.	1. Some events have changed.
2. Cheating, nationalism, and professionalism occurred in both ancient and modern games.	2. There were no female contestants in the ancient games.
	3. Athletes competed nude in the ancient games.

Pattern	Description	Cue Words	Graphic Organizer	Sample Passage
Description	The author describes a topic by listing characteristics, features, and examples.	*for example* *characteristics are*		The Olympic symbol consists of five interlocking rings. The rings represent the five continents—Africa, Asia, Europe, North America, and South America—from which athletes come to compete in the games. The rings are colored black, blue, green, red, and yellow. At least one of these colors is found in the flag of every country sending athletes to compete in the Olympic games.
Sequence	The author lists items or events in numerical or chronological order.	*first, second, third* *next* *then* *finally*	1. _____ 2. _____ 3. _____ 4. _____ 5. _____	The Olympic games began as athletic festivals to honor the Greek gods. The most important festival was held in the valley of Olympia to honor Zeus, the king of the gods. It was this festival that became the Olympic games in 776 B.C. These games were ended in A.D. 394 by the Roman Emperor who ruled Greece. No Olympic games were held for more than 1,500 years. Then the modern Olympics began in 1896. Almost 300 male athletes competed in the first modern Olympics. In the games held in 1900, female athletes were allowed to compete. The games have continued every four years since 1896 except during World War II, and they will most likely continue for many years to come.
Comparison	The author explains how two or more things are alike and/or how they are different.	*different* *in contrast* *alike* *same as* *on the other hand*		The modern Olympics is very unlike the ancient Olympic games. Individual events are different. While there were no swimming races in the ancient games, for example, there were chariot races. There were no female contestants and all athletes competed in the nude. Of course, the ancient and modern Olympics are also alike in many ways. Some events, such as the javelin and discus throws, are the same. Some people say that cheating, professionalism, and nationalism in the modern games are a disgrace to the Olympic tradition. But according to the ancient Greek writers, there were many cases of cheating, nationalism, and professionalism in their Olympics, too.

Cause and Effect	The author lists one or more causes and the resulting effect or effects.	*reasons why* *if . . . then* *as a result* *therefore* *because*

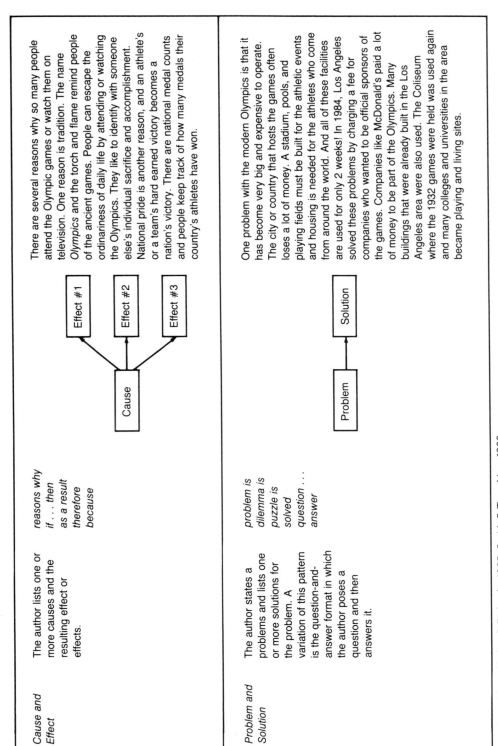

There are several reasons why so many people attend the Olympic games or watch them on television. One reason is tradition. The name *Olympics* and the torch and flame remind people of the ancient games. People can escape the ordinariness of daily life by attending or watching the Olympics. They like to identify with someone else's individual sacrifice and accomplishment. National pride is another reason, and an athlete's or a team's hard earned victory becomes a nation's victory. There are national medal counts and people keep track of how many medals their country's athletes have won.

Problem and Solution	The author states a problems and lists one or more solutions for the problem. A variation of this pattern is the question-and-answer format in which the author poses a question and then answers it.	*problem is* *dilemma is* *puzzle is* *solved* *question . . .* *answer*

One problem with the modern Olympics is that it has become very big and expensive to operate. The city or country that hosts the games often loses a lot of money. A stadium, pools, and playing fields must be built for the athletic events and housing is needed for the athletes who come from around the world. And all of these facilities are used for only 2 weeks! In 1984, Los Angeles solved these problems by charging a fee for companies who wanted to be official sponsors of the games. Companies like McDonald's paid a lot of money to be part of the Olympics. Many buildings that were already built in the Los Angeles area were also used. The Coliseum where the 1932 games were held was used again and many colleges and universities in the area became playing and living sites.

Adapted from McGee & Richgels, 1985; Smith & Tompkins, 1988.

FIGURE 9–3 The Five Expository Text Structures

Diagrams called graphic organizers can be created to help students organize ideas for the other four organizational patterns as well (Smith & Tompkins, 1988). Sample diagrams of the graphic organizers are presented in Figure 9–3.

Reading researchers identified these patterns by examining content area reading materials to devise ways to help students comprehend those materials more easily. Most of the research on expository text structures has focused on older students' use of these patterns in reading; however, elementary students also use the patterns and cue words in their writing.

A class of second graders examined the five expository text structures and learned that authors use cue words as a secret code to signal the structures. Then they read informational books using each of the expository text structures. After reading, the second graders wrote paragraphs to share what they had learned. Working in small groups, they developed graphic organizers and wrote paragraphs to exemplify each of the five organizational patterns. These graphic organizers and paragraphs are presented in Figure 9–4. The secret code (or cue) words in each paragraph appear in boldface type.

Teaching Students to Use Expository Text Structures

Students can learn to recognize these patterns and to use them to improve their reading comprehension as well as to organize their writing (Flood, Lapp, & Farnan, 1986; McGee & Richgels, 1985; Piccolo, 1987). The steps in the instructional strategy are:

1. *Introduce an organizational pattern.* Explain the pattern and when writers use it, note cue words that signal the pattern, share an example of the pattern, and then describe the graphic organizer for that pattern.
2. *Analyze examples of the pattern in tradebooks.* Students locate examples of the expository text structure in informational books, not in stories. Sometimes the pattern is signalled clearly using titles, topic sentences, and cue words, and sometimes it is not. Students identify cue words when they are used, and they talk about why writers may or may not explicitly signal the structure. They also diagram the structure using a graphic organizer.
3. *Write paragraphs using the pattern.* After students analyze examples of the pattern in informational books, they write paragraphs using the pattern. The first writing activity may be a whole class activity. Later, students write paragraphs in small groups and individually. For prewriting activities, students choose a topic, gather information and organize it using a graphic organizer. Next they write a rough draft of the paragraph, inserting cue words to signal the structure. Then they revise, edit, and write a final copy of the paragraph.
4. *Repeat for each pattern.* Repeat the first three steps for each of the five expository text structures. Once students have learned the organizational patterns, they are ready to use them in their writing.
5. *Choose the most appropriate pattern to communicate effectively.* After students learn to use each of the five expository text structures, they need to learn to choose the most appropriate pattern to communicate effectively. Students

can experiment to see the appropriateness of various patterns by taking one set of information and writing paragraphs using different organizational patterns. For example, information about igloos might be written as a description, as a comparison with Indian teepees, or as a solution to a housing problem in the arctic region.

Assessing Students' Use of Expository Text Structures. When students write paragraphs using an expository text structure, they:

- Choose the most appropriate structure.
- Develop a graphic organizer before writing.
- Write a topic sentence that identifies the structure.
- Use cue words to signal the structure.

These four components can be used to develop a checklist to assess students' use of expository text structures. Also, teachers may want to monitor students' use of the five structures in research reports and other across-the-curriculum writing.

Knowledge of these organizational patterns is also valuable in writing groups. When students offer compliments, they can compliment a classmate on sequence or the use of cue words to signal the cause and effect pattern. Similarly, when offering suggestions for improvement, they can suggest that a classmate try a specific pattern or add cue words.

WRITING ABOUT LITERATURE

When students read, they engage in a transaction or interaction with the text. According to Louise Rosenblatt, a piece of literature is only alphabetic symbols printed on a page until a reader transforms them into meaning, and "the literary work exists in the live circuit set up between reader and text" (1983, p. 25). She describes the reader's role as that of an active co-creater rather than a re-creator because "every time a reader experiences a [piece of literature], it is in a sense created anew" (p. 113). In contrast to the traditional approach to reading in which the focus was on the text, and students were required to decipher the author's meaning from the symbols on the page, this new approach, called *response to literature,* involves a negotiation of meaning between reader and text. Readers bring their own experiences to the text, and "the live circuit" interaction that is created through reading depends on the reader as well as the author's text and varies as readers' experiences vary.

Aesthetic Reading and Response

Louise Rosenblatt (1978) makes the distinction between efferent and aesthetic stances to reading. In *efferent reading,* students focus on the information they are to use during or after reading while in *aesthetic reading* they co-create the piece

Description

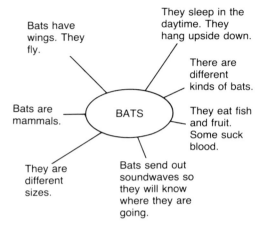

Bats have wings. They fly.

They sleep in the daytime. They hang upside down.

There are different kinds of bats.

Bats are mammals.

BATS

They eat fish and fruit. Some suck blood.

They are different sizes.

Bats send out soundwaves so they will know where they are going.

Bats

All bats are mammals. Bats sleep upside down in the daytime. These animals make sounds to know where they are going. Bats find food by sending out soundwaves. They eat fish, blood, insects, rodents, fruits, and nectar. Bats are all different sizes. Some bats have wings that are five feet wide.

Sequence

1. male and female mate
2. female lays eggs
3. eggs hatch
4. a caterpillar eats and grows
5. it sheds its skin several times
6. caterpillar forms a crysalis
7. butterfly hatches
8. start all over again

The Life of a Monarch Butterfly

A butterfly makes a lot of changes in its life. First the male and the female mate. Next the female lays eggs. The eggs stick to milkweed leaves for three days. Then the eggs hatch into little caterpillars. For five weeks, the caterpillar eats and grows. After shedding its skin several times, the caterpillar forms a crysalis. After two weeks, the butterfly hatches out of the crysalis. Then it starts all over again when a butterfly finds a mate.

Comparison

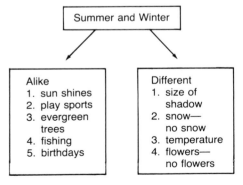

Summer and Winter

Alike
1. sun shines
2. play sports
3. evergreen trees
4. fishing
5. birthdays

Different
1. size of shadow
2. snow— no snow
3. temperature
4. flowers— no flowers

Summer and Winter

Summer and winter are alike in a lot of ways. In the winter and the summer the sun shines. You can play sports in both of these seasons. You can have birthdays in the winter and summer. In the winter you can go ice fishing and in the summer you can go fishing. Evergreens stay green in both seasons.

Summer and winter are different in a lot of ways. In the winter it snows and in the summer it doesn't. In the winter we have big shadows and in the summer we have little shadows. Summer is hot and winter is cold.

FIGURE 9–4 Second Graders' Graphic Organizers and Paragraphs Illustrating the Five Expository Text Structures

Cause and Effect

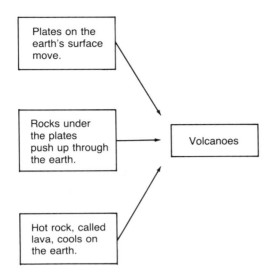

Volcanoes

Do you know what causes volcanoes? The plates on the earth's surface rub together and make hot liquid rock underneath the plates. The hot rock pushes up between the plates. Sometimes it makes a big explosion and the lava comes out onto the earth.

Problem and Solution

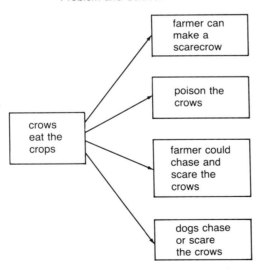

The Problem with Crows

The farmer was having a problem with crows eating the crops. One solution the farmer tried was to put up a scarecrow. Another idea he had up his sleeve was to poison the crows by spraying the crops with chemicals. The farmer thought about chasing the crows away himself. One more idea the farmer had was to let his dog out to chase the crows.

of literature. The aesthetic reading process involves four stages (Corcoran, 1987), and writing can be connected with each stage:

Stage 1: Introducing the Text. Students make connections between their background of experiences and the text they will read. Writing helps to make these connections explicit as well as to heighten anticipation about the literary work. For example, before reading Uri Shulevitz's *The Treasure* (1978), a story about a man who travels to a distant land only to find that the treasure he is seeking is in his house, students in Mrs. Williams' fifth-grade class brainstormed the following list of treasures:

family	dirt bikes	seashells
gold	pets	brothers and sisters
hobbies	friends	rubies
teachers	freedom	Cabbage Patch dolls
baseball cards	summer vacation	parents
diamonds	trophies	my horse
grandparents	pearls	being able to read
money	playing sports	jewelry

Next, students listed in their learning logs at least five things they treasured. Items could come from the class list or from other sources. After reading the story, students reviewed the list and chose one treasure to write about. Matt freewrote about trophies:

■ Trophies are a treasure because they are something that you have earned or worked for. They are something you can show people. You can tell people about them. They make you feel proud because you have worked hard for them.

This writing helped Matt value the story by connecting the treasures in his life to the treasure in the story.

Another way for students to make these connections is by freewriting to relate personal experiences to the theme, characters, plot, or setting of the story. For example, before reading a story in which weather plays an important role, students can write about a time when they were in a storm or weather played a crucial role in their life. Students also can do a cluster about an author, a literary form, or a time period to provide background information before reading.

Stage 2: Reading the Text. Students read the text silently or listen to it read orally by the teacher or by classmates. They also may read it more than once. One way to use writing to help students as they read the text is the *Directed Reading-Thinking Activity (DRTA),* a procedure developed by Russell Stauffer (1975) in which students make predictions about a story and then read to confirm or reject them. This procedure can be easily adapted for writing by having students write their predictions before sharing them orally. The procedure is presented in Figure 9-5, and it works best with stories in which characters must make difficult choices or solve complex problems.

FIGURE 9–5 Steps in the Directed Reading-Thinking Activity

Step 1: Predicting

After showing students the cover of the book and reading the title, the teacher begins by asking students to make a prediction about the story, using questions such as:

- What do you think a story with a title like this might be about?
- What do you think might happen in this story?
- Does this picture give you any ideas about what might happen in this story?

The teacher or students may read the first paragraph or two of the story, if necessary, to provide more information to use in making predictions. Then students write a brief response and read their responses aloud. After sharing their responses, the teacher asks these questions:

- Which of these ideas do you think would be the likely one?
- Why do you think that idea is a good one?

Step 2: Reasoning and Predicting from Succeeding Pages

After setting their purpose for reading or listening, the students or teacher read part of the story, and students begin to confirm or reject their predictions. At crucial points in the story, the teacher asks questions such as:

- What do you think now?
- What do you think will happen next?
- What would happen if . . . ?
- Why do you think that idea is a good one?

Students write brief responses and read them aloud. Then the students or the teacher continue reading the story.

Step 3: Proving

Students give reasons to support their predictions by writing answers questions such as:

- What in the story makes you think that?
- Where in the story do you get information to support that idea?

The teacher can ask these "proving" questions during the story or after it has been read.

A group of fourth and fifth graders in a reading lab class listened to their teacher, Mrs. Pittman, read Leo Lionni's *Tico and the Golden Wings* (1964), a fable about a bird named Tico who was born without wings. He was, however, a happy bird because he had friends who took care of him. One day a wishingbird granted Tico's wish for wings, and he received wings covered with golden feathers. After his jealous friends abandoned him, Tico traveled around the world, giving away his golden feathers to people who needed help. Black feathers grew on his wings in place of the golden feathers, and when he was all black again, Tico's friends welcomed him.

Mrs. Pittman began by reading the title and showing the cover of the picture book. She asked, "What do you think the story will be about?" and the students wrote the following responses:

- Tico will probably have them at the first of the story and then lose them at the end.
- Tico might have regular wings at first and then something drastic might happen and he would get gold wings.
- He'll have them at the beginning and he keeps them forever.
- Tico was just a normal bird and then one day his wings turned to gold.

Soon Tico is given the opportunity to make a wish, and Mrs. Pittman asked, "What do you think Tico will wish for?" Students predicted:

- Tico wants wings so he can fly like the other birds.
- Tico wishes for golden wings and to be able to fly from tree to tree and soar through the sky like other birds.

Later, after Tico gets the golden wings, he meets a poor man with a sick daughter, and Mrs. Pittman asked, "How do you think Tico will help the poor man and his sick daughter?" Students answered:

- Tico would fly to town and get the medicine.
- He could call for that wishingbird and ask her.
- Tico will pick one of his golden feathers off and give it to the man.

After Tico gives away all of his golden feathers, Mrs. Pittman asked, "Will Tico's friends welcome him back now?" and students wrote:

- Yes, because he don't have golden wings no more.
- Yes, because he is just like the other birds now.
- Yes, because his friends won't think he's trying to be better than them.
- Yes, they will because he is different on the outside but still the same on the inside.

After reading the end of the story, students were asked, "Did you like the story? Why or why not?" Before beginning an oral discussion of the story, they reflected:

- Yes, because it told about Tico's ups and his downs.
- Yes, I did because it was interesting.
- Yes, because it was a very exciting book.
- Yes, because Tico is a smart bird to give his golden wings to the poor people so he can be the same as the other birds.
- I liked it because Tico was a likable bird.

After students wrote each response, they read them aloud to the group before the teacher continued reading. Then students had a purpose for listening: to learn if their predictions were correct. Through this activity, students engaged with the text, anticipated story events, and constructed meaning and an emotional response.

A warning is in order. Teachers should not interrupt a story too often because this procedure can become tedious for children who are comprehending and making their own predictions (Corcoran, 1987). This process is more useful with less capable readers who need help in making connections as they read or for students who are reading a complex piece of literature. For the remedial readers who used DRTA in reading *Tico and the Golden Wings,* the procedure encouraged them to probe their thoughts more deeply than if they had simply listened to the story read aloud.

Stage 3: Exploring the Text. Students make tentative and exploratory comments while reading, often using a reading log. According to Davala (1987), when logs become a regular part of classroom activities, students take an active part in their own learning, and they "'tune in' to the curriculum when they explore it personally" (p. 179). As students make connections between their own experiences and the experiences presented in a story, they are creating mental images, anticipating what will happen next, constructing a reaction, and valuing the story.

Mr. Bell read aloud the Howes' hilarious *Bunnicula* (1979) to his second-grade class. In this story, a family finds an abandoned bunny in a movie theater while watching the movie Dracula. They bring the bunny home and name him Bunnicula (Bunny + Dracula). Soon mysterious things begin to happen. The other family pets are convinced the bunny is a vampire, and they attempt to warn the human members of the family. After Mr. Bell read each chapter aloud, he asked the students to write or draw pictures about the chapter. Here are three students' entries from their reading logs:

■ I liked when the mother said, "Let's call him Fluffy," "Or Prince," yelled dad. I liked when both of the boys said, "Get real dad, can't you ever stop!"
Emily

■ I thought it was scary when the moonlight was shining on Bunnicula and he got red eyes and he opened his mouth and had sharp teeth and had a cape thing on his back.
Christen

■ I liked the part where Chester got the towel from Mr. Monroe and acted like a vampire. If oil gets on vampires they will die.
Melissa

In these entries, second graders wrote about what they liked and what scared them in the story. This writing helps them to personalize or co-create the story. For another example of a reading log, check the sixth grader's reading log on *Tuck Everlasting* in Chapter 2.

Another way students reflect on their reading is to compare the piece of literature to the film version, to another book by the same author, or to a book with a similar character, setting, or theme. For example, after listening to *Sounder* (Armstrong, 1969) read aloud and viewing the film version of the book, students in Mrs. Pierce's fifth-grade class made charts in their reading logs to compare the two versions. They then freewrote to decide which version they liked best. One student's comparison and freewriting are presented in Figure 9–6.

Stage 4: Responding to the Text. Students build on the exploratory responses made while reading to create a more extended (and often more formal) response. This response may take many forms, and a list of response activities is presented in Figure 9–7. Examples of responses written at four grade levels are presented in the following paragraphs.

First Grade: Class Collaboration Verse. After reading *Jamberry* (Degen, 1983), a delightful wordplay book using many invented *berry* words, Mrs. Edison's first graders became wordsmiths and added *berry* to almost every word they said. With this much interest in inventing new words, the class decided to write their own *berry* verse. The first graders chose a space theme and dictated "Spaceberry":

One berry	Three berries
Two berries	Four berries
In my rocketshipberry	Landing at Plutoberry
Zoom-zoom berry	Floating out of the doorberry
Going to Plutoberry.	To pick blueberries.
Five berries	Seven berries
Six berries	Eight berries
Going to moonberry	Returning to Earthberry
To pick strawberries	To eat chocolateberries
Never to crashberry!	Yumberry! Yumberry! Yumberry!

Notice that the children followed the same numerical sequence in their version that Degen used in his.

Second Grade: Writing Pattern Books. After reading John Burningham's *Would You Rather . . .* (1978), students made their own pattern books in which they offered readers a series of outrageous choices. Jeff's "Would You Rather . . ." book is presented in Figure 9–8 (p. 338). Like the original, Jeff's book spurs audience participation.

Grade Five: Travel Brochures. After Ms. Edge-Christensen's fifth-grade class read Elizabeth George Speare's *The Witch of Blackbird Pond* (1958), in which a free-spirited young girl, Kit, leaves Barbados after her grandfather's death to live with her Puritan relatives in colonial Wethersfield, Connecticut and is accused of being a witch, one student created a modern-day travel brochure for Wethersfield which is shown in Figure 9–9 (p. 339). As she developed the brochure, Sara consulted maps of Connecticut and examined travel brochures to help her decide what types of information to include in her brochure.

Grade Seven: Interviews. After reading a children's version of the Anglo-Saxon epic *Beowulf* retold by Charles Keeping (1982), seventh-grade Matt wrote and videotaped a television interview with Beowulf in which he asked the hero about his battle with Grendel. This is Matt's script:

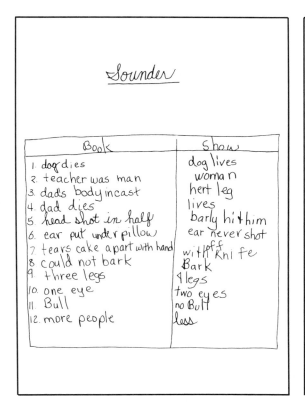

FIGURE 9–6 A Fifth Grader's Comparison of the Book and Film Versions of *Sounder* (Armstrong, 1969)

Interviewer: Today is May 10, 587 AD and our guest today is Beowulf, the greatest of the Geats. Welcome Mr. Wulf. I'm sure there are a lot of people out in the world who would like to know about your battle with Grendel.

Beowulf: Well, it all started when Grendel came to the palace one night a long time ago. The blasted creature broke thirty Thanes' necks! Well, this was totally intolerable, so I got together a group of my best Geats and set out to find Grendel! That night after we had all set up our camp and gone to sleep I was suddenly awakened by a rustling in the bushes. I opened my eyes but I didn't even move a muscle. Then I saw him, the most sickening thing I had ever seen. It was Grendel. Grendel slowly moved toward a Geat. He never had a chance. Grendel grabbed the Geat and before he could even scream, his head was gone! It rolled down beside me. I actually thought I was going to see my supper again. Grendel then turned the geat upside-down and drank and ate all of his internals. Really sickening. He then saw the head laying beside me and moved towards it. He picked the head up

FIGURE 9–7 Response to Literature Activities

Art Activities

Create a series of illustrations for a favorite book or story episode and compile the illustrations to form a wordless picture book.

Practice the illustration techniques (e.g., collage, styrofoam prints, watercolors, line drawing) used in the favorite book. Also, examine other books that use the same illustration technique.

Create a collage to represent the theme of a favorite book.

Design a book jacket for a favorite book, laminate it, and place it on the book.

Construct a shoebox or other miniature scene of an episode from a favorite story.

Create a filmstrip to illustrate a favorite story.

Create a game based on a favorite story or series of stories. Possible game formats include card games, board games, word finds, crossword puzzles, and computer games.

Draw a map or make a relief map of a book's setting. Some stories, such as Kathryn Lasky's *Beyond the Divide* (1983), include a map, usually on the book's end papers.

Create a mobile illustrating a favorite book.

Make a movie of a favorite book by drawing a series of pictures on a long strip of paper. Attach ends to rollers and place in a cardboard box.

Writing Activities

Assume the role of a book character and keep a simulated journal from that character's viewpoint.

Write a book review of a favorite book for the class newspaper.

Write a letter to a pen pal about a favorite book.

Create a poster to advertise a favorite book.

Write another episode for the characters in a favorite story.

Create a newspaper with news stories and advertisements based on characters and episodes from a favorite book.

Write a letter to the author of a favorite book. Check the guidelines for writing to children's authors presented in Chapter 3.

Write a simulated letter from one book character to another.

Select five "quotable quotes" from a favorite book and list them on a poster or in copy books.

FIGURE 9–7 (continued)

Reading Activities

Research a favorite author and compile the information in a brief report to insert in the author's book.

Read other stories by the same author.

Read other stories with a similar theme.

Tape-record a favorite book or excerpts from a longer story to place in a listening center.

Read a favorite story to children in the primary grades.

Compare different versions of the same story.

Talk and Drama Activities

Give a readers theater presentation of a favorite story.

Write a script and produce a play or puppet show about a favorite book.

Dress as a favorite book character and answer questions from classmates about the character and the story.

Retell a favorite story or episode from a longer story using puppets or other props.

Give a chalk talk by sketching pictures on the chalkboard or on a large sheet of paper as the story is retold.

Discuss a favorite book informally with several classmates.

Tape-record a review of a favorite book using background music and sound effects.

Videotape a commercial for a favorite book.

Interview classmates about a favorite book.

Other Activities

Plan a special day to honor a favorite author with posters, publicity information from the author's publishers, letters to and from the author, a display of the author's books, and products from other activities listed above.

If possible, arrange to place a conference telephone call to the author or have the author visit the school on that day.

Conduct a class or school vote to determine students' 10 most popular books. Also, many states sponsor annual book awards for outstanding children's books such as Ohio's Buckeye Book Award and Oklahoma's Sequoia Book Award. Encourage students to read the books nominated for their state's award and to vote for their favorite books.

Cook a food described in a favorite book, such as gingerbread cookies after reading Galdone's *The Gingerbread Boy* (1975) or spaghetti after reading de Paola's *Strega Nona* (1975).

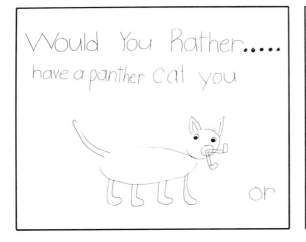

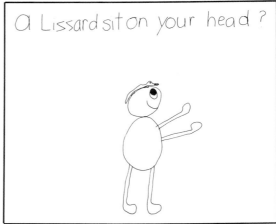

FIGURE 9-8 A Second Grader's "Would You Rather..." Book

and swallowed it with one big gulp. He then reached for me. Suddenly, faster than the eye could see I jumped up and grabbed him by the arm. I yelled, "Surprise Grendel! Your days of terror are over. This is your day—your end." Grendel yelled in agony like he had never yelled before. For the first time he was feeling pain. He was feeling the strength of thirty me in one. I twisted his right arm until it finally popped off. Blood dripped from his body and his arm. The beast walked only a short distance and then died.

Interviewer: Well, well, that's quite a scary story you have told, Mr. Wulf. I'm sure you'll never forget it. Did you do anything with the body or arm?

Beowulf: Well, the Geats and I decided just to let the body lay there and decay; however, we took the arm back for a souvenir.

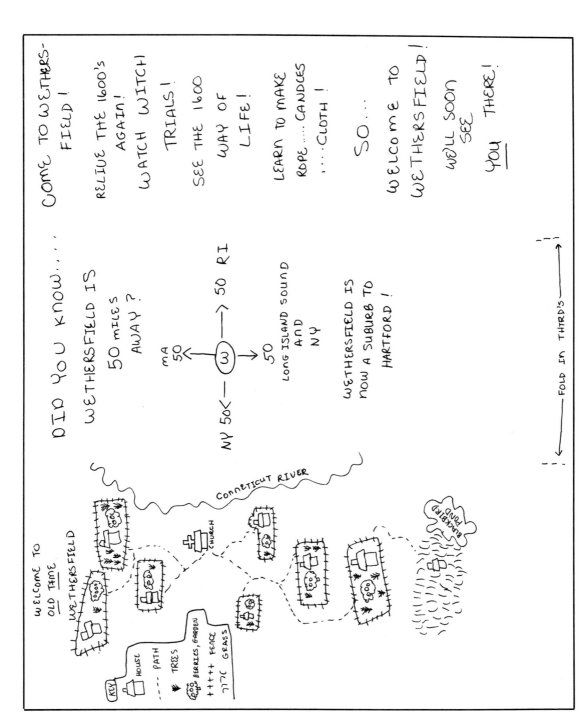

FIGURE 9–9 A Fifth Grader's Travel Brochure for Wethersfield, Connecticut

Interviewer: Do you still have the arm?
Beowulf: Yes, I do. It's hanging in the souvenir room. Would you like to see it?
Interviewer: Yes, indeed I would.
[Beowulf takes Interviewer to view the arm.]
Interviewer: Well, that's the story of Beowulf's greatest adventure. A few years
             later Beowulf was killed by a great dragon. It was the end of Beowulf.
             The end of a legend!

The National Assessment of Educational Progress (1981) examined 9-, 13-, and 17-year-olds' achievement in literature and found that American students in general were unable to read critically or to support or explain their interpretations and responses to literature except in superficial ways. This study documented the need for what Rosenblatt calls aesthetic reading and to teach students strategies that will enable them to engage in a transaction with the text. Writing is an important learning tool in the aesthetic reading process because through writing students explore literature.

Genre Stories

Another component of writing in literature is reading and writing fables, myths, and other genre stories. Just as students read and examine stories to learn about beginning-middle-end and the other elements of story structure, they read genre stories to learn about these unique forms. Then they apply what they have learned in writing their own stories. As children examine the structure and unique forms of these stories, they become better readers and writers (Bosma, 1987).

Fables. *Fables* are brief narratives designed to teach a moral. Authors use the story to teach a lesson and usually state the moral at the end of the fable. Characteristics of fables include:

1. They are short, often less than a page long.
2. The characters are usually animals.
3. The characters are one-dimensional, either strong or weak, wise or foolish.
4. The backdrop setting is barely described.
5. Fables involve only one event.
6. The conflict is between characters.
7. The theme is usually stated as a moral at the end of the story.

Our best-known fables, including "The Hare and the Tortoise" and "The Ant and the Grasshopper," were written by a Greek slave, Aesop, in the sixth century B.C. Collections of Aesop's fables for elementary students include Eric Carle's *Twelve Tales from Aesop* (1980), *Aesop's Fables* selected by Michael Hague (1985), Eve Rice's *Once Upon a Wood: Ten Tales from Aesop* (1979), and *Doctor Coyote: A Native American Aesop's Fables* (Bierhorst, 1987). Also, Arnold Lobel (1980) wrote 20 original fables in Aesop's style with short narratives and clearly stated morals.

Other well-known fables include *Once a Mouse,* an Indian fable retold by Marcia Brown (1961), Hans Christian Andersen's *The Emperor's New Clothes* (Westcott, 1984) and *The Ugly Duckling* (Cauley, 1979), *Doctor De Soto* by William Steig (1982), and Chaucer's *Chanticleer and the Fox* (Cooney, 1958). These fables are longer than Aesop's, and the moral is implied rather than clearly stated in the text.

After students read fables, they choose a moral and construct a brief story to illustrate it, following the instructional strategy presented in Chapter 4, "Narrative Writing." A sixth grader's fable with a modern-day setting—his language arts class—is presented below:

The Peacock and the Mouse

The peacock was a very boastful bird who bragged and spread his feathers whenever he did something. He gave a report in front of our Language Arts class and bragged about it for three weeks.

The mouse was very quiet and never bragged. She was just a quiet person who did her work.

Well, it turned out at the end of the year the mouse's average was an A+ and the Peacock's was a D−.

MORAL: Boastful people don't always come out on top.

Myths. People around the world have created *myths* to explain the origin of the world, how human beings were brought into existence, their relationship to gods, and how the sun and moon originated. Other myths were created to explain the seasons, physical features of the earth, and characteristics of animals and constellations. These myths explained many phenomena that have more recently been explained scientifically. *Gods, Stars, and Computers: Fact and Fancy in Myth and Science* (Weiss, 1980) provides an interesting comparison of ancient beliefs and scientific facts for middle and upper grade students. Characteristics of myths include:

1. Myths explain creations.
2. Characters are often heroes with supernatural powers.
3. The setting is backdrop and barely sketched.
4. Magical powers are required.

Myths about different cultures have been compiled for children, and these myths provide a valuable way to tie literature and writing with history. The D'Aulaires have chronicled Greek myths (1980) and Norse myths (1967), and other myths have been compiled from Native American, Greek, Egyptian, African, and other cultures. One example is Gail Haley's *A Story, A Story* (1970), an African explanation of how stories were hidden from humans, which appeals to primary students because of its repetition.

The myths that students write usually explain how animals acquired their physical characteristics, modeled on Rudyard Kipling's *Just So Stories* (1987). Many picture book versions of the *Just So Stories* are now available and popular with middle grade students. Native American myths, such as *The Fire Bringer* (Hodges, 1972), tell how fire and other natural phenomena came to be. Children read and examine myths, compare myths from various cultures, and write their own myths. Here is a seventh-grade class collaboration myth about the origin of the sun and moon:

■
Suntaria and Lunaria: Rulers of the Earth

Long ago when gods still ruled the earth, there lived two brothers, Suntaria and Lunaria. Both brothers were wise and powerful men. People from all over the earth sought their wisdom and counsel. Each man, in his own way, was good and just, yet the two were as different as gold and coal. Suntaria was large and strong with blue eyes and brilliantly golden hair. Lunaria's hair and eyes were the blackest black.

One day Zeus, looking down from Mount Olympus, decided that Earth needed a ruler—someone to watch over his people whenever he became too tired or too busy to do his job. His eyes fell upon Suntaria and Lunaria. Both men were wise and honest. Both men would be good rulers. Which man would be the first ruler of the earth?

Zeus decided there was only one fair way to solve his problem. He sent his messenger, Postlet, down to earth with ballots instructing the mortals to vote for a king. There were only two names on the ballot—Suntaria and Lunaria.

Each mortal voted and after the ballots were placed in a secure box, Postlet returned them to Zeus. For seven years Zeus and Postlet counted and recounted the ballots. Each time they came up with the same results: 50% of the votes were for Suntaria and 50% were for Lunaria. There was only one thing Zeus could do. He declared that both men would rule over the earth.

This is how it was, and this is how it is. Suntaria still spreads his warm golden rays to rule over our days. At night he steps down from his throne, and Lunaria's dark, soft night watches and protects us while we dream.

It is interesting to compare this myth with the sun and moon myths told by aboriginal Australians, Native Americans, Nigerians, and Polynesians and collected in the Hadleys' *Legends of the Sun and Moon* (1983).

Fantasies. In *fantasies,* authors create another world for their characters, and readers must believe this other world exists. These stories may be about personified animals that talk as well as science fiction set in the future. Examples include A. A. Milne's *The House at Pooh Corner* (1956), C. S. Lewis' *The Lion, the Witch and the Wardrobe* (1981) and other stories in the Narnia series, and Mary Norton's *The Borrowers* (1981). In these stories, readers must suspend disbelief to enjoy the story. Characteristics of fantasies include:

1. The events in the story are fantastic; things happen that could not happen in today's world.
2. The setting is realistic.
3. Main characters are people or personified animals, and many have magical qualities.

4. Themes often deal with conflict between good and evil.
5. In science fiction, characters use scientific processes in resolving the conflict.

A list of fantasies appropriate for elementary students is presented in Figure 9-10. After reading and examining the characteristics of these stories, children write class collaborations and individual stories, incorporating as many of the characteristics as they can.

Mysteries. Many mystery stories have been written for elementary students, and like people of all ages, they enjoy reading these suspense stories. The Nate the Great series of stories by Marjorie Weinman Sharmat (c.f. *Nate the Great Goes Undercover,* 1974) is popular with beginning readers, and middle grade students enjoy the Encyclopedia Brown series by Donald J. Sobol (c.f., *Encyclopedia Brown, Boy Detective,* 1963). Characteristics of mystery stories include:

FIGURE 9–10   A List of Fantasy Stories Appropriate for Elementary Students

---

Alexander, L. (1964). *The book of three.* New York: Holt. (U)

Baum, L. F. (1982). *The Wizard of Oz.* New York: Holt. (M)

Bond, M. (1960). *A bear called Paddington.* New York: Houghton Mifflin. (P)

Boston, L. M. (1955). *The children of Green Knowe.* New York: Harcourt. (M–U)

Brittain, B. (1983). *The wish giver.* New York: Harper. (M)

Cleary, B. (1965). *The mouse and the motorcycle.* New York: Morrow. (P–M)

Cooper, S. (1973). *The dark is rising.* New York: Atheneum. (U)

Dahl, R. (1961). *James and the giant peach.* New York: Knopf. (M)

Ehrlich, A. (1979). *Thumbelina.* New York: Dial. (M)

Grahame, K. (1940). *The wind in the willows.* New York: Shepard. (M)

Hodges, M. (1984). *Saint George and the dragon.* Boston: Little, Brown. (P–M)

Juster, N. (1961). *The phantom tollbooth.* New York: Random House. (M–U)

L'Engle, M. (1962). *A wrinkle in time.* New York: Farrar. (U)

Lewis, C. S. (1950). *The lion, the witch and the wardrobe.* New York: Macmillan. (M–U)

Milne, A. A. (1954). *Winnie-the-Pooh.* New York: Dutton. (P)

Norton, M. (1953). *The borrowers.* New York: Harcourt. (P–M)

O'Brien, R. C. (1971). *Mrs. Frisby and the rats of NIMH.* New York: Atheneum. (M)

Sleator, W. (1984). *Interstellar pig.* New York: Dutton. (M)

Tolkien, J. R. R. (1938). *The Hobbit.* Boston: Houghton Mifflin. (M–U)

Van Allsburg, C. (1981). *Jumanji.* Boston: Houghton Mifflin. (M)

Volen, J. (1974). *The girl who cried flowers.* New York: Crowell. (P–M)

P = Primary (grades K–2)
M = Middle (grades 3–5)
U = Upper (grades 6–8)

1. Mysteries have crimes or problems to solve.
2. Main characters are detectives who work to solve crimes or problems.
3. Detectives are integral characters with unusual names, special traits, and equipment.
4. Plot develops as clues are introduced and detectives follow up on them.
5. Some clues are "true" clues which lead the detective toward solving the crime or problem; other clues are "false" clues which lead the detective astray.

After students read mystery stories and examine the characteristics of this genre, they write collaborative and individual stories. Here is a collaborative mystery story, "Edith, No!" composed by Mr. McCracken's third-grade class:

The mud oozed around Ed Trail's boots as he beached his canoe. It was 10:00 Saturday evening as Ed made his way home through the woods from his fishing trip. He only walked a few steps when . . . SNAP . . . an old trap caught his foot and pulled him down. As he turned over to free himself, the last thing he saw was a rock.

From the other side of the woods, Sam Baker, well-known detective, was searching for Ed at the request of his worried wife, Sally. He found the place where Ed docked his boat and followed the path from there. A short distance up the path led Sam to where Ed Tail lay dead with a rock crushing his head. While Sam was running to tell what had happened, he discovered a torn scarf stuck on a bush. As he observed the scarf, he discovered the initials E. T. Sam stuck the scarf in his pocket because he knew it was a clue and went to tell Sally Trail what had happened.

Out of breath, Sam arrived at the Trails' and told Sally the horrible details. When Sam showed her the scarf, Sally got a far away look in her eyes and went upstairs. Finding this strange, Sam Baker waited outside the Trail home to see what he might find.

Meanwhile, Sally went upstairs to the room of Aunt Belle who lived with the Trails. Aunt Belle had taken care of Sally as a little girl and knew everything about Sally. Now she was crippled and in a wheelchair.

"Well, hello dear," said Aunt Belle. "What are you doing here? Where are you taking me?" said Aunt Belle worriedly as Sally wheeled her to the stairs. As Sally gave the final shove Aunt Belle screamed, "EDITH, NO!"

At that moment Sam Baker knew that the initials stood for Sally *E*dith *T*rail. The *S* had been ripped off in her rush to leave the place of the crime. Sam rushed in just in time to catch Aunt Belle before Sally Edith Trail sent another victim to her death. Quickly Sam grabbed Sally and took her to the police station.

At the station house the chief found out that Sally killed her husband to keep him from giving all his money to Aunt Belle to take care of her. Sally tried to kill Aunt Belle because she was the only one who could connect Sally with the initials E. T.

Another case wrapped up by Sam Baker.

Notice that the students included almost all of the characteristics of mysteries. This story is more compact than many mysteries that children write, and in keeping it short, solving the crime takes precedence over Sam Baker's character development.

WRITING IN OTHER CONTENT AREAS

Students use writing to learn and to demonstrate learning in the content areas. Three content areas—science, math, and social studies—will be considered in this section. The Tchudis (1983) point out that content area learning must be at the center of content area writing activities and set four guidelines for across-the-curriculum writing:

1. Plan at least one formal writing project in each content area unit.
2. Include informal writing-to-learn activities daily.
3. Choose writing activities that incorporate a variety of forms (see Figure 9–2) during the school year.
4. Focus on content as well as quality of writing when assessing students' writing in content area classes.

Writing About Science

Students participate in both informal and formal writing activities when they learn science. Students keep learning logs to record observations, detail experiments, and explore other information related to the unit. Students also write collaborative and individual reports in which they share what they have learned in a science unit. One popular format for these reports is an ABC book.

Learning Logs. In learning logs, students write about what they are learning, and these logs can take several different forms. One type of learning log is an observation log in which students make daily entries, tracking the growth of a plant or animal. Figure 9–11 presents first-grade Tyler's seed journal. In this journal, Tyler makes each entry on a new page and drawing is as important as writing. He uses invented spelling. Because several pages are difficult for adults to decipher, the text on each page has been translated into standard orthography.

A second type of learning logs are those in which students make daily entries during a unit of study. Students may take notes during a presentation by the teacher or a classmate, after viewing a film, or at the end of each class period. Sometimes students make entries in list form, sometimes in clusters or charts, and at other times in paragraphs.

Lab reports are a third type of learning logs. In these logs, students list the materials and procedures used in the experiment, present data on an observation chart, and then discuss the results. A fourth grader's lab report for an experiment with hermit crabs is presented in Figure 9–12 (p. 350).

Reports. Similarly, students demonstrate what they have learned by writing reports. Young children can write "All About _____" books or dictate reports (Armes & Sullenger, 1986; Fehrenbach et al., 1986). Older children can write collaborative and individual reports. For example, Mrs. Jordan's second-grade class researched quails as they waited for the quail eggs in their classroom incubator to hatch, and six students compiled what they had learned in a collaborative report. Students each wrote one page, stating and illustrating a fact about quail. Here is their report:

Quails

Page 1: The quail in Oklahoma is also called a "bobwhite."
Page 2: Quail help farmers by eating insects and weed seeds.
Page 3: A quail is about ten inches long. It has a fat body. Its color is reddish-brown.
Page 4: Quail live on the ground and their nests are on the ground.
Page 5: The baby quail hatch out in 24 days and they take care of themselves.
Page 6: People hunt the quail for food.

Integrating Writing in a Science Unit. Writing activities can be integrated into a science unit to help students better understand the science content. A cluster that delineates possible informal and formal writing activities that can be integrated with a second-grade unit on weather is presented in Figure 9–13. Nine writing activities are included in the cluster, and while it is unlikely that all the activities would be incorporated in any one unit, the cluster does illustrate a range of options available to teachers. Student samples illustrating four of the activities are presented in Figure 9–14. Two activities are informal and two are formal. The learning log and vocabulary list are informal writing-to-learn activities, and the D page from a class ABC book on weather and the page from a class report on their interview of a local TV weather forecaster are formal activities in which students demonstrate their learning.

Writing About Math

Writing about mathematics? At first the relationship between writing and math may not be apparent, but students can do meaningful writing in math class, writing that will improve their learning. When students can write clearly about the mathematical concepts they are learning, it is apparent they understand them. Christine Evans (1984) conducted a teacher-researcher project with her fifth-grade math classes, and she found that students who wrote during math learned mathematical concepts better than students who did not write. Her students wrote simulated letters describing procedures for solving math problems, defined and illustrated mathematical terms, and explained errors on homework or quizzes. Interestingly, Evans found that these writing activities were most valuable for her weaker math students.

Learning Logs. Upper grade students keep learning logs in which they write about what they are learning during the last 5 minutes of class (Salem, 1982; Schubert, 1987). Students can write what they have learned during that class, the steps involved in solving a problem, definitions of mathematical terms, and things that confuse them. Writing in learning logs has several advantages over class discussion (Greesen, 1977). All students participate simultaneously in writing, and teachers can review written responses more carefully than oral ones. Also, students use mathematical vocabulary and become more precise and complete in their answers.

Figure 9–15 presents an entry from a sixth grader's learning log in which she describes how to change improper fractions. Notice that after she describes the steps in sequence, she includes a review of the six steps.

In addition to the benefits to students, teachers use learning logs to informally assess student's learning. Through students' journal entries, teachers:

- Assess what students already know about a concept before teaching.
- Help students integrate what they are learning and make the knowledge a part of their lives.

FIGURE 9–11 A First Grader's Seed Journal (pp. 347–349)

3-2‑7‑87

we PIAt DIAIPIAt

(We planted a plant.)

2

3-30-87

we dUpthe PIAt
it I3 fAt

(We dug up the plant.
It is fat.)

3

4-1-87.

we Du‑GUP
the UPThe
PAtitdIAl Not
CACAEC

(We dug up the plant.
It did not crack open.)

4

4-2-87

we DAG
UPThePLut
it DID M0t
GRO

(We dug up the plant.
It did not grow.)

5

FIGURE 9–11 (continued)

348

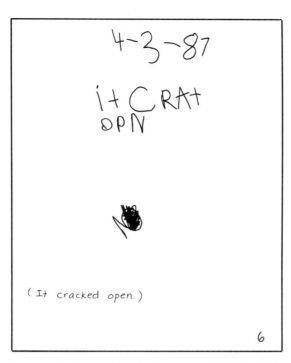

4-3-87

it CRAt
OPN

(It cracked open.)

6

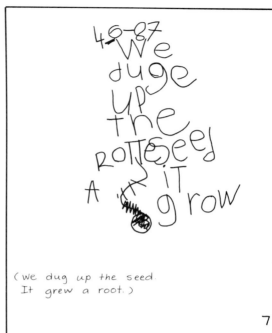

4-6-87
We
duge
UP
the
RottSeeJ
A it
grow

(we dug up the seed.
It grew a root.)

7

4-7-87

iT GOT F ATR
iT GR ROS

(It got fatter.
It grew roots.)

8

4-12-87
The PAt
GRUOl
RUS
it iTGRUOl
LLS

(The plant grew roots.
It grew leaves.)

9

FIGURE 9-11 (continued)

Lab Report

Do hermit crabs prefer a wet or dry habitat?

Materials
  trough
  trough cover
  2 paper towels
  water sprinkler

Procedures
  1. Put one wet and one dry paper towel in the trough.
  2. Place the hermit crab in the center of the trough and put on the cover.
  3. Wait 60 seconds.
  4. Open the cover and observe the location of the hermit crab.
  5. Mark the location on the observation chart.
  6. Do the experiment 6 times.

Observation Chart

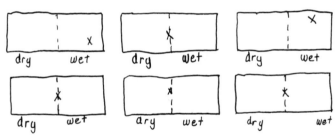

Results
  Wet: 2
  Dry: 0
  Center 4

Our hermit crab liked the center part best. 4 out of 6 times it stayed in the center. Then it liked the wet part next best. It didn't like the dry part at all.

FIGURE 9–12 A Fourth Grader's Lab Report

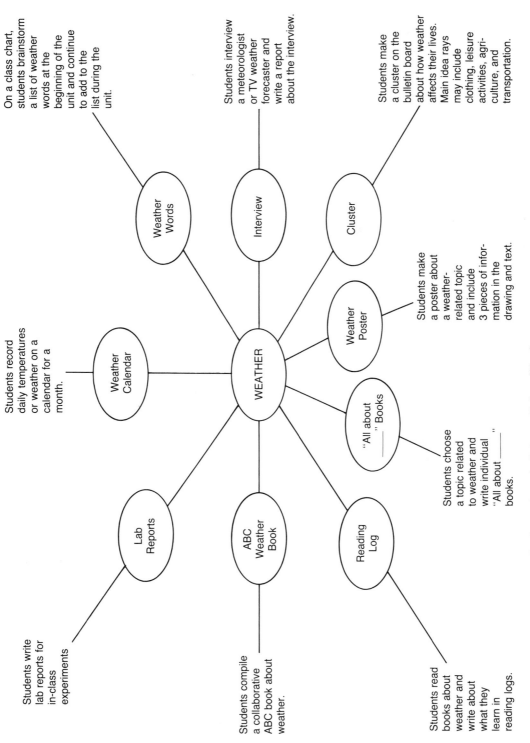

On a class chart, students brainstorm a list of weather words at the beginning of the unit and continue to add to the list during the unit.

Students interview a meteorologist or TV weather forecaster and write a report about the interview.

Students make a cluster on the bulletin board about how weather affects their lives. Main idea rays may include clothing, leisure activities, agriculture, and transportation.

Weather Words

Interview

Cluster

Students make a poster about a weather-related topic and include 3 pieces of information in the drawing and text.

Weather Calendar

Students record daily temperatures or weather on a calendar for a month.

WEATHER

Weather Poster

"All about ___" Books

Students choose a topic related to weather and write individual "All about ___" books.

Lab Reports

ABC Weather Book

Reading Log

Students write lab reports for in-class experiments

Students compile a collaborative ABC book about weather.

Students read books about weather and write about what they learn in reading logs.

FIGURE 9–13 Writing Activities for Second-grade Science Unit on Weather

Weather Words

thunderstorm	drizzle
snow	climate
clouds	cold air
Blizzard	warm air
flood	storms
lightning	meteorologist
thunder	weather forecaster
hurricanes	jet stream
tornadoes	freezing
Hail	thermometer
sleet	Temperature
sunny	Dopler Radar
snowflakes	Cirrus Clouds
precipitation	Stratus Clouds
	Cumulus Clouds
fog	evaporates
wind	water droplets
down pour	miles Per Hour — M.P.H
dew	gusts
ice	funnel
	air

Learning Log

Apr. 7

We woched a film today and it said that we live under water. That means we live under little water droplets that come down from the sky. The sientists have a spesal microscope to test the droplets. I think it is real neat.

FIGURE 9–14 Second Graders' Informal and Formal Writings about Weather

Changing to Improper Fractions

To Change a mixed number such as: $5\frac{2}{3}$, you must must multiply the denominator, which is the bottom number, times the whole number which is 5. So now we have : $3 \times 5 = 15$, Next you add the numerator to the problem like this! $15 + 2 = 17$. Put the same denominater, the bottom number, and it should look like this! $\frac{17}{3}$. To check your answer, find out how many times 3 , the bottom number, goes into the top number, 17. It goes in 5 times. There are two left over, so the answer is $5\frac{2}{3}$, It is correct.

6 Steps!

1. $5\frac{2}{3}$
2. $3 \times 5 = 15$
3. $15 + 2 = 17$
4. $\frac{17}{3}$
5. $3 \overline{)17}^{\,5\,\,2} = 5\frac{2}{3}$
6. $5\frac{2}{3}$ — Correct

FIGURE 9–15 A Sixth Grader's Math Learning Log

- Discover what students are really learning.
- Check on confusions and misconceptions.
- Monitor students' self-images and attitude toward math.
- Assess students' learning of a concept after teaching. (McGonegal, 1987)

Sometimes teachers simply read these entries, and at other times, these learning logs become dialogue journals as teachers respond to students to clarify misconceptions and offer encouragement.

Story Problems. Students can write story problems in which they apply the mathematical concepts they have been learning. In the process of writing the problems, they must consider what information to include and how to phrase the question. Audience is especially important in writing story problems because if students do not write clearly and completely, classmates may not be able to solve the problem.

In a sixth-grade class, students clipped advertisements from the local newspaper and used them in writing story problems. One student used an ad for aspirin: The 72-count package was on sale for $2.99 and the 125-count package for $4.66. Using this information, she composed the following problem:

■ Sarah went to the drugstore to buy some aspirin. She found a bottle of aspirin with 125 count for $4.66 and a bottle of aspirin with 72 count for $2.99. Which one should she buy to get the most for her money? (Answer: the bottle of 125 count.)

Other Math-Writing Activities. Students can connect math and writing in a variety of more formal ways. They can write "All About _____ " books about sets and numerals, geometric shapes, or telling time, write letters to request free or inexpensive math materials, make posters comparing Arabic and Roman numerals, and write raps or songs about math concepts. They can also participate in more complex projects that integrate writing and math. In a seventh- and eighth-grade class for children with learning disabilities, students designed research questions, such as "What is your favorite sport?" "What is your favorite television show?" or "What is your favorite soft drink?" and surveyed 50 students. They collected their data, transferred the data to a graph, computed percentages, and summarized the results in a paragraph. The results of Phillip's survey about soft drink preferences is presented in Figure 9–16. These seventh and eighth graders were familiar with surveys, and through this activity, they gained a new appreciation for math and writing.

Writing About Social Studies

- First graders take a field trip to a circus, and afterwards they write a collaborative letter to their pen pal class, telling their pen pals about the circus. They make a chart to compare the zoo and the circus.
- Fifth graders keep simulated journals in the role of a historical figure as they study the American Revolution. They publish a simulated newspaper that might have been published during the war.

survey
What is your favorite soft Drink?

A: DR Pepper
B: CoKe Classic
C: DiET COKE
D: Diet Pepsi

1. D	15. B	29 C	43 B
2. A	16. B	30 A	44 B
3. B	17. A	31 A	45 A
4. B	18. C	32 B	46 A
5. A	19. C	33 B	47 A
6. B	20 C	34 B	48 C
7 A	21 B	35. C	49 A
8. A	22 A	36 A	50. A
9. B	23. A	37 C	
10 B	24 A	38 A	
11 C	25 B	39 C	
12 C	26 A	40 C	
13 A	27 C	41 B	
14. A	28. D	42. B	

What Are people's favorite soft Drinks?

Dr. Pepper 40%
Coke Classic 32%
Diet Coke 24%
Diet Pepsi 4%

MY REPORT

I surveyed 50 other people. I asked what is your favorite soft drink. I surveyed mostly girls this time. The results are Dr. Pepper is the favorite. 40% of the people liked it best. Coke is in second place with 32%. Diet Coke with 24% is third. The last one is Diet Pepsi with 4%. That's only 2 people who like it best.

FIGURE 9—16 A Seventh Grader's Survey Data and Summary Paragraph

■ Eighth graders freewrite about their dreams before viewing a videotape of Martin Luther King's "I Have a Dream" speech. They later choose another black man or woman who made a significant contribution to this country about whom to research and write a report.

Letters, charts, simulated journals and newspapers, freewriting, and reports are valuable ways to learn social studies. In these examples, students used both informal and formal writing activities to learn social studies content in a first-grade unit on the circus, a fifth-grade unit on the American Revolution, and an eighth-grade unit on Martin Luther King. A list of writing activities that might accompany these three social studies units is presented as clusters and discussed in the following sections. The three clusters are presented in Figure 9—17.

First-grade Unit: The Circus. A cluster of writing activities that first graders might engage in during a unit on the circus is presented in Figure 9–17. These writing activities augment other content area activities, tradebooks, informal drama, and field trips that students are involved in. Because drawing is such an important prewriting activity for primary grade students, writing and art are integrated in several activities, such as the poster and "All About the Circus" books. Many of the activities involve collaborative writing in which the teacher takes children's dictation. In this way, children express what they have learned about the circus without the constraints that writing can impose on some young children. Through brainstorming, clustering, and writing learning logs, students are introduced to three of the informal writing strategies that are so valuable as writing-to-learn tools.

Fifth-grade Unit: The American Revolution. Figure 9–17 presents a cluster of writing activities for a fifth-grade unit on the American Revolution. Some of these activities are whole-class activities while others are small-group or individual activities. For the cluster, they work together as a class with the teacher serving as scribe to record students' ideas on the chalkboard. Students work in groups as they publish a newspaper that might have been written after the battles of Lexington and Concord. A sample simulated newspaper is presented in Figure 9–18. And students work individually on simulated journals, learning logs, and reports. This cluster includes both informal writing activities, such as clusters, learning logs, and simulated journals as well as formal writing activities, such as persuasive essays, simulated newspapers, and reports.

Eighth-grade Unit: Martin Luther King. A cluster of writing activities for a unit on Martin Luther King is also presented in Figure 9–17. At the upper grade level, students participate in individual projects in addition to the other informal and formal writing activities. These projects are similar to the response to literature activities presented in Figure 9–7 because, in these projects as in response to literature activities, students are valuing and demonstrating their learning.

■ ANSWERING TEACHERS' QUESTIONS ABOUT WRITING ACROSS THE CURRICULUM

1. How do I grade students' informal writing in science?

I recommend that you grade students' learning logs as done or not done rather than trying to assess the quality of the entries. Teachers can give a checkmark or a specified number of points if the work is done and no credit if it is not done. Lab reports can also be graded as done or not done, or teachers can check that students have included each required part. For example, if students are required to have materials, procedures, observation chart or illustration, and results, then four parts are required; the grade is based on whether or not students included each part. Additional credit can be given for exceptional reports and credit can be subtracted from poorly written reports. For informal writing to be effective in ele-

First-grade unit

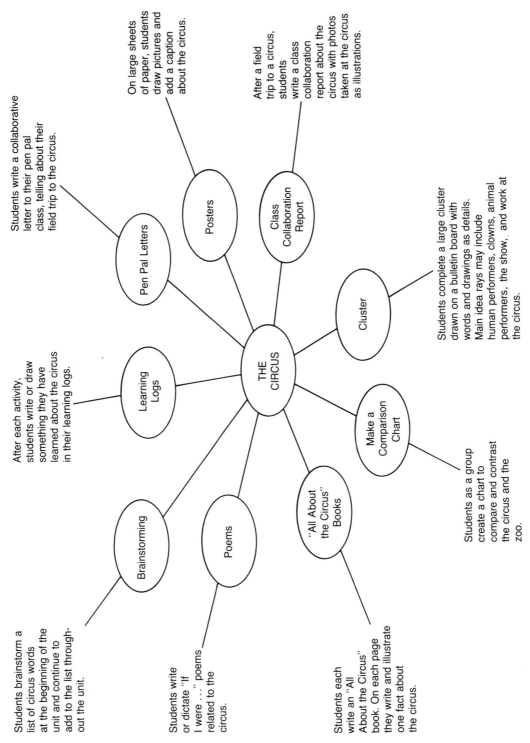

Students brainstorm a list of circus words at the beginning of the unit and continue to add to the list throughout the unit.

Students write a collaborative letter to their pen pal class, telling about their field trip to the circus.

On large sheets of paper, students draw pictures and add a caption about the circus.

After a field trip to a circus, students write a class collaboration report about the circus with photos taken at the circus as illustrations.

After each activity, students write or draw something they have learned about the circus in their learning logs.

Students write or dictate "If I were ..." poems related to the circus.

Students each write an "All About the Circus" book. On each page they write and illustrate one fact about the circus.

Students as a group create a chart to compare and contrast the circus and the zoo.

Students complete a large cluster drawn on a bulletin board with words and drawings as details. Main idea rays may include human performers, clowns, animal performers, the show, and work at the circus.

Pen Pal Letters

Posters

Class Collaboration Report

Learning Logs

THE CIRCUS

Cluster

Brainstorming

Poems

"All About the Circus" Books

Make a Comparison Chart

FIGURE 9–17 Three Clusters Illustrating Ways to Use Writing to Learn Social Studies

Fifth-grade unit

Students cluster what they have learned about the American Revolution to review for the unit test. Main idea rays may include causes, battles, end of the war, famous personalities, Declaration of Independence, and results of the war.

Students write in their learning logs at the end of each activity. They include new words and information, reactions, and questions.

Students create maps of the American colonies and identify locations of noteworthy events during the War.

Students read a biography about an historical figure of the period and keep a simulated journal while they read.

Students write reports about the American Revolution. They create research questions, search for answers, and then share the answers in the report.

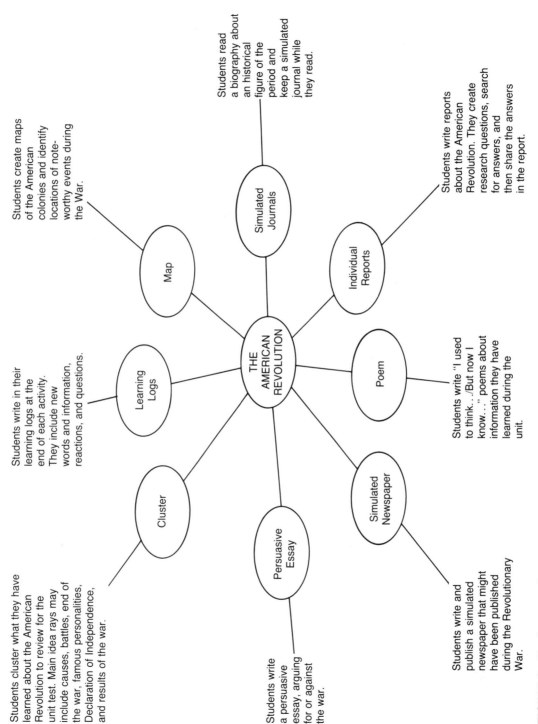

Students write a persuasive essay, arguing for or against the war.

Students write and publish a simulated newspaper that might have been published during the Revolutionary War.

Students write "I used to think.../But now I know..." poems about information they have learned during the unit.

FIGURE 9–17 (continued)

Eighth-grade unit

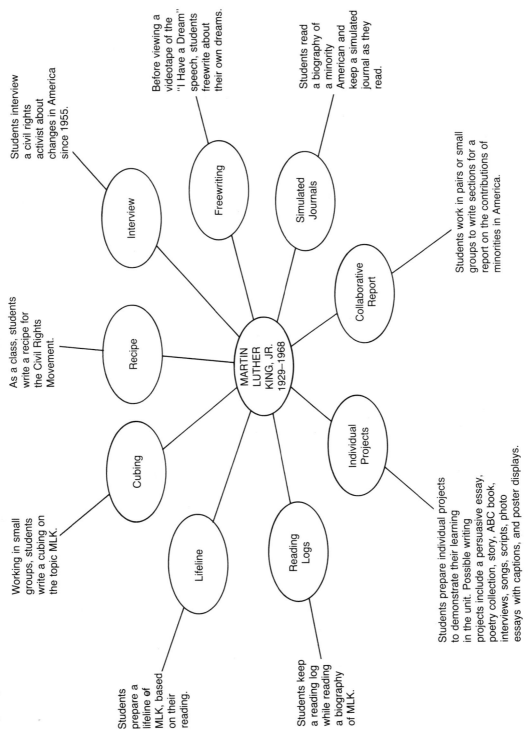

Students interview a civil rights activist about changes in America since 1955.

Before viewing a videotape of the "I Have a Dream" speech, students freewrite about their own dreams.

Students read a biography of a minority American and keep a simulated journal as they read.

Students work in pairs or small groups to write sections for a report on the contributions of minorities in America.

As a class, students write a recipe for the Civil Rights Movement.

Working in small groups, students write a cubing on the topic MLK.

Students prepare a lifeline of MLK, based on their reading.

Students keep a reading log while reading a biography of MLK.

Students prepare individual projects to demonstrate their learning in the unit. Possible writing projects include a persuasive essay, poetry collection, story, ABC book, interviews, songs, scripts, photo essays with captions, and poster displays.

Interview

Freewriting

Simulated Journals

Collaborative Report

Recipe

MARTIN LUTHER KING, JR. 1929–1968

Cubing

Lifeline

Reading Logs

Individual Projects

FIGURE 9–17 (continued)

REVOLUTIONARY TIMES

SUMMER QUARTERLY 1775　　　**LEXINGTON MASS.**　　　3¢

LOCAL PATRIOTS WARN OF BRITISH ONSLAUGHT

On 17 April William Dawes rode to Lexington to warn the colonists there that the British would soon be coming from Boston. The route which they would be traveling by was not yet known.

The following day, 18 April, Boston's Minutemen realized the British were leaving by boat. With that knowledge, Paul Revere, a local silversmith, crossed the Charles River in a rowboat. By wrapping the oars with cloth he was able to pass the armed English transport which was anchored in the river.

At Lexington, Revere was met by William Dawes and Dr. Sam Prescott. Together they set off toward Concord.

During the trip to Concord, they were stopped by British patrols. Revere and Dawes were captured, but Prescott escaped and made it to Concord.

While Revere and Dawes were being escorted to Lexington by the British patrols, along with other prisoners, a volley of gunfire was heard. Revere told the patrols it was a signal to the colonists.

The prisoners were then released, but their horses were taken by the patrols.

BUNKER HILL CLOSEUP

I'm at Bunker Hill. As I got up this morning, it looked like it was going to be a boring day. We were behind the earthworks, then the British soldiers arrived. General William said, "Don't fire until you see the whites of their eyes." Then the British soldiers arrived. As the British got closer and closer, we got more and more nervous. I heard a voice yell "Fire!" The Battle had begun. Guns fired, when the smoke cleared I could see many British soldiers dead. I was standing by my best friend John Wilson. Then I heard a big boom! Part of the earthwork collapsed. My friend was down for two minutes. I knew he was dead, but I kept fighting. I was shot in the shoulder. While I was being carried to a safer place, the blood was seeping out. I could still hear the guns firing. The sick wagon came to pick me up for the long and ruff journey home.

NEW MEMBERS JOIN CONGRESS

On 10 May, 56 delegates of the Continental Congress met to vote three new delegates who were John Hancock, Benjamin Franklin, and Thomas Jefferson. Some of the wisest men voted George Washington Commander in Chief of Continental Army. The Congress said they would take on duties of a government, uniting the colonies for the war effort.

WOMEN CONTRIBUTE TO BATTLES

The women of the surrounding colonies have had to consistently manage the men's trades as well as their own households. This is due to the fact that the men are engaged in the battle against Britain. While worried about their husbands' welfare, the women have many new responsibilities. But because of their determination to do their part, they have so far kept up their towns, businesses, and farms.

Along with the pressures of new trades and responsibilities, the women have had to contribute their personal possessions to supply the Continental Army with needed provisions. Clothing, food, water, pewter pots and pans, and dishes have all helped the army's success. The women are playing a very important role in fighting the battles.

In the Battle of Bunker Hill 10 very important soldiers died. Let's remember them.

ACTION AT BREEDS HILL

The battle of Bunker Hill is actually being fought at Breed's Hill. 1,000 Redcoats led by Gen. Howe and Gen. Pigot marched up the hill. When the British were within 40 paces, Americans opened fire. Possibly 1,000 Britains are dead. It could be the bloodiest encounter of the war.

[MYSTIC RIVER / CHARLES RIVER map]

LETTERS TO THE EDITOR

Dear Editor

I think I or anyone else important should have warned the colonists. Paul Revere is just a silversmith. William Dawes is a smuggler. I am a captain of an army. If somebody more organized warned us we would have more people successful in the Battle of Lexington. We also would have been more alert. Captains are important people not silversmiths or smugglers. William Dawes should be sent to gaol.

Signed, Captain Williams

Dear Editor

Why did the Battle of Bunker Hill start? The British commander decided it was time for action. So the British marched up the hill on 17 June 1775. The American's were behind their earthworks and fired their muskets and killed some of the British. The British won, but I believe it was a victory to the Americans. We killed half of the British army. Very few Americans got killed. We showed the British that we had strength and that we were brave.

Molly Cline

Did You Know?

Did you know, out of all the colors that you can think of black draws more sunlight. You can tell by laying an assortment of cloth on the ground of all different colors. Be sure you lay them apart. Put some black with the colors. Come back in about one hour and feel them. That's how you can tell.

Benjamin Franklin

An Interview with G. Washington

When did you observe your soldiers at their best?

I observed my army at their best when they had a conflict on a public common.

Were you pleased with the results of your army's efforts?

My army was not very disciplined, but they sometimes fought as a team and won a great deal.

Were you mad at your army for not working as a team?

I was not mad, but probably the most embarrassed general in the army.

I met George Washington at the 2 Star Inn. We talked over some glasses of ale. We had a long and cheerful talk.

Was the Lexington Battle Worth it?

The Lexington Battle I know was very important. The battle was fought so Americans could have their rights.

My husband Thomas Madden was 1 out of the 49 American soldiers that were killed. I loved my husband. He was a strong, brave man. He went out on the battle field and fought the Lobster Backs to get our freedom. He never even got to see our little girl Mary.

I asked myself was it worth losing my husband and gaining freedom? I guess it was really worth it. At least now I know my baby will grow up and be free from the king.

Martha Madden

PEOPLE CONFUSED ABOUT BUNKER HILL

It was 17 June when the battle began. Thoughts about King George are half and half. Some think that he is an intelligent person but others are still very angry at him.

Most of the other colonists thought that Bunker Hill would be a good risk. Even with this difference of opinion, the colonists no longer doubted that the Americans must break all ties with Great Britain. General Washington is working hard to turn the volunteers into a efficient fighting force.

Rumor has it Washington is planning to drive the British out of Boston forever!!

FIGURE 9–18 A Fifth-grade Simulated Newspaper

LOCAL NEWS

DOG—MAN'S BEST FRIEND

It started when Paul Revere said, "Put two lanterns in the church steeple, the sounds of bells might alert the British." After a few long nights of watching from a nearby hill, Paul Revere noticed the lanterns were finally lit. Revere then went home, got his jacket and said good-bye to his wife and children. He took out the door and apparently was followed by his dog. Revere told the dog to return home but the dog would not go. Lucky for Revere his dog was with him as he later discovered he had forgotten his spurs. He tied a note to his dog telling his wife to get his spurs, fasten them to the dog's neck and send the dog back to him. The dog went home and returned with the spurs. Revere took the spurs, got on his horse and was on his mission. He warned the colonists of the British arrival. Revere did his job well.

FASHION

Fashions - A new fashion has just arrived from France. Hats that look like bonnets with lace strings that you can tie around your neck. They also have pocket-hoop farthingales to make your dress stick out. You can get the set at Southern Belle and at Jan's Tailor Shop.

SHOES

Women's shoes - Women wear shoes that look like sandals and high heels. You can find them at the Shoe Shop.

New leather shoes have just arrived from France. These shoes have gold or silver buckels. The colors are brown, dark blue, and black. You can find the shoes at Mr. Brown's shoe shop.

BOONE AND THE WILDERNESS ROAD

On 16 March 1775 Daniel Boone and a group of pioneers set out to settle Kentucky. Problems arose along the way. Some problems were Indians and wild animal attacks. Other problems were getting wagons and herds through the long travel. With these problems a road was built.

After the road was built Daniel Boone returned to North Carolina. He gather his relatives and neighbors to make a party. They had a rough and difficult trip. Daniel Boone and the pioneers finally settled. People from all around started settling in Kentucky.

ENTERTAINMENT

Picnic - 15 August Village Commons

Horse race on 2 July was held by Clark Stone. Twenty people came and afterwards they ate cake and drank lemonade.

Climbing greased poles. Running after a greased pig is some of the activities, there are also Music and contests. The prices are 5¢ for adults and 3¢ for children.

30 August ballroom of Black Horse New York held by Clint Adams - noon

WEATHER

This summer's weather has been primarily mild, sunny, and calm. The evenings have been warm and partly cloudy. The expected weather for August and September will be mostly sunny with a greater chance of rain. Farmers be sure to plant early this fall.

Inventions

Bow Beater
by George Herald

A new egg beater has been made. It is a bow drill mixed with an egg beater to make a bow beater. To see how you can build your own, come to the farm by the courthouse.

Benjamin Franklin invented a chair with a table hooked onto it. It looks like this.

LOCAL NEWS

George Adams can walk again after his leg got wounded in the Battle of Bunker Hill.

Kristie and Bill Stockup had twins. The babies and mother died. Bill killed himself.

Peter's Cafe is open now on Elm Road by Linda Cowitt's house.

Linda Cowitt is opening a store by Peter's Cafe on Elm Road.

Foy Hunting was held on 20 May by John Clark on his plantation.

Greg Blame has opened a war supplies store by Steve's Black Carriage Store and his store is called Greg's War Supplies.

HORSE KILLS LOCAL MAN

On Tuesday 5 July Tom Haley was killed by a horse. Tom was behind his horse putting medicine on the horse's leg. Tom's brother Jason witnessed the scene of the tragedy. Jason said all of the sudden the horse kicked him in the jaw. The horse was real sick and needed medicine thats probably why it started kicking. Tom's funeral will be 8 July, Saturday.

NEW SCHOOL THREATENED

The G. W. Honeywitt School of Concord opened on 7 September 1774. George Windsor Honeywitt, a former student of the British Conservatory of London, is the headmaster. Twenty students successfully completed their first year.

Honewitt is teaching the students about unfair taxes and unreasonable acts passed by Parliament.

After receiving recent threats from British officers, Mr. Honeywitt is concerned that his school may be destroyed.

Honeywitt, although fearful of the threats, takes pride in his new school, and because of his patriotism, continues to educate his students in the ways of the colonial patriots.

WIGS

New powdered or non-powdered men's or women's wigs just came in. You can find these wigs at Lucy's wig shop.

THE WAR HAS BEGUN!

FIGURE 9–18 (continued)

DEATHS

John Brona was in a horse accident. He died the next day.

Jamie Marshall is dead after fighting a sickness for four years.

We regret the passing of Benjamin Franklin's wife.

Rachel Fire had a sister named Sunshine Fire. She died after riding in a carriage. The horse went wild. They wrecked. She broke her neck and died.

Crystal Winter was a spy for England. She was killed at Lexington.

Julie Hardie dressed up like a British soldier. She died after killing a British officer. We will all remember her.

Sally Winters has been run over by a wild horse on 20 July. Her funeral is on 24 July, Thursday. Her family needs help.

Connie Bloom died in a British attack.

After Leslie Johnson was born, her mother Crystal Johnson died.

Jennifer Ponca fell off her horse and died. Please remember her.

Shelly Dovale dies after falling off a cliff.

Fred Johnson was killed at Bunker Hill.

BIRTHS

Monica and Jason Benkin had a baby girl.

Jamie and Harold Sane had twins on 16 June and their names are Caroline and Mary Sane.

Misty Flagstaff had twins that were girls. Their names are Tuesday and Thursday.

Jane and Billy Sample had a boy on 5 July. His name is Robert.

WEDDINGS

John Hancock married Dolly Quincy this summer.

Kevin Suref married Jenny Harp on 10 June.

Robert Green was married to Julie Center on 2 June.

Bill Bond is going to marry Jenny Dye on 2 August. The wedding will be held at the Colonial Church.

Carriage Tips and Kills

On 7 July in Pennsylvania John Johnson was killed by a carriage falling on him while walking down Main Street. The coach driver was also killed. The other passengers were badly injured. This is bad news to the colonists for John was running for office. The mayor warned the colonists that while driving a carriage, if they hit a dog, cat, livestock, or person, they will be prosecuted.

POPULATION AND LABOUR

The Population of the Colonies in 1774-1775

COLONY	WHITE	NEGRO	TOTAL
New Hampshire	80,000	500	80,500
Massachusetts	355,000	5,000	360,000
Rhode Island	54,500	5,000	59,500
Connecticut	191,500	8,000	199,500
New York	161,000	21,000	182,000
New Jersey	117,000	3,000	120,000
Pennsylvania and Delaware	298,000	2,000	300,000
Maryland	190,000	60,000	250,000
Virginia	300,000	200,000	500,000
North Carolina	260,000	10,000	270,000
South Carolina	120,000	80,000	200,000
Georgia	18,000	15,000	33,000
TOTAL	2,145,000	409,500	2,554,500

BUY TOBACCO

Smoke or Chew YOUR LOCAL General Store

SECOND CONTINENTAL CONGRESS MEETS IN PHILADELPHIA

On 8 July 1775 the Second Continental Congress met in Philadelphia. John Dickinson was chosen leader because of his prestige and influence. Congress agreed to a second petition to the king. The petition was almost solely Dickinson's work. The colonists and Congress wanted peace with Britain. They wanted freedom, liberty, and independence. The Congress said, "The king had no right to make war on us. We should be allowed to make our own rules." American people expressed their hope for the restoration of harmony and begged the king to prevent further hostile actions against the colonies until a reconciliation was worked out. On 6 July, Congress adopted another important resolution that said Americans were ready to die rather than be enslaved. The Olive Branch Petition demanded that Britain leave the door open for reconciliation.

THE KING?

ACCOUNT OF SALES OF CARGO OF ANDERSON

Date	Men	Women	Men Boys	Small Boys	Girls	Small Girls	Ft. of Boards	Slaves	Shingles	Water Casks	Prices	£.s.d
June 18 1775	10	4	11								£35	875
												30
												35
											29	58
												28
												30
		2		1								22 10
		1		1								22 10
		2		2	1	2						22 10
												29
												24 24
						1					Only £35	21
												10
											Only £35	100
												400
					2	3						15
Total	14	9	11	8	2	3	4,256 1,350	8,500		20	6¼ per m.	22 13 6
											8½s and 5	1,437 12 6
												11 7 6
											Total	£1,464 13 6

Too many "slaves" have been sold to our new country. This graph shows a ship load of goods.

YOU SCOUNDREL KING GEORGE

You scoundrel King George,
You put us to work,
When you made us pay taxes.

We will not pay your taxes,
We will get out our axes,
We will fight for our freedom and win.

Aaron Ochs

Teachers: Charlotte Fleetham
Polly Madden

Boles, Teresa
Brown, Amber
Esquivel, Tracy
Fields, Rachel
Gaddis, Chrystal
Hainline, Jamie
Lawson, Julie
McNabb, Bree
Marshall, Erin
Simms, Alisha
Vaughan, Vesper**
Vass, Christopher**
Wallis, Ryan

Bettis, Brad
Clement, Chrissy
Garayua, Richard
Kennedy, Steven*
Levings, Brian
McCrory, Kevin
Murphy, Michael*
Murphy, Patrick*
Nelson, Neil
Ochs, Aaron*
Pierce, Jamie
Windsor, Justin

*Student Editors
**Illustrator

FIGURE 9–18 (continued)

mentary classrooms, the burden of grading the writing cannot be allowed to become burdensome. Therefore, teachers must develop an efficient system of handling the paper load, even if it means not being able to read and respond to every piece of writing.

2. I am a middle school math teacher. Why should I teach writing?

While some language arts educators argue that every teacher is a teacher of writing (and reading) because literacy is everyone's concern, I'll take the opposite position and agree with you. It isn't your responsibility to teach writing, but it is your responsibility to teach math, and by using writing your students will learn mathematics better. Informal writing activities, such as learning logs, require little instruction to get students started, and then only periodic monitoring is needed. Researchers have documented the value of informal writing activities in math class to help students clarify their knowledge, apply specialized vocabulary, and monitor their own learning.

3. I'd like to use writing in my second-grade social studies and science classes, but where do I begin?

You begin small by choosing one or two activities from the list in Figure 9–2 or from one of the social studies or science unit clus-

ters presented in this chapter. A good way to begin is by incorporating one informal writing activity and one formal activity into a unit. Students might keep a learning log in which they write sentences and draw pictures after each content-related activity. You might also try a class collaboration report or an ABC book in connection with the unit. As you and your students become familiar with these activities, add another activity or two to your next unit. Before long, the students will suggest writing activities to you. For example, they will say, "Can't we cluster what we've learned about trees?" or "I think we ought to write a report for the first graders to read about the five senses." Then you know they value writing as a tool for learning and documenting learning.

4. I can't take time away from teaching content for more of this writing.

These writing-across-the-curriculum activities don't take time away from content area learning; they enhance that learning. Through the informal and formal writing activities discussed in this chapter, students think more deeply about what they are learning, and they synthesize and apply this knowlege. Rather than stealing time from instruction, writing across the curriculum makes instruction more meaninful.

■ *REFERENCES*

Armes, R. A., & Sullenger, K. (1986, April). Learning science through writing. *Science and Children, 23,* 15–19.

Armstrong, W. M. (1969). *Sounder.* New York: Harper.

Bierhorst, J. (Trans.) (1987). *Doctor coyote: A native American Aesop's fables.* New York: Macmillan.

Bosma, B. (1987). *Fairytales, fables, legends, and myths: Using folk literature in your classroom.* New York: Teachers College Press.

Britton, J. L., Burgess, T., Martin, N., McLeod, A., & Rosen, H. (1975). *The development of writing abilities, 11–18.* London: Macmillan.

Brown, M. (1961). *Once a mouse.* New York: Scribner.

Burningham, J. (1978). *Would you rather . . .* New York: Crowell.

Carle, E. (1980). *Twelve tales from Aesop.* New York: Philomel.

Cauley, L. B. (1979). *The ugly duckling.* New York: Harcourt.

Cooney, B. (1958). *Chanticleer and the fox.* New York: Crowell.

Corcoran, B. (1987). Teachers creating readers. In B. Corcoran & E. Evans (Eds.), *Readers, texts, teachers* (pp. 41–74). Upper Montclair, NJ: Boynton/Cook.

D'Aulaire, I., & D'Aulaire, P. E. (1967). *Norse gods and giants.* New York: Doubleday.

D'Aulaire, I., & D'Aulaire, P. E. (1980). *D'Aulaires' book of Greek myths.* New York: Doubleday.

Davala, V. (1987). Respecting opinions: Learning logs in middle school. In T. Fulwiler (Ed.), *The journal book* (pp. 179–186). Portsmouth, NH: Boynton/Cook.

Degen, B. (1983). *Jamberry.* New York: Harper.

Emig, J. (1977). Writing as a mode of learning. *College Communication and Composition, 28,* 122–128.

Evans, C. S. (1984). Writing to learn in math. *Language Arts, 61,* 828–835.

Fehrenbach, C. R., Greer, F. S., & Daniel, T. B. (1986, February). LEA on the moon. *Science and Children, 23,* 15–17.

Flood, J., Lapp, D., & Farnan, N. (1986). A reading-writing procedure that teaches expository paragraph structure. *The Reading Teacher, 39,* 556–562.

Fulwiler, T. (1987). Introduction. In T. Fulwiler (Ed.), *The journal book* (pp. 1–4). Portsmouth, NH: Boynton/Cook.

Gere, A. R. (1985). Introduction. In A. R. Gere (Ed.), *Roots in the sawdust: Writing to learn across the disciplines* (pp. 1–8). Urbana, IL: National Council of Teachers of English.

Greeson, W. E. (1977). Using writing about mathematics as a teaching technique. *Mathematics Teacher, 70,* 112–115.

Hadley, E., & Hadley, T. (1983). *Legends of the sun and moon.* Cambridge, England: Cambridge University Press.

Hague, M. (1985). *Aesop's fables.* New York: Holt.

Haley, G. (1970). *A story, a story.* New York: Atheneum.

Hembrow, V. (1986). A heuristic approach across the curriculum. *Language Arts, 63,* 674–679.

Hodges, M. (1972). *The fire bringer.* Boston: Little, Brown.

Howe, D., & Howe, J. (1979). *Bunnicula.* New York: Atheneum.

Keeping, C. (1982) *Beowulf.* Oxford, England: Oxford University Press.

Kipling, R. (1987). *Just so stories.* Harmondsworth, England: Penguin.

Lewis, C. S. (1981). *The lion, the witch, and the wardrobe.* New York: Macmillan.

Lionni, L. (1964). *Tico and the golden wings.* New York: Knopf.

Lobel, A. (1980). *Fables.* New York: Harper.

McGee, L. M., & Richgels, D. J. (1985). Teaching expository text structure to elementary students. *The Reading Teacher, 38,* 739–748.

McGonegal, P. (1987). Fifth-grade journals: Results and surprises. In T. Fulwiler (Ed.), *The journal book* (pp. 201–209). Portsmouth, NH: Boynton/Cook.

Meyer, B. J., & Freedle, R. O. (1984). Effects of discourse type on recall. *American Educational Research Journal, 21,* 121–143.

Milne, A. A. (1956). *The House at Pooh Corner.* New York: Dutton.

Moffett, J. (1968). *Teaching the universe of discourse.* Boston: Houghton Mifflin.

Myers, J. W. (1984). *Writing to learn across the curriculum* (Fastback #209). Bloomington, IN: Phi Delta Kappa Educational Foundation.

National Assessment of Educational Progress. (1981). *Reading, thinking and writing: Results from the 1979–1980 national assessment of reading and literature.* Denver: National Educational Commission of the States.

Ness, E. (1966). *Sam, Bangs, and moonshine.* New York: Holt.

Niles, O. S. (1974). Organization perceived. In H. L. Herber (Ed.), *Perspectives in reading: Developing study skills in secondary schools.* Newark, DE: International Reading Association.

Norton, M. (1981). *The borrowers.* New York: Harcourt.

Ogle, D. M. (1986). K-W-L: A teaching model that develops active reading of expository text. *The Reading Teacher, 39,* 564–570.

Piccolo, J. A. (1987). Expository text structures: Teaching and learning strategies. *The Reading Teacher, 40,* 838–847.

Proett, J. & Gill, K. (1986). *The writing process in action: A handbook for teachers.* Urbana, IL: National Council of Teachers of English.

Rice, E. (1979). *Once upon a wood: Ten tales from Aesop.* New York: Greenwillow.

Rosenblatt, L. (1978). *The reader, the text, the poem: The transactional theory of literary work.* Carbondale: Southern Illinois University Press.

Rosenblatt, L. (1983). *Literature as exploration* (4th ed.). New York: Modern Language Association.

Salem, J. (1982). Using writing in teaching mathematics. In M. Barr, P. D'Arcy, & M. K. Healy (Eds.), *What's going on? Language/learning episodes in British and American classrooms, grades 4–13* (pp. 123–134). Monclair, NJ: Boynton/Cook.

Sanford, B. (1988). Writing reflectively. *Language Arts, 65,* 652–657.

Schubert, B. (1987). Mathematics journals: Fourth grade. In T. Fulwiler (Ed.), *The journal book* (pp. 348–358). Portsmouth, NH: Boynton/Cook.

Sharmat, M. W. (1974). *Nate the great goes undercover.* New York: Coward.

Shulevitz, U. (1978). *The treasure.* New York: Farrar.

Smith, P. L., & Tompkins, G. E. (1988). Structured notetaking: A new strategy for content area readers. *The Journal of Reading, 32,* 46–53.

Sobol, D. J. (1963). *Encyclopedia Brown, boy detective.* New York: Dutton.

Speare, E. G. (1958). *The witch of Blackbird Pond.* Boston: Houghton Mifflin.

Stauffer, R. G. (1975). *Directing the reading-thinking process.* New York: Harper.

Steig, W. (1982). *Doctor De Soto.* New York: Farrar.

Tchudi, S. N., & Tchudi, S. J. (1983). *Teaching writing in the content areas: Elementary school.* Washington, DC: National Education Association.

Weiss, M. E. (1980). *Gods, stars, and computers: Fact and fancy in myth and science.* New York: Doubleday.

Westcott, N. B. (1984). *The emperor's new clothes.* Boston: Little, Brown.

Zinsser, W. (1988). *Writing to learn.* New York: Harper.

Assessing Students' Writing

Sixth-grade Megan looks at the grade on the biography project her teacher has just returned to her. The grade is U (unsatisfactory). She is incredulous; she has never received anything lower than a C +. She looks as though she is about to cry. Then she rips a sheet of paper out of her spiral-bound journal notebook and she quickly writes this poem:

> A, B, C, D, or U
> A, I jump for joy.
> B, well, that's ok with me.
> C, I'd rather get a B.
> D, there must be something wrong with me.
> But U, if I get a U,
> I really feel bad, I really feel sad.
> I know that if I get a U, I could have made a D,
> or a C, or goodness gracious me, a B.
> So, B is fine with me.

Megan rereads her poem and shares it with her teacher. They talk about her grade and the reason for it: the prewriting and rough drafts were not turned in with the project. Megan locates the missing materials in her desk, and her teacher agrees to reconsider the grade. The next day, Megan gets her biography folder back and the grade is now a B +.

The traditional purpose of assessment has been to determine grades, and grading often has the deleterious effects that Megan described in her poem. Rather, assessment should be viewed as a component of the writing process, something that both students and teachers do during writing and after the writing has been completed. As students draft, revise, and edit their writing, they assess their own efforts to communicate effectively, meet with classmates for their assessments at writing group sessions, and have conferences with the teacher for encouragement and suggestions. Yetta Goodman (1989) describes assessment as an integral part of curriculum: "It cannot be divorced from classroom organization, from the relationship between teacher and student; from continuous learning experiences and activities" (p. 4). The important thing to remember is that assessment leads to action—revision, teaching, or future writing. Assessment need never be a dead end.

According to Kenneth Goodman (1989), the characteristics of assessment are:

- Assessment should be holistic, using natural language taken from authentic contexts.
- Assessment should treat students with respect and reveal their writing competencies.
- Assessment should be consistent with what researchers have learned about teaching, learning, and language development.
- Assessment should be innovative, creative, and dynamic.
- Assessment should be open-ended, allowing for change and individual differences.

This chapter focuses on three types of assessment. The informal monitoring of student writing is one type, and teachers use these procedures daily to keep track of students' progress. The second and third types, process and product assessment, are more formal measures and are appropriate when students use the process approach to writing. In process assessment, teachers monitor the process that students use as they write, while product assessment deals with the quality of students' finished compositions. In all three types of assessment, however, the goal is to help students become better writers.

Teachers use the three types of assessment for a variety of purposes. Among these are:

- Compare instructional practices.
- Identify students' strengths and weaknesses.
- Judge the relative worth of compositions.
- Compare compositions with specified criteria.
- Identify students' mechanical errors.
- Inspire risk-taking.
- Develop students' sense of audience.
- Build students' self-confidence.
- Determine the level of writing achievement of a large group of students.
- Identify specific writing problems.
- Evaluate the effectiveness of an instructional program.
- Informally monitor student progress.
- Check mastery of skills.
- Verify students' application of content.
- Determine achievement levels.
- Provide positive feedback.
- Examine students' critical thinking skills.
- Encourage students to write.

Through informal assessment, for example, teachers inspire risk-taking and provide positive feedback; in process assessment, teachers identify strengths and weaknesses and build self-confidence; and through product assessment, they judge the relative worth of compositions and identify errors. Some of the reasons that teachers assess writing are intended to help students grow as writers, such as encouraging risk-taking and identifying strengths and weaknesses, while others, such as giving grades and determining achievement levels, are imposed by school districts and state departments of education.

Frank Smith (1988) regards assessment as the greatest danger in education today, and he cautions teachers that even when their purpose in assessing writing is to benefit the writer, negative consequences are inevitable:

> When evaluation and grading are unavoidable, as they so often are, it can be made clear to the student that the "mark" is given for administrative or bureaucratic purposes that have nothing to do with "real world" writing. Grading never taught a writer anything. Writers learn by learning about writing, not by getting letters or numbers put on their efforts and abilities. (p. 30)

INFORMAL MONITORING OF STUDENT WRITING

Keeping track of students' progress in each curricular area is one of the more complex responsibilities facing elementary teachers, and this ongoing assessment is more difficult in writing than in other areas. Writing is multidimensional and not adequately measured simply by counting the number or quality of compositions a student has written. Three procedures for daily monitoring of students' progress in writing are observing, conferencing, and collecting writing in folders. These informal procedures allow teachers to interact daily with students and to document the progress students make in writing.

Observing

Careful, focused observation of students as they write (and keeping detailed notes of these observations) is part of good teaching as well as part of assessment in writing classrooms. Teachers watch students as they write, participate in writing groups, revise and proofread their writing, and share their finished compositions with genuine audiences. Teachers observe to learn about students' attitudes toward writing, the writing strategies that students use, how students interact with classmates during writing, and whether classmates seek out particular students for assistance or sharing writing.

While observing, teachers may ask questions (e.g., "Are you having a problem?" "What are you planning to do next?") to clarify what they have observed. Observing is not necessarily time-consuming. Even though teachers watch and interact with students throughout their reading and writing projects, these observations take only a few minutes, and for experienced teachers who know their students well, a single glance may provide the needed information about the student's progress.

In general, the richest source of information will be close attention to students as they respond to instructions and as they read and write. Graves (1983) suggests that teachers should observe the class as a whole during writing as well as spend approximately 5 minutes observing each individual student. This "close-in" observation, as Graves calls it, involves sitting next to or across from students as they write. Graves recommends that teachers tell students why they are observing by saying, "I'm going to watch as you write for a few minutes so that I can help you become a better writer. Pretend that I'm not here, and just continue with what you are doing." Teachers may do this "close-in" observation only once or twice during the school year as students write for varied purposes and audiences.

Conferencing

As students write, teachers often hold short, informal conferences to talk with them about their writing or to help them solve a problem related to their writing. These conferences can be held at students' desks as the teacher moves around the classroom, at the teacher's desk, or at a special writing conference table. Some occasions for these conferences include:

1. *On the spot Conferences.* Teachers visit briefly with students at their desks to monitor some aspect of the writing assignment or to see how the student is progressing. These conferences are brief with the teacher often spending less than a minute at a student's desk before moving away.
2. *Prewriting Conferences.* The teacher and student make plans for writing in prewriting conferences. They may discuss possible writing topics, how to narrow a broad topic, or how to gather and organize information before writing.
3. *Drafting Conferences.* At these conferences, students bring their rough drafts and talk with the teacher about specific writing trouble spots they are having. Together the teacher and the student discuss the problem and brainstorm ideas for solving it.
4. *Revising Conferences.* A small group of students and the teacher meet together in a revising conference to get specific suggestions about how to revise their compositions. These conferences offer student writers an audience to provide feedback on how well they have communicated.
5. *Editing Conferences.* In these individual or small-group conferences, the teacher reviews students' proofread compositions and helps them to correct spelling, punctuation, capitalization, and other mechanical errors.
6. *Instructional "Mini-lesson" Conferences.* In these conferences, teachers meet with individual students to provide special instruction on one or two skills (e.g., capitalizing proper nouns, using commas in a series) that are particularly troublesome for individual students.
7. *Assessment Conferences.* In assessment conferences, teachers meet with students after they complete their compositions to talk with them about their growth as writers and their plans for future writing. Teachers ask students to reflect on their writing competencies and to set goals for their next writing assignment. For more information about each type of conference as well as for information about other types of student-led conferences, see Chapter 3 "The Writing Process."

At these conferences, the teacher's role is to be a listener and guide. Teachers can learn a great deal about students and their writing if they listen as students talk about their writing. When students explain a problem they are having to the teacher, teachers are able often to decide on a way to work through their problem. A list of questions that teachers can use in conferences to encourage students to talk about their writing is presented in Figure 10–1. Graves (1983) suggests that teachers balance the amount of their talk with the child's talk during the conference and then at the end, reflect on what the child taught them, what responsibilities the child can take, and whether the child understood what to do next.

Collecting Writing in Folders

Students keep their writing in manila folders called writing folders. These folders, which contain everything students have written except for books and other finished products that are displayed elsewhere, are stored near the teacher's desk in a box that is accessible to both students and the teacher. Writing should be dated

FIGURE 10–1   Questions Teachers Ask in Writing Conferences

As students begin to write:

What are you going to write about?
How did you choose (or narrow) your topic?
What prewriting activities are you doing?
How are you gathering ideas for writing?
How will you organize your writing?
How will you start writing your rough draft?
What form will your writing take?
Who will be your audience?
What problems do you think you might have?
What do you plan to do next?

As students are drafting:

How is your writing going?
Are you having any problems?
What do you plan to do next?

As students revise their writing:

What questions do you have for your writing group?
What help do you want from your writing group?
What compliments did your writing group give you?

What suggestions did your writing group give you?
How do you plan to revise your writing?
What kinds of revisions did you make?
What do you plan to do next?

As students edit their writing:

What kinds of mechanical errors have you located?
How has your editor helped you proofread?
How can I help you identify (or correct) mechanical errors?
What do you plan to do next?
Are you ready to make your final copy?

After students have completed their compositions:

What audience will you share your writing with?
What did your audience say about your writing?
What do you like best about your writing?
If you were writing the composition again, what changes would you make?
How did you use the writing process in writing this composition?

and all pieces related to one project clipped together. It is also helpful to staple a sheet of paper to the inside cover of the writing folder and have students list each piece of writing as it is added to the folder. A sample list is presented in Figure 10–2. The many pieces of writing contained in the folders illustrate all stages of the writing process so that student's progress can be traced by months or semesters of the school year. Many characteristics of writing progress can be documented through writing folders, including topics and themes, writing forms, organizational strategies, details, topic sentences, types of revisions, accuracy of proofreading, grammar and usage, and handwriting.

Writing folders can also be used for parent conferences and as part of the assessment at the end of each grading period. Parents may need help in understanding what the pieces of writing in the writing folders demonstrate. Rynkofs (1988) recommends that parents and teachers examine folders together for what they show that children *do* know and apply rather than what they *don't* know. Also, when writing folders are sent home for parents to examine at the end of a grading period, Rynkofs suggests preparing a cover sheet that describes the types of writing parents will see in the folder, the competencies the student demonstrated in the writings, and goals for the upcoming grading period. After viewing the folder, parents may make comments or ask questions on the cover sheet and return the folder to school.

Writing folders can also be passed from teacher to teacher to provide a developmental perspective to students' growth as writers, and the summary sheets written at the end of each grading period will provide useful information for teachers as well as parents. Bingham (1988) explains that writing folders are useful because they provide accountability by documenting the writing program and individual students' progress.

In a writing process classroom, students rarely throw away a piece of writing or take it home because, if rough drafts are discarded or finished pieces are sent home, part of the record of the child's writing development is lost. Also, these pieces of writing may be used in the classroom for mini-lessons on specific writing skills.

FIGURE 10-2   List for the Inside Cover of a Writing Folder

Writing Folder Table of Contents			
Writer: _____ Grading Period 1 2 3 4			
Title/Topic	Date	Pages	Comments

Keeping Records

Teachers need to document the data collected through observations, conferences, and writing folders. Simply recording a grade in a grade book does not provide an adequate record of a student's writing progress. Instead, teachers should keep a variety of records to document students' writing progress, including copies of students' writing; anecdotal notes from observations and conferences; and checklists of skills taught in mini-lessons, skills applied in students' writing, and writing process activities that students participate in while writing.

Anecdotal Records. Teachers should make brief anecdotal records in which they record samples of a student's behavior and information gathered through observations, conferences, and reviews of writing folders. A year-long collection of these records provides a comprehensive picture of a student's development as a writer. Instead of recording random samples, teachers should choose events that are characteristic of each student's writing.

Several organizational schemes are possible, and teachers should use the format that is most comfortable for them. Some teachers make a cardfile with dividers for each child and write anecdotes on notecards. They feel comfortable jotting notes on these small notecards or even carrying around a set of cards in their pockets. Some other teachers divide a spiral-bound notebook into sections for each child and write the anecdotes in the notebook that they keep on their desks. A third scheme is for teachers to write anecdotes on sheets of paper and clip these sheets to the students' writing folders. Another possibility is the small pads of paper that can be stuck to notecards or in notebooks and writing folders. Like notecards, these little pads are small enough to fit into a pocket and can easily be carried around and used when needed.

An excerpt from a fifth grader's anecdotal record is presented in Figure 10–3. In this excerpt, the teacher has dated each entry and used writing terminology such as *cluster, drafting, compliments.* Each entry provides information about the abilities and skills the child has demonstrated. This information is useful in documenting the child's progress in writing.

Checklists. Teachers can develop a variety of checklists to use in assessing students' progress in writing. Some of the possible checklists include an inventory of:

- Writing forms
- Punctuation marks and other mechanical skills
- Writing topics or themes
- Writing process activities
- Misspelled words by category of invented spelling
- Types of revisions
- Writing competencies

Four sample checklists are presented in Figure 10–4. Teachers add checkmarks, dates, comments, or other information to complete these checklists. The forms can be clipped inside students' writing folders or they can be kept in separate assessment folders for each student.

FIGURE 10–3 Excerpt from a Fifth Grader's Anecdotal Writing Record for an American Revolution Unit

AMERICAN REVOLUTION UNIT—SIMULATED JOURNALS AND BIOGRAPHIES

March 5	Matthew selected Ben Franklin as historical figure for American Revolution projects.
March 11	Matthew fascinated with information he has found about B. F. Brought several sources from home. Is completing B. F.'s lifeline with many details.
March 18	Simulated journal. Four entries in four days! Interesting how he picked up language style of the period in his journal. Volunteers to share daily. I think he enjoys the oral sharing more than the writing.
March 25	Nine simulated journal entries, all illustrated. High level of enthusiasm.
March 29	Conferenced about cluster for B. F. biography. Well developed with five rays, many details. Matthew will work on "contributions" ray. He recognized it as the least-developed one.
April 2	Three chapters of biography drafted. Talked about "working titles" for chapters and choosing more interesting titles after writing that reflect the content of the chapters.
April 7	Drafting conference. Matthew has completed all five chapters. He and Dustin are competitive, both writing on B. F. They are reading each other's chapters and checking the accuracy of information.
April 12	Writing group. Matthew confused Declaration of Independence with the Constitution. Chapters longer and more complete since drafting conference. Compared with autobiography project, writing is more sophisticated. Longer, too. Reading is influencing writing style—e.g., "Luckily for Ben." He is still somewhat defensive about accepting suggestions except from me. He will make 3 revisions—agreed in writing group.
April 15	Revisions: (1) eliminated "he" (substitute), (2) re-sequenced Chapter 3 (move), and (3) added sentences in Chapter 5 (add).
April 19	Proofread with Dustin. Working hard.
April 23	Editing conference—no major problems. Discussed use of commas within sentences, capitalizing proper nouns. Matthew and Dustin more task-oriented on this project; I see more motivation and commitment.
April 29	Final copy of biography completed and shared with class.

PROCESS ASSESSMENT MEASURES

Until recently, the formal assessment of student writing has focused on the quality of students' finished compositions; however, the writing process and its emphasis on what students actually do as they write has spawned a new approach to writing

FIGURE 10-4 Checklists for Monitoring Students' Writing

Punctuation Mark Skills Checklist			
Name: _____ Grading Period 1 2 3 4			
Skill	Introduced	Practiced	Applied in Writing
Period at the end of a sentence			
after abbreviations			
after numbers in a list			
after an initial			
Question Mark at the end of a question			
Exclamation Mark after words or sentences showing excitement or strong feeling			
Quotation Marks before/after direct quotations			
around title or a poem, short story, song, or TV program			
Apostrophe in contractions			
to show possession			
Comma to separate words in a series			
between day and year			
between city and state			
after greeting in a friendly letter			

assessment. This new approach is called process assessment, and it is designed to probe how students write, the decisions they make as they write, and the strategies they use rather than the quality of their finished products. Three measures of process assessment are writing process checklists, student and teacher assessment conferences, and self-assessment by students. Information from these three measures together with the product assessment measures provides a more complete assessment picture or "portfolio" (Flood & Lapp, 1989).

FIGURE 10-4 (continued)

Punctuation Mark Skills Checklist			
Name: _____ Grading Period 1 2 3 4			
Skill	Introduced	Practiced	Applied in Writing
after closing of a letter			
after an initial *yes* or *no*			
after a noun of direct address			
to separate a quote from the speaker			
before the conjunction in a compound sentence			
after a dependent clause at the beginning of a sentence			
Colon before a list			
in writing time			
after the greeting of a business letter			
after an actor's name in a script			
Parentheses to enclose unimportant information			
to enclose stage directions in a script			
Hyphen between parts of a compound number			
to divide a word at the end of a line			
between parts of some compound words			

Writing Process Checklists

As teachers observe students while they are writing, they can note how students move through the writing process stages, from gathering and organizing ideas during prewriting, to pouring out and shaping ideas during drafting, to meeting in writing groups to get feedback about their writing and making substantive changes during revising, to proofreading and correcting mechanical errors in editing, and to publishing and sharing their writing in the last stage (McKenzie &

FIGURE 10-4 (continued)

	1 Add	2 Substitute	3 Delete	4 Move	TOTAL

Revision Checklist

Name: _____ Grading Period 1 2 3 4

Type of Change

Level of Change	1 Add	2 Substitute	3 Delete	4 Move	TOTAL
1 Word					
2 Phrase/ Clause					
3 Sentence					
4 Multi- sentence/ Paragraph					
5 Entire Text					
TOTAL					

Tompkins, 1984). The checklist presented in Figure 10–5 lists several character-istic activities for each stage of the writing process. Teachers observe students as they write and participate in other writing process-related activities and place checkmarks and add comments as necessary for each observed activity. Students can also use the checklist for self-assessment to help make them aware of the activities involved in the writing process. Temple and his colleagues (1988) advocate periodic process assessments to determine whether students are using the writing process.

The writing process checklist can also be adapted for various types of writing projects. For example, if students are writing autobiographies, items can be

FIGURE 10-4 (continued)

Writing Forms Checklist	
Name: _____	Grading Period 1 2 3 4
ABC book	learning log
ad/commercial	letter—business
autobiography	letter—friendly
biography	letter—simulated
book/film review	lifeline/timeline
brainstormed list	map
cartoon/comic	myth/legend
chart/diagram/poster	newspaper
cluster	newspaper—simulated
comparison	persuasive essay
cubing	poem
directions	puzzle
fable	research report
greeting card	script
interview	story
journal-dialogue	other
journal-personal	
journal-simulated	

Adapted from Faigley & Witte, 1981, pp. 400–414; Tompkins & Friend, 1988, pp. 4–9.

added in the prewriting stage about developing a lifeline and clustering ideas for each chapter topic. In the sharing stage, items focusing on adding a table of contents, an illustration for each chapter, and sharing the completed autobiography with at least two other people can be included. Checklists for an autobiography project and for a project on fables are presented in Figure 10–6 to show how the basic writing process checklist can be adapted for two types of writing.

Writing process checklists can also be used in conjunction with product assessment. Teachers can base a percentage of students' grades on how well they used the writing process and the remaining percentage on the quality of the writing.

FIGURE 10-5 A Writing Process Checklist

	Dates						
Student: _____							
Prewriting Can the student identify the specific audience to whom he/she will write?							
Does this awareness affect the choices the student makes as he/she writes?							
Can the student identify the purpose of the writing activity?							
Does the student write on a topic that grows out of his/her own experience?							
Does the student engage in rehearsal activities before writing?							
Drafting Does the student write rough drafts?							
Does the student place a greater emphasis on content than on mechanics in the rough drafts?							
Revising Does the student share his/her writing in conferences?							

Assessment Conferences

Language arts educators such as Nancy Atwell (1988a) argue that to encourage students to take risks and experiment in their writing, not every piece of writing should be graded. Instead, through an assessment conference, teachers meet with individual students, and together they discuss the student's writing, examine papers from the writing folder, and decide on a grade based on their goals for the writing project or grading period. These discussions may focus on any aspect of the writing process including topic selection, prewriting activities, word choice, writing group activities, types of revisions, consistency in editing, and degree of effort and involvement in the writing project. Atwell uses these questions to encourage students to reflect on their writing:

- What does one have to do to be a good writer?
- What is the hardest part of writing for you?
- What is the easiest part?
- Which are your best pieces of writing this grading period (or year)?

FIGURE 10-5 (continued)

Student: _____	Dates					
Revising Does the student participate in discussions about classmates' writing?						
In revising, does the student make changes to reflect the reactions and comments of both teacher and classmates?						
Between first and final drafts, does the student make substantive or only minor changes?						
Editing Does the student proofread his/her own papers?						
Does the student help proofread classmates' papers?						
Does the student increasingly identify his/her mechanical errors?						
Sharing Does the student publish his/her writing in an appropriate form?						
Does the student share this finished writing with an appropriate audience?						

McKenzie & Tompkins, 1984, p. 211.

- What makes them best?
- Which piece or pieces are you least satisfied with? Why?
- Where do your ideas for writing come from?
- Do you have any plans for what you want to write next?
- How do you go about making changes in your writing?
- Can you tell me why you made this change on your draft of this piece?
- What problems are you experiencing with your writing?
- What kinds of response help you most as a writer?
- Who gives you helpful responses? (Atwell, 1988b, p. 239)

Additional possible questions include:

- Of all the kids in the class, which one writes in a way you especially like?
- What makes you like his or her way of writing?
- Of all the authors you read, which one writes in a way you especially like?

FIGURE 10-6 Process Checklist for an Autobiography Project and a Fables Project

---

Autobiography Checklist

Writer: _____

Prewriting	_____	Created a lifeline
	_____	Brainstormed eight chapter topics
	_____	Chose four topics for chapters
	_____	Clustered each topic for a chapter
Drafting	_____	Wrote a draft of each chapter
	_____	Wrote on every other line and marked papers as a ROUGH DRAFT
Revising	_____	Participated in a writing group
	_____	Made at least three changes in the draft
Editing	_____	Completed an editing checklist with a partner
	_____	Had a conference with the teacher
Sharing	_____	Added a title page and a table of contents
	_____	Recopied the autobiography
	_____	Added an illustration for each chapter
	_____	Shared the autobiography with two other people

1. _____

2. _____

- What makes you like his or her writing?
- What do you think would make your writing even better?
- What are the strengths of your writing? The weaknesses? (Calkins, 1986, p. 150)

Through the judicious use of these questions, students probe their understanding of the writing process and their own competencies. Atwell keeps these conferences brief, spending only 10 minutes with each student, and at the end of the meeting, she and the student develop a set of goals for the following writing project or grading period. This list of goals can be added to the student's writing folder and used to begin the next assessment conference. An upper grade student's list of goals might include the following:

- I will have my rough drafts ready for my writing group on time.
- I will write five poems during the next grading period.

FIGURE 10-6 (continued)

Fables Project Checklist			
Writer: _____			
		Student	Teacher
Prewriting	Read 5 fables and took notes in your reading log.	☐	☐
	Drew a story cluster of one fable.	☐	☐
	Copied the list of characteristics of fables that we developed together.	☐	☐
	Listed morals from 10 fables.	☐	☐
	Planned a fable and drew a story cluster.	☐	☐
Drafting	Wrote a rough draft from your story cluster.	☐	☐
Revising	Participated in a writing group and compared your fable with the list of characteristics of fables.	☐	☐
	Made at least one revision.	☐	☐
Editing	Proofread with a partner and corrected spelling and other errors.	☐	☐
	Had a conference with the teacher.	☐	☐
Sharing	Wrote the final copy in your best handwriting.	☐	☐
	Added an illustration.	☐	☐
	Shared with classmates from the author's chair.	☐	☐

- I will locate 75% of my spelling errors when I proofread.
- I will explain the purpose in the first two paragraphs of the essays I write.

Self-assessment

Temple and his colleagues (1988) recommend that we teach students self-assessment through writing conferences so they can learn to assess their own writing and writing processes. In self-assessment, students assume responsibility for assessing their own writing and for deciding which pieces of writing they will share with the teacher and classmates. This ability to reflect on one's own writing promotes organizational skills, self-reliance, independence, and creativity.

Students can assess their rough drafts as well as their finished compositions. Before sharing their writing with classmates in a writing group, students need to examine the rough draft and make some preliminary assessments. This self-assessment may deal with the quality of writing; that is, whether or not the writing communicates effectively and how adequately the writing incorporates the requirements of the composition as stipulated by the teacher. For example, third graders can check to see that their animal reports answer these questions:

- Where does the animal live?
- What does the animal eat?
- What does the animal look like?
- How does the animal protect itself?

Similarly, fifth graders who are writing reports on states can check to see that they have included geographic, historical, and economic information as well as other information that the teacher has specified. Teachers can guide students as they assess their writing by listing questions on the chalkboard or developing a checklist for students to complete as they consider their writing. A sample checklist for fifth graders who are writing state reports is presented in Figure 10–7.

After students meet in a writing group, they use self-assessment again as they decide which revisions to make. This assessment is often difficult for students as they struggle to deal with their own egocentricity as well as the sometimes laborious suggestions made by others. They also consider the teacher's revision

FIGURE 10-7   Checklist for a Report on a State

Name: _____   State: _____

After you have written the rough draft of your state report, complete this checklist to make sure that you have included all the necessary information.

Yes	No	
☐	☐	Have you written information about the **geography** of the state?
☐	☐	Have you drawn a **map** of the state?
☐	☐	Have you written information about the **history** of the state?
☐	☐	Have you made a **timeline** of the state?
☐	☐	Have you written information about the **economy** of the state?
☐	☐	Have you written information about **places to visit** in the state?
☐	☐	Have you written **something special** about the state?
☐	☐	Have you included maps and other information that the **state tourist department** sent to you?

suggestions but in the end may choose to make a revision suggested by a class-mate instead. Teachers are often distressed as they realize that students' revisions are influenced more by classmates' comments than by teachers' suggestions.

Teachers can develop a self-assessment questionnaire for students to com-plete after sharing their writing. Some questions should deal with the writing process and others with the composition students have just completed. A sam-ple self-assessment questionnaire for fourth graders is presented in Figure 10–8. The questions on this questionnaire require only short answers. As stu-dents gain experience with self-assessment, they can write more sophisticated reflections. Completing the self-assessment questionnaire—sharing their reflec-tions—can be considered as one of the steps in the sharing stage of the writing process.

FIGURE 10-8 Self-Assessment Questionnaire

Name: _____ Title: _____ Date: _____	No	Some	Yes
Topic			
Is my topic interesting?	_____	_____	_____
Did I prewrite to gather ideas for the topic?	_____	_____	_____
Have I kept to my topic?	_____	_____	_____
Do all my paragraphs relate to my topic?	_____	_____	_____
Does my title relate to the topic?	_____	_____	_____
Organization			
Does my introduction grab a reader's attention?	_____	_____	_____
Did I organize my writing into paragraphs?	_____	_____	_____
Does my conclusion summarize the topic?	_____	_____	_____
Content			
Did I use descriptive words?	_____	_____	_____
Did I use synonyms so that I did not use the same word too often?	_____	_____	_____
Is my point of view consistent?	_____	_____	_____
Did I combine short, choppy sentences?	_____	_____	_____
Did I make changes based on suggestions from my writing group?	_____	_____	_____
Mechanics			
Did I locate and correct misspelled words?	_____	_____	_____
Did I choose the correct spelling of homonyms?	_____	_____	_____
Did I check punctuation marks?	_____	_____	_____
Did I capitalize proper nouns?	_____	_____	_____
Do all sentences have subject-verb agreement?	_____	_____	_____

A second application of self-assessment is more specific and can be related directly to a particular writing project. Students in the intermediate and upper grades can use a self-assessment checklist similar to the one presented in Figure 10–9 to assess how well they have applied the elements of story structure in their writing. When students complete the checklist after writing a rough draft, they can use the information they learn to guide their revisions. When students complete the checklist after writing the final draft of their story, they use the information to assess the quality of the story or to set goals for their next story.

Self-assessment can also be used for an end-of-the-school-year assessment. Coughlan (1988) asked his seventh-grade students to "show me what you have learned about writing this year" and "explain how you have grown as a written language user, comparing what you knew in September to what you know now" (p. 375). These upper grade students used a process approach to develop and refine their compositions and they submitted all drafts with their final copies. Coughlan examined both the content of their compositions and the strategies they used in thinking through the assignment and writing their responses. He found this "test" to be a very worthwhile project because it "forced the students to look within themselves . . . to realize just how much they had learned" (p. 378). Moreover, the students' compositions verified that they had learned about writing and that they could articulate that learning.

PRODUCT ASSESSMENT MEASURES

Even though assessments about the process that students use when writing may be of greater importance in assisting students to improve their writing, it is the finished composition—the product—by which parents, teachers, and employers judge writing achievement (Bean & Bouffler, 1987). Product assessment focuses on the quality of students' compositions and often is equated with assigning a grade.

Assessing the quality of student writing is one of the most laborious and time-consuming responsibilities of teachers; so much so that some teachers assign very few writing projects in order to avoid assessment. Teachers can decrease the time spent assessing students' writing in two ways. First, teachers can teach students to use a process approach to writing. When students use the writing process, assessment is not as difficult because students write better compositions. Second, teachers can identify the requirements of the writing project for students when it is assigned, and when students understand the requirements of the project *before* they write, the finished compositions are easier to grade because they more closely meet the requirements of the project.

When teachers assess students' writing, they should have specific criteria in mind. These criteria vary according to the writing project and the purpose of the assessment, but they should get to the heart of writing and not focus just on mechanical errors. No matter what type of assessment measure is used, the goal of assessment should be to help students to improve as writers and feel successful.

FIGURE 10-9 Self-Assessment Questionnaire for Stories

Name: _____ Story: _____ Date: _____

1. **Beginning-Middle-End**
   Describe the beginning, middle, and end of your story in a nutshell:

   Beginning   *Middle*   *End*

2. **Plot**
   Which conflict situation did you use in your story?
   ☐ Conflict between a character and nature
   ☐ Conflict between a character and society
   ☐ Conflict between characters
   ☐ Conflict within a character

   On the back of this sheet, draw a plot diagram of your story and mark with a red pen the three or more roadblocks included in your story.

3. **Setting**
   What is important about the setting in your story?
   ☐ Location   ☐ Weather   ☐ Time of Day
   ☐ Historical/futuristic time period   ☐ Setting is not important

4. **Characters**
   List the main characters in your story. Write three words or phrases to describe each character.

   Character #1   *Character#2*   *Character #3*

   How did you develop your characters?

Character	#1	#2	#3
By what the characters look like?	☐	☐	☐
By what the characters say?	☐	☐	☐
By what the characters do?	☐	☐	☐
By what the characters think?	☐	☐	☐

5. **Theme**
   What is the theme of your story?

6. **Point of View**
   What viewpoint did you use? Why?

All too often, the most common way to assess student papers is for teachers to mark mechanical errors, make a few comments, assign a grade, and return the composition to the student. However, writing is a complex cognitive activity, and measuring only one or two dimensions of a student's work as this common procedure does is inadequate. Four product measures that provide a broader assessment of writing and attempt to deal with its multiple dimensions are (a) holistic scoring, (b) primary trait scoring, (c) analytic scoring, and (d) error analysis. Also included in this section are brief discussions about responding to students' writing and assigning grades.

Holistic Scoring

In holistic scoring, teachers read students' writing for a general or "whole" impression, and according to this general impression, they sort compositions into three, four, five, or six piles from strongest to weakest. Then the compositions in each pile can be awarded a numerical score or letter grade. Every aspect of the composition—both content and mechanical considerations—affects the teacher's response, but none of them are specifically identified or directly addressed using a checklist. Instead, the focus is on overall writing performance.

Holistic scoring is often used for large-scale school district or national writing assessments, and for these assessments, readers are carefully trained. Compositions are typically rated on four- or eight-point numerical scales. Even-number scales are favored so that there will be no middle number for average compositions. Before the scoring begins, trainers review a small group of compositions to identify anchor papers representative of each point on the scale. All compositions are read by at least two readers and numerical scores are either averaged or added together for a cumulative score.

The holistic approach is rapid and efficient and is used to judge overall writing performance without emphasis on any particular writing skill. However, it is not an appropriate measure to use when teachers want to assess how well students have used a particular writing form or applied specific writing skills in a composition. The major drawback of this approach in elementary classrooms is that teachers may unknowingly place too much emphasis on mechanical correctness—particularly spelling, grammar/usage, and handwriting—and therefore bias their assessment (Rafoth & Rubin, 1984; Searle & Dillon, 1980).

Primary Trait Scoring

In primary trait scoring teachers focus on specific writing or rhetorical skills in assessing a composition. The most important—or primary—traits in one writing form or for one audience will be different than in another. For example, the primary traits that teachers want to assess in friendly letters written to pen pals will be different from those in business letters written to state departments of tourism. Similarly, the primary traits assessed in tall tales that students write are different from those for myths.

The primary trait assessment is based on two ideas: first, that compositions are written using specific forms for specific functions and audiences, and second, that writing should be judged according to situation-specific criteria. Because the criteria are specific, primary traits differ from one writing project to another, depending on the nature of the assignment. Strong compositions will exemplify the primary traits and weak compositions will not, no matter how well written the weaker papers may be.

The first step in primary trait scoring is to determine which traits are essential to a specific writing project, and these are the traits that will be scored. The next step is to develop a scoring guide with a list of the primary traits to use in assigning scores. Teachers distribute the scoring guide to students before they begin writing so that they know the criteria the teacher will use to assess their finished compositions.

As with holistic scoring, this measure was first used for large-scale writing assessments, but teachers use it too, when they specify what students are to include in the writing project. For example, if students are writing a research report and they are directed to include the answers to at least three research questions and a bibliography, these are primary traits, and students' compositions can be assessed as to whether each component was included. In large writing assessments, if students include one item, they receive a score of one, a two for two items, and so on. Usually a four-point system is used, but the number of points depends on the number of traits being assessed.

A primary trait scoring guide for reading logs written by fifth graders is presented in Figure 10–10. The criteria are divided into two parts. The reading log must meet the basic criteria presented in the first part before the quality of the entries can be assessed using the criteria in the second part. The criteria in the second part are listed in order of increasing difficulty. For students to receive the highest grade, the entries must exhibit almost all of the criteria.

Analytic Scoring

In analytic scoring teachers score compositions against a range of writing skills. This traditional form of assessment is most appropriate when teachers want to compare students' writing against a standard of excellence. Paul Diederich (1974) developed an analytic scoring system for high school and college students that divided writing into two main categories, general merit and mechanics, and he identified several specific traits related to each category. The specific traits for general merit are ideas, organization, wording, and flavor. The specific traits related to mechanics are usage and sentence structure, punctuation and capitalization, spelling, and handwriting and neatness. Diederich's two categories, general merit and mechanics, are comparable to the two categories, content and mechanics, discussed in this book. Perhaps the most significant drawback of this system is that equivalent weight is given to the two categories even though writing educators recommend that greater emphasis be given to content than to mechanics.

FIGURE 10-10 A Primary Trait Scoring Guide

Reading Log Scoring Guide

Name: _____ Book: _____

Part 1: Required Criteria

_____ Complete bibliographic information about the book.

_____ A list of 20 interesting or new words found in the book.

_____ At least 8 written entires. (Other entries may be written or drawn.)

_____ Cover with title and illustration.

Part 2: Grading Criteria (1 for C; 2 for B; 3 or 4 for A)

_____ Entries summarize the chapter.

_____ Entries include opinions and feelings.

_____ Entries incorporate 10 interesting or new words from the book.

_____ Entries include comparisons of characters, setting, or plot with other books or with the reader's life.

One analytic scoring system, adapted from Diederich's scale, that can be used to assess the quality of elementary students' compositions is presented in Figure 10–11. In this system, the traits of good writing are divided into four categories: (a) ideas, (b) organization, (c) style, and (d) mechanics. This arrangement emphasizes mechanics less than do some other analytic scoring systems, such as Diederich's. Percentage values can also be assigned to each category to determine a grade. Some teachers may assign 25% value to each of the four categories while other teachers may assign 30% to each of the first three categories and 10% to mechanics.

This factor analysis of writing is more time-consuming than other assessment measures, and it has been criticized for several reasons. Edward White (1985, p. 124) characterizes this approach as "pedagogically destructive and theoretically bankrupt" even though it is the most commonly used measure in schools today. Analytic scoring is subjective, and the categories may not be appropriate for some writing forms or may not reflect what students are learning about writing as a primary trait scoring system would. Also, students who are rated high on one trait tend to be rated high on other traits, thus producing a "halo" effect.

Error Analysis

Simply identifying and counting the number of errors in students' compositions is a useless measure of writing quality, but analyzing the types of errors that students make can provide valuable information about students' writing. However, the term *error* has a negative connotation, and Kenneth Goodman (1973) coined the more neutral term *miscue* to describe another type of language error—those made by students as they read aloud. A reading miscue is defined as any oral reading response that does not match the text, and specific categories of miscues have been delineated. All readers produce miscues as they read, and categorizing them and analyzing possible patterns provides information about readers' thought processes during reading. Goodman found that good readers' miscues were more often related to meaning than poor readers', which tended to be related to phonics.

Just as teachers gain a better understanding of students' reading behaviors through a careful analysis of students' oral reading miscues, teachers can gain

FIGURE 10-11   An Analytic Scoring System

	Strong	Average	Weak
Ideas			
1. Ideas are creative.	_____	_____	_____
2. Ideas are well developed.	_____	_____	_____
3. Audience and purpose are considered.	_____	_____	_____
Organization			
1. An organizational pattern is used.	_____	_____	_____
2. Ideas are presented in logical order.	_____	_____	_____
3. Topic sentences are clear.	_____	_____	_____
Style			
1. Good choice of words.	_____	_____	_____
2. Use of figurative language.	_____	_____	_____
3. Variety of sentence patterns.	_____	_____	_____
Mechanics			
1. Most words are spelled correctly.	_____	_____	_____
2. Punctuation and capitalization are used correctly.	_____	_____	_____
3. Standard language is used.	_____	_____	_____

Comments:

similar insight into students' development as writers by observing, categorizing, and analyzing writing miscues. In miscue analysis, only those miscues that alter the meaning of the text are considered important because the goal of reading comprehension is meaning. The decision of whether or not to correct a student's miscue depends on how seriously the miscue alters the meaning of what is being read and on the possibility that the student may self-correct the miscue. These same guidelines should apply for writing, and many teachers find it more useful to talk with students about miscues in assessment conferences than to try to guess at the students' reasoning and write a reaction on the compositions. Also, students often self-correct their writing miscues when they reread their compositions.

Teachers can categorize writing miscues and examine the list to discover patterns of error. This information is then used to make instructional decisions. In Chapter 8, "Writers' Tools," information was presented about analyzing students' invented spelling errors to understand their stage of spelling development and to plan appropriate writing projects and spelling instruction.

Responding to Student Writing

When teachers assess students' compositions, they often feel compelled to respond to the writing with comments. Too often these comments translate into either a justification for the grade assigned or to trite "good work" or "I liked it" compliments. Searle and Dillon (1980) examined the comments middle and upper grade teachers made on writing and found that four categories of comments accounted for more than 86% of all written responses made by the teachers in the study. The four categories were (a) grades for content and mechanics, (b) corrections of most mechanical errors, (c) comments about sentence, paragraph, and other structural errors, and (d) comments such as "good work" to encourage students. This overwhelming attention to error led the researchers to conclude that the message students seemed to receive from these comments was that correctness of form was more important than audience, purpose, and content.

Other researchers have suggested that teachers should not write comments on student writing after it has been completed (Gee, 1971). Instead, Donald Graves (1983) and Eileen Tway (1980a, 1980b) recommend that comments about writing be shared with students orally in writing groups and conferences. Tway also recommends that teachers find and encourage the "nuggets" of possibility in their writing as a way to foster growth in writing. She lists these nuggets:

- Original comparisons
- Interesting observations
- Elaborations
- Unusual treatment or twist to a usual idea or expression
- Creative spin-off from traditional or popular stories
- Word play
- Contrived spelling for effect
- Spoof on vagaries of life
- Vivid impressions
- Surprise ending (1980a, p. 304)

She suggests a variety of ways that teachers foster these nuggets, including encouraging students as they write, using questions to probe students' thinking, demonstrating how to support general statements with details, helping students to expand the nucleus of an idea, using literature as a model, and enjoying writing and the empowerment of language with students.

Assigning Grades

"Grading is a fact of life," according to Donald Graves (1983, p. 93), but he adds that teachers should use grades to encourage students as they write, not to hinder their achievement. Teachers gather information to use in grading students' progress in writing from a variety of sources, including observations, checklists, conferences, and the writing in writing folders. An adequate assessment of students' writing should include informal monitoring of student writing and process assessment measures as well as product assessment measures.

When students' writing is graded using product assessment measures, only compositions that students have revised and edited should be graded, and only those papers that students identify as their best papers from all the writing they have done during a grading period—and only these best papers—be graded. It is unfair to grade all writing and then average the grade, according to Graves because "dry periods, slumps, high peaks are the pattern for writers of all abilities" (p. 93). Further, Tom Romano (1987) explains that grades don't teach nearly as much as teachers think, but they do have far-reaching effects on students' attitudes toward writing and on their willingness to write.

REPORTING TO PARENTS

Reporting to parents is crucial in a process-oriented writing program because the approach to language learning is different from what parents experienced in school. It is only natural that they question the rough draft papers that children bring home with unmarked errors, or that, if they visit the classroom, they are surprised by the movement around the classroom and the accompanying noise as students write collaboratively. Moreover, parental participation in schooling is a key factor in children's academic achievement according to the United States Department of Education's booklet *What Works: Research About Teaching and Learning* (Office of Educational Research and Improvement, 1986). Three components of the reporting program are (a) explaining the rationale, (b) demonstrating the program, and (c) displaying results (adapted from Busching, 1979). The fourth component of any reporting program is communicating students' achievement through report cards.

Gill Potter (1989) argues that parents should be participants, not just involved, in their children's schooling. He points out that there is a subtle difference between *involvement* and *participation,* with the later term indicating a more in-depth relationship. Educators have articulated hierarchical models of this participatory relationship between parents and schools (Wood, 1974; Petit, 1980) to describe how parents move from attendance at parent-teacher meetings to participation in curriculum planning. At the most basic level, parents monitor school activities by chatting informally with the teacher before and after school or by exchanging informal notes. At the next level, teachers strive to inform parents about the instructional program and their child's achievement through hallway displays, parent-teacher conferences, report cards, and other printed materials distributed by the school. At the third level, parents participate in the instructional program by volunteering in the classroom and providing special expertise for content area instruction. At the highest, most formal level, parents develop the curriculum through their participation in curriculum planning committees and textbook selection committees.

Explaining the Rationale

When any new educational program is being implemented, parents will be curious about it, and to the extent that it differs from what they recall from their elementary school experience, they will be more concerned about it. Too often parents expect their children to be educated as they were educated (e.g., "If it was good enough for me, then . . . ").

The process approach to writing is predicated on a new view of language learning, and introducing parents to a new writing program begins with an overview of psycholinguistic and sociolinguistic theories of learning (Fields, 1988). Comparing how children learn to talk to how they learn to write and describing the type of environment that supports language learning are important components of this overview. Understanding the rationale for the program and the contribution of writing to literacy as well as how it relates to higher level thinking skills and learning across the curriculum is important if parents are to accept the new writing program.

Parents will also be interested in some of the specifics of the program. They will want to know about the process approach to writing and the five stages of the writing process, the types of writing activities involved, how the program will be implemented, and, in particular, how this new emphasis on writing will benefit their children.

One way to describe the process approach to writing is by showing videotapes of the program in schools where it has already been implemented. Videotapes of the writing process classrooms that Donald Graves has worked with in New Hampshire ("The Writing and Reading Process: A New Approach to Literacy" developed by Jane Hansen and Donald Graves) and Jerome Harste's series "The Authoring Cycle: Read Better, Write Better, Reason Better" are available from Heinemann Educational Publishers (70 Court Street, Portsmouth, NH 03801). Others documenting writing activities in classrooms of teachers who have participated in National Writing Project summer institutes are available from the National Council of Teachers of English (1111 Kenyon Road, Urbana, IL 61801). Other videotapes can be made of classrooms in local schools that have implemented a process approach to writing.

Another way to involve parents is by talking to them about how they can help at home to encourage writing. Just as children need to see their parents reading for enjoyment and for genuine communicative purposes, they need to see them writing in order to appreciate writing as a genuine, functional communicative tool rather than only as something teachers make them do in school. A brochure developed by the National Council of Teachers of English, "How to Help Your Child Become a Better Writer" is presented in Figure 10–12. Copies of this brochure can be ordered from the NCTE and used in a workshop for parents. Knowledge about the writing program their child is involved in and ways they can support that learning empower parents so that they can participate meaningfully in their child's education (Allen & Freitag, 1988).

Parents may feel uncomfortable about the amount of responsibility children assume in writing process classrooms or that skills are not taught in a definite sequence using a workbook. However, taking time to explain the rationale, describe the program, and invite parents to observe the program in action will help to allay some of these fears.

Demonstrating the Program

Having parents visit in classrooms and observe as students use the writing process approach is the best way to demonstrate the program. Students are enthusiastic and more committed to their writing, and as they talk about their writing, they use terms such as *clustering, rough draft, bibliography,* and *proofreading* that provide additional evidence of the value of the program. Parents who visit classrooms see their children assuming more responsibility, working cooperatively, and taking risks as they extend their knowledge. When it is not possible for parents to view a classroom during the school day, students can demonstrate a writing group or a class collaboration activity for parents at an evening meeting. Also, writing activities in classrooms can be videotaped and then shown for parents at a later date. A teacher or student can narrate the videotape explaining what parents are seeing and why the activities are valid ones.

Displaying the Results

The results of a process-oriented writing program can be displayed in many ways. During parent-teacher conferences, parents can examine students' writing folders and the many pieces of writing that they contain. Class newspapers and anthologies are two ways to publish student writing and, at the same time, communicate with parents. Also, in class newspapers, students can explain writing projects in progress and enlist parental support. Writing should also be displayed in the hallways and as bound books in the school library. When students write scripts for skits, plays, puppet shows, or commercials they should be performed for parents. Inviting parents to view the presentations is a convincing way to display the results of writing.

Through these three ways, teachers explain to parents why their children don't bring work home every day, why they may need to go to the public library to research or to check out a book to read, why misspelled words have not been corrected on rough drafts, and that there is an important difference between revising

NCTE National Council of Teachers of English
1111 Kenyon Road, Urbana, Illinois 61801

How to Help Your Child Become a Better Writer

**Suggestions for Parents
from the National Council of Teachers of English**

Dear Parent:

We're pleased you want to know how to help the NCTE effort to improve the writing of young people. Parents and teachers working together are the best means for assuring that children and youth will become skillful writers.

Because the situation in every home is different, we can't say when the best time is to pursue each of the following suggestions. In any case, please be aware that writing skill develops slowly. For some, it comes early; for others it comes late. Occasionally a child's skill may even seem to go backwards. Nonetheless, with your help and encouragement, the child will certainly progress.

The members of the National Council of Teachers of English welcome your involvement in your child's education in writing. We hope you will enjoy following these suggestions for helping your child become a better writer, both at home and at school.

Sincerely,

Executive Director

Things to Do at Home

1. Build a climate of words at home. Go places and see things with your child, then talk about what has been seen, heard, smelled, tasted, touched. The basis of good writing is good talk, and younger children especially grow into stronger control of language when loving adults—particularly parents—share experiences and rich talk about those experiences.

2. Let children see you write often. You're both a model and a teacher. If children never see adults write, they gain an impression that writing occurs only at school. What you *do* is as important as what you say. Have children see you writing notes to friends, letters to business firms, perhaps stories to share with the children. From time to time, read aloud what you have written and ask your children their opinion of what you've said. If it's not perfect, so much the better. Making changes in what you write confirms for the child that revision is a natural part of writing—which it is.

3. Be as helpful as you can in helping children write. Talk through their ideas with them; help them discover what they want to say. When they ask for help with spelling, punctuation, and usage, supply that help. Your most effective role is not as a critic but as a helper. Rejoice in effort, delight in ideas, and resist the temptation to be critical.

4. Provide a suitable place for children to write. A quiet corner is best, the child's own place, if possible. If not, any flat surface with elbow room, a comfortable chair, and a good light will do.

5. Give the child, and encourage others to give, the gifts associated with writing:
- pens of several kinds
- pencils of appropriate size and hardness
- a desk lamp
- pads of paper, stationery, envelopes—even stamps
- a booklet for a diary or daily journal
(Make sure that the booklet is the child's private property; when children want to share, they will.)

- a dictionary appropriate to the child's age and needs. Most dictionary use is for checking spelling, but a good dictionary contains fascinating information on word origins, synonyms, pronunciation, and so forth.
- a thesaurus for older children. This will help in the search for the "right" word.
- a typewriter (even a battered portable will do), allowing for occasional public messages, like neighborhood newspapers, or play scripts.
- erasers or "white-out" liquid for correcting errors that the child wants to repair without rewriting.

6. Encourage (but do not demand) frequent writing. Be patient with reluctance to write. "I have nothing to say" is a perfect excuse. Recognize that the desire to write is a sometime thing. There will be times when a child "burns" to write; others, when the need is cool. But frequency of writing is important to develop the habit of writing.

7. Praise the child's efforts at writing. Forget what happened to you in school and resist the tendency to focus on errors of spelling, punctuation, and other mechanical aspects of writing. Emphasize the child's successes. For every error the child makes, there are dozens of things he or she has done well.

8. Share letters from friends and relatives. Treat such letters as special events. Urge relatives and friends to write notes and letters to the child, no matter how brief. Writing is especially rewarding when the child gets a response. When thank-you notes are in order, after a holiday especially, sit with the child and write your own notes at the same time. Writing ten letters (for ten gifts) is a heavy burden for the child; space the work and be supportive.

9. Encourage the child to write for information, free samples, and travel brochures. For suggestions about where to write and how to write, purchase a copy of the helpful U.S. Postal Service booklet *All about letters* (available from NCTE @ $2.50 per copy; class sets of 20 or more, $1.50 each).

10. Be alert to occasions when the child can be involved in writing, for example, helping with grocery lists, adding notes at the end of parents' letters, sending holiday and birthday cards, taking down telephone messages, writing notes to friends, helping plan trips by writing for information, drafting notes to school for parental signature, writing notes to letter carriers and other service persons, and preparing invitations to family get-togethers.

Writing for real purposes is rewarding, and the daily activities of families present many opportunities for purposeful writing. Involving your child may take some coaxing, but it will be worth your patient effort.

Things to Do for School Writing Programs

1. Ask to see the child's writing, either the writing brought home or the writing kept in folders at school. Encourage the use of writing folders, both at home and at school. Most writing should be kept, not thrown away. Folders are important means for helping both teachers and children see progress in writing skill.

2. Be affirmative about the child's efforts in school writing. Recognize that for every error a child makes, he or she does many things right. Applaud the good things you see. The willingness to write is fragile. Your optimistic attitude toward the child's efforts is vital to strengthening his or her writing habit.

3. Be primarily interested in the content, not the mechanics of expression. It's easy for many adults to spot misspellings, faulty word usage, and shaky punctuation. Perfection in these areas escapes most adults, so don't demand it of children. Sometimes teachers—for the same reason—will mark only a few mechanical errors, leaving others for another time. What matters most in writing is words, sentences, and ideas. Perfection in mechanics develops slowly. Be patient.

4. Find out if children are given writing instruction and practice in writing on a regular basis. Daily writing is the ideal; once a week is not often enough. If classes are too large in your school, understand that it may not be possible for teachers to provide as much writing practice as they or you would like. Insist on smaller classes—no more than 25 in elementary schools and no more than four classes of 25 for secondary school English teachers.

5. Ask if *every* teacher is involved in helping youngsters write better. Worksheets, blank-filling exercises, multiple-choice tests, and similar materials are sometimes used to *avoid* having children write. If children and youth are not being asked to write sentences and paragraphs about science, history, geography, and the other school subjects, they are not being helped to become better writers. *All* teachers have responsibility to help children improve their writing skills.

6. See if youngsters are being asked to write in a variety of forms (letters, essays, stories, etc.) for a variety of purposes (to inform, persuade, describe, etc.), and for a variety of audiences (other students, teachers, friends, strangers, relatives, business firms). Each form, purpose, and audience demands differences of style, tone, approach, and choice of words. A wide variety of writing experiences is critical to developing effective writing.

7. Check to see if there is continuing contact with the imaginative writing of skilled authors. While it's true that we learn to write by writing, we also learn to write by reading. The works of talented authors should be studied not only for ideas but also for the writing skills involved. Good literature is an essential part of any effective writing program.

8. Watch out for "the grammar trap." Some people may try to persuade you that a full understanding of English grammar is needed before students can express themselves well. Some knowledge of grammar *is* useful, but too much time spent on study of grammar steals time from the study of writing. Time is much better spent in writing and conferring with the teacher or other students about each attempt to communicate in writing.

9. Encourage administrators to see that teachers of writing have plenty of supplies—writing paper, teaching materials, duplicating and copying machines, dictionaries, books about writing, and classroom libraries of good books.

10. Work through your PTA and your school board to make writing a high priority. Learn about writing and the ways youngsters learn to write. Encourage publication of good student writing in school newspapers, literary journals, local newspapers, and magazines. See that the high school's best writers are entered into the NCTE Achievement Awards in Writing Program, the Scholastic Writing Awards, or other writing contests. Let everyone know that writing matters to you.

By becoming an active participant in your child's education as a writer, you will serve not only your child but other children and youth as well. You have an important role to play, and we encourage your involvement.

Single copies of this statement are available free upon request, and may be copied without permission from NCTE. Multiple copies are available at a bulk rate of U.S. $5 per 100, prepaid only. Send request to NCTE Order Department, 1111 Kenyon Road, Urbana, IL 61801.

FIGURE 10–12 How to Help Your Child Become a Better Writer: Suggestions for Parents

and editing. A summary of ways to encourage parents' participation in a school writing program is presented in Figure 10–13.

Communicating Through Report Cards

Report cards remain a part of the school life, and they are probably the most obvious form of communicating with or reporting to parents. Even though teachers change how they teach students when they implement the process approach to writing, the report cards often remain the same with space for a single letter or number grade in language arts or writing. What does change is the way teachers determine these grades. Teachers use informal monitoring procedures, process measures, and product measures to determine grades. Many teachers also insert a sheet describing the informal and formal writing projects students were involved in during the grading period or the specific writing skills that students demonstrated through these projects. Students may also take home their writing folders for their parents to review and then return them to school.

FIGURE 10–13 Ten Ways to Encourage Parents' Participation in a School's Writing Program

1. **Open Houses.** Invite parents to attend open houses to view recently completed writing projects.
2. **Writing Folders.** Send writing folders home for parents to review at the end of each grading period.
3. **Videotapes.** Plan viewings of videotapes (either those that are commercially available or made locally) to show the writing process in action.
4. **Professional Library.** Lend books about writing such as Judith Newman's *The Craft of Children's Writing* (1984) from a professional library established in the school.
5. **Newsletters.** Prepare weekly or monthly newsletters for parents which describe the writing program and explain new terminology and activities.
6. **Displays.** Display student writing in school hallways, the public library and other community buildings, and shopping malls.
7. **School Assemblies.** Celebrate writing in weekly assemblies that all students in the school attend and participate in.
8. **Interview Community Persons.** Interview community persons with special expertise in various content areas as a part of writing projects.
9. **Anthologies.** Publish an annual anthology of student writing which includes entries written by each student in the school.
10. **Volunteers.** Invite parents to serve as volunteers in the classroom to assist with writing projects.

■ ANSWERING TEACHERS' QUESTIONS ABOUT ASSESSING STUDENTS' WRITING

1. Don't I have to grade every paper my students write?

No, in a writing process classroom, students write many more papers than teachers can read and critique. As often as possible, students should write for themselves, their classmates, and other genuine audiences rather than for the teacher. Teachers need to ask themselves whether assessing each piece of writing will make their students better writers, and most teachers will admit that such a rigorous critique will not. More likely, grading every composition will clear teachers' conscience about whether they are good teachers; it will not, however, do much to improve students' writing. Teachers should use the informal monitoring procedures and process assessment measures discussed in this chapter as well as grades. Donald Graves (1983) further recommends that teachers grade only the compositions that students identify as their best ones.

2. There are so many ways to assess writing, I don't know which one to use.

How you assess a piece of writing depends on the writing project and on your reason for assessing it. Informal monitoring of student writing provides one measure that students are writing and completing assignments. Using process measures can help assess students' use of the writing process and various writing strategies. Process assessment should be used when teachers want to measure how well students are using the writing process. Most teachers are more familiar with product assessment and more inclined to use a product-oriented measure. If the goal of the assessment is to determine the relative merits of one composition over another, then a product measure is appropriate. Over the grading period, teachers should use a variety of assessment measures to have a more complete picture or portfolio of students as writers.

3. If I don't correct students' errors, how will they learn not to make the errors?

Children construct their own knowledge of the world through experience, according to Jean Piaget (1975) and other cognitive theorists. The application of this theory to writing instruction is that through experiences with reading and writing, students construct knowledge of writing and mechanical conventions of written English. Writing researchers have documented that students with differing amounts of writing experience make different kinds of writing errors, and that the errors of inexperienced writers are less sophisticated than those made by more experienced writers. Learning is more complex than simply identifying errors and marking corrections on students' papers. Teachers can make a far more important contribution to students' learning by structuring worthwhile writing experiences, providing instruction in writing as it relates to the writing projects that students are involved in, and by providing opportunities for students to share their writing with classmates than by correcting students' errors after the writing has been completed.

4. I just don't agree with you. The mechanics are important—they are the mark of a good writer—and they should receive more importance in grading. I think mechanics should count the most in grading a student's writing.

I agree that using correct spelling, grammar, and other mechanics is one indication of a good writer, and when the conventions of written English are used correctly, the writing is easier to read. However, literary prizes are not awarded for technically correct writing; they are awarded for writing that exhibits unique content. I would rather read writing that is clever and creative, well organized, or makes me laugh or cry even if it has some mechanical errors than a bland, error-free composition. Think for a moment about book reviews. Are books ever recommended because they don't have mechanical errors,

or are they recommended because of their memorable characters or vivid language? The mechanics of writing are important, but they are better dealt with in the editing stage after students have drafted and revised their writing than in the early stages of the writing process when students are concerned with gathering and organizing ideas and finding the words to express those ideas.

■ REFERENCES

Allen, J. M., & Freitag, K. K. (1988). Parents and students as cooperative learners: A workshop for parents. *The Reading Teacher, 41,* 922–925.

Atwell, N. (1988a). *In the middle.* Portsmouth, NH: Heinemann.

Atwell, N. (1988b). Making the grade: Evaluating writing in conference. In T. Newkirk and N. Atwell (Eds.), *Understanding writing: Ways of observing, learning, and teaching, K-8* (pp. 236–244). Portsmouth, NH: Heinemann.

Bean, W., & Bouffler, C. (1987). *Spell by writing.* Rozelle, New South Wales (Australia): Primary English Teaching Association.

Bingham, A. (1988). Using writing folders to document student progress. In T. Newkirk & N. Atwell (Eds.), *Understanding writing: Ways of observing, learning, and teaching K-8* (2nd ed.) (pp. 216–225). Portsmouth, NH: Heinemann.

Busching, B. (1979). Not grading writing: How to get parents to like it. In *How to handle the paper load* (Classroom practices in teaching English, 1979–1980). Urbana, IL: National Council of Teachers of English.

Calkins, L. M. (1986). *The art of teaching writing.* Portsmouth, NH: Heinemann.

Coughlan, M. (1988). Let the students show us what they know. *Language Arts, 65,* 375–378.

Diederich, P. B. (1974). *Measuring growth in English.* Urbana, IL: National Council of Teachers of English.

Faigley, L., & Witte, S. (1981). Analyzing revision. *College Composition and Communication, 32,* 400–414.

Fields, M. V. (1988). Talking and writing: Explaining the whole language approach to parents. *The Reading Teacher, 41,* 898–903.

Flood, J., & Lapp, D. (1989). Reporting reading progress: A comparison portfolio for parents. *The Reading Teacher, 42,* 508–514.

Frank, M. (1979). *If you're trying to teach kids how to write, you've gotta have this book!* Nashville, TN: Incentive Publications.

Gee, T. C. (1971). *The effects of written comment on exposition composition.* Doctoral dissertation, North Texas State University. *Dissertation Abstracts International, 31,* 3412A.

Goodman, K. S. (1973). Windows on the reading process. In K. S. Goodman and O. S. Niles (Eds.), *Miscue Analysis.* Urbana, IL: National Council of Teachers of English.

Goodman, K. S. (1989). Preface. In K. S. Goodman, Y. M. Goodman, & W. J. Hood (Eds.), *The whole language evaluation book* (pp. xi–xv). Portsmouth, NH: Heinemann.

Goodman, Y. M. (1989). Evaluation of teachers: Teachers of evaluation. In K. S. Goodman, Y. M. Goodman, & W. J. Hood (Eds.), *The whole language evaluation book* (pp. 3–14). Portsmouth, NH: Heinemann.

Graves, D. H. (1983). *Writing: Teachers and children at work.* Portsmouth, NH: Heinemann.

McKenzie, L., & Tompkins, G. E. (1984). Evaluating students' writing: A process approach. *Journal of Teaching Writing, 3,* 201–212.

Newman, J. (1984). *The craft of children's writing.* Portsmouth, NH: Heinemann.

Office of Educational Research and Improvement. (1986). *What works: Research about teaching and learning.* Washington, DC: United States Department of Education.

Petit, D. (1980). *Opening up schools.* Harmondsworth, England: Penguin.

Piaget, J. (1975). *The development of thought: Equilibration of cognitive structures.* New York: Viking.

Potter, G. (1989). Parent participation in the language arts program. *Language Arts, 66,* 21–28.

Rafoth, B. A., & Rubin, D. L. (1984). The impact of content and mechanics on judgments of writing quality. *Written Communication, 1,* 446–458.

Romano, T. (1987). *Clearing the way: Working with teenage writers.* Portsmouth, NH: Heinemann.

Rynkofs, J. T. (1988). Send your writing folders home. In T. Newkirk & N. Atwell (Eds.), *Understanding writing: Ways of observing, learning, and Teaching K-8* (2nd ed.), (pp. 226–235). Portsmouth, NH: Heinemann.

Searle, D., & Dillon, D. (1980). Responding to student writing: What is said or how it is said. *Language Arts, 57,* 773–781.

Smith, F. (1988). *Joining the literacy club.* Portsmouth, NH: Heinemann.

Temple, C., Nathan, R., Burris, N., & Temple, F. (1988). *The beginnings of writing* (2nd ed.). Boston: Allyn and Bacon.

Tompkins, G. E., & Friend, M. (1988). After your students write: What's next? *Teaching Exceptional Children, 20,* 4–9.

Tway, E. (1980a). How to find and encourage the nuggets in children's writing. *Language Arts, 57,* 299–304.

Tway, E. (1980b). Teacher responses to children's writing. *Language Arts, 57,* 763–772.

White, E. M. (1985). *Teaching and assessing writing.* San Francisco: Jossey-Bass.

Wood, A. J. (1974). Some effects of involving parents in the curriculum. *Trends in Education, 35,* 39–45.

Appendix

ADDITIONAL SAMPLES OF STUDENTS' POEMS

Additional samples of formula poems, free-form poems, syllable- and word-count poems, rhymed poems, and model poems are presented in this appendix. Some poems were written by primary grade students; others by middle and upper grade students. Teachers may want to share these poems with their students as part of the instructional strategy presented in Chapter 5.

FORMULA POEMS

"I Wish . . ."Poems

I wish I were an astronaut
I wish the stars were touchable.
I wish I could float.
I wish I could not burn by the sun.
I wish I could go to Planet Pluto.
I wish I could touch the stars.
I wish I were an astronaut.

David, grade 5

I wish I could fly
high in the sky.
I wish I could soar,
fly above the sea.
I wish I were a bald eagle
and eagles were not endangered.
I wish I could fly.

Josh, grade 5

I Wish . . .

I wish
That a magical rain
Would sweep across the earth
Turning war to peace
And nuclear missiles to dust.

Craig, grade 8

I wish
Our heads could pop off
So we could fix our insides
If they were damaged.

Becky, grade 6

Color Poems

Blue Is

Blue is an ice cube
melting in my hand
Blue is a tuba
playing in a band
Blue is a waterbed
that feels like silk
Blue is a blueberry
floating in milk.
Blue is an ocean
crashing on the shore
Blue is a bluejay
coming back for more.

David, grade 4

White

White is my paper
that floats gently
off the corner of my desk.

White is a pampered,
fat, house cat climbing
on the back of the chair

White is the fluffy clouds
hovering over me
for what seems like Eternity.

White is the snow
falling gently to its fate
along the busy highway.
                    Todd, grade 7

Yellow

Yellow is shiny galoshes
splashing through mud puddles.
Yellow is a street lamp
beaming through a dark, black night.
Yellow is the egg yolk
bubbling in a frying pan.
Yellow is the lemon cake
that makes you pucker your lips.
Yellow is the sunset
and the warm summer breeze.
Yellow is the tingling in your mouth
after a lemon drop melts.
                    Class collaboration, grade 7

Five Senses Poems

Red

Tastes like hot sauce on a taco
Looks like blood
Feels like when I'm angry
Smells like a red, red rose
Sounds like a fire crackling
                    Class collaboration, grade 5

Being Heartbroken

Sounds like thunder and lightning
Looks like a carrot going through a blender
Tastes like sour milk
Feels like a splinter in your finger
Smells like dead fish
It must be horrible!
                    Kim, grade 6

Electricity

Feels like ants crawling over me
Sounds like people running

Tastes like old stale bread
Looks like dancing fire
It's a shocking experience!
Don, grade 6

"If I were . . ." Poems

If I were a pig
I would play in the mud.
I would live at a farm
I would love to eat corn.
And I would lay pork chops.
Kevin, grade 1

If I were . . .

If I were a dragon,
I would breathe fire at people.

If I were a snake,
I would slither around people
and bite them.

If I were a wild horse,
I would buck off people
who tried to ride me.

If I were a mouse,
I would eat all the cheese
and never get caught in a trap.

If I were a baby,
I would squeal
and cry all day long.

If I were a billionaire,
I would spend the money
with my friends.

If I were a pencil,
I would stay dull all the time.
Leslie, grade 4

If I were a glove
I'd catch fly balls all day.
If I were a bat
I wouldn't let a ball cross the plate
If I were a ball
I would fly over the fence

If I were a home-plate
I wouldn't let people step on me.
Devin, grade 5

"I used to/But now" Poems

I used to be a cat
But now I am a dog.

I used to be a gorilla
But now I am a kangaroo.

I used to be a moon
But now I am a planet

I used to be a person
But now I am a Martian.

I used to be a Martian
But now I am a wallabangoo.

I used to be on earth
But now I live with the fairy folk.
Third-grade class collaboration

Me

I used to be a lightbulb,
But now I am a star.
I used to think the world was a kitten,
But now I know it's a lion.
I used to think I was so large
But now I know I am small.
I used to be a fool,
But now I go to school.
I used to just see myself,
But now I see others.
I used to live in Canada,
But now I live in the USA.
I used to not know who I was,
But now I know I am Cassidy.
Cassidy, grade 6

I used to be a giraffe
Walking high and proud
Touching the sky
Skimming the clouds.

But now I'm a snake
Slithering from place to place.
Everyone's scared.
I've no pride at all.
                              Kevin, grade 8

Lie Poems

Our Freaky Family

I know a green alien's alphabet.
My baby cousin is old
because his vocabulary is "goo-goo-gaa-gee."
My Mom is rainbow-colored
because she's a gardener.
Our purple and silver dog
had blue and gold kittens.
Our maroon and gold house
is set on a zebra-colored yard.
                              Amber, grade 4

Me

I live in an orange and pink pepperoni hotdog.
I eat red dogs and purple cats.
I am married to a white raincoat
I work in the middle of yellow Earth to keep it moving.
I play on an orange and black Venus space hockey team.
                              Eric, grade 4

The Whole Truth and Nothing But the Truth

The world is a square, purple desert.
The year is 2000 in black oil Oklahoma.
I can fly in the blue sky on the beach
Alaska is as hot as the Amazon River is pink.
I'm 556 blue years old.
My brother is sailing on 50 maroon yachts.
I can fly in two silver boats inside a ham.
My room is a small fuchsia morgue.
I drink flourescent pink Scope inside my locker.
Our polka-dotted school is as tiny as a Georgia peanut.
                              Sixth-Grade class collaboration

——————— *"is" Poems*

Thunder is . . .

Thunder is someone bowling.
Thunder is a hot cloud bumping against a cold cloud.
Thunder is someone playing basketball.
Thunder is dynamite blasting.
Thunder is a Brontosaurus sneezing.
Thunder is people moving their furniture.
Thunder is a giant laughing.
Thunder is elephants playing.
Thunder is an army tank.
Thunder is Bugs Bunny chewing his carrots.

Second-Grade class collaboration

Sadness Is

Sadness is a dropping tear hitting the ground
Sadness is a dark cloud drifting in the sky
Sadness is a gloomy day just starting

Chelsa, grade 5

What is Misery?

Misery is . . .
Falling in a deep mud hole
Getting sick while eating lunch
Stepping on thin ice
Wrecking your new bike
Eating corned beef and cabbage

Anonymous, grade 7

Preposition Poems

Beside the building I saw a deer.
Near the deer I saw something
above him. It was a fly, flying
around his head.

Before he ran I walked
toward him.
But when I got three feet
from him, he ran away.

Kevin, grade 4

Dear Teacher,
    I know I had it,
    I just know I did.
    It wasss—

Beside my bed
Above the desk
Against the wall
Among the books
Behind the door
Below the table
    Unless—my little brother ate it!
    Oh no!
          Brandon, grade 7

Superman
Within the city
In a phone booth
Into his clothes
Like a bird
In the sky
Through the walls
Until the crime
Among us
   Is defeated!
     Mike, grade 7

Free-Form Poems

The Dinosaur Poem
Millions of years ago
It was breakfast time.
The meat-eating dinosaurs,
Tyrannosaurus and Allosaurus,
   walked on their two legs
   looking for food
   in the swamp where
   they lived.

They found a Brontosaurus
And they ate him,
   clawing and
   hissing—
   Chomp! Chomp!
They spit out a bone
And went home.
                John, age 5 (dictated)

Hershey's Kiss

M-M-M
delicious and scrumptious
Hershey's Kisses
When you plop it into your mouth
your tastebuds have a ball.
First you have it—
then it's gone.
When you eat chocolate, you're going to say,
YUM YUM

I love it!
                      Mark, age 7

Odes

Ode to the American Flag

Oh, American Flag, American Flag,
you have seen the beautiful firecrackers
bursting in the air on the fourth of July.
You have seen the new lands
and the rippling oceans.

Oh, American Flag, American Flag,
you hear jets and airplanes flying overhead.
You hear gunshots during the wars
and best of all, you hear the beautiful song,
the "Star Spangled Banner"
that tells you your country is free.

Oh, American Flag, American Flag,
your country tastes delicious pies
and yummy pizza and fried chicken
that makes your mouth water.
And don't forget your delicious hamburgers.

Oh, American Flag, American Flag,
you smell the fresh spring air
and the sweet smell of flowers
You smell the pine trees that are green
all through the year and the fresh air
that surrounds the pine trees

Oh, American Flag, American Flag,
you have felt sadness when you see
the Americans die and you feel pride
after a war when the Americans win.
You have felt honor when
American citizens are honored.

Oh, American Flag, American Flag,
you love your country so.
You have felt the tears and the pains
of all the USA and your country loves you so.
Jenny, grade 5

Ode to Grass

Oh grass,
Why do you whisper
and call to me?
At times you are short
and other times you are long.
You smell like a pine
in a farm field.
You feel so soft
and so fluffy to me.
Grass, how do you taste?
Sixth-grade class collaboration

Found Poems

(The following poem was written in response to a newspaper article about people forming a human conveyor belt to rescue books from a flooded library storage room.)

A Human Conveyor Belt

Students
Teachers
Parents
Transfer—
A human chain
Anonymous, grade 7

(The following poem was written in response to a movie review of a horror film.)

An innocent victim, asleep
only to awake to another
"Bad Dream."
I watched with a tide,
a tide of unease rising
within me
shrinking.

Angela, grade 7

Acrostics

Jeff

J azzy
E nchanting
F unny
F abulous

Jeff, grade 5

Ghost

G host creeping down the
H all
O h, what's that grabbing my neck?
S h-h-h! It's after me
T hump! It got my neck—
Oh, heck!

Kelsey, grade 5

Chicago

C ity of
H ardworking people.
I ndustries everywhere,
C onstantly noisy streets, three-story buildings.
A thick cloud of fog covers the city.
G reat things to see,
O verlooking Lake Michigan.

April, grade 6

Mosquito

M ost
O f the time they
S warm
Q uietly above and
U nder your hand
I f
T hey would
O nly leave you alone!

Jeff, grade 7

SYLLABLE- AND WORD-COUNT POEMS

Haiku

Spider web shining
Tangled on the grass with dew
waiting quietly.

Candice, grade 4

A crafty sea gull
Soars through the wind, plunges for prey
Splash, gulp, satisfied.

Amy, grade 5

Icicles

The icicles hang
From the low roof of the house
Like glittering stars

Jason, grade 8

Fall

Multi-colored leaves
covering the cool, brown earth
winter's patchwork quilt

Vickie, grade 8

Tanka

Butterflies

Delicate and quick
Fluttering through the blue sky

In rainbow colors
Darting between the flowers
Gracefully landing on them
Amy, grade 6

The rose seems anxious
For the first spring rain to come
And give her a drink
Of its crystal clear water
So her leaves can breathe again
Tiffany, grade 7

Cinquain

Brother
Fun, pesky
Crying, walking, talking
I love my brother
Jeffrey
Audrey, grade 3

Pool
Fun, hard
Swimming, jumping, diving
You can make friends
Y.M.C.A.
Amanda, grade 3

Raccoon
Fuzzy soft sleek
Climbing crawling drinking
cheerful playful
Black mask

Twister
Dangerous Wind
Moving Destroying Turning
Scary Speeding
Funnel
Josh, grade 5

Abandoned House

Cobwebs
Hanging about
Furniture full of dust
Windows broken from strong winds
Dirty

Jennifer, grade 8

Diamante

PEOPLE
cool, dirty
running, playing, buying
clothes,hat, antenna, spacesuit
talking, walking, running
green, ugly
ALIEN

Gabriel, grade 3

FEET
stinky, sweaty
running, hurting, kicking
shoes, socks, hair, hat
thinking, concentrating, hurting
smart, hard
HEAD

Third-grade class collaboration

ICE
cold solid
Freezing chilling hardening
snow streets stoves camp-outs
burning sizzling frying
hot flames
FIRE

Fourth-grade class

CAT
pretty soft
running jumping eating
whiskers milk bones dirt
running jumping eating
loyal brave
DOG

Russell, grade 5

RHYMED POEMS

Limericks

There once was a thing at the zoo
I think that it's from Kalamazoo
It has a big nose
And ears I suppose
And for dinner, it eats airplane glue.

Jason, grade 6

Mrs. Hobb has a hat with a feather
That can even tell the weather.
It's pink when it's hot
and grey when it's not.
(By the way, it's made of leather.)

Carrie, grade 6

The Egyptian Mummy
There once was an Egyptian mummy
Who found himself next to a dummy.
Said the mummy, "Don't move
While I find a new groove,
For I don't find this situation funny."

Nicole, grade 8

Clerihews

Albert Einstein
His genius did shine.
Of relativity and energy did he dream
And scientists today hold him in high esteem.

Heather, grade 6

Mickey Mouse
Lives in a paper house
With a comical wife
In a cartoon life.

Carrie, grade 8

Clint Eastwood
All his movies, really good

I would gladly pay to hear him say,
"C'mon punk, make my day!"
Bobby, grade 8

MODEL POEMS
Apologies

Oh cookie jar,
oh cookie jar,
will you ever forgive me?
I opened your mouth
and put my hand
down your tonsils
to get some cookies.
Please, oh please,
forgive me
and my hand.
Soon I will fill you up
  again
      and again
          and again
Krystal, grade 4

Dear Chair,
I'm so-oo-oo sorry
Day after day
I sit on you.
I didn't know
I weighed 72 pounds
until just this morning.
Please,
I beg you,
please forgive me.
Tony, grade 5

The Truck
Dad,
I'm sorry
that I took
the truck
out for
a spin.

I knew it
was wrong.
But . . .
The exhilarating
motion was
AWESOME!
                    Jeff, grade 7

Invitations

My Place
Come take a ride on my seagull's back.
To a magical land where the color is pink
and love is extreme.
Come study the twinkle in the cold, blue stars.
Come wade on the clear water's waves.
Come sit under the green lacy trees.
Come to this island where the meadows are cool,
and people are everything.
                    B. J., grade 7

Come with Me
Come with me and fly above
        the shores of hope, the sea of love.
And land where people know no pain
        where no one's selfish, no one's vain.
Where mountains greet you with a colorful view,
        and seagulls and bluebirds are singing to you.
A place where animals roam about free,
        a place where everyone longs to be.
                    Amy, grade 7

Prayers from the Ark

The Kangaroo's Prayer
Dear Lord,
I thank you for making me live in Australia.
I thank you for giving me a pouch for my joey.
I forgive you for making me so ugly.
I forgive you for making my arms so short.
I thank you for making the grass so fresh.
Oh, I almost forgot, thank you very much
for giving me such powerful legs for jumping
so high and so far.
                    Chad, grade 2

The Mouse's Prayer

Dear Lord,
I am glad I am a mouse.
Thank you for making me quiet
and giving me sharp teeth.
I can sneak up on a cat and bite his tail.
I can also chew holes in the walls.
And thank you very much for the cheese.
I love cheese!

Jason, grade 2

Elephant's Prayer

Dear God,
I am the elephant.
Why did you make me so fat?
The ground moans when I walk.
Yet I thank you for keeping the grass
sweet and green so I can be strong.
Thank you for keeping the mud puddles soft.
I ask you one favor.
Could you keep me with this fine herd
for as long as I live?

Mattson, grade 6

If I Were in Charge of the World

If I Were in Charge of the World

I would make a law that everyone over five could drive.
I would be rich.
I would make it hot all the time, even if it snows.
I would put Alaska and Hawaii very close to the main United States.
I would let no one die.
I would make it so that kids could boss adults around.
I would make everyone look like Cookie Monster.
I would let all the animals go free.
I would get rid of people who tease people.
I would build no more schools.
I would make spring break three weeks long.
I would make people know everything when they were born
so they didn't have to go to school.
I would make people not smoke, drink, or get hooked on drugs.
I would make kids their own boss.
That's what I would do
if I were in charge of the world.

Fourth-grade class collaboration

If I were in charge of the world, I . . .
   would make it where you didn't have to miss recess
   and where you wouldn't get in trouble.
If I were in charge of the world, I . . .
   would make it where cake was a fruit
   and broccoli wasn't anything to do with food.
If I were in charge of the world, I . . .
   would make it where anyone over ten could drive a car
   and your parents would have to buy you the car you wanted.
That's what I would do
If I were in charge of the world.

Jack, grade 5

If I Were in Charge of the World

If I were in charge of the world,
there wouldn't be Brussels sprouts,
there wouldn't be quiet,
there wouldn't be homework, and
there would be more recess.

There wouldn't be long lunch lines,
there wouldn't be any days but Saturday and Sunday,
there wouldn't be chores for kids, and
there would be desserts instead of full meals.

There wouldn't be any certain bed times,
there wouldn't be cooked carrots,
there wouldn't be prunes, and
that's almost all there would be
if I were in charge of the world!

Tracy, grade 5

Title and Author Index

Subject Index

ABC Books 162, 209, 213, 346
Advertisements 267–273
"All About ____" Books 204,
  206–207, 346, 354
"All About the Author" 94, 95,
  209
"All About Me" Books 219,
  223–224
Alliteration 191–192
Analytic Scoring 389–390, 391
  (see also Assessment)
Anecdotal Records 374, 375
Assessment
  Advertisements 273
  Assigning Grades 393
  Autobiographies and
    Biographies 231–232, 233
  Characteristics of 368
  Danger of 369
  Expository Text Structures 327
  Goal of 20–21, 368
  Handwriting 300–301
  Informal Monitoring 370–375
  Journals 48–49
  Large Scale 22, 388, 389
  Letters 246–247
  Persuasive Essays 265–266
  Poems 189
  Portfolio 376
  Process Assessment 375–386,
    387
  Product Assessment 386,
    388–392

Research Reports 217–218
Responding to Student Writing
  39, 97, 99–100, 392–393
Self-Assessment 383–386
Stories 145, 148–149, 387
Audience 3, 18, 75, 76, 78, 252
Authentic Writing 17
Author's Chair 9, 84, 93–94, 116
Autobiography 218, 219,
  220–222, 223–224, 228,
  232–233

Beginning-Middle-End (see
  Story Structure)
Bibliographies 200, 202, 203,
  205, 209, 216, 217, 248
Big Books 112–113, 137
Biography 2, 44, 79, 218, 219,
  225–227, 229
Blank Page Syndrome 56
Booklists
  about Writing 25
  Autobiographies 228
  Beginning-Middle-End Stories
    123
  Biographies 229
  Characters in Stories 131
  Conflict in Stories 126
  Fantasies 343
  Folktales 142
  Point of View in Stories 134
  Repetition Stories 125
  Setting in Stories 131

Stories in Which Characters
  Keep Journals 35
Theme in Stories 133
Wordplay 156–157
Bookmaking 94, 96
Books About Writing 25
Brainstorming (see Informal
  Writing Strategies)

Capitalization 21
Cartoons 164, 165
Characters (see Story Structure)
Class Collaborations 19, 21, 48,
  63, 66, 102, 137, 144,
  146–147, 154, 155, 159,
  168–169, 170, 173, 174,
  181, 187, 188, 192,
  193–194, 195, 204, 208,
  210–211, 213–214, 216,
  226, 242, 311, 334, 342,
  344, 346
Clustering 50–55, 66, 67, 113,
  122, 124, 141, 143, 188,
  200, 201, 205, 210, 215,
  230, 232, 238, 259, 262,
  275
Collaborative Writing (see Class
  Colaborations)
Commercials 268, 271
Comparison 190–191
Computers and Writing 22, 280,
  303–311 (see also Word
  Processing)

Author Profile

Gail E. Tompkins is an Associate Professor of Teacher Education at California State University, Fresno, where she teaches reading and language arts courses. Formerly, she taught at the University of Oklahoma and was Director of the Oklahoma Writing Project. Dr. Tompkins enjoys working side by side with teachers, kindergarten through college level, sharing her strategies for teaching writing and giving demonstration lessons in their classrooms.

Teaching Writing is Dr. Tompkins' second college textbook published by Merrill. She is also co-author of the popular core text, *Language Arts: Content and Teaching Strategies*. In addition, Dr. Tompkins has written more than 25 articles on topics related to writing, reading, and language arts that have been published in *Language Arts, The Reading Teacher, Childhood Education, Teaching Exceptional Children,* and other professional journals.

Dr. Tompkins also shares her interest in writing with teachers who want to write for publication in professional journals. She chairs the National Council of Teachers of English Professional Writing Networks Committee and serves on the Editorial Review Board of *The Reading Teacher.*

Dr. Tompkins is married and lives in Fresno, California, with her husband, two step-children, two dogs, and a cat.